First World War

and Army of Occupation

War Diary

France, Belgium and Germany

61 DIVISION
182 Infantry Brigade
Royal Warwickshire Regiment
2/8th Battalion
1 September 1915 - 22 February 1918

WO95/3057/1

The Naval & Military Press Ltd
www.nmarchive.com
Published in association with The National Archives

Published by

The Naval & Military Press Ltd

Unit 10 Ridgewood Industrial Park,

Uckfield, East Sussex,

TN22 5QE England

Tel: +44 (0) 1825 749494

www.naval-military-press.com

www.nmarchive.com

This diary has been reprinted in facsimile from the original. Any imperfections are inevitably reproduced and the quality may fall short of modern type and cartographic standards.

© Crown Copyright

Images reproduced by permission of The National Archives, London, England, 2015.

Contents

Document type	Place/Title	Date From	Date To
Heading	WO95/3057/1		
Heading	61st Division 182nd Infy Bde 2-8th Bn R. Warwicks 1915 Sep-1918 Feb		
Miscellaneous	2nd. 8th. Battalion The Royal Warwickshire Regiment	04/09/1915	04/09/1915
War Diary	Maldou	01/09/1915	30/11/1915
Heading	War Diary of 2nd 8th Battalion The Royal Warwickshire Regiment From 1st December 1915 To 31st December 1915		
War Diary	Maldou	01/12/1915	31/12/1915
Miscellaneous	Appendix A		
Miscellaneous	2nd 8th Battalion The Royal Warwickshire Regiment	01/01/1916	01/01/1916
Heading	War Diary of 2/8th Battalion The Royal Warwickshire Regiment From 1st January 1916 To 31st January 1916 Vol 3		
War Diary	Maldon	01/01/1916	31/01/1916
Miscellaneous	Appendix 1	05/01/1916	05/01/1916
Operation(al) Order(s)	White Force Orders No.1	05/01/1916	05/01/1916
Miscellaneous			
Heading	War Diary of 2/8th Battn The Royal Warwickshire Regt. From May. 22nd 1916 To May. 31st.1916 (Volume 1)		
War Diary	Perham Down Salisbury	22/05/1916	22/05/1916
War Diary	Southampton Dock	22/05/1916	22/05/1916
War Diary	Havre	23/05/1916	24/05/1916
War Diary	Berguette	25/05/1916	25/05/1916
War Diary	L'Ecleme	26/05/1916	31/05/1916
Heading	War Diary of 2/8th Battalion The Royal Warwickshire Regiment From June 1/16 To June 30/16 Volume II		
War Diary	L'Ecleme	01/06/1916	02/06/1916
War Diary	Gonnehem	02/06/1916	02/06/1916
War Diary	L'Ecleme	03/06/1916	07/06/1916
War Diary	Le Quesnoy	07/06/1916	10/06/1916
War Diary	Robermetz	13/06/1916	17/06/1916
War Diary	Riez Bailleul	18/06/1916	21/06/1916
War Diary	Neuve Chapelle (Right Sub sector)	22/06/1916	29/06/1916
War Diary	Croix Barbee	30/06/1916	30/06/1916
Operation(al) Order(s)	2/8 Warwicks Operation Orders No.1		
Operation(al) Order(s)	Operation Orders No.2 by Lieut Colonel E.C. Cadman Commanding 2nd 8th Battalion The Royal Warwickshire Regt	17/06/1916	17/06/1916
Operation(al) Order(s)	Operation Orders No.3 by Lt Col E.C. Cadman Commanding 8th Warwicks	30/06/1916	30/06/1916
Operation(al) Order(s)	Operation Order No 4 by Lt Col E.C. Cadman Cdg S Warwicks	23/06/1916	23/06/1916
Operation(al) Order(s)	Operation Orders No.5 by Lt Col E.C. Cadman Commanding 2nd 8th Battalion The Royal Warwickshire Regt	28/06/1916	28/06/1916
Heading	War Diary of 2/8th Battalion The Royal Warwickshire Regt From July 1st.1916 To July 31st 1916 Volume 3.		
War Diary	Croix Barbee	01/07/1916	03/07/1916

War Diary	Neuve Chapelle	04/07/1916	15/07/1916
War Diary	Lagorgue	15/07/1916	19/07/1916
War Diary	Fauquissart Section Of Trenches	20/07/1916	23/07/1916
War Diary	Fauqissart	24/07/1916	24/07/1916
War Diary	Robermetz	24/07/1916	31/07/1916
Operation(al) Order(s)	2nd 8th Battalion The Royal Warwickshire Regiment. Operation Order No. 8	03/07/1916	03/07/1916
Miscellaneous	Operation Orders No.8 by Lt Col E.C. Cadman Commanding 2nd 8th Battalion The Royal Warwickshire Regt	11/07/1916	11/07/1916
Operation(al) Order(s)	2nd 8th Battalion The Royal Warwickshire Regiment. Operation Order No. 11	19/07/1916	19/07/1916
Heading	War Diary Of 2/8th Battalion The Royal Warwickshire Regiment Period August To 31st-1916. Volume IV		
Miscellaneous			
War Diary	Robermetz	01/08/1916	01/08/1916
War Diary	Riez Bailleul	01/08/1916	09/08/1916
War Diary	Neuve Chapelle And Moated Grange	10/08/1916	19/08/1916
War Diary	Riez Bailleul	19/08/1916	25/08/1916
War Diary	Robermetz	26/08/1916	31/08/1916
Miscellaneous	Battalion Orders by Lieut Col E.C. Cadman Commanding 2/8 Battalion The Royal Warwickshire Regiment	09/08/1916	09/08/1916
Operation(al) Order(s)	Battalion Order No. 14	09/08/1916	09/08/1916
Operation(al) Order(s)	Battalion Order No. 30	18/08/1916	18/08/1916
Miscellaneous	Raid Orders		
Miscellaneous	2nd 8th Battalion The Royal Warwickshire Regiment. Battalion Order By Lt. Col. E.C. Cadman. Commanding. Friday 25th Augst 1916.	22/08/1916	22/08/1916
Heading	War Diary Of 2/8th Battalion The Royal Warwickshire Regiment Volume 5 Period Sept 1/16 To Sept 30/16		
War Diary	Robermetz	01/09/1916	02/09/1916
War Diary	Fauquissart Left Sector	03/09/1916	12/09/1916
War Diary	Laventie	13/09/1916	18/09/1916
War Diary	Fauquissart Left Sector	19/09/1916	24/09/1916
War Diary	Laventie	25/09/1916	30/09/1916
Miscellaneous	Battalion Order By Lt Col E.C. Cadman Commanding	02/09/1916	02/09/1916
Operation(al) Order(s)	Battalion Order No. 41	08/09/1916	08/09/1916
Operation(al) Order(s)	Battalion Order No. 44	10/09/1918	10/09/1918
Miscellaneous	Battalion Order By Lt Col E.C. Cadman Commanding	18/09/1916	18/09/1916
Operation(al) Order(s)	Battalion Operation No 50 by Lt. Col. E. C. Cadman. Sunday 24-9-16.	24/09/1916	24/09/1916
Heading	War Diary Of 2/8th Battalion The Royal Warwickshire Regiment Period Oct 1/16 To Oct 31/16 Volume VI		
War Diary	Fauquissart Left Sector	01/10/1916	07/10/1916
War Diary	Laventie	08/10/1916	12/10/1916
War Diary	Fauquissart Left Sector	13/10/1916	18/10/1916
War Diary	Laventie (Billers)	19/10/1916	23/10/1916
War Diary	Fauquissart (Left Sector)	24/10/1916	28/10/1916
War Diary	Laventie	28/10/1916	28/10/1916
War Diary	Robermetz	29/10/1916	31/10/1916
Operation(al) Order(s)	Battalion Order 53 By Lt Col E.C. Cadman Commanding	03/10/1916	03/10/1916
Operation(al) Order(s)	Battalion Order 54 By Lt Col E.C. Cadman Commanding	06/10/1916	06/10/1916

Operation(al) Order(s)	2nd 8th Battalion The Royal Warwickshire Regiment Operation Order 56 by Lt Col E.C. Cadman Commanding	12/10/1916	12/10/1916
Miscellaneous	2nd 8th Battalion The Royal Warwickshire Regiment Operation Order No. 56 by Lt Col E.C. Cadman Commanding	18/10/1916	18/10/1916
Operation(al) Order(s)	Battalion Order No. 57 By Lt Col E.C Cadman Commanding	22/10/1916	22/10/1916
Operation(al) Order(s)	Battalion Order 58 By Lt Col E.C. Cadman Commanding	27/10/1916	27/10/1916
Operation(al) Order(s)	Battalion Order 59 By Lt Col E.C. Cadman Commanding	28/10/1916	28/10/1916
Heading	War Diary Of 2/8th Battalion The Royal Warwickshire Regt Volume VII Period Nov 1/16 To Nov 30/16		
War Diary	Robermetz Near Merville	01/11/1916	01/11/1916
War Diary	L'Ecleme	02/11/1916	02/11/1916
War Diary	Floringhem	03/11/1916	03/11/1916
War Diary	Marquay	04/11/1916	04/11/1916
War Diary	Sericourt	05/11/1916	05/11/1916
War Diary	Mezerolles	06/11/1916	14/11/1916
War Diary	Candas	15/11/1916	15/11/1916
War Diary	Halloy	16/11/1916	16/11/1916
War Diary	Herisart	17/11/1916	17/11/1916
War Diary	Warloy	18/11/1916	20/11/1916
War Diary	Bouzincourt	21/11/1916	26/11/1916
War Diary	Hedauville	27/11/1916	30/11/1916
Heading	War Diary of 2/8th Bn The Royal Warwickshire Regt From December 1. 1916 To December 31st 1916 Volume 8		
War Diary	Hedauville	01/12/1916	01/12/1916
War Diary	Martinsart	02/12/1916	10/12/1916
War Diary	Wellington Huts	11/12/1916	15/12/1916
War Diary	Ravine	16/12/1916	19/12/1916
War Diary	Martinsart Wood W.2660	20/12/1916	21/12/1916
War Diary	Hedauville	22/12/1916	29/12/1916
War Diary	Martinsart Wood	30/12/1916	31/12/1916
Operation(al) Order(s)	Battalion Order No. 73 By Lt Col E.C. Cadman Commanding	09/12/1916	09/12/1916
Miscellaneous	Battalion Order No. 73 By Lt Col E.C. Cadman Commanding	15/12/1916	15/12/1916
Operation(al) Order(s)	2/8th Warwick Order No. 78	21/12/1916	21/12/1916
Operation(al) Order(s)	Battalion Order No. 80	29/12/1916	29/12/1916
Heading	War Diary Of 2/8th Battalion The Royal Warwickshire Regiment Volume IX Period January 1/17 January 31/17		
War Diary	Martinsart Wood	01/01/1917	05/01/1917
War Diary	Warwick Huts	06/01/1917	10/01/1917
War Diary	Rt Subsector Mouquet	11/01/1917	15/01/1917
War Diary	Rubempre	16/01/1917	17/01/1917
War Diary	Candas Carmont	18/01/1917	18/01/1917
War Diary	Canchy	19/01/1917	31/01/1917
Operation(al) Order(s)	Battalion Order No. 81		
Operation(al) Order(s)	122nd Infantry Brigade Order No. 70.	10/01/1917	10/01/1917
Operation(al) Order(s)	18th Divisional Operation Order No. 197	19/01/1917	19/01/1917
Operation(al) Order(s)	Special Order No. 38	10/01/1917	10/01/1917

Operation(al) Order(s)	2nd 8th Battalion Royal Warwickshire Regiment Order No. 82	09/01/1917	09/01/1917
Miscellaneous	Appendix To Order 82	09/01/1917	09/01/1917
Miscellaneous	Supply Arrangements To Accompany B.O 82		
Miscellaneous	Report on Raid on entry on morning	11/01/1917	11/01/1917
Operation(al) Order(s)	Battalion Order No 84	14/01/1917	14/01/1917
Miscellaneous	Battalion Order No 84	14/01/1917	14/01/1917
Miscellaneous	Battalion Order 84	16/01/1917	16/01/1917
Operation(al) Order(s)	Battalion Order No. 85	17/01/1917	17/01/1917
War Diary	Canchy	01/02/1917	05/02/1917
War Diary	Buigny L'Abbe	06/02/1917	15/02/1917
War Diary	Camp No 101 Near Cayeux	20/02/1917	25/02/1917
War Diary	Framerville	26/02/1917	28/02/1917
Miscellaneous	2nd 3rd Battalion The Royal Warwickshire Regiment. Battalion Order By Lt. Col. E.C. Cadman. Commanding.	02/02/1917	02/02/1917
Operation(al) Order(s)	Battalion Order No. 90 By Lt Col E.C Cadman Commanding	04/02/1917	04/02/1917
Miscellaneous	Battalion Order No. 90 By Lt Col E.C Cadman Commanding	12/02/1917	12/02/1917
Miscellaneous	2nd 6th Battalion The Royal Warwickshire Regiment. Battalion Order By Lt. Col. E.C. Cadman. Commanding.	18/02/1917	18/02/1917
Miscellaneous	Operation	13/02/1917	13/02/1917
Operation(al) Order(s)	Battalion Order No. 97 By Lt Col E.C Cadman Commanding	13/02/1917	13/02/1917
Miscellaneous	All Coys	13/02/1917	13/02/1917
Miscellaneous	App VI	13/02/1917	13/02/1917
Operation(al) Order(s)	Battalion Order 99 By Lt Col E.C. Cadman Commanding	23/02/1917	23/02/1917
War Diary	War Diary of 2/8th Battalion The Royal Warwickshire Regiment Volume XI Period From March 1/17 To March 31/17		
War Diary	Framerville	01/03/1917	03/03/1917
War Diary	Chaulnes	04/03/1917	08/03/1917
War Diary	Framerville	09/03/1917	15/03/1917
War Diary	Right Subsector Ablaincourt (Spuds)	15/03/1917	17/03/1917
War Diary	B.2.A.9.9	18/03/1917	19/03/1917
War Diary	C.14.A.2.4	20/03/1917	23/03/1917
War Diary	Falvy	24/03/1917	27/03/1917
War Diary	Fourques	28/03/1917	30/03/1917
War Diary	Soyecourt	30/03/1917	31/03/1917
Operation(al) Order(s)	Battalion Order 111 By Lt Col E.C. Cadman Commanding	29/04/1917	29/04/1917
Heading	War Diary Of 2/8th Bn. The Royal Warwickshire Regt For Period April 1st 1917 To April 30th 1917 Volume XII		
War Diary	Soyecourt	01/04/1917	01/04/1917
War Diary	Tertry	02/04/1917	07/04/1917
War Diary	Villeveque	07/04/1917	09/04/1917
War Diary	Left Subsector Line	10/04/1917	10/04/1917
War Diary	Left Sub sector Berthaijourt Court	10/04/1917	11/04/1917
War Diary	Villecholles	12/04/1917	12/04/1917
War Diary	Vaux	13/04/1917	21/04/1917
War Diary	Map 62 B SW S.17.A.0.3	22/04/1917	24/04/1917
War Diary	Savy	25/04/1917	27/04/1917

War Diary	Brown Line S20 A 4.8 (Map 62 B S W)	28/04/1917	30/04/1917
Miscellaneous	Advance Order By Major W.E.Phillips	18/04/1917	18/04/1917
Operation(al) Order(s)	Battalion Order 118 By Major W.E. Phillips. Commdg.	20/04/1917	20/04/1917
Miscellaneous	Supply Arrangements Battalion Order 118	20/04/1917	20/04/1917
Miscellaneous	Commanding Officer's Trench Notes	20/04/1917	20/04/1917
Operation(al) Order(s)	Battalion Order No. 119	14/04/1917	14/04/1917
Operation(al) Order(s)	Battalion Order No 120 By Major W.E. Phillips Commdg	27/04/1917	27/04/1917
Heading	War Diary Of 2/8th Battalion The Royal Warwickshire Regt Volume XIII Period May 1/1917 To May 31/1917		
War Diary	Brown Line S20a5.5 Map 62 B S W	01/05/1917	03/05/1917
War Diary	Outport Line Savy Sector	04/05/1917	06/05/1917
War Diary	Savy	07/05/1917	09/05/1917
War Diary	Savy Wood (Brown Line)	10/05/1917	14/05/1917
War Diary	Germaine	15/05/1917	15/05/1917
War Diary	Nesle	16/05/1917	17/05/1917
War Diary	Flesselles	18/05/1917	21/05/1917
War Diary	Longuevillette	22/05/1917	24/05/1917
War Diary	Berneville	25/05/1917	31/05/1917
Operation(al) Order(s)	Battalion Order 124 By Lt Col E.C. Cadman Commanding	09/05/1917	09/05/1917
Operation(al) Order(s)	Battalion Order No. 125	14/05/1917	14/05/1917
Operation(al) Order(s)	Battalion Order No. 126	15/05/1917	15/05/1917
Operation(al) Order(s)	Battalion Order No. 127 By Lt Col E.C Cadman Commanding	16/03/1917	16/03/1917
Operation(al) Order(s)	Battalion Order 128 By Lt Col E.C. Cadman Commanding	20/05/1917	20/05/1917
Operation(al) Order(s)	Battalion Order No. 129 By Lt Col E.C Cadman Commanding	22/05/1917	22/05/1917
Operation(al) Order(s)	Battalion Order 130 By Lt Col E.C. Cadman Commanding	23/05/1917	23/05/1917
Miscellaneous	2/8th Battn Royal Warwickshire Regiment		
Miscellaneous	Battalion Order XXX By Lt Col E.C Cadman Commanding	30/05/1917	30/05/1917
Miscellaneous	Training Scheme For Trench Attack		
Miscellaneous	2nd 8th Battalion The Royal Warwickshire Regiment Battalion Order By Lt. Col. E.C. Cadman. Commanding.	29/05/1917	29/05/1917
Heading	War Diary Of 2/8th Battalion The Royal Warwickshire Regt Volume XIV Period June 1/17 To June 30/17		
War Diary	Berneville	01/06/1917	01/06/1917
War Diary	Arras	02/06/1917	10/06/1917
War Diary	Duisans	11/06/1917	23/06/1917
War Diary	Fontaine	24/06/1917	26/06/1917
War Diary	Fontaine L'Etalon	27/06/1917	30/06/1917
Operation(al) Order(s)	Battalion Order 131 By Lt Col E.C. Cadman Commanding	31/05/1917	31/05/1917
Miscellaneous	2/8th Bn Royal Warwickshire Regiment		
Operation(al) Order(s)	Battalion Order 134 By Lt Col E.C. Cadman Commanding	10/06/1917	10/06/1917
Miscellaneous	2nd 8th Battalion The Royal Warwickshire Battalion Order By Lt Col E.C Cadman D.S.O. Commanding 15th June 1917	15/06/1917	15/06/1917
Diagram etc			
Miscellaneous	App V Tactical Scheme for Coy Commanding of The 2/8. Battalion. The Royal Warwickshire Regiment.		

Miscellaneous	Battalion Order 134 By Lt Col E.C. Cadman Commanding	22/06/1917	22/06/1917
Heading	War Diary Of 2/8th Battalion The Royal Warwickshire Regt Volume XV Period July 1/17 To July 31/17		
War Diary	Fontaine L'Etalon	01/07/1917	24/07/1917
War Diary	Bonnieres	25/07/1917	25/07/1917
War Diary	Rubrouck	26/07/1917	31/07/1917
Miscellaneous	Supplement To Battalion Orders By Lt.Col.E.C.Cadman.D.S.O. Battalion Platoon Competition. App I	02/07/1917	02/07/1917
Miscellaneous	App II 2nd 8th Battalion in Royal Warwickshire Regiment.		
Diagram etc	Brigade Attack		
Miscellaneous	Battalion Order 0000. By Lt Col E.C. Cadman Commanding	20/07/1917	20/07/1917
Diagram etc	Diagram		
Operation(al) Order(s)	Battalion Order 156 By Lt Col E.C. Cadman Commanding	23/07/1917	23/07/1917
Operation(al) Order(s)	Battalion Order 157 By Lt Col E.C. Cadman Commanding	24/07/1917	24/07/1917
Heading	War Diary Of 2/8th Battalion The Royal Warwickshire Regt Volume XVI Period Aug 1/17 To Aug 31/17		
War Diary	Hofland Near Roubrouck	01/08/1917	16/08/1917
War Diary	Camp B Brandhoek	17/08/1917	20/08/1917
War Diary	B Camp Brandhoek No 1 Area	21/08/1917	25/08/1917
War Diary	Camp Ypres N.	26/08/1917	30/08/1917
War Diary	Call Reserve Trench	31/08/1917	31/08/1917
Miscellaneous	Battalion Order Z.Z.Z by Capt J Mungle M.C. Commanding	01/08/1917	01/08/1917
Operation(al) Order(s)	Battalion Order 203	15/08/1917	15/08/1917
Operation(al) Order(s)	Battalion Order 167	20/08/1917	20/08/1917
Heading	War Diary Of 2/8th Battalion The Royal Warwickshire Regt. Volume XVII Period Sept 1/17 To Sept 30/17		
Heading	2nd-8th Battalion The Royal Warwickshire Regt War Diary Volume XVII Period 1st To 30th September 1917		
War Diary	Call Reserve C.23.c.8.6 Map Sheet 28	01/09/1917	02/09/1917
War Diary	Capricorn Keep C.18.d.6.6	03/09/1917	04/09/1917
War Diary	Left Support Batt H.Q.C.2308.6 Call Farm	06/09/1917	08/09/1917
War Diary	Batt H.Q Brandhoek No1 Area B. Camp	09/09/1917	13/09/1917
War Diary	Watou No 1 Area ESK Camp	14/09/1917	16/09/1917
War Diary	No 3 Camp EECKE Q.19.a.4.7 (Sheet 27)	17/09/1917	19/09/1917
War Diary	Camp At Dainville L.28.a4.2	20/09/1917	21/09/1917
War Diary	Lancaster Camp H.11.c.1.1.	22/09/1917	22/09/1917
War Diary	Chemical Works Sector H.18.6.6.8	23/09/1917	29/09/1917
War Diary	H.11.a.6.2	30/09/1917	30/09/1917
Miscellaneous	2/8th Bn Royal	02/09/1917	02/09/1917
Miscellaneous	Battalion Order No	05/09/1917	05/09/1917
Operation(al) Order(s)	Battalion Order No. 167	08/09/1917	08/09/1917
Miscellaneous	War Diary	13/09/1917	13/09/1917
Operation(al) Order(s)	Battalion Order No. 170	18/09/1917	18/09/1917
Operation(al) Order(s)	Battalion Order 171 By Lt Col E.C. Cadman Commanding	18/09/1917	18/09/1917
Operation(al) Order(s)	Battalion Order 173 By Lt Col E.C. Cadman Commanding	23/09/1917	23/09/1917
Operation(al) Order(s)	Battalion Order 172 By Lt Col E.C. Cadman Commanding	21/09/1917	21/09/1917

Operation(al) Order(s)	Battalion Order 174	28/09/1917	28/09/1917
Heading	War Diary of 2/8th Battalion The Royal Warwickshire Regiment For Period From 1st October 1917 31st October 1917 Volume 18		
War Diary	H.11.a.6.2 Fampoux)	01/10/1917	06/10/1917
War Diary	Cudis Reserve	07/10/1917	11/10/1917
War Diary	H.11.a.64	12/10/1917	16/10/1917
War Diary	Levis Barracks Area	17/10/1917	28/10/1917
War Diary	Right Bn Greenland Hill Sector	28/10/1917	31/10/1917
Operation(al) Order(s)	Batt. Order No. 175	05/10/1917	05/10/1917
Operation(al) Order(s)	Battalion Order No. 176	10/10/1917	10/10/1917
Operation(al) Order(s)	2/8th Bn. Royal Warwickshire Regt Battalion Order No. 17	15/10/1917	15/10/1917
Miscellaneous	8th Battalion Royal Warwickshire	27/10/1917	27/10/1917
Operation(al) Order(s)	2nd 8th Battalion The Royal Warwickshire Regiment Operation Order No. 179	27/10/1917	27/10/1917
Miscellaneous	2/8th Battalion The Royal Warwickshire Regiment	27/10/1917	27/10/1917
Heading	War Diary Of 2/8th Batt. R. Warwickshire Regt Volume XVIII Period Nov 1/17 To Nov 30/17		
Miscellaneous	Messages And Signals		
War Diary	Right Bn Greenland Hill Sector	01/11/1917	03/11/1917
War Diary	Left Support Greenland Hill Sector	04/11/1917	09/11/1917
War Diary	Left Battn Greenland Hill Sector	09/11/1917	12/11/1917
War Diary	Right Bn Greenland Hill Sector	12/11/1917	15/11/1917
War Diary	Rt Support Bn Greenland Hill	15/11/1917	21/11/1917
War Diary	Levis Barracks Arras	21/11/1917	28/11/1917
War Diary	Wanquetin	28/11/1917	30/11/1917
Operation(al) Order(s)	Battalion Order No. 180	02/11/1917	02/11/1917
Operation(al) Order(s)	Battalion Order No. 181	08/11/1917	08/11/1917
Operation(al) Order(s)	Battalion Order No. 182	14/11/1917	14/11/1917
Operation(al) Order(s)	Battalion Order No. 183	20/11/1917	20/11/1917
Heading	War Diary Of 2/8th Battalion The Royal Warwickshire Regiment Volume XX Period Dec 1/17 To Dec 31/17		
War Diary	Metz-En-Couture	01/12/1917	01/12/1917
War Diary	Heudicourt	02/12/1917	02/12/1917
War Diary	Front Line	03/12/1917	05/12/1917
War Diary	Rhondda Tr.	06/12/1917	06/12/1917
War Diary	Havrincourt Wood	07/12/1917	10/12/1917
War Diary	Rhondda Trench	11/12/1917	11/12/1917
War Diary	Line	12/12/1917	14/12/1917
War Diary	Line to Support Havrincourt Wood	15/12/1917	17/12/1917
War Diary	Manancourt	18/12/1917	23/12/1917
War Diary	Cerisy	24/12/1917	30/12/1917
War Diary	Beaucourt	30/12/1917	31/12/1917
Operation(al) Order(s)	Battalion Order No. 186	08/12/1917	08/12/1917
Miscellaneous	2/8 R Warwicks Regt Battalion Order 186		
Miscellaneous	2nd 8th Batt The Royal Warwickshire Regt		
Operation(al) Order(s)	Battalion Order No. 189	09/12/1917	09/12/1917
Operation(al) Order(s)	2/8 Battn Royal Warwick Regt Order No. 191	12/12/1917	12/12/1917
Miscellaneous	Messages And Signals		
Operation(al) Order(s)	2nd 8th Battalion Royal Warwick Regt Order No. 192	15/12/1917	15/12/1917
Operation(al) Order(s)	2nd 8th Battalion Royal Warwick Regt Order No. 193	16/12/1917	16/12/1917
Operation(al) Order(s)	2nd 8th Battalion Royal Warwick Regt Order No. 194	18/12/1917	18/12/1917
Operation(al) Order(s)	2nd 8th Battn The Royal Warwickshire Regt Battalion Order 195	29/12/1917	29/12/1917

Heading	War Diary Of 2/8th Battalion Royal Warwickshire Regt. Volume XXI Period Jan 1/18 To Jan 31/18		
War Diary	Beaucourt En Santerre	01/01/1918	07/01/1918
War Diary	Rethonvillers	07/01/1918	09/01/1918
War Diary	Etreillers	09/01/1918	10/01/1918
War Diary	Line	11/01/1918	13/01/1918
War Diary	Line Fayet Sector	13/01/1918	16/01/1918
War Diary	Holnon Wood	16/01/1918	18/01/1918
War Diary	Vaux	19/01/1918	26/01/1918
War Diary	Line Right Subsector Gricourt	27/01/1918	29/01/1918
War Diary	Line	29/01/1918	30/01/1918
War Diary	Rt. Support Quarry On Fresnoy Rd and Dug-Out By Otter Copse	31/01/1918	31/01/1918
Operation(al) Order(s)	Battalion Order No. 198	06/01/1918	06/01/1918
Operation(al) Order(s)	Battalion Order No. 199	08/01/1918	08/01/1918
Operation(al) Order(s)	Battalion Order No. 201	10/01/1918	10/01/1918
Operation(al) Order(s)	Battalion Order No. 202	10/01/1918	10/01/1918
Miscellaneous	Administrative Order	10/01/1918	10/01/1918
Miscellaneous	2/8th Battn Royal Warwickshire Regiment Battalion Order no 202	12/01/1918	12/01/1918
Operation(al) Order(s)	Battalion Order No. 203	14/01/1918	14/01/1918
Miscellaneous	B.O 203	14/01/1918	14/01/1918
Operation(al) Order(s)	Battalion Order No. 204	17/01/1918	17/01/1918
Miscellaneous	Administrative Orders To Accompany From Order 204	17/01/1918	17/01/1918
Operation(al) Order(s)	Battalion Order No. 205	24/01/1918	24/01/1918
Heading	To Report To T.M.S Today 29643 Pte H Harrison		
Operation(al) Order(s)	Battalion Order No. 206	25/01/1918	25/01/1918
Operation(al) Order(s)	Battalion Order No. 207	29/01/1918	29/01/1918
War Diary	Support Area Badger Copse Near Fresnoy Le-Petit	01/02/1918	03/02/1918
War Diary	Gricourt Sector	03/02/1918	04/02/1918
War Diary	Otter Copse In Support	08/02/1918	11/02/1918
War Diary	Ugny	12/02/1918	22/02/1918
Operation(al) Order(s)	Battalion Order No. 208	02/02/1918	02/02/1918
Operation(al) Order(s)	Battalion Order No. 211	10/02/1918	10/02/1918
Operation(al) Order(s)	Battalion Order No. 212	13/02/1918	13/02/1918
Operation(al) Order(s)	Battalion Order No. 213	16/02/1918	16/02/1918
Operation(al) Order(s)	2nd 8th Battalion Royal Warwickshire Regiment Order No. 214	21/02/1918	21/02/1918

WO/95/3057/1

2/8 Royal Warwickshire Reg.

61ST DIVISION
182ND INFY BDE

2-8TH BN R. WARWICKS

~~MAY 1916 - FEB 1918~~

1915 SEP - ~~1916 JAN~~

~~1916 MAY~~ - 1918 FEB

(1916 FEB, MAR, APR DIARIES MISSING)

DISBANDED

2ND. 8TH. BATTALION THE ROYAL WARWICKSHIRE REGIMENT.

SUMMARY OF WAR DIARY for month of August. 1915.

2ND. 8TH. BATTALION THE ROYAL WARWICKSHIRE REGIMENT.

182 ND. INFANTRY BRIGADE,

61ST. (SOUTH MIDLAND) DIVISION.

MOBILISATION CENTRE. Aston Barracks, Birmingham.
TEMPORARY WAR STATION. Maldon, Essex.
STATIONS OCCUPIED subsequent to Concentration.

1. Northampton. Feb. 4th. to March. 24th.
2. Coggeshall. Mar. 24th. to Apr. 28th.
3. Billericay. Apr. 28th. to May 12th.
4. Colchester. May. 12th. to June 18th.
5. Chelmsford. June 18th. to July 27th.
6. Epping. July 27th. to September. 3rd.
7. Maldon. September. 3rd.

A. MOBILISATION. - NIL.

B. CONCENTRATION AT WAR STATION.
September 3rd. the Battalion moved to Maldon.

C. ORGANISATION FOR DEFENCE.
Inlying picquet detailed daily for firing on hostile aircraft.

D. TRAINING.
This is severely handicapped owing to greatly depleted numbers.

E. DISCIPLINE.
Satisfactory.

F. ADMINISTRATION.
1. Medical Services. - Satisfactory.
2. Veterinary Services. - Satisfactory.
3. Supply Services. - Satisfactory.
4. Transport Services. Satisfactory.
5. Ordnance Services - Satisfactory.
6. Billeting and Hutting. - Nil.
7. Channels of Correspondence. - Nil.
8. Range Construction. - Nil.
9. Supply of Remounts. - Satisfactory.

G. REORGANISATION OF T.F. INTO HOME AND IMPERIAL SERVICE.
Reorganisation completed.

H. PREPARATION OF UNITS FOR IMPERIAL SERVICE.

Maldon.
September. 3rd. 1915.

J. R. Nuttall
Major,
Cmmndg., 2/8 R. War. R.

2/8 Royal Warwickshire Regiment

Army Form C. 2118.

WAR DIARY ~~or~~ ~~INTELLIGENCE SUMMARY~~.

(*Erase heading not required.*)

Instructions regarding War Diaries and Intelligence Summaries are contained in F. S. Regs., Part II. and the Staff Manual respectively. Title pages will be prepared in manuscript.

[Stamp:] OCT 1915 No. 456/15 THE ROYAL WARWICKSHIRE REGT.

Place	Date	Hour	Summary of Events and Information	Remarks and references to Appendices
	1915			
Maldon	Sept 2	3-0 a.m.	Battalion left Epping and marched to Brentwood Entrained there for Maldon. Arrived Maldon midday.	
	10th	9.30 p.m.	Proceeded to Man Trenches	
	11th		Remained in Trenches until noon.	
	14th		Adjutant examined all Officers below rank of Captain in Company Drill	
	15th	7.45 a.m.	Brigade Field Day. Tactical Scheme	
	22nd	6.15 a.m.	Brigade Field Day. Tactical Scheme carried out near Boreham.	
	30th	2.30 p.m.	Visit of Sir George Markham with reference to Munition Workers	
	Oct 1		Brigade Field Day. Tactical Scheme continued	
	Sept. 20		Two mules transferred to 2/7th R. War. R.	
	Sept. 24		Nineteen mules taken on Strength	

Maldon
Oct. 2/1915.

J. R. Nuttall Major,
Commdg. 2/8 R. War. R.

T2134. Wt. W708–776. 500000. 4/15. Sir J. C. & S.

Instructions regarding War Diaries and Intelligence Summaries are contained in F. S. Regs., Part II. and the Staff Manual respectively. Title pages will be prepared in manuscript.

WAR DIARY

~~or~~

~~INTELLIGENCE~~ ~~SUMMARY~~.

(Erase heading not required.)

Army Form C. 2118.

Place	Date	Hour	Summary of Events and Information	Remarks and references to Appendices
	1915			
Maldon	Oct. 7th		Brigade Field Day	
	12th		1 mule transferred to 61st S.M. Divn Hospital Chelmsford	
	14th		Brigade Field Day	
	16th		1 mule taken on strength from Hospital	
	19th		Army Exercise. Divisional Field Day. Battn. moved by march route to Tiptree	
	20th		Continued — from Tiptree to Great Totham	
	21st		Continued — Battalion returned to Camp	
	26th		Battalion struck camp & moved into billets at Maldon	
	28th		36 rifles (Japanese) transferred to 81st Prov. Batt. at Southminster.	
	28th		75 rifles & 22.500 rounds of Ammunition transferred to 64th Prov. Batt.	

Maldon
Novr. 1st 1915

J. Keady Simcox Major
for O.C. Comndg 2/8 R. War. R

T2134. Wt. W708–776. 500000. 4/15. Sir J. C. & S.

Instructions regarding War Diaries and Intelligence Summaries are contained in F. S. Regs., Part II. and the Staff Manual respectively. Title pages will be prepared in manuscript.

WAR DIARY

~~INTELLIGENCE SUMMARY~~.

(Erase heading not required.)

Army Form C. 2118.

7 ... - 3 DEC 1915 5207/15 THE ROYAL ...

Place	Date	Hour	Summary of Events and Information	Remarks and references to Appendices
	November 1915			
Maldon	2nd		Tactical Scheme. Brigade Field Day.	
	4th.		1 man temporarily released for Munition Work.	
			Tactical Scheme. Brigade Field Day.	
	8th.		1 Officers Charger destroyed by order of Veterinary Officer.	
	14th.		Lieut. Col. S. Freer Ash. T.D. transferred to Territorial Force Reserve.	
	16th.		Tactical Scheme. Brigade Field Day.	
	18th.		525 Rifles ·303 and 157,920 Rounds of ·303 Ammunition Received.	
	20th.		1 Cart. Tank water. received from 2/5 R. War. R	
	22nd		9 wagons G.S. received from A.O.C. Chelmsford.	
	23rd		9 wagons Limber transferred to O/C 2nd Army Camp Depot. Tunbridge Wells.	
	25th.		502 J.P. Rifles, 474 J.P. Bayonets. 1 J.P. Carbine despatched.	
			158,050 Rounds of J.P. Ammunition despatched.	
	30th.		19 J.P. Rifles. 25 J.P. Bayonets despatched.	
			6 Officers transferred to 3rd line	
Maldon			December 3rd 1915	J. R. Nuttall Major Cmdg 2/8 R. War R.

T2134. Wt. W708–776. 500000. 4/15. Sir J. C. & S.

Confidential.

War Diary of

2nd. 8th. Battalion The Royal Warwickshire Regiment.

from 1st. December. 1915 to 31st. December. 1915.

Instructions regarding War Diaries and Intelligence Summaries are contained in F. S. Regs., Part II. and the Staff Manual respectively. Title Pages will be prepared in manuscript.

WAR DIARY

~~or~~

~~INTELLIGENCE SUMMARY~~

(Erase heading not required.)

Army Form C. 2118

Place	Date	Hour	Summary of Events and Information	Remarks and references to Appendices
	Dec			
Maldon	1st.		Individual Training 2/Lieut. A.L. TOSLAND reported for duty.	JRS
	2nd		Individual Training	JRS
	3rd.		Individual Training	JRS
	4th.		Individual Training	JRS
	5th	9.25	Church Parade.	JRS
	6th.		Individual Training Major J.R. NUTTALL having proceeded on leave, Major J.R. SIMCOX assumes Command. Regimental Courses of Instruction in Musketry and Physical Training Commenced.	JRS
	7th.		Route March. Route: HEYBRIDGE — COBB'S FARM — FALCON'S HALL FARM LITTLE RENTER'S FARM — BROAD ST. GREEN — HEYBRIDGE — MALDON	JRS
	8th.		Individual Training. 1 man rejoined from Desertion.	JRS

1875 Wt. W593/826 1,000,000 4/15 J.B.C. & A. A.D.S.S./Forms/C. 2118.

Army Form C. 2118

Instructions regarding War Diaries and Intelligence Summaries are contained in F. S. Regs., Part II. and the Staff Manual respectively. Title Pages will be prepared in manuscript.

WAR DIARY
~~or~~
~~INTELLIGENCE SUMMARY~~

(Erase heading not required.)

Place	Date	Hour	Summary of Events and Information	Remarks and references to Appendices
Maldon	Dec. 9th.		Individual Training. 5 men proceeded to CHELMSFORD for examination as Cold Shoers. Passed as efficient.	WS
	10th.		Individual Training 1 man struck off strength under Para: 392 (VI.) (a.) K.R.	WS
	11th.		Individual Training. 9 Heavy draught Horses received from 2/6th. R. War. R.	WS
	12th.		Church Parade.	WS
	13th.		Major J.R. NUTTALL, having returned from leave, resumes Command. 2/Lieut. J.J. SLATER. proceeded to CHELSEA to attend Course of Instruction.	WS
	14th.		3 men temporarily released for Employment at STEWARTS and LLOYDS, GLASGOW. 1 N.C.O. for employment with the ARCHER STAMPING Co. BIRMINGHAM. Route March. Route: HEYBRIDGE — LANGFORD GROVE — CROSS ROADS ½ MILE E. of S. in WICKHAM BISHOPS — E. TO BEACON HILL AND INN — S. TO LITTLE TOTHAM — CHIGBOROUGH FARM — HEYBRIDGE.	WS

1875 Wt. W593/826 1,000,000 4/15 J.B.C. & A. A.D.S.S./Forms/C. 2118.

Instructions regarding War Diaries and Intelligence Summaries are contained in F. S. Regs., Part II. and the Staff Manual respectively. Title Pages will be prepared in manuscript.

WAR DIARY

or

~~INTELLIGENCE SUMMARY~~

(Erase heading not required.)

Army Form C. 2118

Place	Date	Hour	Summary of Events and Information	Remarks and references to Appendices
Maldon	Dec. 14th.		2/Lieuts D. MACNIVEN & F.A. BRETTELL transferred to 3/8 R. WAR. R.	WS
	15th.		Individual Training	WS
	16th.		Individual Training	WS
	17th.		Individual Training. District Court Martial: President: Lieut. Col. J. SHANNESSY. 2/6 R.WAR.R. Members: Major. G. BLAKELEY. 2/5 R.WAR.R. Capt. A.L.T. BRONETT. 2/4 R.WAR.R. assembled at Battalion Hqrs. for trial of No. 3095 Pte. F. GOLDSBY 2/8 R.WAR.R.	WS
	18th		Individual Training 2 chargers received from 2/6 R.WAR.R making No. of animals in possession = 62.	WS
	19th	9.15	Church Parade. Guards of 2 N.C.O's and 9 men found at HEYBRIDGE BASIN. of 1 N.C.O and 3 men at MARINE LAKE for the week ending 26.12.15.	WS

1875 Wt. W593/826 1,000,000 4/15 J.B.C. & A. A.D.S.S./Forms/C. 2118.

Army Form C. 2118

Instructions regarding War Diaries and Intelligence Summaries are contained in F. S. Regs., Part II. and the Staff Manual respectively. Title Pages will be prepared in manuscript.

WAR DIARY
or
~~INTELLIGENCE SUMMARY~~

(Erase heading not required.)

Place	Date	Hour	Summary of Events and Information	Remarks and references to Appendices
Maldon	Dec 20th.		One Company instructed in Transport Duties at MALDON WEST STATION	WS
	21st.		Individual Training	WS
	22nd		Individual Training.	
			Audit Board assembled at Battn. Hdqrs. in accordance with Para: 104 K.R.	WS
	23rd		Individual Training	
		3pm	Lecture by Officers of ROYAL ENGINEERS. All Officers attended.	WS
	24th		1 man struck off Strength under Para: 392 (VI.) (a) K.R.	WS
	25th.		Christmas Day. special arrangements, dinner, free entertainments for troops.	
		9.30	Church Parade.	WS
	26th	9.30	Church Parade	WS

1875 Wt. W593/826 1,000,000 4/15 J.B.C. & A. A.D.S.S./Forms/C. 2118.

Army Form C. 2118

Instructions regarding War Diaries and Intelligence Summaries are contained in F. S. Regs., Part II. and the Staff Manual respectively. Title Pages will be prepared in manuscript.

WAR DIARY

or

~~INTELLIGENCE SUMMARY~~

(Erase heading not required.)

Place	Date	Hour	Summary of Events and Information	Remarks and references to Appendices
Maldon	Dec. 27th.	10.30	Physical Training.	JRS
	28th.		Individual Training	JRS
		12.10	Special train for men proceeding on leave	
	29th.		Individual Training	JRS Appendix A
			Secret Operation Orders received from Brigade	
	30th.		Individual Training.	JRS
	31st.		2 men medically unfit for Imperial Service, transferred to 81st. PROVNL BATTN.	JRS
			Brigade Concentrated: tactical exercise for Field Officers	

J. Ready Simcox Major.
for O.C. Commdg. 2/8 Bn. R. War. R.

1875 Wt. W593/826 1,000,000 4/15 J.B.C. & A. A.D.S.S./Forms/C. 2118.

Appendix A.

Brigade Concentration.
31st. Dec. 1915.

Alarm orders by

Lieut. Col. J.R. Nuttall
Commanding 2/8. R.War.R.

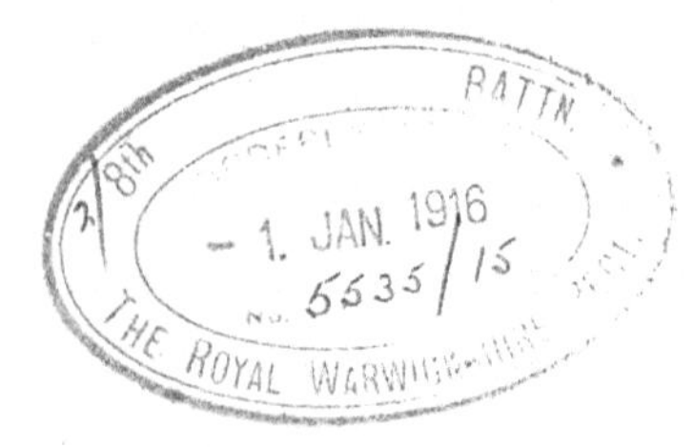

Sheet I. No.308/15.

2ND 8TH BATTALION THE ROYAL WARWICKSHIRE REGIMENT.

BATTALION ORDERS by Lieut.Col. J.R.Nuttall, Commanding.
Headquarters. Maldon.
Thursday 30th December 1915.

PART I.

2.PARADES. The Battalion will parade tomorrow as for Alarm. Alarm Orders will be strictly adhered to excepting in the following paras. Kits of N.C.O's and men will not be stored. The Guard on duty at present will remain behind, prisoners will not be taken. No Fatigue parties required.

The Battalion will be ready to move at 8-40 a.m.

(sgd). J.Ready Simcox. Major & Adjt.,
2/8th.R.War.R.

BATTN. 2/8th THE ROYAL WARWICKSHIRE REGT. -1 JAN. 1916 5535/15

2ND 8TH BATTALION THE ROYAL WARWICKSHIRE REGIMENT.

ALARM ORDERS.

ALARM POST.	On the alarm sounding or an order is issued to assemble either by day or night, the Battalion will form up in close column of Companies, on the Battalion Alarm Post facing the road in the following order:- "A" "B" "C" and "D" Companies. Companies will atonce detail a N.C.O. as right marker. Strictest silence must be maintained.
DRESS.	Full Marching Order, waterproof sheets to be folded up under the flap of the valise. Water Bottles will always be kept filled both by day and by night. Attention is directed to page 19, 20, 21 of the Field Service Manual 1914.
INDENT RATIONS. AMMUNITION.	The first duty of the O.C.Company is to notify the Adjutant and Quartermaster of the numbers parading stating numbers of Officers and other ranks.
BLANKETS.	O.C. Companies will atonce arrange for one blanket per man to be rolled in bundles of 10 to which must be attached a wooden label with the Company marked on it, these will be handed to the Transport Officer on his arrival at the Company Storeroom, for loading on the 1st Line Transport. Kits of N.C.O's and men moving out with the Battalion will be stored under Company arrangements, in the Company Storerooms. The Kits of all Details at Headquarters will be stored under the orders of 2/Lieut.B.K.Parsons. at Musketry Storeroom.
AMMUNITION.	O.C.Companies will arrange to draw from the Quartermaster 120 rounds per rifle and issue the same to the men previous to parading on the Alarm Post, and this will be kept on the Company charge. The Quartermaster will arrange for the loading of 100 rounds per N.C.O. and man moving out with the Battalion which will be loaded on the Regimental Transport, also 60 rounds per N.C.O. and man to be handed over to the Brigade Transport.
RATIONS.	When ordered to move the N.C.O's and men will carry the unconsumed portion of the previous days ration, the Quartermaster will arrange for the issue of an Iron ration, which will be issued in bulk by the Quartermaster. O.C. Companies will detail a party to draw these rations.
COOKS.	The Sergeant Master Cook will atonce pack his cooking utensils on the Field Kitchen and be ready to move with the Battalion.
ENTRENCHING TOOLS.	The Quartermaster will arrange for the loading of Entrenchin Tools.
TRANSPORT½	Officer in charge Transport will detail the Transport drivers where they are to proceed to for loading.
DETAILS.	All N.C.O's and men medically unfit to move out with the Battalion will parade in clean fatigue dress in the rear of the Battalion. O.C.Companies will render rolls of those left behind to the Adjutant on parade.
TO REMAIN BEHIND.	Sergeant as Acting Sergt. Major. The Guard which is on at the time the Battalion is ordered to assemble will proceed with the Battalion. A Guard will be detailed from those staying behind.

ALARM ORDERS----- continued.

PRISONERS. All prisoners in the Guard Detention Room will be handed over to O.C. Companies by Sergt. Mason and a receipt obtained for them. O.C.Companies will take the necessary precautions for their safety.

MEDICAL STORES. The Medical Officer will have the Medical Boxes and Stores ready to be loaded on the Medical cart at Headquarters.

STRETCHERS. Stretchers will be carried on the Medical Cart.

SIGNALLERS. The Officer in Charge of Signallers will arrange to have the Signalling Equipment readynpacked for loading on the Medical Cart.
Attention is directed to page 55 Field Service Manual 1914.

OFFICERS' BAGGAGE. A Transport Cart will be at the Headquarters for the loading of Officers kits, Officers will make their own arrangements for conveying their k ts there and loading them.

COMPANY STATIONERY BOX. O.C.Companies will arrange to take the necessary stationery required, including billeting book, in a small box, which should be kept ready to move.

ORDERLY ROOM EMERGENCY BOX. The Orderly Room Sergeant will arrange to have an emergency box packed for the necessary stationery and on the order to move will send it to the Medical Room to be loaded on the Medical Cart.

NOMINAL ROLLS. Nominal rolls in duplicate will be kept by O.C.Companies of every Officer, N.C.O. and man of their Company and in the column of remarks, which should be in blacklead, stating if on Command, Hospital, Detention, Leave (with or without) which should be kept strictly up to date.

BAGGAGE GUARD. O.C.Companies will each detail 4 men per Company to report to Sergt. Hopkin at the Quartermaster's Stores, who will be in charge of the Baggage Guard.

FATIGUE PARTIES. O.C. "C" Company will detail 1. N.C.O. and 2 men to load the Battalion Ammunition.
O.C. "D" Company will detail 1 N.C.O. and 4 men to load rations picks and shovels.
The above fatigues will report to the Quartermaster immediately the Battalion is ordered to assemble.

The Transport Officer will arrange to draw from the Quartermaster 1 Blanket, 1. Oil Sheet, and 120 rounds per rifle for men on Transport Duty. This is to be in his charge and kept in ~~the~~ his own storeroom.
Rations will be drawn from Companies.

Confidential

War Diary

of

2/8TH. BATTALION THE ROYAL WARWICKSHIRE REGIMENT,

from 1st. January. 1916 to 31st. ~~November~~ January JB. 1916.

Vol 3.

Ref. O.S. map Sheet 30 - 1/2"

Instructions regarding War Diaries and Intelligence Summaries are contained in F. S. Regs., Part II. and the Staff Manual respectively. Title Pages will be prepared in manuscript.

WAR DIARY

or

~~INTELLIGENCE SUMMARY~~

(Erase heading not required.)

Army Form C. 2118

Place	Date	Hour	Summary of Events and Information	Remarks and references to Appendices
	JANUARY			
MALDON	1st.		Individual Training	J.R.S.
"	2nd.	9.45.	Church Parade	J.R.S.
"	3rd.		Individual Training	J.R.S.
"	4th.	11.0 am	District Court Martial at HEADQUARTERS 2/8 R. WAR. R. for trial of NO. 3741. PTE. SMITH. J. 2/8 R. WAR. R. President: MAJOR E.A.M. BINDLOSS, Members. A CAPTAIN, R.E., a CAPTAIN. 2/6 R. WAR. R.	J.J.S.
			LIEUT-COL. J. R. NUTTALL, having proceeded on leave of absence, MAJOR J. REABY SIMCOX assumes command of the Battalion from this date: 2/LIEUT. J. J. SLATER becomes ADJUTANT, during time that MAJ. J.R. SIMCOX is in Command.	
		9.0 am	ROUTE MARCH:- HEYBRIDGE — SOUTH WOOD — GREAT TOTHAM — LANGFORD GROVE — HAY GREEN — HOME (abt 12 miles) Bde. letter. 4373/15, dated 14-12-15 + W.A. 153 of even date received.	
"	5th.	10.0 am	Battalion paraded with the 2/6 R. WAR. R., and took part in a scheme set by the G.O.C. 182nd. INF. BDE: and encountered the 2/5 and 2/7. R. WAR. R.	J.J.S. Appendix A.
"	6th.	9.0 am	BOARD OF SURVEY on Clothing and Equipment on charge of the Battalion assembled at the QUARTERMASTER'S STORES. President:- CAPT. H.E. TEMPLE. Members. LIEUT. G.C. FIELD, 2/LIEUT. R.V. GUEST. Individual Training	J.J.S.
"	7th.		Individual Training.	J.J.S.
"	8th.		Individual Training.	J.J.S.

1875 Wt. W593/826 1,000,000 4/15 J.B.C. & A. A.D.S.S./Forms/C. 2118.

Army Form C. 2118

Instructions regarding War Diaries and Intelligence Summaries are contained in F. S. Regs., Part II. and the Staff Manual respectively. Title Pages will be prepared in manuscript.

WAR DIARY
or
~~INTELLIGENCE SUMMARY~~
(Erase heading not required.)

Place	Date	Hour	Summary of Events and Information	Remarks and references to Appendices
	JAN.			
MALDON.	9th.	a.m. 9.45	Church Parade LIEUT. COL. J. R. NUTTALL, having returned from leave of absence, resumed Command of Battalion. MAJOR. J. READY SIMCOX resumes his duties as ADJUTANT.	JRS.
"	10th.		Individual Training	JRS
"	11th.	9.0 a.m	Route march: LONDON ROAD – LODGE FARM – RUNSELL GREEN – WARREN FARM – SPRING ELMS – MANOR FARM – BEELEIGH ROAD – HOME. L.D. HORSE. No. 4681 met with an accident on route.	J.R.S
"	12th.	p.m. 2.30	1 man temporarily released for employment with The HUGHES-STUBBS METAL COMPANY, BIRMINGHAM, and transferred to ADMINISTRATIVE CENTRE, 8. R. WAR. R. Individual Training COURT OF INQUIRY, President, CAPT. P. H. WHITEHOUSE, assembled at the QUARTERMASTER'S STORES to enquire into and report upon the circumstances under which certain articles of equipment became deficient L.D. HORSE. No. 4681 destroyed, as the result of an accident, under instructions of Veterinary Officer. Individual Training	JRS
"	13th.		BRIGADE paraded on WOODHAM WALTER GOLF COURSE, and were exercised under the GENERAL OFFICER COMMDG.	JRS
"	14th.		7 men, found medically unfit for service abroad, transferred to 81st PROVISIONAL BATTN. (T.F) at GATESHEAD. 1 man discharged under Para. 392 (xvi) K. Regs: one N.C.O transferred to 2/6 R. WAR. R. Individual Training	J.R.S.
"	15th		Individual Training	JRS
"	16th	10.0.	Church Parade.	JRS

1875 Wt. W593/826 1,000,000 4/15 J.B.C. & A. A.D.S.S./Forms/C. 2118.

Instructions regarding War Diaries and Intelligence Summaries are contained in F. S. Regs., Part II. and the Staff Manual respectively. Title Pages will be prepared in manuscript.

WAR DIARY
or
~~INTELLIGENCE SUMMARY~~
(Erase heading not required.)

Army Form C. 2118

Place	Date	Hour	Summary of Events and Information	Remarks and references to Appendices
MALDON.	JAN. 17th	a.m. 11.0	District Court Martial, President, COLONEL H.J.NUTT, members CAPT. E. ROTHERHAM, 2/7 R.WAR.R. CAPT. M.C. WADE 2/6 R.WAR.R. assembled at HEADQUARTERS, 2/8 R.WAR.R. for the trial of No. 3213. PTE. A.J. MILNER, 2/8 R.WAR.R. CAPT. T.E. LEFROY, 2/8 R.WAR.R. attended for instruction. Individual training.	HCS
"	18th	pm 6.30	Arrival of 180 recruits from 3rd line DEPOT, 8. R.WAR.R. Individual training	HCS
"	19th		Inspection by Major-General S.J. DICKSON, Inspector of Infantry. Medical Inspection of Recruits.	HCS
"	20th.	noon 12	Battalion inspected by the INSPECTOR of PHYSICAL TRAINING AND BAYONET FIGHTING. LIEUT. COL. J. B. NUTTALL and CAPT. H.E. TEMPLE attended Court Martial at R.E. HEADQUARTERS WITHAM as President and member respectively. Medical Inspection of Recruits (concluded)	HCS
"	21st.	9.30am	Route march: WOODHAM MORTIMER HALL — TYN DALES — DANBURY — RUNSELL GREEN — LODGE FARM — LONDON ROAD — HOME (about 12 miles)	HCS
"	22nd.		Individual training.	HCS
"	23rd.	10.20am	Church Parade at the Regimental Institute, HIGH STREET, MALDON.	HCS

1875 Wt. W593/826 1,000,000 4/15 J.B.C. & A. A.D.S.S./Forms/C. 2118.

Instructions regarding War Diaries and Intelligence Summaries are contained in F. S. Regs., Part II. and the Staff Manual respectively. Title Pages will be prepared in manuscript.

WAR DIARY
or
~~INTELLIGENCE SUMMARY~~
(Erase heading not required.)

Army Form C. 2118

Place	Date	Hour	Summary of Events and Information	Remarks and references to Appendices
MALDON.	JAN 24th	10.0 a.m.	GARRISON BOARD assembled at HEADQUARTERS, 2/6 R.WAR.R., to enquire into the circumstances under which L.D. HORSE. No 4081 on charge of 2/8 R.WAR.R., became so injured as to necessitate its destruction. President: CAPT. E.H. WATHES, members 2/LIEUT. W.R. SHUTT, VETERINARY SURGEON.	JRS
			1 N.C.O. temporarily released for employment with MESSRS. H.J. GRIFFITHS, LIVERPOOL, and transferred to ADMINISTRATIVE CENTRE, 8 R.WAR.R.	
		3 pm.	Lecture by LT.COL. J. SHANNESSY, 2/6 R.WAR.R. on his visit to FRANCE, in the BRITISH SCHOOLS, MALDON. All available officers attended. 100 rifles ·303. Mk III* received	
"	25th		Individual training 2/LIEUT. S.E. PARSONS attended a Regimental Court martial at the HEADQUARTERS, 2/6 R.WAR.R. as member.	JRS
"	26th		Individual training	JRS
"	27th.		Individual training Enquiry at 2/8 BATTN HEADQUARTERS to enquire into the Deficiencies of Kit and Equipment.	JRS
"	28th.		Individual training 1 N.C.O. temporarily released for employment with MESSRS ROSTON PROCTOR & Co, LINCOLN, & transferred to ADMINISTRATIVE CENTRE, 8 R.WAR.R. 1 man discharged under Para 392(vi)(a) K.R.: 4 men transferred to 81. Prov. Batt (T.F.)	JRS
		2.0 pm.	Medical Inspection under Battalion arrangements	
"	29th		Individual training. LT.COL. J. SHANNESSY, 2/6 R.WAR.R. having proceeded on leave of absence, LT.COL. J.R. NUTTALL assumes command of TROOPS in MALDON.	JRS
"	30th		Church Parade Lieut. G.C. FIELD and 44 N.C.O.s and men proceeded to WOODHAM FERRIS for instruction in wood-clearing.	JRS

Army Form C. 2118

Instructions regarding War Diaries and Intelligence Summaries are contained in F. S. Regs., Part II. and the Staff Manual respectively. Title Pages will be prepared in manuscript.

WAR DIARY

or

~~INTELLIGENCE SUMMARY~~

(Erase heading not required.)

Place	Date	Hour	Summary of Events and Information	Remarks and references to Appendices
MALDON	1916 JAN. 31st		MAJOR J. READY SIMCOX, having proceeded on leave of absence, 2/LIEUT. J.J. SLATER. assumes duties of adjutant.	J.J.S.
			2/LIEUT. H.T. CHIDGEY, 2/8 R.WAR.R. attended as member a COURT of ENQUIRY, assembling at HEADQUARTERS, No. 2. COMPANY 61st. DIVISIONAL TRAIN, A.S.C. at HEYBRIDGE	
			Individual training.	

J. R. Nuttall Lieut. Col.,
Commanding. 2/8 R. Warwick. Regt.

1875 Wt. W593/826 1,000,000 4/15 J.B.C. & A. A.D.S.S./Forms/C. 2118.

Appendix. "A" 1.

Copy no ....

White Force Orders. No. 1.

Ref. ½" O.S. Sheet. 30. 5th. January. 1916.

INFORMATION. The enemy credibly estimated at 2 Battalions Infantry is known to be in the vicinity of and is advancing on MALDON.

INTENTION. The O.C. intends to advance on CHELMSFORD.

DETAIL

2/8 R. WAR. R. (less 1 company)

2/6 R. WAR. R.

Troops detailed in margin will advance along the WOODHAM MORTIMER Road.

Head of the main body will pass the starting point, MALDON WORTHOUSE at 10. a.m.

O.C. 2/8 R. WAR. R. will detail one Company as Advance Guard.

Reports to head of main body.

J. J. Slater

2/ Lieut & A/Adjt.,
2/8 R. War. R.

Time. 9. a.m.

Copy. No. 1. filed
" 2 O.C. 2/6 R. War. R.
" 3 O.C 2/8 R. War. R

COPY No. 2.

APPENDIX I.

WHITE FORCE ORDERS NO. 1.

Ref. ¼" O.S. Sheet 30. 5th January,1916.

INFORMATION.	The enemy, credibly estimated at 2 Battalions Infantry is known to be in the vicinity of and is advancing on Maldon.
INTENTION.	The O.C. intends to advance on Chelmsford.
DETAIL. 2/8th R.War.R. (less 1 Coy.) 2/6th R.War.R.	Troops detailed in margin will advance along the Woodham Mortimer Road. Head of the main body will pass the starting point, Maldon Workhouse at 10 a.m. O.C. 2/8th R.War.R. will detail one Company as Advance Guard. Reports to head of main body.

(Signed) J.J. Slater,
2/Lieut. & A/Adjt.,
2/8th Batt.R.War.R.

Copy No. 1 Filed.
" " 2.O.C. 2/6th R.War.R.
" " 3.O.C. 2/8th R.War.R.

✓ WHEN MARKING UP DOCUMENTS FOR COPYING PLEASE TICK THE APPROPRIATE BOX ON THE OPPOSITE SIDE OF THIS MARKER. THIS INFORMATION IS ESSENTIAL TO ALLOW US TO PROVIDE YOU WITH THE COPIES YOU REQUIRE INFORMATION SHEETS ARE AVAILABLE FROM THE RECORD COPYING COUNTER SHOULD YOU NEED FURTHER ASSISTANCE. *

Feb/Mar/Apr 1916 missing

When marking up documents for copying please tick the appropriate box.

- ☐ Right hand page only
- ☐ Left hand page only
- ☐ Right hand page start
- ☐ Left hand page start
- ☐ Right hand page stop
- ☐ Left hand page stop

Please use a separate slip for each instruction.

e.g. If copying several continuous pages you require one slip to indicate where to start copying and another slip to indicate where the copying should end.

Confidential

31 MAY 1916
No. E61/16

W.O. 1 182/61

War Diary

of

2/8th. Battn. The Royal Warwickshire Regt.

from May. 22nd. 1916 to May. 31st. 1916.

(Volume 1).

May 16
1
Feb 18

1

Army Form C. 2118.

WAR DIARY
or
INTELLIGENCE SUMMARY.
(Erase heading not required.)

Instructions regarding War Diaries and Intelligence Summaries are contained in F. S. Regs., Part II. and the Staff Manual respectively. Title pages will be prepared in manuscript.

Place	Date	Hour	Summary of Events and Information	Remarks and references to Appendices
PERHAM DOWN SALISBURY	20/5/16	9.30 am.	17 Officers and 482 Other Ranks, 9 4-wheeled wagons, 2 2-wheeled wagons, 32 horses, 8 bicycles entrained for port of Embarkation.	E.B.X
		11.0 am.	15 Officers and 505 Other Ranks, 8 4-wheeled wagons, 2 2-wheeled wagons, 32 horses entrained for port of embarkation.	
SOUTHAMPTON DOCK		11.0 am.	9.30 am. train arrived	E.B.X
		12.30 pm.	11.0 am. train arrived	
		4.0 pm.	3 horses exchanged for 3 suffering from colds.	
		7.0 pm.	23 Officers 855 Other ranks, 3 of 1/6th R. War. R attached embarked on Princess CLEMENTINE.	
		7.0 pm.	9 Officers, 132 other ranks, 17 4-wheeled wagons, 4 2-wheeled wagons 64 horses, 8 cycles embarked on the City of BENARES.	
HAVRE	23/5/16	3.0 a.m.	PRINCESS CLEMENTINE and CITY OF BENARES arrived. Disembarkation commenced at 7 a.m.	E.B.X
		8.15 am.	Battalion proceeded by march route to No 1 Rest Camp HAVRE, arriving 10.15 am.	

T2134. Wt. W708—776. 500000. 4/15. Sir J. C. & S.

Instructions regarding War Diaries and Intelligence Summaries are contained in F. S. Regs., Part II. and the Staff Manual respectively. Title pages will be prepared in manuscript.

WAR DIARY
or
~~INTELLIGENCE SUMMARY.~~
(Erase heading not required.)

Army Form C. 2118.

2

Place	Date	Hour	Summary of Events and Information	Remarks and references to Appendices
HAVRE	23/5/16	3pm.	3 sick horses Exchanged at Remount Depot for 3 sound horses	E.B.D.
		6.30pm.	Muster Roll Call. Strength of Bn as follows. 33 Officers (includes Lt Morton Advance Officer)	
			988 Other Ranks (includes 5 RAMC, 4 ASC Attached)	
			8 on command in France	
HAVRE	24/5/16	9.30a.m.	(1) Entrained at GARE LES MARCHANDISES Point 3. Bn less 6 Officers & 150 Other Ranks.	E.B.D.
		11.0a.m.	Above train left station	
		12.0noon	(2) 6 Officers & 250 men entrained at GARE LES MARCHANDISES. Point 1.	
		10.0a.m.	Orderly Room Sergt Beverley left the Bn. to proceed to A.G's Office at the Base	
BERGUETTE	25/5/16	8.37a.m.	1st Train arrived. Train load proceeded by March Route to L'ECLEME Arrived 1.5pm. Bn. HQrs. V4.c.10.8. (Ref. Map 36a $\frac{1}{40,000}$)	E.B.D.
	"	2.45pm	2nd Train arrived. Train load proceeded by March Route to L'ECLEME, Arrived 5.35pm	
			Whole Battalion billeted in and around V.4. (Ref Map 36a $\frac{1}{40,000}$)	

T2134. Wt. W708–776. 500000. 4/15. Sir J. C. & S.

Instructions regarding War Diaries and Intelligence Summaries are contained in F. S. Regs., Part II. and the Staff Manual respectively. Title pages will be prepared in manuscript.

WAR DIARY
or
INTELLIGENCE SUMMARY.
(Erase heading not required.)

Army Form C. 2118.

2/8th Warwicks

Place	Date	Hour	Summary of Events and Information	Remarks and references to Appendices
L'ECLEME	26/5/16	9.30am	Inspections of Arms, equipment, Gas helmets etc.	
		11.0am	Bathing Parade. Whole battalion bathed in LA BASSÉE CANAL at P.28.d.9.3. (Map 36A)	
		2.30–4pm	Coys under Coy Commanders.	
		2.30pm–6pm	The Brigadier General Commanding inspected billets of 'A' 'C' & 'D' Coys.	E.S.D.
L'ECLEME	27/5/16	7-8am	Physical Training	
		9.30-10.30	Rifle Exercises, Rapid loading etc.	
		11am	Bathing Parade.	
		2.50pm	Lecture for all Officers by General Haking at GONNEHEM. Wooden Theatre.	E.S.D.
L'ECLEME	28/5/16	9.30am	Church Parade (2/7th & 2/8th Warwicks) at BUSNETTES	
		3.0pm	Inspection of Cookers by Commanding Officer.	
		9.0pm	Lt MORTON (& batman) returned from doing M.L.O. work.	E.S.D.

T2134. Wt. W708–776. 500000. 4/15. Sir J. C. & S.

Instructions regarding War Diaries and Intelligence Summaries are contained in F. S. Regs., Part II. and the Staff Manual respectively. Title pages will be prepared in manuscript.

WAR DIARY
or
INTELLIGENCE SUMMARY.
(Erase heading not required.)

Army Form C. 2118.

Place	Date	Hour	Summary of Events and Information	Remarks and references to Appendices
	29/5/16	7.30pm	Receipt of 39th Divisional Order No 19 dated 29.5.16 (Orders for Training in Trenches)	
L'ECLEME		7-8am	Physical Training	
		9.30-11am	Musketry, Rapid Loading, fire Control, Picking up targets etc.	
			Specialists under Specialist Officers	
		11.30am	Practice in Embussing for whole Bn.	
		2.30-4pm	Coy Training. Competition in 'Guards'.	G.S.D.
L'ECLEME	30/5/16	7-8am	Physical Training. Heavy rain during night & early morning 29/30.5.16	
		9.30-11am	Musketry etc. Specialists under Specialist Officers	
		11.30-1pm	Under Coy Commanders.	
		2.30-4pm	Coy Training	
			Lecture to Officers & NCOs of 'C' & 'D' Coy on Trench Discipline by C.O.	
		All day	'B' improves 30x Range at P.29.c.9.2.	G.S.D.
L'ECLEME	31/5/16	7-8am	Physical Training	
		9.30am -5.45pm	Route March. L'ECLEME - LILLERS - BOURECQ - NORRENT FONTES - HAM-EN-ARTOIS - L'ECLEME. Bathing at NORRENT FONTES	
		6.30pm	4 men received for England (in hospital on day of Embarkation).	G.S.D.

Sd. C. Coldman
LIEUT. COLONEL,
COMMANDING 2/8TH R. WAR. R.

T2134. Wt. W708-776. 500000. 4/15. Sir J. C. & S.

2H 17

61

Vol 2

Confidential

War Diary of:-

2/8th Battalion The Royal Warwickshire Regiment.

From June 1/16 to June 20/16.

Volume II.

907

Army Form C. 2118.

Instructions regarding War Diaries and Intelligence Summaries are contained in F. S. Regs., Part II. and the Staff Manual respectively. Title pages will be prepared in manuscript.

WAR DIARY
or
INTELLIGENCE SUMMARY.
(Erase heading not required.)

Place	Date	Hour	Summary of Events and Information	Remarks and references to Appendices
L'ECLEME	1/6/16	5.15 am	Lt. B.K. Parsons and 20 men proceeded to Forest Control Office for Forest work	
		7-8 am	Physical Exercise.	
		9.30-12.30	Musketry & bomb throwing from prone position } C & D Coy on 30× Range	
		2.30-4 pm	Coy Training	
		6 pm	24 men inoculated 1st dose	
			Weather very fine. Rough cloudy in evening	E.S.D.
do:	2/6/16	7-8	Physical Exercises	
		9.30-12.30	Musketry & bombing 'A' Coy on 30× Range.	
		9.30 am	5370 Pte Taylor W / 4351 " Hulme R } 'B' Coy awarded 14 days' F.P. No 1. for "Absence without leave".	
		2.30-4 pm	Coy Training. 'B' Coy on 30× Range.	
		12.15 pm	Accident with Lewis Gun. resulting in death of No 1919 Pte Tate J. and injury to to No 1868 Pte Hobson E, both of D Coy.	
		3 pm	Inquiry into Lewis Gun Accident. Capt W Mackay, President; { Capt W.R.T. Whatmore, 2/Lt C.R. White Members.	E.S.D.

T2134. Wt. W708–776. 500000. 4/15. Sir J. C. & S.

Instructions regarding War Diaries and Intelligence Summaries are contained in F. S. Regs., Part II. and the Staff Manual respectively. Title pages will be prepared in manuscript.

WAR DIARY
or
INTELLIGENCE SUMMARY.
(Erase heading not required.)

Army Form C. 2118.

Place	Date	Hour	Summary of Events and Information	Remarks and references to Appendices
GONNEHEM	2/6/16	4 p.m.	F.G.C.M. on Cpl Bridgwater A. 2/6th Warwicks President Major H.H. Beer 2/8th Warwicks Members { Capt. H.T. Hewins 2/8th Warwicks { Officer of 2/6th Warwicks.	E.G.D.
L'ECLEME	3/6/16	7-8am	Physical Exercise.	
		9.30-12.30	Coy Training. Bombing Practice. 30x Range 'A' Coy's poor shots.	
		9.15am	6 men (1 from 'A'+'B', 2 from 'C'+'D') proceeded to AIRE on Anti-gas Course.	
		12.15am	Lt GUEST + 4 men proceeded to Snipers Course at STEENBECQUE.	E.G.D.
L'ECLEME	4/6/16	9.0am	Funeral of 1919 Pte Tate. J. in Roman Catholic Church of ROBECQ. Buried in S.W. Corner of ROBECQ Cemetery. Bde Band attended.	
		2.0am	Lt Garland and batman proceed to St VENANT. on Medium Trench Mortar School (10 days)	
		3.0am	2/Lts. Stone, Morton & Hamilton & 12 men (3 per Coy) proceeded to 39th Div. Bombing School (E. of HINGES at W11 b 2.6 Map 36A)	E.G.D.

T2134. Wt. W708-776. 500000. 4/15. Sir J. C. & S.

Instructions regarding War Diaries and Intelligence Summaries are contained in F. S. Regs., Part II. and the Staff Manual respectively. Title pages will be prepared in manuscript.

WAR DIARY
or
INTELLIGENCE SUMMARY.
(*Erase heading not required.*)

Army Form C. 2118.

Place	Date	Hour	Summary of Events and Information	Remarks and references to Appendices
L'ECLEME	5/6/16	7-8 am	Running Drill	
		7.15 am	Revolver accident to 3643 Pte BICKNELL E. 'B' Coy. Wound through back & neck. Removed to Field Ambulance at ROBECQ.	
		10.0 am	Board of Inquiry on above accident. Major Beer. Pres. Capt Whatmore } Lt Slater } Members	~~Proceedings marked Appendix II~~
		9.30-12.30 } 2.30-4.30 }	Coy Training. 30x Range for poor shots. Bombing & bayonet fighting	
			Raining hard during night 5/6 June 1916	E.G.D
L'ECLEME	6/6/16	7-8 am	Running Drill	
		9.30-12.30 } 2.30-6 pm }	30x Range. Each man fires 5 rounds. Coy Training Etc.	
		4 pm	Bombing accident at CENSE LA VALLEE. Lt J.S. Morris } 2589 Pte F.E. Workman } injured. in leg, right hand & face / in right arm.	
				E.G.D

T2134. Wt. W708-776. 500000. 4/15. Sir J. C. & S.

Instructions regarding War Diaries and Intelligence Summaries are contained in F. S. Regs., Part II. and the Staff Manual respectively. Title pages will be prepared in manuscript.

WAR DIARY
or
INTELLIGENCE SUMMARY.
(Erase heading not required.)

Army Form C. 2118.

Place	Date	Hour	Summary of Events and Information	Remarks and references to Appendices
L'ECLEME	7/6/16	9.55am	Left L'ECLEME for Instruction in Trenches. Route via GONNEHEM – BETHUNE	
			Arrived BETHUNE 12.50pm. Dinners in Horse market.	
			Left BETHUNE 2.0pm.	
			Arrived LE QUESNOY. 2.45pm.	
"	"	2.30pm	Instruction re attachment in Trench Warfare Recd. (S1608. 116 Bde 6/6/16.)	E.S.D.
LE QUESNOY	"	3.45pm	Billeting of Bn. completed. H.Qrs. at F9.a.0.9.	
"	"	6.30pm	½ Offrs & N.C.O's of all Coys. proceeded to trenches till 6pm. 8/6/16	E.S.D.
F LE QUESNOY	8/6/16	9.30–12.30 2–4.	Instruction in Gas Helmet uses.	
"		5.0pm	Receipt of March Orders for occupation of trenches by Whole Bn.	~~Operation Orders Appendix III~~ E.S.D.
"		7.50pm	Remaining Offrs & N.C.O's of all Coys. proceeded to Trenches.	
"		7.20pm	Started to rain heavily.	E.S.D.

T2134. Wt. W708–776. 500000. 4/15. Sir J. C. & S.

Instructions regarding War Diaries and Intelligence Summaries are contained in F. S. Regs., Part II. and the Staff Manual respectively. Title pages will be prepared in manuscript.

WAR DIARY
or
INTELLIGENCE SUMMARY.
(*Erase heading not required.*)

Army Form C. 2118.

Place	Date	Hour	Summary of Events and Information	Remarks and references to Appendices
LE QUESNOY	9/6/16	7-8	Running Drill	
		9.30-12.30 p.m.	Gas helmet instruction Etc.	
		2 pm.	C & D Coys. moved to trenches	
		9–3 pm.	C.O. & Adjutant visited the trenches.	
		6.30.	A & B Coys. moved to trenches.	
		12 m/n	Orders received for Bn to return to GONNEHEM billeting area.	~~App. II attached~~ E.S.D.
				E.S.D.
LE QUESNOY	10/6/16.	9 am. 10 am 12 noon 2 pm.	A, B, C. & D returned from the Trenches.	
		5.30 pm.	Bn returned by march Route to L'ECLEME arriving 9.5 pm. Ras en route.	
L'ECLEME		9.50 pm.	182 Bde Operation Order No 1. received (Copy No 4) (re move to LA GORGUE & MERVILLE area).	App. I attached. (1)
				E.S.D.

T.1134. Wt. W708–776. 500000. 4/15. Sir J. C. & S.

Instructions regarding War Diaries and Intelligence Summaries are contained in F. S. Regs., Part II. and the Staff Manual respectively. Title pages will be prepared in manuscript.

WAR DIARY
or
INTELLIGENCE SUMMARY.
(Erase heading not required.)

Army Form C. 2118.

Place	Date	Hour	Summary of Events and Information	Remarks and references to Appendices
L'ECLEME	11/6/16	9.30.a	Coy Inspections of Kit, Arms, Equipment, Gas helmets etc	
		2.30pm	D Coy had Church Parade followed by Holy Communion	ESD
		7.30.a	4 men proceeded to XI Corps HQrs for duty.	
L'ECLEME	12/6/16	9.0 am	Bn. moved by March Route to ROBERMETZ. HQrs. at K 24. d 3.5. (36A Map) ESD	
			Arrived 11.40.a.m.	ESD
			Lt. Prosser & 70 men proceeded to be attached to 3rd Aust. Tunnelling Coy at LAVENTIE.	
ROBERMETZ	13/6/16	ESD	Musketry of LESART 400x Rifle Range. A ESD 8am - 12 noon. B. 12 - 4 pm. C 4 pm - 8 pm	
		8 am.	Raining all day	
			Coy Training when not firing	ESD
ROBERMETZ	14/6/16	7-8.	Physical Exercises	
		9.30-12.30 2.30-4.30	} Coy Training.	ESD

Instructions regarding War Diaries and Intelligence Summaries are contained in F. S. Regs., Part II. and the Staff Manual respectively. Title pages will be prepared in manuscript.

WAR DIARY
or
INTELLIGENCE SUMMARY.
(*Erase heading not required.*)

Army Form C. 2118.

Place	Date	Hour	Summary of Events and Information	Remarks and references to Appendices
ROBERMETZ.	15/6/16	7-8.	Brisk Running & Physical Exercises	
		9.30 – 1.	A. C. & D. – Independent Route March.	
			'B'. Miniature Range.	
		2.30-4.30.	Snipers used Range. Coys did Coy Training.	E.S.D.
ROBERMETZ.	16/6/16	7-8.	Running Drill	
		9.30-12.30 } 2.30-4.30 }	Bombing for Bn & Coy Bombers 30x Range for C & D Coys. Barbed Wiring for A & B Coys.	
		5.30.	Lt Garland left to be appointed to Medium Trench Mortar School. Move Orders received (see App. II)	App. II. E.S.D.
ROBERMETZ.	17/6/16	7-8	Running Drill	
		9.30.	Lecture to all Platoons on Health & Sanitation.	
		2.0.	Bn moved by march Route to RIEZ BAILLEUL.	
		4.30	Arrived BAILLEUL.	
		2.0.	Lts Morton & While, & 22 NCOs & men proceeded to join Bde Machine Gun Companies	E.S.D.

T2134. Wt. W708–776. 500000. 4/15. Sir J. C. & S.

Instructions regarding War Diaries and Intelligence Summaries are contained in F. S. Regs., Part II. and the Staff Manual respectively. Title pages will be prepared in manuscript.

WAR DIARY
or
INTELLIGENCE SUMMARY.
(Erase heading not required.)

Army Form C. 2118.

Place	Date	Hour	Summary of Events and Information 2/8 Battn R. WARWICKS	Remarks and references to Appendices
RIEZ BAILLEUL	18/6/16	3.15am	Battalion furnished carrying party of 16 Officers, 16 NCOs & 640 men. Last parties arrived back in billets at 2.15 p.m.	
		7pm	15 men transferred to 3rd Australian Tunnelling Coy	
		7pm	1 NCO & 3 men manned post at Q.12.b.50.	[illegible]
RIEZ BAILLEUL	19/6/16	9.30-12.30 / 2.30-8	Coy training & Musketry on 30x Range	
		8pm-10pm	Bombing with live bombs.	
		11.50pm	182 Inf. Bde Operation Order No 5, Copy No 6 received.	
		12.15pm	3 men proceeded on Lewis Gun Course at CAMIERS.	[illegible]
RIEZ BAILLEUL	20/6/16	8am	Company Commanders, Sniping, Signalling & Machine Gun Officers reconnoitred Trenches (Right, NEUVE CHAPELLE Section)	908
		9.30am	6 men, temporarily unfit, attached to 61st Divisional Sanitary Section	[illegible]
		All day	Musketry & bombing on Ranges.	
		4.30pm	Operation Order No 3 issued.	App III

T2134. Wt. W708-776. 500000. 4/15. Sir J. C. & S.

Army Form C. 2118.

WAR DIARY
or
INTELLIGENCE SUMMARY.
(Erase heading not required.)

Instructions regarding War Diaries and Intelligence Summaries are contained in F. S. Regs., Part II. and the Staff Manual respectively. Title pages will be prepared in manuscript.

Place	Date	Hour	Summary of Events and Information	Remarks and references to Appendices
RIEZ BAILLEUL	21/6/16		Bn moved to the trenches. Right (NEUVE CHAPELLE) Subsection. Bays 110 – 236.	See Appendix VII.
			Coys. reached barrier EUSTON POST at 5.30am, 8.30am, 11.30am, 2.30pm.	
			Relief reported complete at 3.55pm. 1/4th Bln on right. 2/5th Warwicks on our left.	
		5am.	Situation report normal. No wind	S.S.D.
NEUVE CHAPELLE (Right Subsection)	22/6/16		Bn in Trenches. Situation report – normal. Wind S.W. light	
"	23/6/16.		Bn in Trenches. Situation Report normal except for shelling of CHURCH (M.35.c.5.2.) REDOUBT, Artillery O.P. & 'B' line by 9 inch guns.	
			About 40 shells 2.20pm — 4.45pm. First 4 failed to explode. Parapet of CHURCH	
			REDOUBT demolished. Slight head wound casualty.	S.S.D.
" Delete S.S.D.		10am.	~~'D' Coy moved to LAVENTIE for training. 2/6 Warw. relieved 'C' Coy in Redoubts~~	Appendix VIII
"			~~'C' Coy took over D Coy's Frontage. (See Appendix VIII. for Oper. Order No 4.)~~	S.S.D.
		11.0pm	12 rounds from Medium Trench Mortar Battery	
		11.2pm	12 rounds from C 306 Battery S.M. Division.	
		6.50pm	Heavy thunderstorm. Lasting about 25 minutes.	

T2134. Wt. W708—776. 500000. 4/15. Sir J. C. & S.

909

Army Form C. 2118.

Instructions regarding War Diaries and Intelligence Summaries are contained in F. S. Regs., Part II. and the Staff Manual respectively. Title pages will be prepared in manuscript.

WAR DIARY
or
INTELLIGENCE SUMMARY.
(Erase heading not required.)

Place	Date	Hour	Summary of Events and Information	Remarks and references to Appendices
	24/6/16			
NEUVE CHAPELLE		10 am	'D' Coy moved to LAVENTIE. 'C' Coy relieved 'D' in the line. 1/6th Relieved 'C' Coy in Reserve. (see Operation Order No. 4 App. VIII)	App. XV E.S.D.
		[illegible]	[illegible] E.S.D.	
"	25/6/16	—	Bn in Trenches	
		5.45	G.O.C. Division visited HQrs & rounds of Trenches.	
		4.30 pm	[illegible] Five Shells fired by enemy on our aeroplanes	
		5.40 pm	Heavy bombardment of NEUVE CHAPELLE Village	E.S.D.
	26/6/16		Raid on enemy's Trenches at S.5.b.5.1. Raining hard from 5 pm — 11 pm	
		11.40 pm	Artillery bombarded enemy's front line trenches. 12.10 pm. Artillery lifted to enemy's support trenches.	
		1.1 am	Artillery lowered to enemy's front line trenches 1.15 am. artillery ceased fire	
		11.46 pm	'D' Coy advanced on enemy's trenches. Returned 12.55 am.	
			Casualties Killed. Offrs 1. (2nd Lt WHILE). O.R. 2: Wounded Offrs. nil. O.R. 20. (includes 1 missing) Missing Offrs. 2. (Capt FIELD, Lt HOOTON) O.R. 15	E.S.D.

T2134. Wt. W708—776. 500000. 4/15. Sir J. C. & S.

Instructions regarding War Diaries and Intelligence Summaries are contained in F. S. Regs., Part II. and the Staff Manual respectively. Title pages will be prepared in manuscript.

WAR DIARY
or
INTELLIGENCE SUMMARY.
(Erase heading not required.)

Army Form C. 2118.

Place	Date	Hour	Summary of Events and Information	Remarks and references to Appendices
NEUVE CHAPELLE	27/6/16	3.50 pm	Major BEER left to assume command of 2/4th BUCKS.	
			Trenches in bad state owing to wet.	
	28/6/16		Bn in trenches. Offrs of 2/7th Warwicks reconnoitred trenches.	G.S.D.
			Trenches in bad state owing to wet.	
	29/6/16		Bn. relieved by 2/7 Warwicks (vide Operat Orr. No 5 attached)	App. 5
			Bn. reported completion of relief 3.59 pm.	
CROIX BARBEE	30/6/16		Bn in Reserve for Bde.	
			Fatigue parties during day & night.	
		2.50 am	Smoke bomb attack 2.50 – 3.25 am along whole Brigade Front. [illegible] 29/30.	G.S.D.
			Weather fine.	

[illegible signature]
Lieut. Colonel,
Commanding 2/8th R. War. R.

T.1834. Wt. W708–776. 500000. 4/15. Sir J. C. & S.

App I

2/8 Warwicks. OPERATION ORDERS. NO. 1. SECRET.

The Battalion will match on the 12th. inst. to new Billeting area (LA GORGUE & MERVILLE AREA) as under:-

Billeting area. Headquarters. K.24.c.4.6. Ref. Map 36a

ROUTE.	STARTING POINT.	TIME.
via ROBECQ & CALLONNE	BATTALION HEADQUARTERS.	Head of 'C' Coy. will pass starting point at 8-40 a.m., followed by "D" Coy. "A" and "B" Coys will join the Column at respective billets. Headquarters, Signallers & Pioneers will precede "B" Coy, Drums and Buglers =C= Coy. Quartermaster to arrange to carry Drummers packs. Lewis Gun Section in rear of "B" Coy.

Rear party of three men per company will be left behind to clear up billets, especially latrines. This party will be under L/C Twamley.

O.C. Companies are again reminded that they are personally responsible that 2nds. in Command carefully inspect billets before leaving, special attention being paid to latrines.

O.C. Transport will be held responsible that all Transport Lines are left perfectly clean. Sergt. Shale will be held responsible for Headquarters.

sgd. E.G. Davis., Capt. and Adjt.,
2/8 Warwicks.

E.S.D. F.D.

App II

2ND. 8TH. BATTALION THE ROYAL WARWICKSHIRE REGT.

OPERATION ORDERS. NO.2.
by Lieut. Colonel E.C. Cadman, Commanding.

1. The Battalion will move into new billets on Saturday, June 17th

2. The Battalion will form Column of route facing South.
Starting point. K.30.d.2.2. (Ref. 36a.)
Time. 2 p.m.
Order of march. Signallers. etc. B.,A.,D.,C.,M/G Section, Transport.
Drums between ~~A~~ B and ~~B~~ A Coys.

17-6-1916.

Copies to
1. All Companies.
2. Quartermaster.
3. Transport Officer.
4. M/G Officer.
5. Signalling Officer.
6. File.
7. War Diary.

E.S. Davis
Capt. and Adjt.,
2/8 Warwicks.

Appendix VIII

SECRET. Copy No. 9

914

OPERATION ORDERS NO 3.

BY LT. COL. E.C. CADMAN COMMANDING 8TH WARWICKS. DATED JUNE 20/16.

1. The Battalion will take over Right (NEUVE CHAPELLE) sub section of Trenches on June 21.

2. Right Coy. (Bays 110-160) - D Coy. meet guides at EUSTON POST 5.30 a.m.
Left Coy. (Bays 202-236) - A Coy. .. .. 8.30 a.m.
Support Coy. - C Coy. .. .. 11.30 a.m.
Centre Coy. (Bays 161-201) - B Coy. .. .. 2.30 p.m.

ROUTE 3. PONT DU HEM - ROUGE CROIX - EUSTON POST (M.27.d.7.2.)

MOVEMENT. 4. Movement along or East of BELLE CROIX - LA BASSEE RD. will be by platoons at 100 yds. distance by day and 50 yds. distance by night. Wagons and Carts will move by threes at same distance.

SUPPORT COY. 5. (a) The support Coy. will man:-
(1) CURSON REDOUBT)
(2) CHATEAU DO.)
(3) CHURCH DO.)
Minimum Garrison of each Redoubt 1? N.C.O's and men (includes 8 Bombers.)

(b) The Support Coy. will also find the following:-
(1) Patrol of 6 men - from extreme left of "B" LINE to DEAD HUN CORNER.
(2) 1 Sentry group at junction of "B" LINE and BALUCHI RD. - 1 N.C.O. and 3 men.
(3) 1 Sentry group at MOGGS HOLE - 1 N.C.O. and 3 men.
(4) 1 sentry group at DEAD HUN CORNER - 1 N.C.O. & 3 men.

6. Steel Helmets only will be taken in trenches.

7. Each man will carry one empty sandbag.

8. One Officer and one N.C.O. per Coy., the Bombing Officer and Sniping Officer, the Lewis Gun Section and Batt. Signallers, will proceed with "A" Coy. and will report at Batt. Hdqtrs. of sub section on arrival, for purpose of taking over all Trench Stores, Maps, Ammunition Grenades etc.

Receipts for all Trench Stores, Maps, Ammunition, Grenades etc. will be sent to Batt. Hdqtrs. by 9 a.m. June 22.

(Signed) E.G. Davis.
Capt. & Adjt. 1/8th Warwicks.

Issued at 4.30 p.m.

Copies 1-4 to Coys.
5 .. Q.M.
6 .. L.G. Section.
7 .. Signals.
8 Office
9 War Diary
10 .. 7th Worcs.

Each party will start from RIEZ BAILLEUL 1½ hrs. before time due at EUSTON POST. O.C.A Coy. will issue orders for all details going with his Coy. mentioning his starting point.

App. IV

Operation Orders No 4
by
[illegible] Cdg. 8 Warwicks 9/12

1. 2 Officers (Capt Hawkins & Lt Morton)
2 Sergts & 52 other ranks
will relieve D Coys. front, less
Bays 110-130 10 bays to-morrow, Sat June 24.

Movement. 2. 'C' Coy to relieve 'D' Coy by 10 a.m.
D Coy to start filing out at 10 a.m.

Cookers 3. Capt Fields will meet D Coy's
Cookers at PONT DU HEM X Rds
M 15 C 4 at 10 a.m. June 24 & guide
into fields.

Rations 4. QrMr has been asked to send
up only breakfast rations in
the morning, but if the whole
days rations are sent, they
men must carry the uneaten
portion with them.

Limbers. 5. Two limbers will be at
ROUGE CROIX at 11 a.m. Sat.
for carrying kits & other loads
6. O.C. D Coy will arrange for
his dinners to be eaten about
1 p.m.

7. O.C. 'B' Coy will take over 913 from 'D' Coy, Lamps Nos 157–160 by 9 am. Sat June 24

Issued at
7.25 p.m.
June 23.

[illegible] Davis
Capt. [illegible]

SECRET. 2ND 8TH BATTALION THE ROYAL WARWICKSHIRE REGIMENT. 915

App V

OPERATION ORDERS NO. 5. COPY NO. 7
BY LT. COL. E.C. CADMAN COMMANDING.
June 28/16.

---

1. a. 8 Warwicks will be relieved in right sub section on June 29th, by the 7 Warwicks.
   b. Company Commanders will collect their Coys. on the road running west at ROUGE CROIX.

RELIEF 2. Right Coy. ("D" 8 War bays 110-160) will be relieved by "C" Coy. 7 War.
ROUTE. HUN STREET. COVERED WAY. ROUGE CROIX.

3. Left Coy. ("A" Coy. 8 War. Bays 202-236) by "A" Coy. 7 War. ROUTE. CHATEAU ROAD. BALUCHI ROAD.

4. Support Coy. ("C" Coy 8 War. B Lines) by "D" Coy. 7 War. ROUTE. As per left Coy.

5. Centre Coy. ("B" Coy. 8 War. bays 160-202) by "B" Coy. 7 War. ROUTE. As per left Coy.

POSTS. 6. Posts as per attached table will be taken over from 7 War. by Coys. as under.
Nos. 1 & 2 by "C" Coy.
.. 3 & 4, 11 - 16 by "D" Coy.
.. 5 - 7 by "B" Coy.
.. 8 - 10 by "A" Coy.
O. C. Machine Guns will send his men to report to Officer i/c EUSTON by 2 p.m.
Garrisons will be sent to their respective posts immediately the Coys leave the trenches.

GUIDES. 7. O.C. Right Coy. will detail 1 guide per platoon to be at EUSTON POST at 5.30 a.m. 29/6/16.
O.C. Left Coy. .... at 8.30 a.m. ..
O.C. Support Coy. .... at 11.30 a.m. ..
O.C. Centre Coy. .... at 2.30 p.m. ..

TRENCH STORES. 8. Receipts for Trench Stores, Maps, Ammunition, Grenades etc. will be handed over as usual, and duplicates forwarded to Hdqtrs. by noon June 30.

BILLETS. 9 Billeting representatives to report to Lt. Middleton at Batt. Hdqtrs. at 6 a.m. They will meet Coys. at ROUGE CROIX and conduct them to Billets.

BAGGAGE 10. Baggage will be man handled to Billets except that heavy baggage can be dumped at ration dump and fetched by dusk.

HDQRS. 11. Trench Hdqtrs. will close at 2.30 p.m. Batt. Hdqrs. will be opened at RUE DU PUITS M.26.d.5.7. as soon as possible.

RATIONS. 12. A special memo respecting Rations has been issued.

(Signed) E. G. DAVIS.
Capt & Adjt.
2/8th Warwicks.

Issued at 9.45 p.m.

Copies.
1-4 to Coys.
5 .. 7 Warwicks.
6 .. Lt. Chidgey.
7 .. War Diary
8 .. Office.

2H 15

61

Confidential.

Vol III

War Diary of:-

2/8th Battalion The Royal Warwickshire Regt.

From July 1st 1916 to July 31st 1916

Volume 3.

Instructions regarding War Diaries and Intelligence Summaries are contained in F. S. Regs., Part II. and the Staff Manual respectively. Title pages will be prepared in manuscript.

WAR DIARY or INTELLIGENCE SUMMARY.

(*Erase heading not required.*)

Army Form C. 2118.

Place	Date	Hour	Summary of Events and Information	Remarks and references to Appendices
CROIX BARBEE	1/7/16		Fatigue Parties all day.	
			Capt. LAPHAM & 2Lt SE PARSONS for instruction with Artillery, 6pm 1/7/16 – 6pm 2/7/16.	
		9:30pm	Artillery activity, CROIX BARBEE under shell fire. 2 casualties slight 'B' Coy.	
			Readiness A. Ordered 10:50pm	
			Stand Down Ordered 12:45am. 2/7/16.	E.G.D.
	2/7/16.		Fatigue Parties all day	
		6pm	Capt Lefroy & Lt Rice for instruction with artillery 6pm. 2/7/16 – 6pm 3/7/16	E.G.D.
	3/7/16.		Fatigues cancelled.	
		10–11:30 pm	Heavy shelling along RUE DE PUITS. 2 slightly wounded.	E.G.D.
NEUVE CHAPELLE	4/7/16	4. a.m.	Bn relieved 2/5th Warwicks in Centre Subsector. Relief commenced 4 a.m. completed 12:30pm.	
			One casualty during night 3/4 July (killed) O.O. No 6	App. I
			Two men accidentally wounded. Sent to Special Hospital at BUSNES. F.G.C.M. held	E.G.D.

T2134. Wt. W708—776. 506000. 4/15. Sir J. C. & S.

Army Form C. 2118.

Instructions regarding War Diaries and Intelligence Summaries are contained in F. S. Regs., Part II. and the Staff Manual respectively. Title pages will be prepared in manuscript.

WAR DIARY
or
INTELLIGENCE SUMMARY.
(Erase heading not required.)

Place	Date	Hour	Summary of Events and Information	Remarks and references to Appendices
NEUVE CHAPELLE	5/7/16		Instructions re Smoke bombs received.	
		11 pm.	Gas helmets in alert position 11 pm. 5/7/16 — 4 pm. 6/7/16. 1 Casualty (wounded)	
			Lt Rich went sick	E.G.D.
	6/7/16	3 pm	Brigadier visited H.Qrs.	
		1 pm.	Carrying parties for Smoke bombs, fusees, etc. to front line. Several shells aimed at party. 1 wounded.	E.G.D.
	7/7/16		Bn in trenches. Contd	
	8/7/16	9.30 pm	Following officers of 3rd S. Lancs repd for duty: 2/Lt. A.L. Clayson, H.M. Adams ('A' Coy); 2/Lt. [illegible] Harrison ('B' Coy) left sick at ETAPLES; 2/Lt. E.L. Lloyd, A.V. Rushforth, R.C. Watson ('C' Coy); 2/Lt. A. McClure, R.E. Sloane (D Coy)	
		12 noon.	CAPT. W.T. HEWINS proceeded to join Machine Gun Depôt	E.G.D.
	9.7.16	9.30 am	Lt PROSSER rejoined Bn. from duty with 3rd Australian Mining Coy.	
		10 am.	One Coy 1/5 Warwicks raided Enemy's trench at M.36.a.0.5	E.G.D.

T2134. Wt. W708—776. 500000. 4/15. Sir J. C. & S.

918

Instructions regarding War Diaries and Intelligence Summaries are contained in F. S. Regs., Part II. and the Staff Manual respectively. Title pages will be prepared in manuscript.

WAR DIARY
or
INTELLIGENCE SUMMARY.
(Erase heading not required.)

Army Form C. 2118.

Place	Date	Hour	Summary of Events and Information	Remarks and references to Appendices
NEUVE CHAPELLE	10/7/16	9 am	Lt. W.S. FARMER & 2 O.R proceeded to STEENBECQUE for Sniping Course.	
		10.0 morning	Brigade Trench Front readjusted.	E.S.D.
			7/8 Warwicks allotted from CHURCH Rd to COLVIN Trench C, D, 2 plats A & B in Front Line, 2 plats. of A in Reserve	
	11/7/16		Shelling of back areas especially near HQrs. 8.0 am & 12.15 pm. Mine blown up by enemy S.E. of DUCKS BILL 5.50 am	
		3.50 pm	2/Lt Rich returned from [illegible] hospital	
		7.0 pm	2 platoons of 'A' withdrawn from fire trench & posted in Reserve. (Op. O. No 8.)	App. II
				E.S.D
	12/7/16	10-12 noon	Shelling of EBENEZER Farm — no casualties though a working party was there all the morning.	
		6.50 pm	Commenced raining.	E.S.D.

919

T2134. Wt. W708—776. 500000. 4/15. Sir J. C. & S.

Instructions regarding War Diaries and Intelligence Summaries are contained in F. S. Regs., Part II. and the Staff Manual respectively. Title pages will be prepared in manuscript.

WAR DIARY
or
INTELLIGENCE SUMMARY.
(Erase heading not required.)

Army Form C. 2118.

Place	Date	Hour	Summary of Events and Information	Remarks and references to Appendices
NEUVE CHAPELLE	13.7.16.	7.50am	2/Lt R.V. GUEST wounded in head. Sent to A.D.S, thence to No 2 C.C.S. MERVILLE	
		11.0pm	2/4 BERKS (1 Coy) carried out Raid on our Left. 2/8 Warwicks cooperated with Trench Mortar, machine gun & rifle fire	E.S.D.
"	14.7.16.	10.30am	F.G.C.M. on 947 Pte Redpath R. } 5767 Pte Hunlove J. } for self-inflicting a wound, at Special hospital BUSNES. Witnesses 4 men from C Coy. 3123 Pte G. Yates, 5751 Pte L. Holt, 5730 Pte G. McAndrew, 5683 Pte R. Rice.	
		11pm	Smoke attack due to take place. Postponed owing to wind dropping	
		12m/n	Left Coy of 1/4 Oxfords came under orders of O.C. 2/8 Warwicks	E.S.D.
"	15.7.16		Bn. relieved from Trenches. 13th Yorks & Lancasters took over from Oxford St to CHATEAU Rd HQrs at HUSH HALL	
			14th Yorks & Lancasters — CHATEAU Rd (exc) to S. TILLELOY Trench HQrs EBENEZER FARM	E.S.D.

T2134. Wt. W708—776. 506000. 4/15. Sir J. C. & S.

Instructions regarding War Diaries and Intelligence Summaries are contained in F. S. Regs., Part II. and the Staff Manual respectively. Title pages will be prepared in manuscript.

WAR DIARY
or
INTELLIGENCE SUMMARY.
(Erase heading not required.)

Army Form C. 2118.

Place	Date	Hour	Summary of Events and Information	Remarks and references to Appendices
LA GORGUE	15/7/16	6 pm.	Bn. moved into billets at LA GORGUE HQrs. L 34 d. 3.6. Divisional Reserve	
			Last Coy. 'C' arrived at 11.30 pm.	E.S.D.
			~~[illegible]~~ E.S.D.	
"	16/7/16.	6.30 am.	Rest in billets. Fatigue party of 3 Offrs & 100 men. (A & D Coys)	
			Receipt of Secret Orders for advance of 61st Division. (BMWO 551 & 552. B.O.O. No 22 Copy 7)	
			Baths for whole Bn less those on fatigue.	E.S.D.
"	17.7.16	8 am	A & D Coys at disposal of 182 Bde. Paraded 8 am & marched to LAVENTIE.	
			HQrs, B & C in Divisional Reserve at LA GORGUE. Readiness 'B'.	
		6.55 pm.	Bde Order 24. Copy No 7 received which postpones 'Attack' till 19th inst.	E.S.D.
		11.30 pm.	A & D Coys returned to billets in LA GORGUE	
"	18.7.16.		Training. Bayonet fighting for B & C Coys.	
		1.30 pm.	Bde Order 25. Copy No 7 received giving orders for 'Attack' on 19th	
			Secret maps received (G.C. 9/7/1)	E.S.D.
		9.15.	Fatigue party of 7 Offrs & 240 men sent up to trenches. Returned 5 a.m.	

T2134. Wt. W708—776. 500000. 4/15. Sir J. C. & S.

946

Instructions regarding War Diaries and Intelligence Summaries are contained in F. S. Regs., Part II. and the Staff Manual respectively. Title pages will be prepared in manuscript.

WAR DIARY
or
INTELLIGENCE SUMMARY.
(Erase heading not required.)

Army Form C. 2118.

Place	Date	Hour	Summary of Events and Information	Remarks and references to Appendices
LA GORGUE	19/7/16	9.45 am	Notification that Zero time is 11 a.m.	
			B & C Coys in Bde Reserve at LAVENTIE (Bn Operation Order No 11)	App. III
			HQrs & A & D Coys in Div. Reserve at LA GORGUE.	
			Readiness 'B' from 9.30 am.	S.S.D.
		11 am	Baths for A & D Coys 11 a.m. – 2.35 p.m.	
		8.30 pm	Orders received to move to trenches & relieve 2/6 & 2/7 Warwicks.	
			Arrived trenches 11. pm. Relief completed 1.15 am. FAUQUISSART Section	
		7.45 pm	Aeroplane dropped 3 bombs on LA GORGUE.	
FAUQUISSART Section of Trenches	20/7/16	12.50 am	2/LT. M. D RICH. wounded. 7 men suffered from Shell Shock during relief.	
		7.0 pm.	Capt (Temp Major) W. E. PHILLIPS. reported at Trench HQrs for duty.	
		11. pm.	Raiding party under 2 Lt D STONE. went out.	
			2LT D STONE badly wounded & died on way to Dressing Station.	
		Midnight.	Parties patrolled for killed & wounded of 2/6 & 2/7 Warwicks. Many bodies brought in.	S.S.D.

922

T2134. Wt. W708—776. 500000. 4/15. Sir J. C. & S.

Instructions regarding War Diaries and Intelligence Summaries are contained in F. S. Regs., Part II. and the Staff Manual respectively. Title pages will be prepared in manuscript.

WAR DIARY
or
INTELLIGENCE SUMMARY.
(Erase heading not required.)

Army Form C. 2118.

Place	Date	Hour	Summary of Events and Information	Remarks and references to Appendices
FAUQUISSART Section of Trenches	21.7.16	10.30am	Aerial Torpedoes over our right on to Enemies front line.	
			Lt Farmer took over as Sniping Officer.	
		3pm	3 men went over parapet to fetch in a wounded 2/6th War. man.	
		12 m/n	R.A. programme commenced	
		During night	Many bodies recovered from No Man's Land inc. Capt Sims 2/6 War. and Lt Tisoe 2/6 Glos.	S.S.D.
"	22.7.16		Recovery of bodies continued. One wounded fetched from No Man's Land by 3 men of 'C' Coy in daylight.	
		9.30am	Brigadier & Capt Orr went round the trenches.	
		8.0pm	Orders received to take over frontage of Bn on our left.	
		1.15am	Dead German Officer found in No Mans Land & several other bodies of 2/6 & 2/7 Warwicks found.	
	23.7.16.	12 noon	Relief of Bn on our left completed. i.e. from ERITH ST inclusive to FAUQUISSART – TRIVELET Rd. 'A' Coy took over this line.	S.S.D.

T2134. Wt. W708—776. 506000. 4/15. Sir J. C. & S.

923

Army Form C. 2118.

WAR DIARY
or
INTELLIGENCE SUMMARY.
(Erase heading not required.)

Instructions regarding War Diaries and Intelligence Summaries are contained in F. S. Regs., Part II. and the Staff Manual respectively. Title pages will be prepared in manuscript.

Place	Date	Hour	Summary of Events and Information	Remarks and references to Appendices
FAUQISSART	24/1/16	5.0 am	Relief of the Battalion by 2/8 WORCESTERS. Relief completed by 7.30 a.m. Battalion marched to LAVENTIE, embussed there and proceeded to billets at ROBERMETZ	
			CAPTAIN & ADJUTANT. E.G. DAVIS admitted to hospital. 2/LIEUT. W.R MORTON assumed the duties of Adjutant.	WRM
ROBERMETZ.	"	3.0pm	1 Company bathed at MERVILLE	
"	25/1/16.	10.0am	Court Martial on No. Pte. BALL J at Headquarters, 2/6 WARWICKS. MAJOR. W.E. PHILLIPS, 2/8 WARWICKS sat as president of the Court.	
		all day	Cleaning up. Bathing continued	
		9.0pm	LT. J.A.S. HASSAL reported for duty.	
		11.10pm	1 man of B Coy. shot, while on sentry duty, by some person unknown.	WRM.
"	26/1/16	9.0.	Detachment of 25 men sent to 61st DIVISIONAL TUNNELLING DETACHMENT at M2.c.9.1	
		10AM -11.30	Inspection of A+B Coys by Commanding Officer. 'C' Company. Musketry. 'D' - Bathing	
		11.0 Am	COURT OF ENQUIRY on accidental wounding of No. 4205. PTE. A. FORD. President CAPT. W MACKAY, Members LT. F.C.H. THOM 2/LT. H. RUSHFORTH.	

924

T2134. Wt. W708—776. 500000. 4/15. Sir J. C. & S.

Instructions regarding War Diaries and Intelligence Summaries are contained in F. S. Regs., Part II. and the Staff Manual respectively. Title pages will be prepared in manuscript.

WAR DIARY
or
INTELLIGENCE SUMMARY.
(Erase heading not required.)

Army Form C. 2118.

Place	Date	Hour	Summary of Events and Information	Remarks and references to Appendices
ROBERMETZ ~~JULY 27 1916~~	27/7/16	10.0am	Inspection of C+D Companies by COMMANDING OFFICER. Remaining Companies Musketry and Bayonet Fighting.	WRh
		3.0pm	Inspection of transport by Commanding Officer.	
		10.0pm	Night Work for C+D Companies	
	28/7/16	9.30-12.30	Musketry + Bayonet Fighting (Final assault) for all Companies.	
		1.10pm	Bombing accident, owing to premature explosion of Newton Rifle Grenade, involving injuries to 5 men	WRh.
		2.30-4.30	'Attack' by all Coys	
	29/7/16	9.0	Court of Enquiry on Bombing accident at 'A' Coys Orderly Room. President CAPT WHATMORE, Members 2LT. S.E. DARSONS, 2/LT. H.C. WATSON.	WRh.
		9.30-1.0pm	Company Training for A+B Coys. Musketry for 'C'	
		1.0-5pm	Musketry for 'D' Company.	

921

T2134. Wt. W708-776. 500000. 4/15. Sir J. C. & S.

Instructions regarding War Diaries and Intelligence Summaries are contained in F. S. Regs., Part II. and the Staff Manual respectively. Title pages will be prepared in manuscript.

WAR DIARY
or
INTELLIGENCE SUMMARY.
(Erase heading not required.)

Army Form C. 2118.

Place	Date	Hour	Summary of Events and Information	Remarks and references to Appendices
ROBERMETZ	30/7/16	9.0	Battalion proceeded by Route March to LA GORGUE to attend Horse Show	WRM
		7.0pm	Operation order No , detailing move of Battalion to RIEZ BAILLEUL on the 1st. prox. received.	
	31/7/16	all day	'A', 'B' & 'D' Companies – Company training. 'C' Coy. improvement work on LE SART Range	
		9.30am	Billeting Party proceeded to RIEZ BAILLEUL to arrange Billets	WRM
			Meeting of Commanding Officers & Adjt's at Bde Office.	

Sd. C. Cadman
Lieut. Col.,
Comdg 2/8 R. Warwick. R.

T2134. Wt. W708—776. 500000. 4/15. Sir J. C. & S.

App I

Copy No 10

SECRET.

2ND 8TH BATTALION THE ROYAL WARWICKSHIRE REGIMENT.

OPERATION ORDERS NO 6. BY LT. COL. E.C. CADMAN COMMANDING.

DATED July 3/16.

---

1. The Battalion will relieve the 2/5th Warwicks in Centre Subsection on July 4/16.

2. (a) Left Coy. "C" Coy. will meet guides at entrance to S. TILLELOY TRENCH (M22c.5.5.) at 4 a.m. July 4.
   Support Coy. "D" Coy. .... at 5 a.m. .. 4.
   Centre Coy. "B" Coy. .... at 8 a.m. .. 4.
   Right Coy. "A" Coy. .... at 11 a.m. .. 4.

   (b) Lewis Gunners and Batt. Signallers with certain Coy. Signallers will take over day before. They will meet guides at entrance to S. TILLELOY TRENCH at 8 p.m. July 3.

   (c) Bombers and Snipers will move in with "C" Coy.

3. TRENCH STORES ETC.

One Officer and 1 N.C.O. per Coy. will proceed with "C" Coy. to take over during daylight, all Trench Stores ammunition etc. Duplicate receipts to be forwarded to Batt. Orderly Room by noon July 5.

4. DIRECTION AS TO RELIEF OF POSTS.

Company Commanders will arrange for garrisons at EUSTON. LORETTA. MIN. LONELY. ROUGE CROIX, caretakers 1 & 2, to join Companies as soon after stand down as possible. One N.C.O. and 1 man will be left in each post to hand over to relieving unit.
Remaining Posts (i.e. those manned by "D" Coy.) will remain until relieved.
O.C. "D" Coy. will arrange for rendezvous and guides.

5. RATIONS.

Rations for the day will be carried. Dixies etc. will be carried in by Companies.

6. TRANSPORT.
Baskets and any heavy baggage, carefully labelled, will be dumped at Batt. Hdqrs. and brought to S. TILLELOY TRENCH after dark by Transport.

~~XXXXXXXXXXXXXXXXXXXXXXXXXXXXX.~~
Officers baggage and articles not required in the Trenches will be dumped inside railings opposite Sentry at CROIX BARBEE CROSS RD. by 8 a.m. and taken by Transport to Qr. Mr's Stores.

7. POLICE.
A policeman will always be on duty at entrance to S. TILLELOY TRENCH.

8. BATT. HDQRS.
Batt. Hdqrs. will close at 10 a.m. and re-open in the Centre Subsection 11 a.m.

(Signed) E.G. DAVIS.
Capt. & Adjt.
8 Warwicks.

1–4 Coys.
5 Bde.
6. L. Gun Offr.
7 2/5 Warw.
8 Office
9, 10 War Diary

App. II

Copy No.4.

928

2/8TH BATTALION THE ROYAL WARWICKSHIRE REGIMENT.

OPERATION ORDERS NO.8, BY LT. COL E.C. CADMAN. COMMANDING.

DATED JULY11.1916.

1. "A" Coy. will be withdrawn from the Fire Trench to-day.

2. Company Frontages will be re-adjusted as follows:-
"D" Coy. Bays 211 - 236 and Bays 1 - 19.
"B" Coy. Bays 20 - 54.

RELIEF OF "A" COY. (less 2 Platoons).

3. Extra Bays to be taken over and relief completed by 7 p.m. July 11.

4. Responsibilities of "A" Coy. for Trench Stores etc. to be taken over by "D" Coy.

5. 2 Platoons of "A" (less 18 O.R. who will occupy DUCK'S BILL) will move back to "B" Line.

(Signed) Ed. C. Cadman.Lt. Col.
Commanding 2/8 Warwicks.

Copies to.
1 - "A" Coy.
2 - "B" Coy.
3 - "D" Coy.
4 - File.

App VI

Copy No. 9

2/8TH BATTALION THE ROYAL WARWICKSHIRE REGIMENT.

OPERATION ORDERS NO. 11, BY LT. COL. E.C. CADMAN COMMANDING.

DATED July 19/16.

1. "B" & "C" Coys. with three Lewis Guns will be placed at the disposal of the 182nd Inf. Bde. to-day.

Capt Mackay. "B" "C" Machine Guns.

2. Companies will fall in as per margin, at 2 p.m. on road running N. from LA GORGUE Church, column of route facing South, head of column at LA GORGUE Church.

Route. 3. BELLE CROIX - G.32.d.4.6. - LAVENTIE Railway Station, to arrive 2.45 p.m. One Officer will report at Brigade Hdqrs. at 2.45 p.m.

Rations. 4. Rations to be taken as arranged by O.C. party with Qr. Mr. Cookers to be sent to LAVENTIE. Qr. Mr. to send rations nightly to LAVENTIE Station. All ranks will carry the Iron Ration. Water bottles to be filled.

Billets. 5. Party will be billeted in LAVENTIE by 183 Brigade.

6. Headqrs., "A" & "D" Coys. will remain in LA GORGUE in Div. Reserve. On being called upon, they will fall in on Alarm Posts and await orders. Units will report to Batt. Hdqrs. when ready to move.

7. Lt. Hamilton and one Orderly (both mounted on cycles) will report to Div. Hdqrs. at 9 a.m. to-day. Capt. Brock, Lt. Morton, Lt. Sloane, and other surplus officers of Bde. will report to 2/8 Warwicks. Hdqrs. at 9 a.m. to-day.

Dress. 8. Fighting Order.

9. Readiness B will prevail for whole of Battalion from 9.30 a.m. onwards.

10. Brigade Reserve will report to COCKSHY HOUSE M.4.c.1.1.

(sd) E.G. Davis. Capt & Adjt.

Issued at 8.15 a.m. 2/8 Warwicks.

Copies 1-4 Coys.
5 L.G.O.
6 Capt. Mackay.
7 Qr.Mr.
8 Office.
9 & 10 War Diary.

4 H 30

Confidential

Vol 4

War Diary of:-

2/8th Battalion The Royal Warwickshire

Regiment.

Period:- Aug 1st to 31st 1916.

Volume IV

930
4/B

NOTE. Guides for Headquarters 5th GORDONS and 2 Coys ROYAL SCOTS relieving three Coys 2/8.R.WAR.R. will be at KEEPERS HOUSE from 5-30 p.m. onwards. Please inform me if these guides are not required.

sgd. E.C.CADMAN. Lieut.Col.
Commdg. 2/8.R.WAR.R.

VOL 4.

Instructions regarding War Diaries and Intelligence Summaries are contained in F. S. Regs., Part II. and the Staff Manual respectively. Title pages will be prepared in manuscript.

WAR DIARY
or
INTELLIGENCE SUMMARY.
(Erase heading not required.)

Army Form C. 2118.

Place	Date	Hour	Summary of Events and Information	Remarks and references to Appendices
ROBERMETZ	1/8/16.	5.30 am.	Battalion moved by Route march to RIEZ BAILLEUL, — to occupy billets and posts in reserve line. (Operation Order No. 13)	App. I.
RIEZ BAILLEUL	"	9.0 a.m.	Battalion arrived at RIEZ BAILLEUL. Headquarters	
		12 noon.	Relief of following posts completed: LA FLINQUE, PONT DU HEM, CHARTERHOUSE, ETON, HARROW ROUGE CROIX E.W., MIN, LONELY, CHARTERHOUSE. Garrisons found by 'B' Company. LT. SLOANE R.E. proceeded to the FOREST CONTROL, LE PARC to relieve LT. B.H. PARSONS ~~Post~~	WRh.
"	2/8/16	7.0 am – 10.0 am, 4.0 pm – 7.0 pm	Under Company Officers. Construction of Bayonet Fighting Course. Baths at CROIX BARBÉE.	WRh.
			Following R.E. working parties found.	
		11 pm	1 Officer 25 men at LA BASSEE DUMP (M 21. c. 8.9) for carrying work; 1 Officer 40 men " " " " "	
"	3/8/16.	4 a.m.	1 Officer 50 men as R.E. working party at junc. S. TILLELOY & RUE BACQUEROT for work in Reserve line.	WRh.
		11.0 pm	Other working parties as for 2/8/16	

Instructions regarding War Diaries and Intelligence Summaries are contained in F. S. Regs., Part II. and the Staff Manual respectively. Title pages will be prepared in manuscript.

WAR DIARY
or
~~INTELLIGENCE~~ SUMMARY.

(Erase heading not required.)

Army Form C. 2118.

Place	Date	Hour	Summary of Events and Information	Remarks and references to Appendices
RIEZ BAILLEUL	4/8/16	4.0 am – 11.0 pm	R.E. Working parties found as for previous days	
		7.0 pm	Instructions received re repair of emergency roads EBENEZER ROAD	
		8.0 am – 10 am, 4 pm to 7 pm	Work under Company Officers, principally Bayonet fighting and practice in the assault. 1 Company held in readiness B	WRM.
"	5/8/16	4.0 am – 11.0 pm	R.E. working party found as for previous days	
		"	Further garrison of 1 NCO & 3 men found for PONT RIQUELL, (R9 b & 100)	WRM
		8–10 am, 4–7 pm	Company Training – Bayonet Fighting, Form of attack across 'NO MAN'S LAND'	
"	6/8/16	4.0 am – 11.0 pm	R.E. working parties found as for previous days	
		10.0 am	Church Parade (combined 2/6 & 2/E) at Headquarters 2/6 R.W.R. R., RIEZ BAILLEUL	WRM.

Instructions regarding War Diaries and Intelligence Summaries are contained in F. S. Regs., Part II. and the Staff Manual respectively. Title pages will be prepared in manuscript.

WAR DIARY
or
INTELLIGENCE SUMMARY.
(Erase heading not required.)

Army Form C. 2118.

Place	Date	Hour	Summary of Events and Information	Remarks and references to Appendices
RIEZ BAILLEUL	7/8/16		Working Parties found as for previous days	
		8-10 4-6	Company Training Bayonet Fighting	LRM.
	8/8/16		Working Parties, except 4 a.m. cancelled.	
		8-10 4-6	Company Training.	
		6.0pm	CAPT. J. MUNGLE reported from 1st Army School of Instruction	
		10.0am	C.O, COMPANY COMMANDERS proceeded to BDE HDQRS to arrange details of Relief	LRM.
		4.0pm	Order No. 20 regarding Relief received	
	9/8/16	3.30PM 1-30 3-0PM	"D" Coy + 2 platoons of "A" Coy } Relieved 2/5th Warwicks 2 Platoons of "C" Coy } garrisoned S. Tilleloy Post, Rafone Post.	O.A.T. LRM.
		4.15PM	Relief of 2/5th Warwicks complete. Quiet night, no casualties during either the relief or the following night.	Appendix I

Instructions regarding War Diaries and Intelligence Summaries are contained in F. S. Regs., Part II. and the Staff Manual respectively. Title pages will be prepared in manuscript.

WAR DIARY
or
INTELLIGENCE SUMMARY.

(Erase heading not required.)

Army Form C. 2118.

Place	Date	Hour	Summary of Events and Information	Remarks and references to Appendices
NEUVE CHAPELLE and MOATED GRANGE.	10/5/16	10a.m	Remainder of Batt. left RIEZ BAILLEUL & relieved 14th York & Lancs Regt 94th Bde. "C" Coy, in reserve, occupies CHATEAU & CHURCH Redoubts, & garrisoned with 1 platoon MOGG'S HOLE. Remainder of Coy in CARDIFF ROAD in reserve. Enemy shelled between front & support lines at frequent intervals throughout the day; about 30 aerial torpedoes on front line. Two casualties.	App II WRH.
"	11th	9 a.m	Brigadier visited HQRS & front line. Very quiet during morning.	
		2p.m	Enemy shelled HUSH HALL & CHATEAU communication trench; the latter is now almost unusable. Two dug-outs in process of construction with R.Es at HQRS. Capt Lapham went sick. Two	WRH
"		10.30pm	casualties. 2nd Lt. W. Hodgson 7th Lancs. Fus. reported for duty was posted to "D" Coy.	
	12th		Patrols during previous night did good work, put enemy patrol to flight & brought in several bombs etc. Morning quiet but for aerial torpedoes to which we replied with Stokes guns & silenced for a time.	
"		2-4	Transport field at RIEZ BAILLEUL shelled. No damage. Small mine was exploded by us at 7.30 a.m in sector N of this. Quiet evening. 4 casualties during day, 1 died & buried at 8 p.m at POINT-DU-HEM.	WRH
		11.15pm	2nd Lieut W. G. CHAPPLE 7th Lancs Fusiliers reported for duty was posted to "A" Coy.	
	13th	10-12a.m	Frequent shells passing over HQRS & bursting along LA BASSÉE Road. Capt. Brook left battalion on six weeks course. Lt B. K. Parsons in command of "D" Coy. Two officers from "C" temporarily transferred to "D". 50% of all P.S. smoke bombs sent to D.A.C. Helmets in "Gas Alert" position for 8 p.m previous night to 10 a.m 13th owing to 184th Bde carrying out cylinders.	WRH

T2134. Wt. W708—776. 500000. 4/15. Sir J. C. & S.

Army Form C. 2118.

Instructions regarding War Diaries and Intelligence Summaries are contained in F. S. Regs., Part II. and the Staff Manual respectively. Title pages will be prepared in manuscript.

WAR DIARY
or
~~INTELLIGENCE SUMMARY.~~
(Erase heading not required.)

Place	Date	Hour	Summary of Events and Information	Remarks and references to Appendices
NEUVE CHAPELLE and MOATED GRANGE.	13th contd.	7-30 - 8pm	Bombardment by MTMs covered by artillery on enemy front line. After 15 minutes enemy retaliated with T-Ms & artillery damaging our trenches slightly. Night very quiet	
	14th	9-12.	Enemy shelled support lines & put a quantity of aerial torpedoes over front line. Three casualties, 1 Sgt killed. Afternoon quiet.	WRH. WRH
		6. p.m	Draft of two men arrived. One posted to 'A' Coy (for Lewis guns) one to 'A' for Duty.	
		8.15 - 8.45	Short but violent bombardment by our STOKES guns, M.T. Mortars & rifle grenades covered by artillery. Enemy replied after 10 minutes with T.M's, aerial torpedoes & artillery.	
	15th	-	Heavy M-Gun fire during previous night. 10-11.30 a.m. Enemy shelled reserve trenches.	
		9 a.m	Brig-General visited HQRS & went round the front line. Day fairly quiet.	WRH.
		6 p.m	Enemy fired a large mine on our left in NO MAN'S LAND, apparently in reply to one of ours at 6 p.m	
		6 to 6.30	Short but violent bombardment of enemy's front line by MTM's, Stokes covered by our guns.	
		7 p.m	One platoon of "C" relieved one of "D" in the DUCK'S BILL crater. Relief complete 8.15 p.m.	
	16th	--	Very quiet during preceding night.	
		2-4 p.m	Enemy shelled with 5.9 a battery behind LA BASSEE ROAD, & also 'B' lines & MOGG'S hole, at the latter place doing some damage.	WRH.
		8.15 p.m	Orders for relief on 19th by 2/5th R. War. R came from Bde. Enemy's machine-guns very active.	[illegible]

T2134. Wt. W708-776. 500000. 4/15. Sir J. C. & S.

Instructions regarding War Diaries and Intelligence Summaries are contained in F. S. Regs., Part II. and the Staff Manual respectively. Title pages will be prepared in manuscript.

WAR DIARY
or
~~INTELLIGENCE SUMMARY.~~
(Erase heading not required.)

Army Form C. 2118.

Place	Date	Hour	Summary of Events and Information	Remarks and references to Appendices
NEUVE CHAPELLE and MOATED GRANGE.	17th	8 a.m.	Five men returned to Batt. from ROUEN. Working party arrived 4.30 a.m. worked from 4.30–11.30 repairing parapets.	
		11 am.	Bde operation orders for relief issued. From 11 till about 1.30 p.m. 5.9 shells passing over Batt HQrs bursting near LA BASSÉE ROAD, presumably trying for our batteries. Day very quiet.	
"		7–7.30	Combined bombardment by TMs, rifle grenades + Artillery. Enemy retaliated after 5 minutes but did not do much damage. Three casualties during bombardment. G.O.C. Division visited HQRS followed by Brigadier-General.	WRH
"	18th		Enemy shelled a field behind Batt. HQRS at intervals throughout morning; front line very quiet.	
		10 am.	O.C. 2/5th R. War. R. + Company Commanders arrived to arrange details of relief. Capt. Lepony [?] left for Bde HQRS	
		2 pm	2nd Lt A.L. Tosland [?] left for LA GORGUE to draw money from Field Cashier for pay.	
		6–6.30 and 7.30–8	Bombardment of enemy's front line by Trench Mortars, Stokes, rifle grenades assisted by our Artillery. Enemy retaliated chiefly with Shrapnel. Not much damage done by him.	WRH
		9–11.	Our 18 prs. kept up a slow fire on enemy's roads etc in rear of his lines. He retaliated with Shrapnel on LA BASSÉE road.	
		10.15–11.30.	A small raiding party, after blowing in enemy's wire with a Bangalore torpedo, raided his crater next to the DUCK'S BILL. Found it unoccupied but destroyed his work in it + a quantity of timber, planks + stores. The torpedo has destroyed nearly all his wire on one side of the crater.	WRH

Army Form C. 2118.

WAR DIARY
or
INTELLIGENCE SUMMARY.
(*Erase heading not required.*)

Instructions regarding War Diaries and Intelligence Summaries are contained in F. S. Regs., Part II. and the Staff Manual respectively. Title pages will be prepared in manuscript.

Place	Date	Hour	Summary of Events and Information	Remarks and references to Appendices
	18th	11 p.m	The party returned about 11.30 with no casualties.	
	19th	-	The Batt. was relieved by 2/5 R War. R. "B" + "D" Coys relieved by their "A" + "C" Coys at 2.30 p.m "A" Coy by their "B" + "C" (in reserve) by their "D" at 5 p.m. Enemy very quiet during relief. Batt. moved by Coys in parties of 10 at 100x interval to billets at RIEZ BAILLEUL, each Coy being met en route by guide who led them to their billets. All in billets by 6.30 p.m	WRh
RIEZ BAILLEUL			"D" Coy finding garrisons for posts.	App. III
"	20th		Coy's bathing at LA GORGUE Divisional Baths from 10 a.m – 5 p.m.	
		6.15 pm	Voluntary Divine Service at Battalion Headquarters	
		11 pm	Working Parties of 1 officer 40 O.R. found for carrying party at LA BASSÉE DUMP and 1 officer 60 O.R. for EUSTON DUMP.	WRh
			2/LT. E.L. LLOYD attached to R.A (B/170) for 24 hours	
	21st	4.30 am	Working party of 1 Officer, 30 O.R found for HUSH HALL. Other working parties as for 20th. One officer attached to R.F.A for 24 hours	WRh.

T2134. Wt. W708–776. 500000. 4/15. Sir J. C. & S.

Instructions regarding War Diaries and Intelligence Summaries are contained in F. S. Regs., Part II. and the Staff Manual respectively. Title pages will be prepared in manuscript.

WAR DIARY
or
INTELLIGENCE SUMMARY.
(Erase heading not required.)

Army Form C. 2118.

Place	Date	Hour	Summary of Events and Information	Remarks and references to Appendices
RIEZ BAILLEUL.	21/8/16	10.0 A.M	Field General Court Martial on No 5366 SGT P. MORRIS, 2/8TH WARWICKS, at Bde. Hdqrs on a charge of "Disobeying a lawful command given by his superior officer." Found Guilty and sentenced to reduction to the ranks and 90 days F.P. No 2.	
			CAPT. W.R.T. WHATMORE sat as ~~president~~ member of the Court.	WRh
		7-8 am 9.30-12.30 2.30-3.30	Company training for C & A Coys : D Company holding posts : B Coy. special training	
	22/8/16		Working parties as for previous days	
		7-8 am 9.30-12.30 2.30-3.30	do for 21st.	WRh
			2/LT. R.V. HAMILTON, 2/8 WARWICKS returned from hospital.	
			Orders for Raid published (preliminary)	App IV
	23/8/16.		Working parties as for previous days.	
		2.0 p.m	Inter-Battalion Sports (2/6 & 2/8 WARWICKS).	WRh
		12 noon	Promulgation of FGCM sentence on SGT P. MORRIS	

Instructions regarding War Diaries and Intelligence Summaries are contained in F. S. Regs., Part II. and the Staff Manual respectively. Title pages will be prepared in manuscript.

WAR DIARY
or
INTELLIGENCE SUMMARY.
(*Erase heading not required.*)

Army Form C. 2118.

Place	Date	Hour	Summary of Events and Information	Remarks and references to Appendices
RIEZ BAILLEUL	24/8/16		Working Parties as for previous days.	
		11 pm	'B' Coy. raided enemy trenches about M.36.c.9.5. A Bangalore torpedo was exploded to form gap. Enemy trenches entered by LT. E E PARSONS + 2/LT. A L PROSSER who, having expended their store of bombs, returned. Casualties Wounded O.R. 8. Missing O.R. 4. Wounded at duty O.R. 4.	W.R.H. App V
	25/8/16	7-8 9.30-12.30 2.30-3.30	Company training	
		11.45pm	Exploration of NO MAN'S LAND by CAPT. LEFROY + LT WATSON + 32 men to investigating missing. Out of 4 missing 1 returned wounded, 2 found dead, 1 still missing.	
			Orders for move to ROBERMETZ received.	W.R.H.
	26/8/16	8.0 am	Battalion moved by route march to Robermetz.	App VI
ROBERMETZ			Headquarters K.24.d.4.7. (Reference map sheet 36 a)	W.R.H.

99

Instructions regarding War Diaries and Intelligence Summaries are contained in F. S. Regs., Part II. and the Staff Manual respectively. Title pages will be prepared in manuscript.

WAR DIARY
or
INTELLIGENCE SUMMARY.
(Erase heading not required.)

Army Form C. 2118.

Place	Date	Hour	Summary of Events and Information	Remarks and references to Appendices
ROBERMETZ	27/8/16	10.0	Church Parade (2/6th & 2/8th WARWICKS) on the Town Square, MERVILLE.	
		3.0	2/LT. LLOYD. & 10 men proceeded to SNIPING COURSE at LE SART Range.	
	28/8/16	9.0am	MAJ. W.E. PHILLIPS, CAPT T.E. LEFROY, LT. S.E. PARSONS, 2/LT. T. ENTWHISTLE, and 4 NCO's attended B.E. Course at MEURILLON. Course to last 6 working days.	W.R.M.
			Company training	
	29/8/16		All Companies musketry practice on LE SART Range. A Coy. 9am – 11 am. B " 10.30 – 12.30 C. Coy. 2.30 – 4.0 p.m. D " 2.30 – 5.0 p.m.	W.R.M.
		6.30 pm.	Draft of 5 men received.	
	30/8/16	7–8.0 9–12.30 2–4.0	Company training – very much hindered by bad weather.	
		3.0pm.	LT. HODGSON & 1.O.R. proceeded to LA GORGUE for P.T & B.F. Course.	
		2.30pm	Lewis Gunners at Divisional Gas School for demonstration in Gas measures	W.R.M.

940

T2134. Wt. W708–776. 500000. 4/15. Sir J. C. & S.

Instructions regarding War Diaries and Intelligence Summaries are contained in F. S. Regs., Part II. and the Staff Manual respectively. Title pages will be prepared in manuscript.

WAR DIARY
or
INTELLIGENCE SUMMARY.
(*Erase heading not required.*)

Army Form C. 2118.

Place	Date	Hour	Summary of Events and Information	Remarks and references to Appendices
ROBERMETZ	31/8/16.	7-8 am 930-12.30 2.0-5.30	Company Training. Erection of Bayonet Fighting Course	
		10.0 am	20 NCOs & 80 men attended the Divisional Gas School (L.34.C.4.7) for demonstration of Gas attack and Gas Drill.	WRM.
		3.0 pm	Presentation of 'parchments' for Gallantry to 6 N.C.O's & men of Battalion at LA GORGUE	
		10 pm	Five new officers arrived, all from 3/5 R. War. R. 2nd/Lieuts Walker, Kitchin, Tonks, Gibbins & Whiteley and were posted to companies.	WRM.

E. A. Cladmore Lt. Col.,
Comdg 2/8 R. War. R.

941

T.1134. Wt. W708-776. 500000. 4/15. Sir J. C. & S.

BATTALION ORDERS. by LIEUT.COL. E.C.CADMAN.

COMMANDING. 2/8 Battalion THE ROYAL WARWICKSHIRE REGIMENT.
WEDNESDAY 9th AUGUST 1916.

1. The following will take over their portion of the line as allotted to them tomorrow 10th inst as follows:-

2. Remaining two Platoons "A" Coy will be at entrance to S.Tilleloy at 10 a.m.
Remaining two platoons "C" Coy will be at entrance to Baluchi trench at ~~an hour to be issued by O.C. Company.~~ 10 am

3. Officers baggage and Company Stores, properly tied and labelled required for the trenches will be stacked outside Coy Headquarters by 10 a.m..
Companies will arrange for Fatigue parties to carry it from ROUGE CROIX where Transport will convey to by 1 p.m.
Remainder of Officers kit and Company Stores, not required, will be stacked outside Company Headquarters for removal to Quarter-Master's Stores. One man remaining behind until Transport arrive to take it over.

4. Unconsumed portions of the days rations will be carried by the men.
O.C.Companies willarrange for Camp Kettles to be taken into the trenches.

5. O.C. Companies will send one Officer or N.C.O. to take over Trench Stores, ammunition, etc. by 9 a.m.

6. O.C. "C" Coy will detail 1 N.C.O. and 3 men for CURZON REDOUBT.
O.C. "A" " " " 1 N.C.O. and 3 men for CHATEAU REDOUBT.
O.C. "B" " " " 1 N.C.O. and 3 men for CHURCH REDOUBT.

All reliefs will take place by 12 noon.

7. O.C. Coys will ascertain the number of Trench Mortars and Machine Gun personnel in their portion of the line and to which platoon they will be attached and send a report to Battalion Orderly Room as early as possible.

8. All caps will be left behind and handed over to Coy.Qr.Mr.Sergts. for safe custody.

9. When reliefs are complete Companies will notify Battalion Headquarters by code word.

10 Field Cookers must be left clean and nothing will be allowed to be taken from them for use in the trenches.

sgd. E.C.CADMAN. Lieut.Col.
Commdg 2/8 Warwicks.

issued at 12 noon.

Copy No.1/3 "A" "B" "C" Coys.
4. Y. & Lancs.R.
5 War Diary
6 File.

2. (continued). "B" COMPANY will be at entrance to BALUCHI TRENCH at an hour to be issued by O.C. Company.

SECRET.

App. II

BLACK SQUARE BATTALION ORDER No.14. Copy No. 9
Reference:- Bethune Map 1/40000 AUGUST 9TH 1916.

1. The Battalion will take over the line from the 2/8.R.War.R. today M.35.b.8½.6½. to M.35.d.5½.6 ½.

2. Guides will meet the following at entrance to S.TILLELOY STREET as follows:-

Signallers. Snipers. 3 Lewis Guns.	at 9-30 a.m.
Two Platoons. "A" Company.	at 1-30 p.m.
"D" Company.	at 3-30 p.m.
2 Platoons "C" Company.	at 3 p.m.

3. O.C. Company will detail the following:-

S.TILLELOY POST.	1 N.C.O. and 8 men.
LAFONE POST.	1 N.C.O. and 8 men.

4. O.C. Companies will send one Officer or N.C.O. to take over Trench Stores, ammunition, etc. Duplicate receipts will be forwarded to Battalion Orderly Room by 2-30 p.m.

5. All ranks will carry the unconsumed portion of the days rations. O.C.Coys will make the necessary arrangements to take Camp kettles with them.

6. (a). Baskets and heavy baggage correctly labelled will be dumped outside Company and Battalion Headquarters by 2 p.m. Transport will arrange to carry same to ROUGE CRIOX by 3-30 p.m.
O.C. Coys will detail the necessary fatigue parties to carry it to Company Headquarters in the trenches.
(b). Officers baggage and articles not required in the trenches will be stacked outside Coy Headquarters by 10 a.m. and removed by Transport to Q.M.Stores. One man per Coy will remain with it until it is removed.

7. Battalion Headquarters will move to the Trenches at 2-30 p.m.

8. Field Cookers must be left behind clean and no part of the cooker will be allowed to be taken into the trenches.

9. O.C. Coys will ascertain the number of Trench Mortar and Machine Gun personnel is in their portion of the line and notify Battalion Orderly Room to which platoon they are attached to by 4 p.m.

10. All Caps will be left behind and handed over to Coy.Qr.Mr.Sergts. for safe custody.

11. Companies will report relief complete by code word.

signed. E.C.CADMAN. Lieut.Col.
Commdg. Black Square Battalion.

issued at 6 a.m.

Copy No.1/3. "A" "C" "D" Coys.
4. Headquarter Coy.
5. 2/7.Warwicks.
6. Lewis Gun Officer.
7. Signalling Officer.
8. Quartermaster and Transport Officer.
9/10. War Diary.
11. File.

App III

Sheet 1. Copy No. 11

nhb

BATTALION ORDER No.36. by LT.COL. E.C.CALMAN.

COMMANDING. 2/8. BATTALION THE ROYAL WARWICKSHIRE REGIMENT.

FRIDAY 16th AUGUST 1918.

1.RELIEF. The Battalion will be relieved tomorrow by 2/6.WARWICKS.

2. "B" and "D" Companies will be relieved about 1-30 p.m.
Guides for RIGHT Coy ("B") only to be at entrance
of BALUCHI TRENCH at 12-45 p.m.
"B" Coy will move out via NEW CUT and BALUCHI.
"D" Coy via TILLELOY.
The Centre Coy ("A") will be relieved about 3-30 p.m.
Guides to be at entrance of BALUCHI TRENCH at 3-15 p.m.
On relief they will move out via BALUCHI TRENCH.
"C" Company will be relieved about 5-30 p.m. no guides
will be sent. They will move out via TILLELOY.
O.C. "C" Coy will arrange for guides to be at Company
Headquarters to conduct garrisons for CHURCH and CHATEAU
POSTS.

9-30 p.m. Signallers, Snipers and Machine Gunners will
be relieved. Guides to be at entrance of BALUCHI
TRENCH at 9 oclock.

2.POSTS. Immediately on relief "D" Coy will take over Posts as
per attached table.
O.C. "C" Company will detail 1 Officer and 50 men to
report to 3/1st Field Coy.R.E. at 6 p.m. on the day
of relief.

3.RATIONS. Rations for Machine Gun and Trench Mortar personnel
will be found by Relieving Battalion.
A special memo regarding Transport and rations has
been issued.

4.TRENCH STORES. Receipts for Trench Stores will be handed in to
Battalion Headquarters by 9 a.m. 20th inst.

5.HEADQUARTERS. Trench Headquarters will close at 4-30 p.m. and
Battalion Headquarters will open at RUE BAILLEUL
M.14.a.2.6. as soon as possible after relief.

6.BILLETS. The Battalion will move to billets now occupied by
2/6.Warwicks.
Billeting party will report to 2/Lt.Tosland at
Battalion Headquarters at 9-30 a.m. 18th inst. They
will meet Companies at M.14.c.7.6. and lead Companies
to their billets.

O.C.Companies will see that no Battalion Stores are
left in the Trenches.

sgd. W.H.MORTON. 2/Lt. & A/Adjt
2/8.R.Warwick.R.

Copy. No.1/4. Companies.
5. 2/6.R.War.R.
6. Lewis Gun Officer.
7. Sniping Officer.
8. Signalls.
9. Quartermaster.
10. File.
11. War Diary.

"B" COMPANY. 2/8.R.WARWICK.REGT. **SECRET.**

RAID ORDERS.

1. The Company will make a raid on the enemy trenches about M.36.c.9.5.

2. OBJECT. To force an entry at two points and to kill Germans, take prisoners, obtain identifications, destroy Machine Gun and Trench Mortars etc., and general demolition.

3. The Company will leave billets at 6-15 p.m.(via BALUCHI and NEW CUT Alley).

4. DISTRIBUTION OF COMPANY.

Party 1. under Lieut.S.E.Parsons. SUB-DIVIDED.
(a). Sergt.Corless & 13 O.R.
will enter LEFT GAP. (b). Sergt.Green. & 11 O.R.
(c). Sergt.Carter. & 13 O.R.

Party 2 under 2/Lt.A.L.Prosser. SUB-DIVIDED.
(d). Sgt.Chamberlain & 13 O.R.
(e). Sgt.Marsden & 11 O.R.
will enter RIGHT GAP. (f). Sgt.Lofting & 13 O.R.

5. Sub-Party (a) enters gap bombs to LEFT along enemy front trench.
Sub-Party (b).enters gap bombs to RIGHT along enemy trench as far as possible within time limit.
Sub-Party (c) enters gap follows ~~the~~ sub-party (b) along front trench as far as the first trench junction on the left, party (c) then bombs up this trench.
Sub-Party (d) enters gap bombs to the right along enemy front trench.
Sub-Party (e) enters gap bombs to the LEFT along enemy front trench as far as possible within the time limit.
Sub-Party (f) enters gap follows Sub-Party (e) along front trench as far as the first trench junction on the right. Sub-Party (f) then bombs up this trench.

(All parties withdrew over route of entry if possible)

6. TORPEDO COVERING PARTY.
1. N.C.O. and 6 men will act as covering party to LEFT Torpedo Party and a similar number to the RIGHT Torpedo Party.
Covering Parties to report to Bombing Officer by 8 p.m.

After explosion these parties will form a supporting party to assist in the evacuation of prisoners, wounded, etc., They will remain close to enemy's wire, near to respective gaps and be under orders of O.C. Raid.

7. LEWIS GUN.
One Lewis Gun will accompany Party (a) and will remain outside gap to cover withdrawal.

8. Failure of either party will in no way influence action of the other party.
No attempt will be made to explode torpedos simultaneously.
If large or active enemy patrols or covering parties prevent the laying of torpedos ~~by~~ thesecovering parties will be surrounded and vigorously attacked under unders from O.C. Raid.

9. In event of failure to lay torpedos, party withdraws under orders of O.C. Raid.

10. Officers Commanding Parties 1 and 2 will detail a sequence of Commands in event of casualties, and all ranks will be informed of the sequence.

App IV

VERY SECRET

2ND 8TH BATTALION THE ROYAL WARWICKSHIRE REGIMENT.

Copy No. 6

BATTALION ORDER BY LT.COL.E.C.CADMAN COMMANDING.
22ND AUGUST 1916.

On the night 24/25th a raid will be ~~xxxx~~ made on the enemy trenches at about M.36.c.0.5.

2. OBJECT. (a). Kill Germans. (b). Take prisoners. (c) Obtain identifications. (d). Destroy Machine Gun ~~xxxM.G.~~ Emplacements and Trench Mortars and general demolition.
3. The raiding party will force an entry at two points about 25 yards North of Junction SIGN POST LANE and GERMAN FRONT LINE and at a point about 120 yards NORTH of this.
4. O.C. "B" Coy will detail raiding force and will provide covering party for torpedo carriers.
5. The Battalion Bombing Officer will arrange to make two gaps in enemy wire at points indicated above (exact spot to be arranged between O.C. Raiding Party and Battalion Bombing Officer.
6. The Raiding Parties will rush gap the instant the explosions occur.
7. O.C. 182nd L.T.M.B's will co-operate as arranged confining his fire to the flanks of the front to be attacked.
8. One Lewis Gun will accompany and be at the disposal of O.C. Raiding Party.
9. The 182nd Machine Gun Coy will co-operate by indirect fire on back areas under instructions from G.O.C. 182nd Inf.Bde care being taken that up to the explosion of the first torpedo the situation is kept normal.
10. The artillery will co-operate under instructions from G.O.C. 182 Inf.Bde. no action to be taken previous to the exploding of torpedos.
11. Strength of the actual Raiding Party not to exceed 100 men.
12. Signalling Officer will arrange telephonic communications between point of firing fuse and our own front line.
13. O.C. Raiding Party to arrange all details as to arms and equipment.
14. No Identity discs or other means of identification will be worn.
15. The Medical Officer will arrange for the evacuation of casualties from the Front Line to EBENEZER AID POST via LAFONE POST and G.E.R.
16. The Raiding Party will use BALUCHI and NEW CUT C.T's. and will be in our Front Line by 7-30 p.m. 24th inst.

Ed. C. Cadman Lt.Col.
Commanding 2/8.Warwicks.

No.1. 182nd.Inf.Bde.
2. 2/5.Warwicks.
3. O.C. "B" Coy.
4. B.O. 8th.R.War.R.
5. File.
6. War Diary.

11. **SEQUENCE OF EVENTS.**

ZERO. (1), Torpedo parties leave our front trench.
(2). Artillery warned to "STAND BY"

0.20. (1). Parties 1 and 2 leave our front trench to take up positions of assembly in NO MANS LAND (see sketch attached)

0.45. (1). Parties 1 and 2 to be ready in position.

O.x. (1). Torpedo layer reports to Officer in charge of LEFT (or RIGHT) Party "TORPEDO READY"
(2). Officer in Charge of Party, if ready, orders Bombing Officer to fire Torpedo.

O.y. (1). First torpedo is fired.
(2). STOKES Guns open fire to cover flanks. (All Stokes open fire at first explosion)

PARTY RUSHES GAP.
(3). Artillery warned "FIRE"
(4). One red rocket to be fired from our front trench (to confirm (3).

O.z. (1). O.C. Raid reports his parties "ALL IN"
(2). 3 or 4 red rockets fired from our front line (informs artillery to cease fire).
(3). Artillery warned "ALL IN", this by telephone upon receipt of which Artillery will cease fire.

12. Signal for withdrawal will come from O.C. Raid. All ranks to be informed verbally as to what this signal will be.

13. Details of Equipment as below.

PARTY.	Off.	N.C.O.	OR.	RIFLES.	BAYt.	SAA.	Bombs.	Revl.	Amn.	Cutt.	Knob.	Bn. Bombs.
A.	1	3	11	12	14	130.	136.	2.	36.	8	4	
B.	..	3	9	10	12	150	112	2	36	8	4	
C.	1.	3	11	12	14	180	136	2	36	8	4	
D.	1	3	11	12	14	180	136	2	36	8	4	
E.	..	3	9	10	12	150	112	2	36	8	4	
F.	..	3	11	12	14	180	136	2	36	8	4	
COVERING.	1.	2	10	12	14	210.	28.	2	36	12	=	28
TORPEDO.	1.	3	36		33		152	6	108	12		
DEMOLITION.		3	9		12		24	12	216	=	=	

Electric torches to be distributed.
Bayonets carried by frog on belt.

14.DETAILS.

(1). All faces blackened after arrival on our own front line.
(2). No identity discs, papers, numerals, or other means of identification to be worn or carried.
(3). Certain men to be specially detailed to bring back prisoners.
(4). All ranks to be warned that enemy may make use of English words especially the word RETIRE.
(5). All telephone wires to be cut.
(6) Any check be cleared atonce by getting outside trench and taking enemy in flank and rear.
(7). Bombing Officer and 2/Lt.Hassell to arrange for supply of bombs, ammunition, rockets, etc.
(8). 2/Lt.Tosland to arrange Signal Station at CRICHIETH CASTLE O.P. to Front Line and No Mans Land.
(9). Gas Helmets to be worn in the ALERT position (on chest).
(10) Leaders of Parties C and F will detail one man to drop tape-line as he rushes gap.
(11). O.C.Parties 1 and 2 will make arrangements to carry scaling ladders and bridges as required.

Captain,

O.C. "B" Company.

PARTY 1. TO ENTER BY LEFT GAP.

SUB-PARTY "A"

Sgt.Corless.
L/Cpl. Eames.
L/Cpl.Phelps.
Pte.Bratby
" Dawson.
" Gaskell,
" O'Donnell.
" Allan.
" Devey.
" Dunkley.
" Longman.
" Lumsden.
" Such.
" Sykes.

SUB-PARTY "B"

Sgt.A.Green.
Cpl. Scott.
" J.Bailey.
Pte.J.Hughes.
" Brooks
" B.C.Harris.
" Bellows.
" Davis.
" Keeley.
" Tomkinson.
" Smith.T.
" Parker.L.S.

SUB-PARTY "C"

Sgt.Carter.
L/Cpl.Dale.
" Fieldstead.
Pte. T.Parker.
" Cole.
" A.Smith.
" Ratcliff.
" Grimes.
" W.E.Evans.
" J.H.Jones.
" Miller.
" H.Smith.
" Troop.
" Newell.

PARTY 11. TO ENTER BY RIGHT GAP.

SUB-PARTY "D"

Sgt.Chamberlain.
L/Cpl.Gwynne.
" Harris.
Pte. Read.
" Ward.
" Grigg.
" Edge.
" Bowden.
" H.H.Cox.
" Fulbrook.
" Fyles.
" Naylor.
" Tarbuck.
" A.E.Bennett.

SUB-PARTY "E"

Sgt.Marsden.
L/Cpl.Smith.
" Shuck.
Pte. A.Taylor.
" Levy.
" Simpson.
" J.Cox.
" J.Hall.
" W.Price.
" Reynolds.
" Tarrant.
" G.White.

SUB-PARTY "F".

Sgt. Lofting.
Cpl.Kynnersley.
L/Cpl.Rudge.
Pte.Woolf.
" Fitzsimmons.
" Clarke.
" C.Boden.
" Busby.
" Checketts.
" W.B.Hill.
" Hough.
" Pullinger.
" Roach.
" Worthington.

The FIRST THREE NAMED in Sub-Parties will act as leaders in sequence.

COVERING PARTY FOR TORPEDO PARTIES.

PARTY 1.

Cpl.Roberts.
Pte.G.Edwards.
" Halls.
" Bonnell.
" Jones.E. (3690).
" Wilson.
" Waring.

PARTY 11.

L/Cpl. Wiggin.
Pte.Corker.
" Ditchfield.
" R.Hulme.
" Watson.
" Povey.
" Spencer.

She[illegible] No.33/16. 9

2ND 8TH BATTALION THE ROYAL WARWICKSHIRE REGIMENT.

BATTALION ORDER BY LT.COL.E.C.CADMAN. COMMANDING.
FRIDAY 25th AUGUST 1916.

1.MOVE. The Battalion will move to MERVILLE tomorrow 26th Aug. Companies will move indidependantly and will pass cross roads M.7.b.2.2, Ref. Map Bethune (Comb.Sheet) 36A.36B. as follows:-

"C" Coy. 9 a.m. "B" Coy 9-15 a.m.
"A" " 9-30 a.m. "D" " When relieved of Posts.

2.ROUTE. Companies will march R.12.c.7.8.,R.5.a.9.2.,Map Ref 36A. L.34.b.8.3., L.34.d.9.8., L.34,b.2.4., L.28.d.8.5. K.30.d.1.2 K.30.b.3.3.

3.BILLETS. Companies will move into Billets previously occupied.

4.DRESS. Full Marching Order. Water Bottles filled. Steel Helmets will be carried on back of valise.

5.ROUTINE. Breakfast. 7 a.m.
Dinner and Tea at Merville. Cookers will accompany Coys.

6.HEADQUARTERS. Headquarters will leave at 9-45 a.m., open up at MERVILLE 12 noon.

7.TRANSPORT. All Coy Stores and Officers Kits will be stacked outside Coy Headquarters by 9 a.m. When they will be taken over by Officer i/c Transport and conveyed to Company Hdqrs at MERVILLE.
O.C. Coys will detail the necessary fatigue party for loading baggage.
The Quartermaster will arrange withthe Transport Officer for the Transporting of the Quartermaster's Stores baggage.
Battalion Headquarters Baggage will be packed and ready to move at 8 p.m. 25-8-16.
The M.O. will arrange with the Transport Officer for moving Medical Stores.

8.WATER CARTS. One water cart will accompany "C" Coy and "D" Coy respectively.

9.TELEPHONE. Telephones will be disconnected at 9 a.m. Companies will arrange to carry their own phones.
Battalion Headquarters will be at K.24.d.4.7.

10.POSTS. O.C. "D" Company will detail one guide per post to be at cross roads M.7.b.2.2. Ref. Map Bethune Comb Sheet 36A.36B at 9 a.m. to take reliefs to the Posts occupied by their Company.
Relief to be complete by 12 noon.

signed. W.R. MORTON. 2/Lt. & A/Adjt.
2/8.R.Warwick.R.

Copies. 1 to 4. O.C. Coys.
5. Quartermaster.
6. Medical Officer.
7. Bde.
8. File.
9. War Diary.
10. Signals.
11 Transport Officer.

5 H[12]

Vol 5

War Diary of:-

2/8th Battalion The Royal Warwickshire

Regiment

Volume 5.

Period:-

Sept 1/16.
to Sept: 30/16.

Instructions regarding War Diaries and Intelligence Summaries are contained in F. S. Regs., Part II. and the Staff Manual respectively. Title pages will be prepared in manuscript.

WAR DIARY
or
~~INTELLIGENCE SUMMARY.~~
(*Erase heading not required.*)

Army Form C. 2118.

Place	Date	Hour	Summary of Events and Information	Remarks and references to Appendices
ROBERMETZ	1/9/16	7-8 am. 9-12.30 2.30-4.30	A, B & D Companies, Company training	
		7.10 am	The Battalion ran 1000 yards, and were inspected by the G.O.C. 61. Division	
		9.0 am	'C' Company attended two days B.E course at MEURILLON.	
		4.30-8.30.	Companies did 1 hour's practice of the 'attack' at MEURILLON.	WRH.
			2/Lt. E.L. LLOYD & 10 men returned from Sniping Course	
			Orders for relief of trenches (FAUQUISSART ? section) received	
	2/9/16	10.0 am	Commanding Officer, MAJOR PHILLIPS, Company Commanders reconnoitred trenches.	
		9-12.0 am	Company training	WRH.
		6.30 p.m.	Battalion Order No. 37 published. (App I)	App I
FAUQUISSART LEFT SECTOR	3/9/16	9.30	Batt. moved into trenches. All specialists left at 7.30 a.m & relieved 2/4 R. Berks by 12 noon.	
"			Coys moved independently via ESTAIRES & LAVENTIE. Dinners at latter place at 1 p.m.	WRH
			Relief complete at 4.50 p.m. A, B, C coys in line "D" at HQRs. Very quiet night	
"				9/2
	4/9/16.	9.a.m	General visited HQRS.	
"		2.30.	"D" coy moved from HQRS & took over DEAD END, HUGOMONT, PICANTIN Posts from 2/5th R. Warw. R.	WRH

T2134. Wt. W708–776. 500000. 4/15. Sir J. C. & S.

Instructions regarding War Diaries and Intelligence Summaries are contained in F. S. Regs., Part II. and the Staff Manual respectively. Title pages will be prepared in manuscript.

WAR DIARY

~~or~~

~~INTELLIGENCE~~ SUMMARY.

(Erase heading not required.)

Army Form C. 2118.

Place	Date	Hour	Summary of Events and Information	Remarks and references to Appendices
FAUQUISSART. LEFT.	contd. 4/9/16	11.30pm	Two BANGALORE torpedoes successfully exploded under enemy's wire causing gaps. No casualties. Enemy very quiet.	W.R.M. APP II.
	5/9/16	10am	Visits by XIth Corps Staff & C.R.A. 2/Lt Prosser leaves for Lewis-Gun Course.	
		11-12	Enemy's trench mortars fired; silenced by our batteries.	
		5.30-6.30	Artillery bombardment in conjunction with 5th Australian Divl. Artillery. Very wet day.	W.R.M.
		10-11	"A" Coy patrol caught by enemy M-gun. 2nd Lt Chapple wounded, two N.C.O's killed.	
	6/9/16.	9.30	2/Lt PROSSER & 5 men left for L-gun course at ETAPLES.	
		11.30	PICANTIN Trench heavily shelled. Small SAA dump hit by a shell. Four men wounded.	W.R.M.
		4-4.30	Trench mortar bombardment covered by 15 prs. General visited the line.	
		11p.m	Two raids by battalion on enemy's trenches see appendix III. Neither party penetrated his line.	APP III
	7th -	9a.m.	Brig-Gen & G.O.C. Division visited lines. Recd. orders for another small raid. Enemy fairly quiet during day.	
		3pm.	Court-Martial at HQRS. 2/Lt Hassall went into Hospital, sick.	W.R.M.
		6pm	Short artillery bombardment by Australians on our left, enemy retaliated slightly.	
		11-1.	Small raid by "B" Coy Casualties 3 missing 3 wounded	
	8th	10-10.30	Combined bombardment by 18prs & Stokes. Retaliation feeble. Quiet day till 5.30p.m.	
		5.30-6.30	Bombardment by Heavy T M's on WICK. followed by bombardment of M T M's till 7.15p.m.	W.R.M.

T2134. Wt. W708-776. 500000. 4/15. Sir J. C. & S.

Instructions regarding War Diaries and Intelligence Summaries are contained in F. S. Regs., Part II. and the Staff Manual respectively. Title pages will be prepared in manuscript.

WAR DIARY
or
INTELLIGENCE SUMMARY.
(Erase heading not required.)

Army Form C. 2118.

Place	Date	Hour	Summary of Events and Information	Remarks and references to Appendices
FAUQUISSART LEFT.	8/9/16	2.15a.m.	Small raid by 'D' Coy. Failed to get into enemy's trench. 1 casualty. M-Gun fire very intense on spot chosen for raid.	WRh.
"	9/9/16	–	Trench Mortar & Artillery bombardments at intervals throughout day. Retaliation small.	
		2 p.m.	2/Lt Lloyd left trenches.	
"		11.30 p.	Small raid by 2/6 on Right of our front.	WRh.
	10/9/16	–	Courses. 5 men for L-Gun course; 4 for Sniping; 2/Lt Entwistle + 1 Cpl for Divisional Course	
"			2/Lt Walker to LA GORGUE on B.T. + P.T. Course.	
		3.15	TM's fired from 3.13–3.25, 4.15–4.30, 5.20–5.35. Remarkably quiet day.	
"			Operation orders for relief by 2/5 R. Warw. R. issued. General round the trenches	
		8 p.m.	2/Lt Gough leaves for England on leave.	WRh.
		2-6a.m.	18 pdrs firing in conjunction with trench mortars from 2–2.50.	
	11/9/16	–	Batt. relieved by 2/5 R. War. R. at 8.30 p.m. (See App. IV) Coy's moved into billets in LAVENTIE.	App. IV
	12/9/16	–	Fatigues. 5 Officers + 209 men daily. Very few left for parade.	
		5-6 p.m.	Parades. Rifle inspection by Armourer-Sgt. Whole Batt. inspected by M.O. + bathed.	WRh.
		12 m.n.	C.O left on leave.	

914

Instructions regarding War Diaries and Intelligence Summaries are contained in F. S. Regs., Part II. and the Staff Manual respectively. Title pages will be prepared in manuscript.

WAR DIARY
or
INTELLIGENCE SUMMARY.
(Erase heading not required.)

Army Form C. 2118.

Place	Date	Hour	Summary of Events and Information	Remarks and references to Appendices
LAVENTIE	13/9/16.		Parades. 7.15–7.45 Physical Training.	
			9 – 12.30. All available N.C.O's & men under R.S.M. with a view to training young N.C.O's. ~~Fatigues App V~~	WRM. ~~App V~~
			2.30–4. Bayonet fighting under own Officers by Companies.	
			209 men including specialists on fatigue, leaving very few for training.	
		10pm	2/Lt Prosser returns from L-gun Course.	
	14th		Same fatigues. 9.–12.30 All spare N.C.O's & men under R.S.M. L-guns on Range	WRM.
		2.30–4	Bayonet-fighting under Coy. Officers. Capt. Lefroy went on leave.	
	15th	–	Parades as for previous days. All new N.C.O's under R.S.M. in morning. Lewis guns, Snipers & 15 transport men on 25" range. Usual fatigues.	WRM
	16th		Same as previous day.	WRM
	17th	10a.m.	Church Parade at Rest Gardens. 2Lt S. C. Parsons left on Course. Orders for relief of 2/5 R.War.R in FAUQUISSART (left section).	WRM
	18th	11–1	Operation orders from Bde. Coy. Comdrs. & specialists reconnoitre trenches. Very wet day. No parades possible. Lectures, inspections of equipment, gas-helmets etc by Coy.	
		3pm	Officers: Capt. Brock returned from Course. In absence of Capt Lefroy, posted to "C" Coy	WRM

T.2134. Wt. W708–776. 500000. 4/15. Sir J. C. & S.

Instructions regarding War Diaries and Intelligence Summaries are contained in F. S. Regs., Part II. and the Staff Manual respectively. Title pages will be prepared in manuscript.

WAR DIARY or ~~INTELLIGENCE SUMMARY.~~

(*Erase heading not required.*)

Army Form C. 2118.

Place	Date	Hour	Summary of Events and Information	Remarks and references to Appendices
FAUQUISSART LEFT SECTOR.				
"	19/9/16.		Relieved 2/5 R. War. R. in left FAUQUISSART sector; relief complete by 4·10 p.m.) See App. V	App. V.
"		2 p.m.	2/Lt GOUGH returned from leave. Total of 20 officers only in trenches. [2/6 R. War. R on our right, 5th Australian Division on our left. Enemy opposite supposed to be 16th Bavarian Regt. Very quiet day very wet. No casualties. Trench Strength 20 officers 505 men all ranks.	WRM
"	20/9/16.	10 a.m	2/Lt HODGSON left on B.F. course at LA GORGUE; 2/Lt WALKER returned from same course. Quiet morning. A few minenwerfer & aerial torpedoes in afternoon & evening.	WRM
		7.30 – 8.30	1 man wounded. M.T.M, Stokes & M-G bombardment. Retaliation practically nil.	
"	21st	9 a.m	Brig-Gen went round the line. Enemy put over 3 large minnies. No casualties resulting, but some damage. Trenches still very wet after heavy rains.	WRM.
		–		
		9-3 am	Working on Rhondda Sap & mining Bodmin Trench. 2/Lt Hamilton left to join R Flying Corps.	
"	22nd	10 a.m	Two heavy "minnies" on ROTTEN ROW. Fatigue-party from "A" Coy to repair same. Work completed by 1 p.m but knocked to bits again shortly after. Very quiet day. Enemy sends nothing over even in retaliation. Usual Patrols out at night; we fired 500 rifle grenades.	WRM
"	23rd	–	Very quiet day. Party from "D" Coy exploded a Bangalore torpedo under enemy's wire, but did not try to enter trench. No fire against them & no casualties.	WRM
	24th	11 a.m	Sunday. Service at HQRS. Orders for relief came through & O.C. 2/5 R. War. R visited trenches.	WRM.

96

T.2134. Wt. W708–776. 500000. 4/15. Sir J. C. & S.

Instructions regarding War Diaries and Intelligence Summaries are contained in F. S. Regs., Part II. and the Staff Manual respectively. Title pages will be prepared in manuscript.

WAR DIARY or ~~INTELLIGENCE~~ SUMMARY.

(Erase heading not required.)

Army Form C. 2118.

Place	Date	Hour	Summary of Events and Information	Remarks and references to Appendices
FAUQUISSART LEFT.				
"	24th	2 pm.	Capt Lefroy returned from leave. Quiet day. Our Howitzers fired at minnie emplacements but without success. The minnie retaliated.	WRh
LAVENTIE.	25th		Battalion relieved by 2/5th R. War. R. + moved into old billets. See app. VII. Relief complete by 4.10 p.m. 1 Off. + 20 men of "D" Coy left in trenches to work on Rhondda Sap during the night.	App VII WRh.
"	26th		Battalion in same billets as previously. Fatigues + working parties of 150 men daily.	
		8–12.	Bathing, M.O's inspection, rifle inspection + general cleaning up. No parades. –	WRh.
"		1pm–6.	2Lt F. J. Stephens from 3/8 R. War. R. reported for duty have been posted to this batt. Posted to "C" Coy.	
	27th	9–3pm	Usual fatigues. 2 officers + 100 N.C.O's + men digging trenches at LE DRUMEZ for Divl. Bombing Ground. Remainder of battalion, 12 men, on fatigue cleaning billets etc.	WRh.
	28th	–	150 men on fatigue. Remainder. 7.15–8 early morning parade, physical drill.	
		9.30–12.30.	All available N.C.O's + men under R.S.M. for training of young N.C.O.s.	
		2–3.30	Bayonet-fighting by companies. Rhondda Sap fatigues, 1 man killed.	WRh.
		4 p.m	65 men in wagons to Cinema show at LA GORGUE.	
	29th	–	Same programme as previous day. 2/Lts. Clayton and Rushforth on special leave 7 days.	WRh.
	30th	9 a.m	Orders for relief of 2/5. R. War. R. Visited trenches + made arrangements for relief. 7 Officers + 150 men	
		10.30.	to M.S.C. 2.5 for demonstration of "Flamenwerfer". 2/Lt Kitchen leaves on L-Gun Course.	WRh

[signature] Lieut. Colonel, Commanding 2/8th R. War. R.

T2134. Wt. W708–776. 500000. 4/15. Sir J. C. & S.

App. I

Sheet 1 No.37. 10.

2ND 8TH BATTALION THE ROYAL WARWICKSHIRE REGIMENT.

BATTALION ORDER BY LT.COL.E.C.CADMAN. COMMANDING.
SATURDAY 2nd SEPT 1916.

958

1.MOVE. The Battalion will tomorrow 3rd inst. relieve 2/4.R.Berks. Regt in the LEFT FAUQISSART SECTION.
Companies will move in the following order:-

"B" Coy.	9-30 a.m.
"C" "	9-45 a.m.
"A" "	10 a.m.
"D" "	10-15 a.m.

ROUTE. via TRANSPORT FIELD - ESTAIRES - LAVENTIE.
DRESS. Marching Order, without packs (which will be left behind) Greatcoat rolled and fastened on the belt. Mess Tins will be carried.

Companies will rendezvous at G.34.c.4.2. (field near LAVENTIE STATION) where dinners will be ready at 12-30 pm.

Signallers, Snipers, Lewis Gunners, Bombers will move at 7-30 a.m. and proceed straight to RED HOUSE at M.6.d.1.1. where Guides will meet them at 11-30 a.m.

RELIEF.
"A" Coy (LEFT COY) will relieve "D" Coy R.Berks via RED HOUSE - PICANTIN ROAD - BOND STREET.
"C" Coy (CENTRE COY) will relieve "C" and "B" Coys R,Berks via RED HOUSE - GREAT NORTH ROAD - RIFLEMAN'S AVENUE.
"B" Coy (RIGHT COY) will relieve "A" Coy R.Berks.R. via RED HOUSE - GREAT NORTH ROAD - RIFLEMAN'S AVENUE.
"D" Coy (RESERVE COY) will relieve the Reserve Coy of Oxfords.
GUIDES will be at RED HOUSE at 3 p.m.

POSTS.

"A" Coy will occupy	A.1.Post.	Strength	1 Platoon.
"C" " " "	FLANK "	"	1 "
"D" " " "	DEAD END "	"	2 "
	HUGOMENT "	"	1. "
	PICANTIN "	"	1. "

O.C. "D" Coy will arrange to take over all Control Posts.

After leaving LAVENTIE all traffic in parties not exceeding ten with fifty yards interval.

2.RATIONS. Rations for "A" and "C" Coys will come via RED HOUSE and Great Northern Tramway. "B" Coy via Great Central Rly. Coys will asceratin numbers of Machine and Stokes Gunners in their line.

3.PACKS. All Packs will be stacked at Coy Headquarters by 9 a.m. and one man left in charge. Packs will be brought up to the trenches later.

4.RIFLE GRENADE MEN. O.C. Coys will detail the four Rifle Grenade men per Coy. to report to Lieut.Gough at Headquarters immediately on arrival at trenches.

5.WORK. Company Commanders will pay special attention to work in hand in the trenches.

sgd. E.C.CADMAN. Lt.Col.
Commdg 2/8.R.War.R.

Copy No.1 to 4 Coys. No.5.Q.M.
6.Signalls. 7.Bombers.
8.Lewis Gunners. 9.File.
10.War Diary. 11. C.O.
12.Snipers.

Copy No. /

S E C R E T.

App II

BATTALION ORDER by LT.COL.E.C.CADMAN. COMMANDING.

959

1. The Officers Commanding "A" Coy and "C" Coy will each detail a Torpedo Team to prepare, lay and fire two lengths (20 feet) Bangalore Torpedo under the enemy wire on the night 4/5 Sept.

2. The Torpedoes will be laid at any suitable point opposite the respective Company Fronts. B

3. Bangalore Torpedoes, primers and 100 yards instantaneous fuse will be delivered at respective Coy. Headquarters by 9-30 p.m. 4th Sept.

4. A N.C.O. of the Battalion Bombers will report at Coy.Headquarters at 9-30 p.m. he will be available to give any instruction required.

5. Arrangements will be made by respective Company Commanders as to their own covering party.

6. Company Commanders concerned will make their own arrangements as to exploding torpedoes when laid.

7. Patrol will go out after the explosion to reconnoitre and report on gap made. This patrol may go out at any time after the explosion,(but it should be understood that no immediate action following explosion is required)

8. Reports to Battalion Headquarters.

(a). Time of operations commencing Code word. "LONDON"
(b). Explosion of torpedo. " " "BERLIN"
(c). Detailed report by runner as early as possible.

ACKNOWLEDGE.
(by code word "JONES")

Lieut.Colonel.
Commdg 2/8.R.Warwick.Regt.

Issued at 8-40 p.m.

Copy. No.1. Office.
2. "A" Coy.
3. "C" "

App. III

Sheet 1. **SECRET.** Copy No.

BATTALION ORDER No.41. by Lt.Col. E.C.CADMAN. Commanding.

960

1. A Raid will be made on the enemy trenches tonight 7/8th Sept.

2. All Ranks participating will be reminded that the chief object is to procure and bring back some means of identification of the enemy opposite us.

   It will also be pointed out that it is only weakmindedness which frightens active patrols causing them to withdraw because they have suffered small losses and it is expected that all ranks participating will bring the utmost determination to the work in hand and allow nothing to keep them from success.

3. O.C. "B" Coy will detail a party to prepare, lay and fire a Bangalore Torpedo under the enemy's wire at any suitable point, this point to be selected and notified to Battalion Headquarters before 6 p.m.tonight.

   O.C. "B" Coy will also detail a Cutting Out Party to force an entry into the enemy trench after explosion and bring back a GERMAN.

4. O.C. "B" Coy will be responsible for nötifying flank Coys of his final arrangements.

5. O.C. "B" Coy will make his own arrangements for Machine Gun co-operation if required.

6. Strength of Cutting Out Party not to exceed 11 all ranks.

7. Reports to Battalion Headquarters:-

   1. Probable time of party leaving our trench.) "LEEDS....pm"
   2. Actual time of party leaving our trenches.) "HUNSLET,.,.pm"
   3. Explosion of Torpedo...... "BERLIN"
   4. Party all in............... "HANTS"

8. Further details will be the same as for previous raids.

Sd. C. Cadman Lieut.Col.

Issued at 1 p.m. Comdg 2/8.R.Warwick.Regt.

Copy No.1. Office.
2. O.C. "B" Coy.
3. O.C. "C" "
4. 2/6.Warwicks.
5. Bde.

4.(a). Arrangements will be made to ensure explosion before 2 a.m.

Acknowledge

Sheet 1. Secret Copy No. 5

App. IV

961

BATTALION ORDER No.44. by Lt.Col. E.C.CADMAN. COMMANDING.

The Battalion will be releived ~~xxx~~ by the 2/5.Warwicks tomorrow Sept 11th, in accordance with attached table.

2. On relief Companies will move in parties of 10 at 50 paces interval to LAVENTIE. C.Q.M.S's will meet Companies at LAVENTIE POST en route and guide Companies to their billets.

3. Trenches will be left absolutely clean.

4. ALL Maps will be brought out, not handed over.

10-9-16. sgd. W.R.MORTON. 2/8.R.War.R.
2/Lt & A/Adjt.

RELIEF TABLE.

COY.	Relieved by.	ROUTE IN.	ROUTE OUT.	GUIDES.
A.	"D"	PICCADILLY - BOND STREET.	PICANTIN.	2-30 p.m. JUNC BACQUEROT - PICCADILLY.
C.	"B"	GREAT NORTH RD-RIFLEMAN's Av.	PICANTIN.	2-30 p.m. JUNC RUE BACQUEROT - GREAT NORTH RD.
B.	"A"	EDGWARE RD - ROTTEN ROW.	RIFLEMAN'S AVENUE.	2-30 p.m. JUNC RUE BACQUEROT - EDGWARE RD.
D.	"C"	------	------	no guides. Relief complete 3-30 p.m.
SNIPERS SIGNALS LEWIS GUNS.		------	------	11-30 a.m. one guide for each Party at RED HOUSE

One Guide per Platoon from Companies.

Headquarters will close at RED HOUSE at 3 p.m. and open at LAVENTIE at 4 p.m.

Copy. No.1/4. Companies.
5. ~~Ekkx~~.War Diary.
6. Lewis Guns & Snipers.
7. 2/5.Warwicks.

Sheet 1.

Copy No. 7

962

2ND 8TH BATTALION THE ROYAL WARWICKSHIRE REGIMENT.

BATTALION ORDER BY LT.COL.E.C.CADMAN COMMANDING.
18-9-16.

1. The Battalion, tomorrow 19th, will relieve 2/5.WARWICKS in FAUQISSART LEFT SUB-SECTION, in accordance with the following table.

2. Para.10 Div.Trench Standing Orders will be carefully complied with. Stores and Posts will be carefully checked with the inventory boards.
Trench Store Lists will be sent to Battalion Headquarters by 10 am 20th.inst.
Rifle Grenade Stands with details of registration will be handed over.

3. WORKING PARTIES. Permanent R.E.Party of one Officer and 80 men will return to Battalion 8 a.m. tomorrow 19th inst.

4. All Company Stores, Blankets, caps etc. will be stacked at Coy Headquarters by 2-30 p.m.
A special memo has been issued to Transport Officer.

5. All Billets will be left thoroughly clean and a certificate from Companies will be rendered to that effect.

Relieving Coy.	Coy. Reld.	SECTOR.	TIME & GUIDES.
"D"	"D"	BOND ST. to G.N.R. railhead inclusive.	Junct. of PICANTIN & TILLELOY 3-30 p.m.
"C"	"B"	AS BEFORE.& Flank Post.	Junc. PICANTIN & TILLELOY. 2-30 p.m.
"B"	"C"	AS BEFORE.	Junc. GREAT NORTH RD & TILLELOY. 2-30 p.m.
"A"	"A"	1.Platoon. A.1.Post. 1.Platoon. DEAD END. 1.Platoon. PICANTIN. 1. PLATOON. HOUGOMONT.	3-30 p.m. no guides.
SIGNALS. SNIPERS	LEWIS GUNS. BOMBERS.		11 a.m. Guides at RED HOUSE.

Parties after leaving LAVENTIE CHURCH move in parties of 10 at fifty paces interval.

Battalion Headquarters will close at 3 p.m. and re-open at RED HOUSE at 4 p.m.

sgd. W.R.MORTON. 2/Lieut & A/Adjt.

2/8.R.WARWICK.REGT.

Copy. No.1/4. Coys.
5. 2/5.Warwicks.
6. War Diary.
7. File.
8. Signals.
9. Lewis Guns.
10. Bombers.
11. Snipers.
12. C.O.

Sheet 1.

App VII

963 TB

2ND 8TH BATTALION THE ROYAL WARWICKSHIRE REGIMENT.

BATTALION OPERATION NUMBER 50 by Lt.Col.E.C.CADMAN.
SUNDAY 24-9-16.

1. The Battalion will be relieved Monday 25th inst by 2/5.R.WAR.R. according to following table.
2. Trenches and dugouts will be left absolutely clean.
3. 1/10000 Trench Maps will not be handed over. Handing over lists will be handed in by 9 a.m. 26th inst.
4. On relief Companies will move independantly to LAVENTIE to their former Billets.
5. Special care will be taken that fifty yards interval is kept between all parties which must not exceed 10.
6. O.C. "B" Company will detail 1 Officer and 50 men permanent R.E.Party. The Officer detailed will report to O.C. 1/3rd Field Coy. R.E. at 6 p.m. on day of relief.for instructions.

Coy relieved	Coy relieving.	ROUTE. IN.	OUT.	Gruides and Time.
"D"	"A"	PICANTIN.	BOND ST.	Junc.PICANTIN & TILLELOY. 3-30 p.m.
"C"	"D"	PICANTIN.	PICANTIN.	Junc.PICANTIN & TILLELOY. 2-30 p.m.
"B"	"C"	RIFLEMAN'S.	RIFLEMAN'S.	2-30 p.m. Junc. GT N.RD. & TILLELOY.
"A"	"B"			No guides 3-30 p.m.
SIGNALS SNIPERS BOMBERS. L.GUNS.				Guides 11 a.m. RED HOUSE

O.C. "C" Coy will arrange to take over LAVENTIE POST strength 2 N.C.O's and 6 men, by 6 p.m.on day of relief.

24-9-16.

sgd. W.R.MORTON. 2/Lt & A/Adjt.
2/8.R.WARWICK.REGT.

No. 1 to 4 Coys.
5. 2/5.WARWICKS.
6. WAR DIARY.

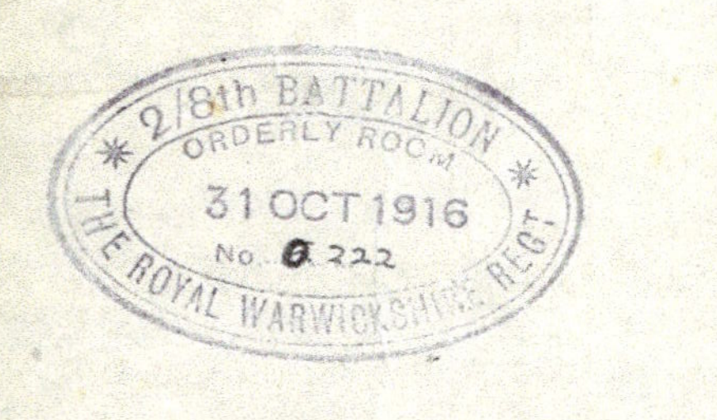

6H 14

Confidential

Vol 6

War Diary of:-

2/8th Battalion The Royal Warwickshire

Regiment

Period:-

Oct: 1/16 to

Oct: 31/16.

Volume VI

964
SB

Instructions regarding War Diaries and Intelligence Summaries are contained in F. S. Regs., Part II. and the Staff Manual respectively. Title pages will be prepared in manuscript.

WAR DIARY
~~or~~
~~INTELLIGENCE SUMMARY.~~
(Erase heading not required.)

Army Form C. 2118.

Place	Date	Hour	Summary of Events and Information	Remarks and references to Appendices
FAUQUISSART. LEFT SECTOR.	Oct 1st 1916	12 noon	Moved by coys into trenches relieved 2/5 R. War. R. Relief complete by 2.45 p.m. Very quiet during relief. HQRS at RED HOUSE. 5th Australian Divn. on our left & 2/7 R. War. R on right	[illegible]
	"	3.45-4.15.	Our H.T.Ms. fired 6 rounds covered by 18 prs & Hows. No retaliation on our front.	
			18 Officers only in trenches; 2/Lts Entwistle & Hodgson to hospital sick.	
	"	9.p.m	Lt-Col. Cadman returned from 1st Army School. Successful raid by 2/7 Warwicks on our right. 1 prisoner captured.	WRM.
	2nd	10 a.m	7 men arrived from base, all but one ex-casualties returned. Very quiet day.	
	"	5.30-6 p.m.	H.T.M. fired on the WICK; MTM's on enemy's mineshafts covered by 18 prs. & LTM's. No retaliation. Each coy. sent out patrols at night but encountered no enemy.)	WRM
	3rd	9.30	Bde Major went round trenches & visited Rhondda Sap.	
	"	11 a.m	2/Lt McClure to LA GORGUE on P.T. & B.F course. 2/Lt GOUGH to Bde to act in place of Bde Bombing Officer killed yesterday	WRM.
	"	4.30p.	M.T.M's registered on enemy mineshafts & at 6.30 fired for ½ hour together with L.T.M's.	
	"	9 and 11.15 p.m	"A" & "C" coys each made a small raid on enemy trenches to obtain identifications. Both entirely successful App. II. No casualties.	App II.
	4th	9 a.m.	Genl. McKenzie, Major Stansfeld visited HQRS. Very quiet day.	

T2134. Wt. W708–776. 500000. 4/15. Sir J. C. & S.

Instructions regarding War Diaries and Intelligence Summaries are contained in F. S. Regs., Part II. and the Staff Manual respectively. Title pages will be prepared in manuscript.

WAR DIARY ~~or~~ ~~INTELLIGENCE~~ ~~SUMMARY~~.

(*Erase heading not required.*)

Army Form C. 2118.

Place	Date	Hour	Summary of Events and Information	Remarks and references to Appendices
FAUQUISSART LEFT.				
	4th	3–4	Enemy sent over several "Minnies"; some artillery fire. Very little damage done.	
"	"		No casualties. Quiet night. Trenches very wet after heavy rains.	WRM.
	5th	–	Very quiet day. Nothing of interest occurred.	
"	6th	8am	Operation orders for relief by 2/5th R War. R. arrived. G.O.C. Division visited trenches.	
			TM's fired 3–3.15 a.m. Enemy put over many "minenwerfer" doing considerable	WRM
"			damage & seriously wounding a C.S.M. Our retaliation appeared ineffective.	
			Brig-Gen Gordon in hospital as a result of motor-accident.	
"	7th	2.30–2.50 a.m.	MTM. bombardment covered by our artillery. Relief by 2/5th R. War. R. See App II	App. II
			Battalion moved back to LAVENTIE to former billets.	WRM.
LAVENTIE.	8th		Bathing, rifle inspections by Armourer Sgt., & cleaning up. M.O's inspection.	
			"C" Coy. struck off all fatigues, & work on Rhondda Sap.	WRM.
"		3pm	2/Lt. KITCHEN returns from Lewis-Gun course. Working parties	
	9th	–	Inspections, bathing etc. 1 off & 35 men to ESTAIRES unloading coal from barges.	
"		4pm	50 men to Div. Pictures at LA GORGUE.	WRM.
	10th	9am	2/Lts. RUSHFORTH & CLAYDON returned from leave to England. All available N.C.O's under	
		3.30pm	R-S-M. All 61st Div. miners returned to units & also those attached to Australian miners	WRM.

T2134. Wt. W708–776. 500000. 4/15. Sir J. C. & S.

966

Instructions regarding War Diaries and Intelligence Summaries are contained in F. S. Regs., Part II. and the Staff Manual respectively. Title pages will be prepared in manuscript.

WAR DIARY
~~or~~
~~INTELLIGENCE~~ SUMMARY.
(*Erase heading not required.*)

Army Form C. 2118.

Place	Date	Hour	Summary of Events and Information	Remarks and references to Appendices
	Oct.			
LAVENTIE	10th contd.		Usual fatigues working-parties, about 185 men including those on Rhondda Sap.	
			2 Offs. (2/Lts WATSON & PROSSER) 2 N.C.O's + 16 men on Bde Bombing Course under 2/Lt GOUGH.	WRM.
"	11th	9–12.30	Usual fatigues. All available men parade under Coy. arrangements. All miners who returned	
			previous night paraded under R.S.M. for Drill & general smartening up. L. Gun's & snipers on	
"		2.15	range. C.O., M.O. 1 Off & 2 N.C.O's per Coy. + transport officer attended demonstration of small	
			box-respirator by Divl. Gas Officer. Coy's meeting at Bde HQ at 11 a.m. 2/Lt RUSHFORTH's leave was	WRM.
"			extended to 25/10/16. Leaves for England tonight. 2/Lt Lloyd to A.P.M. for traffic-control.	
	12th	–	Parades & fatigues as for previous day. Bde operation order for relief of 2/5 R. Warw. R	
"			tomorrow 13th. Arrangements made with 2/5 for the relief. 2/Lt Prosser appointed Batt.	WRM.
			Bombing Officer (temporary)	
FAUQUISSART LEFT SECTOR	13th		Batt. relieved 2/5 R. Warw. R. Relief complete by 2.45 p.m. On our left Australians	
		12–3 p.	were today relieved by New Zealanders 1st Batt. On right 2/7 Warwicks relieved	App. II
"			tomorrow by 2/6th Warwicks. App. III.	WRM
		2 pm	2/Lt Hodgson returned to duty from hospital.	
"	14th	–	Quiet morning. T.M's bombarded enemy's front line from 12.30 – 1 p.m. Enemy	
			retaliated rather heavily from 1–2 pm & again 4–4.30. 1 killed 4 wounded.	WRM.

T2134. Wt. W708–776. 500000. 4/15. Sir J. C. & S.

Instructions regarding War Diaries and Intelligence Summaries are contained in F. S. Regs., Part II. and the Staff Manual respectively. Title pages will be prepared in manuscript.

WAR DIARY

~~or~~

~~INTELLIGENCE SUMMARY.~~

(Erase heading not required.)

Army Form C. 2118.

Place	Date	Hour	Summary of Events and Information	Remarks and references to Appendices
	Oct.			
FAUQUISSART LEFT.—	15th	9 a.m.	G.O.C Divn. visited trenches. Service at HQRS. for those available at 11.30 a.m.	
		1.15– 1.45 }	M.T.M's, L.T.M's bombarded enemy's front line doing much damage to his parapet.	
"	"		Very slight retaliation. 2/Lt TOSLAND attached to "A" Coy for this tour owing to shortage.	
			Major Phillips left on leave to England. M.O. left, transferred to 32nd Division. LT. MACE	WRM.
"	"	7.30 p.	arrived & took up duties as M.O. Quiet night.	
	16th	7–7.30 a.m.	M.T. M's bombardment of enemy line did considerable damage. Enemy very quiet.	
"		12 noon	2/Lt ENTWISTLE reported for duty from Corps Rest Station, & joined his Coy in line.	
"			Three hostile aeroplanes visited our lines during the day.	WRM.
"		10 p.m.	2/6 R. War. R's HQRS at WHITE HOUSE on our right were burnt out.	
	17th	12–12.30 p.m.	Bombardment of enemy's trenches by MTM's & L.T.M's. No retaliation. Very quiet day	
"		5.15	C.O. & adjutant attended lecture at LAVENTIE on lessons from the Somme by G.O.C. 5th Divn.	
			LT. MORRISON (R.A.M.C.) permanently attached to Batt. as M.O. in place of LT. MACE.	WRM.
"	18th	6–6.30 a.m.	Bombardment by M.T.M's. Good results. Orders for relief by 2/5 came through.	App. IV
			Quiet day, Very wet. "D" Coy. made a small raid on enemy's trenches using a	
"		5.30–	Bangalore torpedo. The raid was unsuccessful. On the torpedo exploding, a heavy	[illegible]
		7 p.m.	fire was opened on the gap & raiders were unable to get in. Two casualties.	WRM

968

T2134. Wt. W708—776. 500000. 4/15. Sir J. C. & S.

Instructions regarding War Diaries and Intelligence Summaries are contained in F. S. Regs., Part II. and the Staff Manual respectively. Title pages will be prepared in manuscript.

WAR DIARY

~~or INTELLIGENCE SUMMARY.~~

(*Erase heading not required.*)

Army Form C. 2118.

Place	Date	Hour	Summary of Events and Information	Remarks and references to Appendices
LAVENTIE.	Oct.			
(Billets)	19th	10a.m.	The new Brigadier visited HQRS, having taken over command of the Bde. today. Brig-Gen Nugent.	
"	"	2.30 p.m.	Bde. relieved by 2/5 R. War. R. Relief complete 2.45. Very quiet relief. Batt. went back	WRM.
"			to former billets in LAVENTIE. Draft of 11 men arrived from 4th R. War. R. Posted to "B" Coy.	
	20th	6am.	Fatigues & working-parties; 1 off and 132 men on R.E. working-parties. 1 off & 30 men on fatigue	
"		"	unloading coal at ESTAIRES.	
	"	1030 a.m	Demonstration of Snipers, Bombers & Lewis gun working together at Divl Bombing ground. All	
"			available officers & N.C.O's attended.	WRM.
	"		Bathing, M.O.'s inspection for lice; rifle & equipment inspections.	
"	21st	6a.m.	Usual fatigues. 1 off & 30 men to ESTAIRES unloading coal 11-45am till dark.	
	"		Free preparing for tomorrow's inspection, cleaning up & completing equipment etc.	WRM
"	22nd	10a.m.	Church Parade in Goods yard at Station. Orders for relief of 2/5 R War. R.	
		2.30	Inspection of whole Batt. in full marching order, & also of transport loaded with all	WRM.
"			mobilization stores as if for a move. Capt Whetstone went on leave, 2.30p.m.	
	23rd		Batt relieved 2/5 R. War. R. Relief complete by 2.35p.m.	App. VI
		4.45 – 5.10 p.m	M.T.M. bombardment. No reply – 2Lt. S.E. Parsons returned from 1st Army Course	WRM
		5.30 – 5.35 p.m.	" " " " " Enemy replied with "minnies" & some artillery.	

T2134. Wt. W708—776. 500000. 4/15. Sir J. C. & S.

Instructions regarding War Diaries and Intelligence Summaries are contained in F. S. Regs., Part II. and the Staff Manual respectively. Title pages will be prepared in manuscript.

WAR DIARY
or
~~INTELLIGENCE SUMMARY.~~
(Erase heading not required.)

Army Form C. 2118.

Place	Date	Hour	Summary of Events and Information	Remarks and references to Appendices
FAUQUISSART (LEFT SECTOR)	Oct. 24th	-	Draft of 5 men posted to the Battalion. Very wet – Quiet day.	WRh
"		10am	G.O.C. Divn. visited trenches	
	25th	-	Very wet. Several enemy TM's during morning and some damage. No casualties.	WRh
	26th	9a.m	Orders for relief of Division by 56th Div; the Batt. to be relieved by 1st London Scottish on 28th. Trenches visited by Officers of London Scottish.	WRh
		3pm	Lts. S. E. Parsons & McClure returned from courses. Much enemy TM activity during the day & considerable damage to trenches. We retaliated.	
	27th		Trenches visited by Officers of relieving Bde & Batt. Specialists of London Scottish	
		1pm	came into trenches & spent night with us for instruction.	WRh
		9–11pm	Enemy sent over considerable amount of shells & appeared to be registering on points in back areas.	WRh
	28th	1pm to 3.45 pm	Relief by London-Scottish See App VI. Relief complete by 3.45 p.m. Enemy was thought to know of relief; he shelled communication trenches lightly throughout the day & very heavily about 10 minutes after our last coy. was out. Batt. moved to former billets in LAVENTIE.	App VI
		7p.m	D coy + 2 platoons of A sent up under orders of G.O.C 168 Bde to reinforce London Scottish, remained till stand-to, was	

T2134. Wt. W708–776. 500000. 4/15. Sir J. C. & S.

Army Form C. 2118.

Instructions regarding War Diaries and Intelligence Summaries are contained in F. S. Regs., Part II. and the Staff Manual respectively. Title pages will be prepared in manuscript.

WAR DIARY
or
~~INTELLIGENCE SUMMARY~~.
(Erase heading not required.)

Place	Date	Hour	Summary of Events and Information	Remarks and references to Appendices
LAVENTIE.	Oct. 28		Arrived back at 7.30 a.m. on 29th no casualties & a very quiet night. Preparation for the move	W.R.M.
"	"		on 29th & relief by 12 London Regt.	
ROBERMETZ	29th	9.30 a.m.	Batt less "D" Coy & 2 plts of A marched to ROBERMETZ, inspected on march by Brigadier see app. XXI	2 pp XXI
		1 p.m.	"D" Coy & 2 plts of "A" left 1 pm and arrived at 4 p.m. Billets at LAVENTIE taken over by 165th BDE	W.R.M.
"	"		1/12th London Regt (The Rangers). Major Phillips returned from leave.	
	30th	-	Bathing 11 a.m. – 6 p.m. Snipers & L-gunners on 30x range. Very wet day. Coys under instruction in	
"	"		use of box-respirator. Rifle & kit inspections. Two O.'s inspection. Capt. Whitmore returned from leave.	W.R.M.
	31st	7.10-8	Physical Training by Coys.	
"		9.30-10.30	Coy. Drill inspections. 10.30 – 1 p.m. Batt. paraded marched to MEURILLON. Batt. drill &	
"			artillery formations, under C.O. Lt & Quar G. F. Hodgkins returned from hospital.	W.R.M.

116

[Signature] Lieut Col., Cmdg 2/8 Warwicks.

T2134. Wt. W708–776. 500000. 4/15. Sir J. C. & S.

Sheet 1. SECRET. 7

App I

ub

2ND 8TH BATTALION THE ROYAL WARWICKSHIRE REGIMENT.

BATTALION ORDER 52 by Lt.COL.E.C.CADMAN. COMMANDING.
TUESDAY 3RD OCT. 1916.

1. The Battalion will make two raids on the enemy trenches night 3/4th Oct.

2. The object being to kill Germans, take prisoners, and procure identifications.

3. O.C. "C" Coy will detail a torpedo party to lay and fire Bangalore Torpedo at a point to be chosen by him in the enemy's wire.

   (a). O.C. "C" Coy will also detail cutting out party, not to exceed 10 all ranks, to force an entry into the enemy's trenches and procure identifications.
   (b). O.C. "C" Coy will be responsible for notification of his final arrangements to Flank Coys.

4. O.C. "A" Coy will detail a torpedo party to lay and fire Bangalore Torpedo at a point to be chosen by him in the enemy's wire, opposite RIGHT Coy frontage.

   (a). The explosion of this torpedo will be merely to make a demonstration and to cut wire, and a cutting out party will not be detailed.
   (b). O.C. "A" Coy will be responsible for notification of his final arrangements to Flank Coys.

5. Co-operation of Lewis Guns will be arranged direct between O.C. Coys concerned and Lewis Gun Officer.

6. Artillery, M.T.M. and L.T.M's will <u>not</u> co-operate.

7. Sergt. Ray will arrange to deliver the necessary torpedo tubes, fuse, lighters, etc., to "A" and "C" Coys respectively before 6 oclock 3rd Oct.

8. On return to our trench, raiders will proceed to Battalion Hdqrs where blankets and hot tea etc will be ready for them.

9. It should be understood that no attempt need be made to synchronize these two operations, each being entirely independant.

10. Details as to equipment etc as for past raids.

11. Reports to Battalion Headquarters.

ACKNOWLEDGE . "SMITH"

issued at 3-30 p.m.

Ed. C. Cadman Lieut.Col.

Commdg 2/8.R.WARWICK.REGT.

Copies. 1/4 Companies.
5 Right Battn. Australian Bde.
6.File
7.War Diary. ✓

Sheet 1.

2ND 6TH BATTALION THE ROYAL WARWICKSHIRE REGIMENT.

BATTALION ORDER NO.54 by LT.COL.E.C.CADMAN. COMMANDING.
6th OCTOBER 1916.

1. The Battalion, tomorrow 7th inst., will be relieved by 2/8.WARWICKS according to subsequent table.

2. Coys will move to their former billets in LAVENTIE, keeping usual distances.

3. 1/10000 Trench Maps will not be handed over.

4. Coys will send any heavy stores down to G.N.R. terminus. The Transport Officer will arrange for one limber to call for these at 11 a.m. one limber to be at RED HOUSE at 11 a.m. for specialists, and one limber and the Mess Cart at RED HOUSE at [illegible] p.m.

5. Coys will report relief by code word.

6. O.C. "D" Company will detail one Officer and 50 O.R. as permanent R.E.Party. The Officer will report to O.C. 1/3rd F.Coy. at 6 p.m. on day of relief.

7. O.C. "A" Coy will arrange to relieve LAVENTIE POST EAST by 6 p.m. on day of relief. Strength [illegible] N.C.O's and 6 men.

8. Lists of Trench Stores will be handed into the Orderly Room by [illegible] on 7th inst. IMPORTANT.

Relieving. Coy.	Relieved Coy.	ROUTE OUT.	TIME.
"C"	"A"	RIFLEMAN'S AV.	[illegible] p.m. No Guides.
"B"	"D"	PICANTIN	ditto.
"A"	"C"	BOND STREET.	ditto.
"D"	"B"		ditto.
SPECIALISTS.			Guides RED HOUSE 11 a.m.

sgd. W.R.HORTON. 2/Lieut. & A/Adjt.
2/6.R.WARWICK.REGT.

Copies 1/4. Companies.
5. 2/8.Warwicks.
6. Specialists.
7. File.
8. War Diary.

App III
Sheet 1.

War Diary

2ND 8TH BATTALION THE ROYAL WARWICKSHIRE REGIMENT

OPERATION ORDER No.5 5. by LT.COL.E.C.CADMAN. COMMANDING.

THURSDAY 12th OCT.1916.

1. The Battalion will relieve 2/5.WARWICKS in the LEFT FAUQUISSART SECTION tomorrow Friday 13th inst.

2. Permanent R.E.Working Party will return at 8 a.m. tomorrow 13th.

3. Billets will be left absolutely clean.

4. All Company stores will be stacked at Coy Hdqrs by 12 noon.

5. 2/5.Warwicks. will relieve LAVENTIE POST by 6 p.m. on day of relief.

6. Care will be taken that the proper distance is kept between parties after leaving LAVENTIE CHURCH.

Coy.	Relieves Coy.	SECTOR.	Place and Time.
"D"	"C"	RIGHT.	JUNC.ROTTON ROW & TILLELOY. 1-30 p.m.
"A"	"B"	CENTRE FLANK POST.	JUNC. PICANTIN & TILLELOY. 1-30 p.m.
"B"	"A"	LEFT A.1.POST.	JUNC. BOND ST and TILLELOY. 1-30 p.m.
"C"	"D"	½ pls. DEAD END ½. " HOUGOMONT. 1. " PICANTIN	Relief complete by 2-30 p.m.
SPECIALISTS.			Guides RED HOUSE at 11 a.m.

Headquarters will close at LAVENTIE at 2 p.m. and re-open at RED HOUSE at 3 p.m.

Companies will report relief by Code Word.

sgd. W.R.MORTON. 2/Lt & A/Adjt.

2/8.WARWICKS.

Copies 1/4 Companies.
5. 2/5.WARWICKS.
6 File.
√ 7. War Diary.
8. Specialists.

Sheet 1.

2ND 8TH BATTALION THE ROYAL WARWICKSHIRE REGIMENT.

OPERATION ORDER NO.56. by LT.COL.E.C.CADMAN. COMMANDING.
WEDNESDAY 18th OCTOBER 1916.

1. The Battalion will be relieved by 2/5.WARWICKS tomorrow 19th inst.

2. Coys of 2/5.WARWICKS will be at entrance to C.T's. at 1-30 p.m. No guides.

3. Reserve Coy will be relieved by 2-30 p.m. Specialists will be relieved at 11 a.m. Guides at RED HOUSE at 11 a.m.

4. On relief, Companies will move independantly to former billets at LAVENTIE, keeping usual distances.

5. Two limbers will be at RED HOUSE at 11 a.m. for Specialists, any Heavy Company Stores will be sent down to Headquarters by that time.

6. The new trench maps will not be handed over.

7. O.C. "A" Coy will detail one Officer and 50 men for Permanent R.E.Party. The Officer to report to O.C. 1/3rd Field Coy.R.E. at 6 p.m. on day of relief.

8. O.C. "B" Coy will garrison LAVENTIE POST by 6 p.m. on day of relief. Strength 2 N.C.O's and six men.

9. All sacking and sandbags will be removed from dugouts. M.O. will arrange to spray the dugouts.

10. Relief will be reported by code word "OATS".

11. Headquarters will close at RED HOUSE at 2 p.m. and re-open at LAVENTIE at 3 p.m.

sgd. W.R.MORTON. 2/Lieut & A/Adjt.

2/8. [illegible]WICK.REGT.

Copies 1/4. Coys.
5. 2/5.WARWICKS.
6. File
7. War Diary. ✓
8. Specialists.

97

Sheet 1.

2ND 6TH BATTALION THE ROYAL WARWICKSHIRE REGIMENT.

BATTALION ORDER No.67. by LT.COL.E.C.CADMAN. COMMANDING.
SUNDAY 22nd OCTOBER 1916.

1. The Battalion will relieve 2/5.WARWICKS in the LEFT FAUQUISSART SECTION tomorrow Monday 23rd inst.

2. Relief will be as on former occasions :-
"C" Coy being on the RIGHT
"B" " " " " CENTRE
"A" " " " " LEFT.
"D" " " " " RESERVE.

3. Companies will be at the entrance to the communication trench by 1-30 p.m.
Reserve Company will complete relief by 2-30 p.m.

4. SPECIALISTS will be at RED HOUSE by 11 a.m. Guides will be provided. for Specialists.

5. All working parties are cancelled for tomorrow.

6. Billets will be left absolutely clean.

7. All Company Stores will be stacked at Company HQrs by 12 noon.

8. Headquarters will close at LAVENTIE at 1-45 p.m. and re-open at RED HOUSE. at 2-30 p.m.

9. Companies will report relief by previous code word.

sgd. W.B.NORTON. S/Lt & A/Adjt.

2/6.R.WARWICK.REGT.

Copies. 1/4 Coys.
5. 2/5.WARWICKS.
6. Specialists.
7. War Diary.

VI

Sheet 1.

116

2ND 6TH BATTALION THE ROYAL WARWICKSHIRE REGIMENT.

BATTALION ORDER 96 by LT.COL.E.C.CADMAN. COMMANDING.
OCTOBER 27th 1916.

1. The Battalion will be relieved tomorrow the 28th inst. in the LEFT FAUQUISSART SECTION by 1/14th County of London Regiment (London Scottish).

2. All trench stores will be carefully handed over and all maps with the exception of, HAZEBROUK 5A. and LENS 11.
Trench Store lists will be in Battalion Orderly Room by 9 a.m. 28th inst.

3. Trenches will be left clean and smoking etc. brought out of the dug-outs. The M.O. will arrange to have all dugouts sprayed.

4. On relief Companies will move back to their former billets in LAVENTIE.

5. Both relieving and relieved Battalions will move in parties of not more than 10 in single file, 50 paces between parties, between LAVENTIE CHURCH and the FRONT LINE.

6. Separate orders have been issued to Transport Officer.

Coy. relieving.	Relieved.	ROUTE IN.	ROUTE OUT.	TIME & GUIDES.
"A"	"A"	PICANTIN RD & BOND ST.	BOND ST.	RED HOUSE 1 p.m.
"B"	"B"	PICANTIN RD PICANTIN Trench.	PICANTIN.	RED HOUSE 1-15 p.m.
"C"	"C"	GREAT NORTH RD. ROTTON ROW.	ROTTON ROW.	RED HOUSE 1 p.m.
"D"	"D"	RESERVE COY.		RED HOUSE 1-45 p.m.
SIGNALS SNIPERS LEWIS GUNNERS BOMBERS.				RED HOUSE 11 a.m.

Companies will send one guide per Platoon. in ample time to meet relieving Battalion.

HEADQUARTERS will close at RED HOUSE at 3 p.m. and re-open at LAVENTIE at 4 p.m.

Relief will be reported by code-word.

Sgd. W.R.NORTON. 2/Lt & A/Adjt.
2/6 R.WARWICK.REGT.

Copies 1/4 Coys.
5 London Scottish.
6 Specialists.
7. War Diary.

Sheet 1.

V81

88 826

2ND 8TH BATTALION THE ROYAL WARWICKSHIRE REGIMENT.

BATTALION ORDER 59 by LT.COL.E.C.CADMAN. COMMANDING.
SATURDAY 28th OCTOBER 1916.

1. The Battalion tomorrow 29th inst. will march to ROBERMETZ.

2. Companies will move independantly as follows:-

Snipers and Signallers.	9 a.m.
"B" Company.	9-10 a.m.
"D" "	9-20 a.m.
"A" "	9-30 a.m.
"C" "	9-40 a.m.
Lewis Guns.	9-45 a.m.

Transport will follow behind Lewis Guns.

3. ROUTE. Ref. Sheet 36a.
LA GORGUE - L.28d. - L.27.c. - L.26.c. - L.25.c.

4. At the cross roads at K.30.d.2.2. Companies will concentrate at 12-45 p.m.
The Battalion will then march in the following order:- Snipers,and Signals, "A" "B" "C" "D" Lewis Guns, Transport. to K.30.b.3.3. where they will be inspected on the march by the ~~G.O.C. Division~~. B.G.C.

5. After passing the inspection point, Companies will march off to their billets previously occupied there.

6. Caps will be worn, helmets carried at back of pack, Mess Tin inside helmet.

7. Cookers will be ready to move at 8-45 a.m.
Dinners will be cooked en route and be issued on arrival.

8. Breakfast will be at 7 a.m.

9. Officers kits will be carried by their servants to Q.M.Stores by 8 a.m.
The Company Mess Baskets will be at Headquarter Mess by 9 a.m.

sgd. W.R.MORTON. 2/Lt & A/Adjt.
2/8.R.WARWICK.REGT.

Coys. 1/4. Companies.
5. War Diary
6. Specialists.
7. Transport.Officer.
8. File

K. 29. 6. 8. 7
K. 30. 6. 8. 4

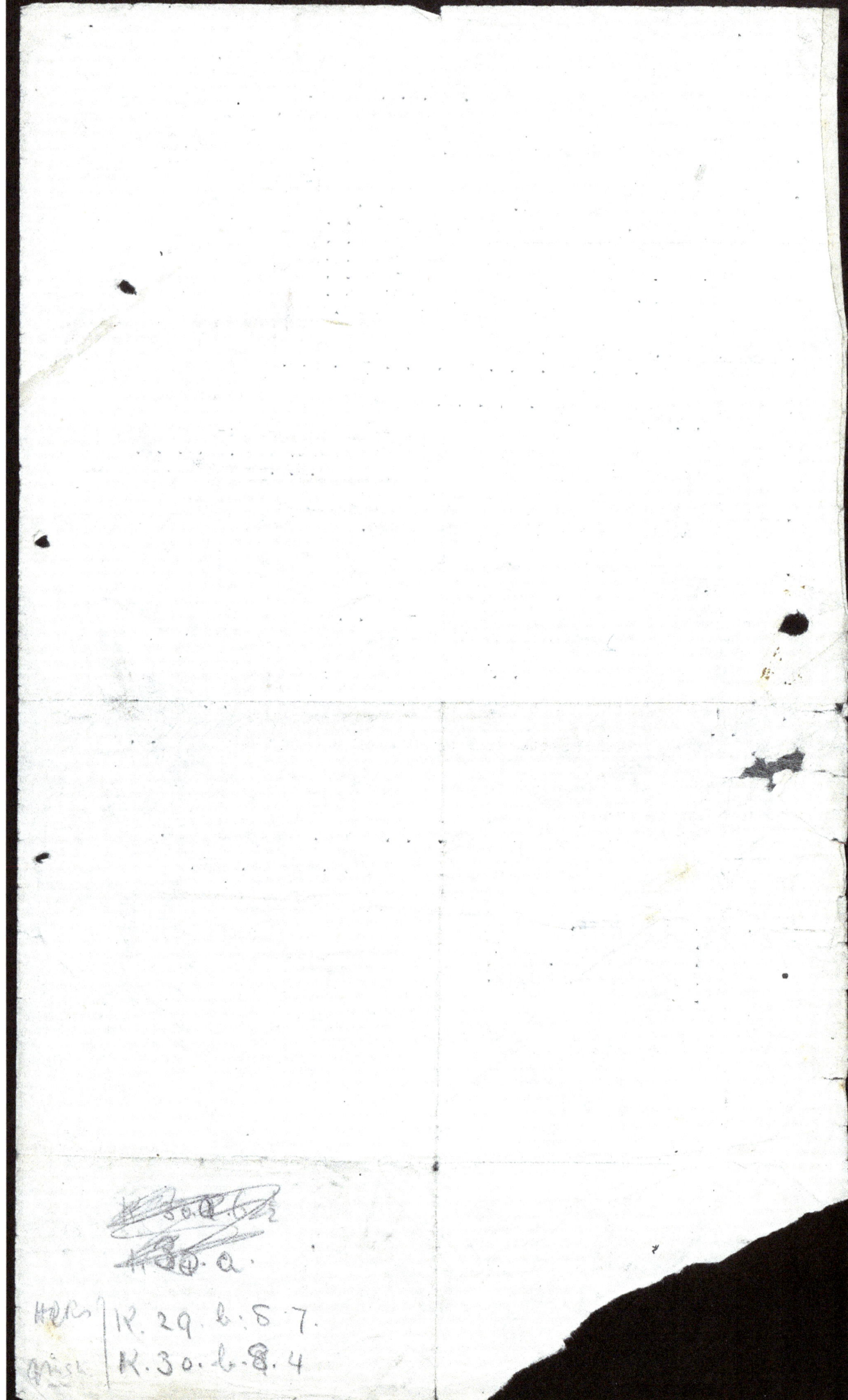

7 H 4

Confidential

Vol 7

War Diary of:

1/8th Battn. The Royal Warwicks Regt

Volume VII

Period:-

Nov: 1/16

To:- Nov: 30/16

Army Form C. 2118.

Instructions regarding War Diaries and Intelligence Summaries are contained in F. S. Regs., Part II. and the Staff Manual respectively. Title pages will be prepared in manuscript.

WAR DIARY
or
~~INTELLIGENCE SUMMARY.~~
(Erase heading not required.)

Place	Date	Hour	Summary of Events and Information	Remarks and references to Appendices
ROBERMETZ near MERVILLE	1916 Nov: 1st	7.15–8am.	Physical Training by Coys.	
"	"	9–1	Shooting on 30x range, bayonet-fighting, drill & box-respirator work, by Coys. No afternoon parade.	
"			Preparation for move tomorrow to new area.	WRM.
L'ÉCLÈME	2nd	9a.m	Marched to L'ÉCLÈME arriving about 12.30p.m & billeted for the night. Bde HQRS at BUSNES.	WRM.
FLORINGHEM	3rd	8.40a.m.	Marched to FLORINGHEM via LILLERS arriving about 1.30 p.m. Good billets.	WRM
MARQUAY	4th	9.30a.m	Batt. marched to MARQUAY, arriving about 2.30 p.m. Very wet; billets very bad indeed.	WRM
SERICOURT	5th	9a.m	Batt. marched to SERICOURT	WRM
MÉZEROLLES	6th	9a.m	Batt. marched to MÉZEROLLES arriving 1.30 p.m.	WRM.
"	7th	.	Day spent in cleaning up, making up deficiencies in kit & in inspections; also in repairs to billets which were in very bad state. Officers communication drill. Box-respirator	
"			practice. F.G.C.M. on Pte. SYKES at HQRS. 2/6 R. War. R at BOMMIÈRES, guilty 21 days F.P. No 1.	WRM.
			Authority to strike off strength 2/Lt RUSHFORTH as unfit for service abroad.	
"	8th	10a.m	Demonstration at REMAISNIL in laying out & consolidation of trenches, attended by C.O, Coy. Comdrs, 5th C.O's	
			per coy. – Construction of miniature rifle-range. Musketry & open formations. Communication	WRM
"			drill for junior officers & N.C.O's. Capt. Lefroy returned from L-Gun Course.	
	9th		As for previous day and Artillery formations.	WRM.

T2134. Wt. W708—776. 506000. 4/15. Sir J. C. & S.

Army Form C. 2118.

Instructions regarding War Diaries and Intelligence Summaries are contained in F. S. Regs., Part II. and the Staff Manual respectively. Title pages will be prepared in manuscript.

WAR DIARY
or
INTELLIGENCE SUMMARY.

(Erase heading not required.)

Place	Date	Hour	Summary of Events and Information	Remarks and references to Appendices
	1916 NOV:			
MÉZEROLLES	10th	7-7.45	Physical Training.	
		9-12.15	Artillery formations. Close-order work - Rapid extensions + opening of fire - Siting of trenches + allotting of	
"			tasks to working-parties. - rapid loading + aiming.	
		2.30 p.m.	Tactical scheme for 2/7 + 2/8 Warwicks. C.O., 2nd in Comd., Adjt + Coy. Comdrs attended. Meeting-place F in	
"			FROHEN-LE-GRAND. Remainder of Batt. musketry on 30× range.	WRh.
	11th		Programme of work as for previous day. Spare L-Gun teams training under L-G. Officer.	
"			In afternoon, bayonet-fighting. Poor shots on range.	WRh.
	12th		Church Parade for all denominations. No other parades.	WRh.
"	13th	9.00 a.m.	Battalion scheme. Attack under Artillery-fire.	
		5.30 p.m.	Siting + digging of trenches by night under R.E's supervision.	WRh.
"	14th	9.0 am	Improving trenches dug previous day. Poor shots on range. Afternoon bayonet fighting	
		8 pm	Filling in trenches preparatory to moving	
CANDAS	15th	10.15 am	Batt marched to CANDAS, arriving 2.30 p.m.	
HALLOY	16th	10.10 am	Batt marched to HALLOY arriving 1.30 pm. - Billets fair.	
HERISSART	17th	10.40 am	Batt marched to HERISSART arriving 2.30 pm. Billets very poor.	
WARLOY	18th	9 am	Batt marched to WARLOY. Weather bad - Snow on ground & sleet falling. Arrived	
			10.45 am. Billets fair. All Coys bathed during evening.	

T2134. Wt. W708—776. 500000. 4/15. Sir J. C. & S.

Army Form C. 2118.

Instructions regarding War Diaries and Intelligence Summaries are contained in F. S. Regs., Part II. and the Staff Manual respectively. Title pages will be prepared in manuscript.

WAR DIARY
or
INTELLIGENCE SUMMARY.
(Erase heading not required.)

Place	Date	Hour	Summary of Events and Information	Remarks and references to Appendices
	1916 NOV			
WARLOY	19th	7am	Fatigue party - All officers of A.B. Coys with 300 men from A B & C. Coys left by motor buses to report to 18th Divn. for loading & unloading fatigues. Returned 7pm	WJJ
"	20th	9 am	Parades under C.C. Coys - Bayonet fighting - Musketry &c	WJJ
BOUZINCOURT	21st	11.30am	Battalion marched to BOUZINCOURT. Coys marched with intervals of 200 yds. - arrived 1.30pm. Billets poor and very dirty. Afternoon fatigues cleaning up	WJJ
"	22nd	9am	Cleaning up billets and removing rubbish. Found fatigue party of 2 Coys made up to 300 O.R. behind the lines.	WJJ
"	23rd	9am	Coys practised formations and the Attack on lines laid down by Division. Afternoon bayonet fighting, musketry &c. - Specialists under Specialist Officers. Found Divn'l Guard.	WJJ
"	24th	7am	Physical Drill & Smartness. 9am Battalion practised the Attack. Afternoon Bayonet fighting. Specialists under own officers. Divisional Guard returned. Found fatigue of 12 O.R. for work under Town Major. C.S.M. McGeorge A.G.S. reported for duty with Batt.	WJJ
"	25th	7 am	Physical Exercise. All Coys did Bayonet fighting under C.S.M. McGeorge A.G.S. Rapid loading practice. Fatigue party of 11 O.R. reported to Camp Commdt. 61 Divn. at 2pm	WJJ
"	26	9a.m.	Working-party of 300 all ranks for unloading at AVELUY RLY SIDING. 2 Off. + 9 O.R. proceeded on leave.	WJJ WRM.

T2134. Wt. W708—776. 506000. 4/15. Sir J. C. & S.

Instructions regarding War Diaries and Intelligence Summaries are contained in F. S. Regs., Part II. and the Staff Manual respectively. Title pages will be prepared in manuscript.

WAR DIARY
or
INTELLIGENCE SUMMARY.
(Erase heading not required.)

Army Form C. 2118.

Place	Date	Hour	Summary of Events and Information	Remarks and references to Appendices
	Nov:			
HEDAUVILLE	27th	8 a.m.	Batt. marched to HEDAUVILLE arriving 9.30 a.m. Camp in very bad condition.	
	"		Fatigue parties cleaning up in afternoon.	W.R.h.
"	28th	9 a.m.	Batt. parade. Practice of attack from trenches.	
		2.30 p.m.	Bombing. Training of new Lewis-Gun Squads.	
		6-8.	Night-patrols.	W.R.h.
"	29th	9 a.m.	Practice "Extension of working-parties" and "The attack from the trenches"	
			Working-party for Town-major of 1 off. + 30 men for cleaning roads.	
		2.30.	Bombing. Officers + N.C.O's map-reading + message writing.	
		6-8.	Night-patrols.	W.R.h.
"	30th	9 a.m.	Bayonet-fighting. Rapid-loading + rapid aim, Artillery formations.	
		2.30	Bombing	
		6-8	Extension of working-parties + allotting of tasks in the dark.	W.R.h.
		8.35 a.m.	Working-party of 100 all ranks for work with 9th Labour Batt. at LEAVILLERS.	
		9 a.m.	" " " 15 O.R. under Capt. Lefroy.	

8H [14]

BATTALION ORDERLY ROOM 1 ... 1917 No. 57/7 ROYAL WARWICKSHIRE

Vol 8

Confidential

War Diary

of

2/8th. Bn. The Royal Warwickshire Regt

from December. 1. 1916 to December, 31st. 1916.

Volume 8.

Instructions regarding War Diaries and Intelligence Summaries are contained in F. S. Regs., Part II. and the Staff Manual respectively. Title pages will be prepared in manuscript.

WAR DIARY
or
~~INTELLIGENCE SUMMARY~~.
(Erase heading not required.)

Army Form C. 2118.

Place	Date	Hour	Summary of Events and Information	Remarks and references to Appendices
HEDAUVILLE	Dec 1st		Batt^n in Brigade Attack for instruction. Repeated by batt^n in the afternoon.	WGP
MARTINSART	Dec 2.	10.15	Marched to huts at MARTINSART via BOUZINCOURT. delayed en route by 7th R.W.R. taking billets originally intended for this batt^n. Arrived 12.15 P.M. AVELOY was shelled during march.	WGP.
		P.M.	Cleaning up of huts.	WGP
	Dec 3		Fatigue parties. 420 all ranks on working parties. ten O.R. & Lt S.E. PARSONS left on leave.	
	Dec 4		Training under Coy arrangements. R.E. start work (flooring huts). (draft of 25 O.R. arrived 6 P.M.)	WGP
	Dec 5th	AM.	300 (B-C-D.) working party at PIONEER STATION. 100 at TULLOCH'S CORNER. this	WGP
		PM	latter party were shelled during day. 1 (Sergt NICHOLLS A Coy) Killed. 1 O.R. wounded.	WGP.
	Dec 6th	AM.	~~[illegible]~~ 2 latest drafts inspected by G.O.C. Bde at 10 AM. Working parties. B Coy burying cable (100 men). C & D. 100 men & 4 officers ammunition carrying at DONNET'S POST. Several small fatigues (1 off. 47 or.) in addition.	
			Repairs to billets by R.E. & Pioneers. Capts. BROCK & MUNGLE & 2 O.R. returned from leave.	RSP
	Dec 7th	AM	1 Company (100 men) at DONNET'S POST on ammunition carrying ~~1 Company (100 men) at AVELUY SIDING [illegible]~~ RSP. 3 Coys (300 O.R.) at PIONEER RD. STN. on work on new Shops. Repairs to billets (flooring huts) were continued.	RSP

T2134. Wt. W708—776. 500000. 4/15. Sir J. C. & S.

Instructions regarding War Diaries and Intelligence Summaries are contained in F. S. Regs., Part II. and the Staff Manual respectively. Title pages will be prepared in manuscript.

WAR DIARY
or
INTELLIGENCE SUMMARY.
(Erase heading not required.)

Army Form C. 2118.

Place	Date	Hour	Summary of Events and Information	Remarks and references to Appendices
MARTINSART	Dec 8th	AM	~~1 Coy at AVELUY SIDING on loading fatigue~~. 3 Companies (300 men) at PIONEER RD STN on Work on new shops. Flooring of huts continued by R.E.'s. 2 O.R. returned from leave. 4 OR proceeded on leave.	A.S.T.
	" 9th	A.M.	2 Companies (250 men) on light Railway grading at end of Standard Gauge Rly. 1 Coy (100 men) burying cable under O/C Signal Coy. 11 O.R. making log road at MARTINSART.	A.S.T.
	" 10th		2 Companies (200 men) at AVELUY SIDINGS loading. 1 Coy (100 men) at PIONEER RD. STN. on New Shops. 1 Coy (100 men) on light Rly. grading.	
		10-30 am	Battalion moved to WELLINGTON HUTS, AVELUY in Brigade Reserve. Fatigue parties proceeded from their fatigues direct to new area. Enemy shelled neighbourhood during the night several times.	App. I A.S.T.
WELLINGTON HUTS	" 11th	A.M	2 Companies (200 men) at TULLOCHS CORNER on various fatigues. Remainder engaged in cleaning camp.	
		3-0 p.m	D Coy proceeded to FABECK TRENCH to relieve a Coy of 2/6 R.W.R. 2 Officers 13 O.R. returned from leave. Enemy shelling of neighbourhood not so frequent. Major SHIACH, 2/6 SEAFORTHS arrived: attached for duty.	A.S.T.
	" 12th	AM.	2 Companies (200 men) at TULLOCHS CORNER on various fatigues.	
		PM	1 Coy proceeded to REGINA TRENCH for construction of wire entanglements. Casualty 1 OR wounded by shellfire	A.S.T.
	" 13th	AM.	1 Company (100 men) at TULLOCHS CORNER on various fatigues. Another party engaged on salvage in the neighbourhood of the huts — 1 OR accidentally wounded by the explosion of a bomb found amongst the salvage.	
		PM	2 Companies wiring at REGINA TRENCH	

T2134. Wt. W708—776. 506000. 4/15. Sir J. C. & S.

Instructions regarding War Diaries and Intelligence Summaries are contained in F. S. Regs., Part II. and the Staff Manual respectively. Title pages will be prepared in manuscript.

WAR DIARY
or
INTELLIGENCE SUMMARY.
(Erase heading not required.)

Army Form C. 2118.

Place	Date	Hour	Summary of Events and Information	Remarks and references to Appendices
WELLINGTON HUTS	1916 Dec 14		Same working parties – hostile shelling round camp at night – no damage	WJT.
			Commanding Officer Second in Command & Coy Commanders – also specialist officers proceeded to trenches to reconnoitre. Orders received to relieve 2/7 R Warwicks in the line	App. II
	15	AM	Party of 200 O.R. to TULLOCH'S CORNER on various fatigues. Relief commenced with specialists at 10 a.m. A Coy relieves D Coy 2/7 ROYAL WARWICKS	WJT.
			B " " A " "	
			C " B " "	App
			D " C " "	
			Relief between Coys. commenced at dusk – going very bad and night dark – considerable hostile shelling near front line – no casualties.	

Instructions regarding War Diaries and Intelligence Summaries are contained in F. S. Regs., Part II. and the Staff Manual respectively. Title pages will be prepared in manuscript.

WAR DIARY
or
INTELLIGENCE SUMMARY.
(Erase heading not required.)

Army Form C. 2118.

Place	Date	Hour	Summary of Events and Information	Remarks and references to Appendices
RAVINE	16/12/16	3.9am	Relieved 2/7 ROYAL WARWICKS - night dark - Relief completed 3.9 a.m. - One casualty (wounded) O.R. Hostile artillery active all day in RAVINE Area and portions of REGINA TRENCH - Wind - North moderate - Shortage of petrol tins for water carrying. Work - getting up wire & stakes, and wiring. Working party of 2 Coys 2/7 R. Warwicks cancelled by Brigade orders.	WB
"	17/12/16		Day misty - No wind. Less enemy shelling than usual during day, principally in DESIRE and HESSIAN Trenches. Wired 300 yds at REGINA Trench during day & 150 yds front line at night. Other work burying bodies - salvaging - clearing trenches & dugouts. 2 patrols out at night. Fatigue of 2 Coys sent by 2/7 ROYAL WARWICKS - Wounded 1 O.R.	WB
"	18/12/16		Hostile artillery active on DESIRE, RAVINE & new wire in front of REGINA - Wind light - Northerly. Air clear. Work 150 yds of wiring in front line & 100x at REGINA. Killed 1 O.R. Wounded 2/Lt R. L. McGUIRE, 9 O.R. Buried 5 bodies. 2 Coys of 2/7 R.W.R carried wire to front line	WB
"	19/12/16		Hostile artillery active all day on RAVINE and W. end of REGINA and DESIRE. Sector quiet. Patrol of L??? to examine CROSS TRENCH and found same occupied. Trench Coy of 2/7 R.W.R wired 130 yds at W end of REGINA. Laid 450 yds armoured cable. Buried 11 bodies.	WB
MARTINSART WOOD W.26.b.0	20		Relieved by 2/5 GLOUCESTERS. Relief complete 7.52 p.m. Weather bright & clear all day - considerable aerial and artillery activity. Proceeded to huts at Martinsart Wood - arrived 10.30 p.m.	WB App III

T2134. Wt. W708—776. 600000. 4/15. Sir J. C. & S.

Instructions regarding War Diaries and Intelligence Summaries are contained in F. S. Regs., Part II. and the Staff Manual respectively. Title pages will be prepared in manuscript.

WAR DIARY
or
INTELLIGENCE SUMMARY.
(*Erase heading not required.*)

Army Form C. 2118.

Place	Date	Hour	Summary of Events and Information	Remarks and references to Appendices
	1916 Dec			
MARTINSART WOOD	21		Resting and cleaning up. Weather very wet.	WH
HEDAUVILLE	22		Moved to HEDAUVILLE - arriving 11.30 a.m. having left 9.30 a.m. 17 O.R. attached to YELLOW LINE permanent fatigue. Fatigue of 1 N.C.O + 3 men for work at Baths, + 1 N.C.O + 2 men for Army P.O. HEDAUVILLE - A Company and half B Coy bathed - cleaning up + resting. 2 officers sent to Corps School.	App. IV
	23		Bathing continued - refitting and cleaning up. Fatigue party of 1 N.C.O + 7 men for work with TOWN MAJOR. Six O.R recommended by C.O. for commissions interviewed by B.G.C. 7 pm. CAPT. T. R. LEFROY selected to attend C.O. Course at ALDERSHOT on 8/1/17 Authority G.H.Q. 777 20/12/16 + struck off strength. Court of Inquiry held on accident to Lt J.S. MORRIS wounded 8/6/16.	WH
	24		Bathing of Battn completed - refitting and resting - Voluntary Services to C of E at 10.30 am + 6.30 pm. Weather showery. Bombing Squad of 1 N.C.O + 8 men to Divnl School. 1 Officer + 2 N.C.O.s to P.T. + B.F. School.	WH
	25		CHRISTMAS DAY - 3 Communion Services - entertainments for troops	WH
	26		Fatigue of 1 Officer + 50 men to Divisional Bombing Officer - 1 N.C.O + 11 O.R. for work under TOWN MAJOR. Training in accordance with Table sent in to Brigade - Games + competitions in afternoon.	WH
	27		Training on same Programme - Close Order Drill - Training for Attack - bombing practice.	WH
	28		C.O. left on 10 days leave. MAJOR PHILLIPS on 4 days tour with 306 ART. BRIGADE at OVILLERS. Training in accordance with Programme. 1 N.C.O to Field Eng. Course at ST RICQUIER. Orders for move to MARTINSART received.	WH

T2134. Wt. W708-776. 500000. 4/15. Sir J. C. & S.

Army Form C. 2118.

WAR DIARY
or
INTELLIGENCE SUMMARY.
(*Erase heading not required.*)

Instructions regarding War Diaries and Intelligence Summaries are contained in F. S. Regs., Part II. and the Staff Manual respectively. Title pages will be prepared in manuscript.

Place	Date	Hour	Summary of Events and Information	Remarks and references to Appendices
HEDAUVILLE	1916 Decr 29	9am	Party of 1 Coy made up to 100 O.R. reported to O.C. "B" Coy 9th LABOUR BATT. BOUZINCOURT for work on roads - returned 5 p.m. Training in accordance with programme. Firing on 100x Rifle Range. L.G's firing on Range. Party of 1 NCO & 11 O.R. worked under CAPT LEFROY, Divn School. 2 O.R. provided to C.R.E. DIVN for work as Carpenters. 1 O.R. to work as Fitter at Divn Theatre.	
		4.30pm	Orders re move to MARTINSART published -	App - V
MARTINSART WOOD	30	9.30am	Battalion marched to canvas huts previously occupied at MARTINSART WOOD - arriving 11 a.m. - Party of 1 Coy made up to 100 O.R. reported to O.C. B Coy 9th Lab Batt BOUZINCOURT for work on roads. Huts very dirty and wet. 1 Officers hut quite uninhabitable. Worked in afternoon cleaning up huts, laying paths, digging trenches round huts.	
	31	4.15am	C Coy and 43 men of "B" Coy (Total 115 O.R.) proceeded to WELLINGTON HUTS to be employed cable burying reporting to 2nd Field Coy. 100 men to Yardmaster AVELUY SIDING for train loading - 100 to C.R.E. AVELUY SIDING for loading stores - R.E. party commenced to lay floor in Officers Hut. 2/Lt WATSON + 1 N.C.O. proceeded to P. & B.T. Course at HEDAUVILLE. 8 O.R. returned from YELLOW LINE working party.	

W. [illegible] Major
Cmdg. 2/8 R. War. R.

T2134. Wt. W708–776. 500000. 4/15. Sir J. C. & S.

Sheet 1.

APP I

2ND 8TH BATTALION THE ROYAL WARWICKSHIRE REGIMENT.

BATTALION ORDER NO. 73. BY LT.COL.E.C.CADMAN. COMMANDING.
FRIDAY 9th DEC. 1916.

1. 182nd Bde relieves 183rd Bde in the line on Dec. 10th-11th 2/8.WARWICKS will relieve 8th WORCESTERS Battalion in Reserve huts at W.12.c.

2. Detail of working parties will be issued later. All ranks proceeding with working parties will be in full marching order and on conclusion of work will rejoin the Battalion in new area (CROMWELL HUTS W.12.c.)

3. <u>BLANKETS.</u> One blanket per man only will be taken by Regimental Transport to new area. <u>One blanket per man</u> will be bundled ~~in~~ and piled together in <u>one hut for each Company</u> before 6-30 a.m. Blankets surplus to one per man will be bundled in tens and all piled in No.1. Hut.

4. The cookers of "A" and "B" Coys will be available for party working at AVELUY STATION tomorrow. Cookers of "C" and "D" Coys will proceed with Transport to new area.

5. Machine Gun Handcarts will be stored at Q.M.Stores and Transport Officer will provide two limbers for transport of guns.

6. Officers Kits, Mess Baskets etc will be piled at Coy. Hdqrs before 9 a.m.

7. 2/Lt.Tosland, four C.Q.M.S's will proceed to new area at 8-30 a.m.

8. Transport ~~xxx~~ for blankets, Lewis Guns and Baggage will be loaded and ready to move off at 9-30 a.m. Limbers will move in pairs at 200 yards interval.

9. Details not proceeding with working parties will clean camp and quarters and will be paraded by 2/Lt Chidgey at 10-30 a.m. ready to march to new area.

10. Battalion Headquarters will close at 10-30 and reopen in new area at same time.

sgd. A.E.TONKS. 2/Lieut & A/Adjt.

2/8.R.WARWICK.R.

ACKNOWLEDGE.

issued at 4 p.m.

2ND 8TH BATTALION THE ROYAL WARWICKSHIRE REGIMENT.

BATTALION ORDER 73. by LT.COL.E.C.CADMAN. COMMANDING.
FRIDAY 15th DEC.1916.

1. The Battalion will relieve 2/7.WARWICKS in the RIGHT SUB-SECTION tonight 15th inst.

2. Relief table:-
"A" Coy. relieves "D" Coy. 2/7.WARWICKS.
"B" " " "A" " "
"C" " " "B" " "
"D" " " "C" " "
Guides TULLOCHS CORNER in order "A" "B" "C" "D". The first Platoon of "A" Coy to reach TULLOCHS CORNER AT 4 p.m. "D" Coy will relieve "C" Coy of 2/7.WARWICKS under arrangements made between Company Commanders concerned. This relief should not be carried out in daylight.

3. ADVANCE PARTIES. Sergt.Smale, Signallers,for H.Q., will move before 10 a.m. to take over from Water Party of the 2/7.Warwicks. 1 N.C.O. and 3 men of "B" Coy will leave here before 1 p.m. to relieve a mixed post on WEST MIRAUMONT ROAD, they will carry two days rations and report at RIGHT Battn Headquarters for instructions,
LEWIS GUNS. One limber will be available to carry Lewis Guns and ammunition, leaving here at [illegible] p.m. it will proceed to TULLOCHS CORNER, guns will be dumped and picked up by teams on their way in under arrangements of L.G.O.
[illegible] Buckets of ammunition will be handed over by 2/7.WARWICKS in the trenches. An equal amount will be left here and handed over to 2/7.Warwicks on arraival.

4. GUM BOOTS. Gum Boots will be drawn at KAY DUMP R.[illegible] from Bde.Transport Officer. via Tramway [illegible]

5. Four Regimental Police will relieve four of 2/7.Warwicks at RIFLE DUMP,

6. TRANSPORT. Blankets will be taken from WELLINGTON HUTS at 12-30 p.m. Packs and spare kit, Coy Cookers and water carts at 4 p.m.
One limber as in para.3. above.
One limber to carry Officers packs etc. at [illegible] p.m. One limber at 4 p.m. Mess Cart at 6 p.m.

7. Receipts for trenches stores and secret documents must be forwarded to Battalion Headquarters by 4 a.m. on 17th Dec.1916..

8. RATIONS. Rations for the first 24 hours will be carried "D" Coy rations will be at TULLOCHS CORNER as usual.

9. CODE WORD for relief ; "GAMMA"

ACKNOWLEDGE.

sgd. A.E.TONKS. 2/Lt. & A/Adjt.
2/8.WARWICKS.

Sheet. 1.

2/8th WARWICK ORDER. No. 78

Ref. 1:20000. Sheet 57d. S.E. APP 3

1. Battalion will be relieved by 5th GLOSTERS on night 20/21st, and on relief will march to billets at Huts in MARTINSART WOOD.

2. Relief table.

POSITION.	2/8 COY	5th GLOSTER
RIGHT COY.	B	D
LEFT "	A	B
SUPPORT "	C	C
RESERVE "	D	A

Order of relief

2/8th Coy	A B C D
5th "	B D C A.

3. GUIDES. 1 Guide per platoon to report to Battn. Hqrs before 4.0 p.m.
Guides for posts etc. will be at COY Hdqrs to meet incoming unit there.

4. LEWIS GUNS.
5th GLOSTER Gun teams will be at Bn. Hdqrs at 3.30 [illegible]
1 Guide for [illegible] each of A. B. C Companie[illegible].

SHEET. 2

Headqrs at 3.00 p.m.

L/G. Ammunition. 40 drums will be handed over to incoming unit, a similar quantity to be taken over on relief. It will be at Q.M. Stores, 5th Glos. in MARTINSART.

5. ROUTE. Outgoing Companies via TULLOCH's CORNER - OVILLERS - CRUCIFIX CORNER - AVELUY - to huts in MARTINSART WOOD.

6. TRANSPORT.

Lewis Guns. 1. limber at 6 p.m.

Hq mess at 6 p.m.

Coys. 2 limbers will be available for carriage of any kits etc at 12 noon. Anything for transport on these limbers to reach Battn Hq before 10 A.M.

7. 2 COOKERS will be at CRUCIFIX CORNER from 9.30 p.m - 12.0 p.m. to provide tea, if required.

2 COOKERS at huts, MARTINSART to provide tea or soup on arrival

SHEET. 3.

8. Two blankets per man to be in Coy huts at MARTINSART as soon as vacated by outgoing unit.

9. RATION PARTIES. Pioneers and all Company cooks etc will leave trenches and proceed to Huts, MARTINSART to take over and prepare huts for men coming at night.

10. Relief will be reported by signal from Coys as soon as complete. CODE word CHRISTMAS.

11. Signals. Incoming units will be at their HQrs before 12 noon.

12. Coy Q.M.S. are responsible for all arrangements to meet incoming Companies.

Issued at 5.15 p.m. 19-12-16.

[signature]
Lt. Col.,
Comdg. 2/8 WARWICKS.

APP IV

Operation Order No 79
by Lt Col C. G. Bowman Commdg
2/5th [illegible] R

Reference Map Sheet 57 D S E 1:20000

1. The Battn. will move tomorrow 22nd inst. to billets at HEDAUVILLE.

2. Starting point. W 2. a. 8. 9. (point in road opposite Coin. Cookers sheds)

3. Order of march Hqrs A. B. C. D. Lewis & Lewis Gunners will march in rear of their Companies, 200 yards interval between Coys.

4. Time – Head of column to pass starting point at 9.27 a.m. Steps must be taken to avoid congestion on road near starting point. Companies will fall in in [illegible] at side of road, and will not be on the road longer than necessary before starting time.

5. Dress: Full marching order – steel helmets to be carried on packs.

6. Billeting party – 2/Lt. [illegible] with 5 O.R (one from each Coy.) will leave at ~~9.30~~ 8.0 a.m.

Sheet 2 O.O. 79

7. Blankets – Officers' kit and men's blankets, as laid down in Standing Orders.

8. Mess Cart, Maltese Cart, 4 cookers, one G.S. wagon for Officers' kit and 2 water carts will proceed with Battalion. Any other transport will proceed in advance.

9. Company Commanders are responsible that huts are left clean and tidy.

W. Barker, Lt & Adjt
for Lt. Col.
Cmdg. 2/8 Warwicks

December 21 1916
Issued at 8.0 p.m.

APP. V

SECRET.

Copy. no 1

Battalion Order. No 80. d/ 29.12.16
by Capt. W. R. T. Whatmore,
Comdg 2/8 R. War. R

1 The Battalion will move tomorrow, the 30th inst., to huts previously occupied at HARTINSART WOOD.

2 Starting point. Cross-roads at P. 34. c. 9 2.

3 Order of march — Hqrs, C, D, A, B, Cookers & L/Gunners will march in rear of their Companies. 200 yds distance between Coys.

4 Head of column to pass starting point at 9.30 a.m. Steps must be taken to avoid congestion on road at starting point. Coys will fall in two deep at side of road, and will not be on the road longer than necessary before starting time.

5. Dress. Full Marching Order. Steel Helmets on packs.

6 Advance party. 2/LT TOSLAND & 5 O.R. (1 per Coy) will leave at 9.0 A.M & will take over huts.

7. Officers' kits & blankets. Arrangements as laid down in Standing Orders.

8. Mess Cart, Maltese Carts, 4 Cookers, one G.S. wagon for Officers' kit and 2 water carts will proceed with Battalion. Any other transport will proceed in advance.

9. Company Commanders are responsible that billets are left clean & tidy.

December. 29th 1916.
Issued at 4.30 p.m.

W. R. T. Whatmore
Capt
~~Lt. Col,~~
Comdg ~~2/8 R~~ War R.

9H 27

War Diary of

Confidential

2/8th Battalion The Royal Warwickshire Regiment

Vol 9

2/8th BATTALION ORDERLY ROOM 31 JAN 1917 No. 183/17 THE ROYAL WARWICKSHIRE REGT.

Volume IX.

Period:-

January 1/17.

January 31/17.

Instructions regarding War Diaries and Intelligence Summaries are contained in F. S. Regs., Part II. and the Staff Manual respectively. Title pages will be prepared in manuscript.

WAR DIARY or INTELLIGENCE SUMMARY.

(Erase heading not required.)

Army Form C. 2118.

Place	Date	Hour	Summary of Events and Information	Remarks and references to Appendices
1917 MARTINSART WOOD	1917 Jany 1		(1) Working party of 115 O.R. Cable burying at X 2 a 3.2 - billeted at WELLINGTON HUTS. (2) Party of 100 O.R. reported to Yardmaster, AVELUY SIDING at 8 a.m. for work on Trains. (3) Party of 100 O.R. reported to C.R.E. AVELUY SIDING at 8.30 am for loading Stores. Party of 33 O.R. reported at DONNETS POST at 8 am. - work unloading ammunition. 8 O.R. returned from YELLOW LINE Fatigue. Draft of 8 O.R. arrived from Base	W.R.
"	2		Working parties (1) (2) & (3) same as yesterday. Work at camp laying floors in huts, cleaning up, burying tins and digging drains	W.R.
"	3		Working parties (1) (2) (3) & (4) as above - 3 Coys & 1 Platoon made up to 348 O.R. - Work at camp laying of floors, building fireplace and sides to hut.	W.R.
"	4		Working parties (1), (2) & (3) as above. 2 Lt ADAMS reported for duty from hospital - 1 O.R. to 29 I.B.D. for dental treatment	W.R.
"	5		Working parties (1) (2) & (3) as above. Also 1 Platoon (30 O.R.) at BLACK HORSE BRIDGE W.5 b.9.1. - work at pontoons. Orders for relief received. Batt. Orders published	W.R. App. 1
WARWICK HUTS	6		1 Coy (100 O.R.) worked at AVELUY SIDING, 1 Platoon (50 O.R.) on POZIERES THIEPVAL Road. Major SHIACH left for 45 H.A. Brigade H.Q. for attachment. B Coy moved to FABECK Trench coming under orders of 2/7 R. Warwicks. Remainder of Batt (less B Coy) to WARWICK HUTS. Relief complete 2.10 p.m. A Coy at MARTINSART WOOD were shelled at 8 p.m. (again at 4 am Jany 7)	W.R.

T. 2134. Wt. W708-776. 500000. 4/15. Sir J. C. & S.

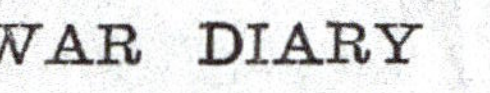

Army Form C. 2118.

WAR DIARY
or
INTELLIGENCE SUMMARY.
(Erase heading not required.)

Instructions regarding War Diaries and Intelligence Summaries are contained in F. S. Regs., Part II. and the Staff Manual respectively. Title pages will be prepared in manuscript.

Place	Date	Hour	Summary of Events and Information	Remarks and references to Appendices
	1917			
WARWICK HUTS	Jany 6		with High Velocity Guns – no casualties but some damage to huts. Work at WARWICK huts laying duckboards, fitting in stoves, erecting latrines &c	WR
"	7		Working parties as follows:– (1) 1 Off + 1 Coy (50 O.R.) at GRAVEL PITS for chalk burying (2) 1 Officer + 1 Platn 30 O.R. at RIFLE DUMP at 8.30 a.m. work on dugouts (3) 1 Sect. (10 O.R.) RIFLE DUMP at 8.30 am. work dugouts (4) 1 Coy (40 O.R.) RIFLE DUMP at 4.30 p.m. chalk burying. A Coy relieved D Coy 2/7 WORC. in ZOLLERN Trench. Draft of 3 O.R. & 1 prisoner arrived. 2LT WATSON retd from P. & B.T. Course. 2/LT GIBBINS left for Batt attached for 14 days	WR
"	8		Working parties as follows:– 1 Coy (50 O.R. + 1 Off) at DONNETS POST 8 a.m. on Ammn Dump (2) 1 Coy (30 O.R.) + 1 Off. at RIFLE DUMP 8 am on dugouts (3) 1 Sect 10 O.R. at RIFLE DUMP at 8 am. dugouts (4) 1 Coy (30 O.R. + 1 Off) at RIFLE DUMP at 4.30 pm – Chalk burying (5) 1 Sect. (10 O.R.) at QUARRY at 8.30 am. Drying room. LT. MORRISON RAMC att left for 2/2 FA. CAPT VICKERS RAMC att. reported for duty. 2 LT. McCLURE reported from Hosp. & left for Rest Station. 10 O.R as pushing party to KAY DUMP (to remain there)	WR
	9		Working parties as follows:– 1 Platoon (30 O.R. + 1 Off) RIFLE DUMP 8 am. dugouts (2) 10 O.R. RIFLE DUMP 8 am – dugouts (3) 10 O.R. QUARRY 8.30 am. drying sheds (4) 1 Platoon (1 Off + 40 O.R.) 4 pm chalk burying (5) 1 Platoon (1 Off + 20 O.R.) 4 pm GRAVEL PIT – work COOKHOUSE ZOLLERN. Brigade Order No 69 in regard to move received; Brigade Order No 70 in regard to raid tomorrow night received. Batt Order No 82 issued detailing A Coy for this. Buried 22 bodies near camp	App No 2 App No 2 App No 2 WR

T.2134. Wt. W708–776. 500000. 4/15. Sir J. C. & S.

Instructions regarding War Diaries and Intelligence Summaries are contained in F. S. Regs., Part II. and the Staff Manual respectively. Title pages will be prepared in manuscript.

WAR DIARY
or
INTELLIGENCE SUMMARY.
(Erase heading not required.)

Army Form C. 2118.

Place	Date	Hour	Summary of Events and Information	Remarks and references to Appendices
WARWICK HUTS	1917 Jany 10		Correction to Brig Orders No 70 received. Working parties as follows:- 1 Plat (1 Off + 30 men) RIFLE DUMP at 8.30 am work at ZOLLERN. (2) 1 Sect (10 OR) RIFLE DUMP 8.30 am work at FABECK (3) 1 Platoon (40 OR & 1 Off) 4.30 pm RIFLE DUMP Chalk carrying	WM
RT SUBSECTOR MOUQUET	11	6.35 am	"A" Coy - made up to 100 strong executed a raid on GRANDCOURT TRENCH - 6 prisoners taken - Operations suspended before reaching objective owing to artillery shooting short - causing casualties 2Lt. C.R. KITCHIN & 13 OR wounded	
		3pm.	2/8 Relieved 2/7 R WARWICKS in line - Some shelling - no casualties - Relief completed 9.30 pm	
		5.30 pm	Artillery active - 1 prisoner questioned - information received reported in I.P.R.	WM
	12	7pm	A Coy relieved A Coy of 2/7 WARWICKS in REGINA - Enemy artillery activity generally below normal. Work of improving & cleaning trenches continued - No casualties. CO made tour of trenches.	WM
	13	4 am	CO made tour of trenches - Draft of 10 OR arrived at Q.M. Stores from Base. 2Lt E.G. STEPHENS to hospital, sick. OC Relieving Batt visited Batt H.Q. - 2 OR proceeded to ST RIQUIER on course. Orders for relief & subsequent moves received from Brigade. Enemy artillery fairly active No casualties. 11 Bodies buried	WM
	14	12 mn	2nd in Command Coy Commanders & Number of OR of 6th NORTHANTS (relieving Batt) made reconnaissance of trenches.	WM

T.1134. Wt. W708-776. 500000. 4/15. Sir J. C. & S.

Instructions regarding War Diaries and Intelligence Summaries are contained in F. S. Regs., Part II. and the Staff Manual respectively. Title pages will be prepared in manuscript.

WAR DIARY
or
INTELLIGENCE SUMMARY.
(Erase heading not required.)

Army Form C. 2118.

Place	Date	Hour	Summary of Events and Information	Remarks and references to Appendices
	1917 Jany			
MOUQUET	14	11pm	Lachrymatory gas shells fired on MOUQUET Farm no Casualties	
		11.30p	Orders for second day of move received.	
		11.40p	Our artillery firing short – reported. 15 bodies buried (unidentified)	WR
	15		Trench Stores handed over – Batt relieved by 6th NORTHANTS – Relief completed 12.40 am (16th)	App. III
			Artillery activity below normal.	WR
RUBEMPRE	16		On relief Batt proceeded to AVELUY & embussed for RUBEMPRE – 1 Officer per Coy – 2 runners	
			1 Batt Signaller remained after Batt relief in the line. CAPT W MACKAY reported from Base	App. IV
			2LT. A L McCLURE reported from Officers Rest Station. Orders for move on 18th & 19th inst received	WR
			& 1 Officer per Coy & Coy runners [illegible] returned from line	
RUBEMPRE	17		Batt moved to CANDAS by march – arrived 4pm 2LT W R MORTON reported from 5th Army School	WR App. V
CANDAS CRAMONT	18		Batt marched to CRAMONT – arrived 11.45am – C.O returned from leave	WR App. VI
CANCHY	19		Batt marched to CANCHY – arrived 1.30pm 2LT WHITELEY to hospital	WR
"	20		Draft of 11 O.R. arrived. Rest & Cleaning up.	WR
"	21		Rest & cleaning up – replacing deficiencies – No blanket parades – Forwarded Training Programme to Brigade	
			for ensuing week	WR
	22		Rest & cleaning up – Inspections – Com. Officer held Conference of Officers – F.G.C.M. on 3463 Pte GOLDSBY.	WR
	23	9a–1p	Close order drill, Handling of arms, saluting & Physical training. Draft of 7 O.R. arrived	WR

Instructions regarding War Diaries and Intelligence Summaries are contained in F. S. Regs., Part II. and the Staff Manual respectively. Title pages will be prepared in manuscript.

WAR DIARY
or
INTELLIGENCE SUMMARY.
(Erase heading not required.)

Army Form C. 2118.

Place	Date	Hour	Summary of Events and Information	Remarks and references to Appendices
CANCHY	1917 Jany 24	9am -1pm	Close Order Drill – Extended order drill [illegible] – P.T. – CPL WHITMORE to Hospital. Visit from B.G.C. on parade & inspected work. Promulgated sentence of 6 months imprisonment with hard labour on No 3443 Pte GOLDBY W.	WB
"	25	9-11am	Musketry – rapid loading – P.T. – Bombing practice – C.O's conference with Officers	
"		8-10pm	Night marching by compass – patrol work. Programme of next week's training to Brigade.	WB
"	26	9-1pm	Running drill – Rapid extensions – handling of arms – Bayt fighting. 2Lt PHIPPS reported for duty & posted to A Coy. 2pm Court of Inquiry – Pres Capt BROCK – Members 2Lts CADBEY & TISLAND on accident to 2Lt WALKER. 2Lt ADAMS to Hosp.	WB
"	27	9am-1pm	Bombing practice – Bayt fighting – Physical Training. C.O. held Conference of Officers	WB
"	28	10am	Church parade – 100 O.R. – Recreation Room. Medical Inspection of Coys for Scabies P. 11am-12 noon C.O's conference	WB
"	29	9-11am	Running drill – fire position – rapid aiming & loading & Bayt fighting – Specialists under Specialist Officers	
		11am-1pm	A Coy firing on Range – [illegible] Coy – Extended order drill – forming up for attack – Coy attack. Capt WHITMORE returned from hospital.	WB
	30	9am-1pm	Bayonet fighting, Extended order, fire discipline – P & B T class under CSM DENYER, Army Gym Staff.	
		11-1pm	Coy attack including reorganisation – B Coy firing on range. Lt Q.M. HODGKINS to Hospital	WB
"	31	9-11am	P.T. Patrols & reconnaissance, map reading & use of ground for N.C.Os & understudies, Bayt Fighting	
		11-1pm	Company attack – C Coy firing on range	WB

[illegible signature]
Lieut Colonel
Commanding 2/8th R. War. R.

T2134. Wt. W708-776. 500000. 4/15. Sir J. C. & S.

App 1

[illegible] Battalion The Royal Warwick[illegible]

[illegible] Order No. 31 by Major [illegible] Commanding [illegible]

Ref. Map 57D S.E. [illegible]

1 [illegible]

2 [illegible] WARWICKS [illegible] WORCESTERS [illegible] following [illegible]

8th WARWICKS	7th WORCESTERS	PLACE	TIME
A Coy	B Coy	ZOLLERN	[illegible] 6th [illegible]
B	C	FABECK	3pm 6th
C			
D	Move to WARWICK HUTS by 3pm 6th inst		
HQ	[illegible]		

3 **DRESS** for A & B Coys [illegible] Coy [illegible] HQ Coy [illegible] B Coy [illegible]

4 [illegible] FABECK & ZOLLERN [illegible] ZOLLERN Coy [illegible]

5 All Coys before leaving camp will [illegible] HUTS [illegible]

6 **RATIONS** B Coy to TULLOCHS CORNER [illegible] 6th inst inclusive C D & HQ Coy to WARWICK HUTS [illegible] 6th [illegible] A Coy to MARTINSART [illegible] 6th inst & to TULLOCHS CORNER from night of 7th [illegible]

[illegible] 7 pm

Lieut & A/Adjt
2/8 R War R

SECRET. Copy No.19. App 2

182nd.Infantry Brigade Order No,70.

1.In connection with an operation undertaken by the 13th Corps North of the Ancre, a bombardment of 48 hours duration commenced at 8 a.m. 9th inst.

2.On the 11th inst. under cover of a rolling barrage of 126 guns which will be carried out on a front R.12.c.9.9. to R.12.a.0.8. the Brigade will carry out a raid on a portion of GRANDCOURT TRENCH and FOLLY TRENCH with the object of killing Germans, taking prisoners, and damaging enemy defences.

3.(a). C.O. 2/8 Warwicks will detail 1 Company, strength 100 other ranks, to raid 250 yards of GRANDCOURT TRENCH from R.16.b.4.8. to SIXTEEN ROAD inclusive.
(b). C.O. 2/6 Warwicks will detail 1 Platoon, strength 34 other ranks, to raid FOLLY TRENCH from SIXTEEN ROAD INCLUSIVE Westwards throughout its length.

4.The rolling barrage will open on a front parallel to GRANDCOURT TRENCH and 240 yards in front of it between R.16.a.0.8. and R.12.c.9.9. at ZERO.
The raiding parties will be in position on a line R.16.b.0.2. to R.16.a.0.5. by ZERO hour.
The signal to advance will be the opening of the barrage.

5.At 0.04 the barrage will advance and will roll by 100 yards into GRANDCOURT TRENCH, pausing for four minutes on each 100 yards and 5 minutes on GRANDCOURT TRENCH.

6.(a). The raiding party of 2/8 Warwicks will not remain in GRANDCOURT TRENCH after 0.40.
(b). The raiding party of 2/6 Warwicks will not leave Folly Trench until the 2/8 Warwicks pass the end of it as they withdraw.
(c). The signal to withdraw will be given by the O.C. Raiding Party by firing Very Lights low towards our own lines.

7.O.C. 182nd M.G.Coy will co-operate by searching the area R.11.a. during the period of the barrage with all available guns.

8.Arrangements will be made to supplement telephone communication with lamps.

9.The Brigade Signal Officer will arrange the synchronisation of watches,

10.Zero time will be notified later.

11.Reports to Brigade Headquarters.

12.Acknowledge.

Issued at 9 p.m. sgd. J.R.HEELIS. Major.
B.M. 182nd. Inf.Bde.

Corrections to Bde.O. 70.

<u>Para.4. second sentence.</u>
For: "The raiding party will be in position on a line R.16.b.0.2. to R.16.a.0.5. by ZERO hour"
Read. "The raiding parties will be in position on a line R.16.b.2.0. to R.16.a.5.0. "

<u>Para. 6. (a).</u>
For:- "0.40."
Read "0.50."

Copy 4.

10-1-17.

Amendment and Additions to 182nd Bde.Order 70.

---

1. For para. 6. (a) read :-

"The raiding party of 2/8 Warwicks will be prepared to leave GRANDCOURT TRENCH at 0.30."

2 To para, 6. (c) add:-

"and long whistle blasts. Both these signals will be repeated by all Platoon Commanders."

3. To para, 8. add:-

"Notification that the raiding parties are back will be sent by telephone and by a signal consisting of red rockets in groups of 5 fired from R.17.a.6.0.

Either of these will be the signal for the barrage to cease.

issued at 5-45 p.m. sgd. J.R.HEELIS. Major.

B.M. 182nd Inf.Bde,

SECRET. Copy No.31.

Artillery
18th Divisional/Operation OrderNo.107 by Brigadier Genl.
S.F.METCALF. D.S.O.

Reference attached diagram.

1. The 61st Division will carry out a raid on (day at the same time as the minor operation by XIII Corps and 11th Division, at a ZERO time to be communicated later.
2. The artilleries of 2nd Division and 18th Division and 61st Division(less 4 batteries) will be at the disposal of 61st Division to carry out the raid.
3. The 182nd Inf.Bde are carrying out the raid as under:-
   (a), One Company 2/8 Warwicks 250 yards of GRANDCOURT TRENCH as shown on attached diagram (R.16.b.4.8. to SIXTEEN ROAD).
   (b). One Platoon 2/6 Warwicks the whole of FOLLY TRENCH as shown on diagram.
4. The signal for withdrawal of raiding parties will be given by the Officer Commanding Raiding Party by firing Very Lights low towards out own lines.
5. The artillery support will consist of a standing barrage along GRANDCOURT TRENCH from EAST MIRAUMONT ROAD to GRANDCOURT ROAD, and a rolling barrage from BOOM RAVINE to GRANDCOURT ROAD.
   The Heavy Artillery will cover the high ground and trenches in R.11a.& b. MIRAUMONT ALLEY and bank in R.4.a.
6. The distribution of front barrages, and times of lifts are shown in attached diagram and table.
7. Tasks of 4.5" Howitzers are shown on attached table.
8. Liason Officers will be found as under:-
   182nd Inf.Bde. H.Q. by 306th Brigade R.F.A.
   2/6. Warwick Battn. H.Q. by 84th Brigade R.F.A.
   2/8 Warwick Battn. by 307th Brigade R.F.A.
   These Officers will report at their respective Infantry Hdqrs on the previous evening.
   The 84th Brigade R.F.A. for the purpose of this operation will communicate with Liason Officer through 308th Brigade R.F.A. forward wire.
9. Observation stations will be manned by 5-30 a.m. on Z day.
10. The following will be the rates of fire"-

18 pndr.			4.5" Howitzer.	
0. to 0.17.....	3 rounds	p.g.p.m.	2 rds.	p.h.p.m.
0.17. to 0.30...	2 "	p.g.p.m.	1½ "	p.h.p.m.
0.30. onwards.	1 "	p.g.p.m.	1 "	p.h.p.m.

11. The 2nd Divisional Artillery and 83rd Brigade. R.F.A. will fire 50% Shrapnel throughout the operation. Remaining Brigades will fire exclusively Shrapnel up to 0.20.
12. Zero hour will be communicated later - Watches will be synchronized by 61st Divisional time.
14. Acknowledge.

sgd. A.T.BROOKS Major R.A.

19-1-17. B.M. 18th Divisional Artillery.

AMENDMENT TO OPERATION ORDER No.107. Copy No.30.

1. Cancel para.4. and substitute"-
   The signal indicating the safe return of raiding party will consist of 5 Red Rockets from R.16.c.9.9.

2. Reference table of tasks forwarded with above order:
   D/83 Battery from 0. to 0.15. will place three Howitzers on task indicated in Table and 1 Howitzer on junction of SIXTEEN ROAD and GRANDCOURT TRENCH R.16.a.8.7.

Copy No.12.

Special Order No. 38.

Orders for raid on enemy trenches on   inst.

Reference LE SARS TRENCH MAP. 1/10000.

1.OBJECT. To afford a left flank cov ering party for raiding party of 2/8 Warwicks.
To enter enemy trench running from R.16.a.7.3. to R.16.a.1.3. (FOLLY TRENCH), and to hold it while operation of 2/8 Warwicks is in progress.
To kill Germans, capture prisones, and obtain identifications, and to destroy his defences.

2.COMPOSITION OF PARTY. Raiding Party will consist of 2/Lieut.F.P.STEPHENS and 34 other ranks, subdivided as follows:-
No.1.Party - 1 Officer, 2 Bayonet men.
2 throwers, 2 car iers, 2 spare men.
2 Party. 1 N.C.O. 1 bayonet man, 1 thro wer, 1 carrier, 1 spare man.
3 Party. 1 N.C.O. and three men.
4 Party. 1 N.C.O. and 3 men.
5 Party. 1 N.C.O. and 3 men.
6.Party. 1 N.C.O. four men and four stretcher bearers.

3.POINT OF EXIT. R.16.a.6.6.

4.POINT OF ENTRY. R.16.a.7.3.

5.OBJECTIVES. No.1. Party will work along trench as far as its junction with GRANDCOURT ROAD.
No.2.Party will work along communication trench for a distance of 50 yards.
No.3. and 4 Parties will follow No.1. Party and deal with any dugouts left by them.
No.5.Party will follow number 4 Party and escort any pri soners taken by them back to our trenches.
No.6.Party will remain at point of entry and be a reserve.

6.PASSWORD. The password will be "BROTHER".

7.WITHDRAWAL. The code word for withdrawal will be "PACK UP".
The time of withdra wal will be left to discretion of O.C. Raiding Party, but withdrawal will not take place until the Raiding Party of the 2/8 Warwicks has withdrawn past FOLLY TRENCH.

8.ARTILLERY. The artillery will open a creeping bar age at Zero hour on a line parellel to and 250 yards SOUTH of GRANDCOURT TRENCH.
The Raiding Party will be in position at approximately R.16.a.7.0. by Zero hour.
The opening of the bar age will be the signal to advance.
At 0.04 the barage will advance by jumps of 100 yards on to GRANDCOURT TRENCH, pausing for four minutes after each jump.

9.SYNCHRONIZATION. Watches will be synchronized under arangements to be made later.

10.ZERO TIME. Zero time will be notified later.

11.REPORTS. Reports will be sent to Coy Hdqrs at R.22.a.3.8. where the C.O. will be during the operation.

11.ARMAMENT. as per attached table.

sgd. J.W. Padmore, Capt. & Adjt
2/8 Warwicks

AMENDMENTS TO SPECIAL ORDER [illegible].

13. COMMUNICATIONS. A telephone wire will be laid from Company Headquarters at N.22.a.3.8. to B Post dugout in DESIRE TRENCH, under arrangements to be made by Sergt [illegible]. Two men here of 2/6 Warwicks will be on duty at this advanced telephone, and will transmit any message received from the Raiding Party to the Coy Hdqrs, when they will in turn be transmitted back to Battalion Headquarters in ZOLLERN REDOUBT.

14. CODES. The following code words will be used:-

(a). "FOLLY" - means 6th Batt. have got in and 8th Battn have passed by FOLLY TRENCH.
(b). "UNKNOWN" - 6th Batt have got in and fortunes of 8th Batt not known.
(c). "DRAWN". 6th Battn have failed.
(d). "ALL IN" - 6th Battalion all in.

15. C.O. The C.O. 2/6th will be at Battalion Hdqrs in ZOLLERN REDOUBT and not as stated in Special Order No.[illegible].

10-1-17. sgd. J.L.[illegible].
2/6 R.War.R.

ST. 2ND 8TH BATTALION THE ROYAL WARWICKSHIRE REGIMENT.

ORDER No.82. 9th January 1917.

REF. Trench Map 1/10000 LE SARS-BEAUMONT.

1. In conjunction with bombardment which commenced at 8 a.m. on 9th inst. and further artillery programme "A" Coy will force an entry into the enemy trenches on the morning of the 11th.

2. INTENTION. To kill Germans. To take prisoners. To obtain an idea of enemy defences and destroy them.

3. OBJECTIVE. GRANDCOURT TRENCH from its junction with SIXTEEN ROAD to a point 240 yards East along that trench.

4. ASSEMBLY MARCH.
(a), "A" Coy will attached details will be in FABECK, ZOLLERN TRENCH until evening of the 10th. They will complete all necessary preliminary arrangements from there.
(b). After dark on the 10th "A" Coy moves to Headquarter dugout of the FRONT LEFT COY, which dugout will then be completely vacated by 2/7 Warwicks.
(c). 7th Warwicks will continue to hold all front line posts.
(d). The move as in (b) above to be complete by 9 p.m.

5. ASSEMBLY POSITION. A line approximately R.16.a.9.0. to R.16.b.1.0. to be reconnoitred by O.C. "A" Coy on night 9/10th and when the exact line has been selected preparations will be made by him to tape or otherwise mark it on night 10/11th.
O.C. "A" Coy will be responsible that all necessary steps are taken to ensure rapid and correct movement of troops concerned to the selected assembly positions.
NOTE. The great importance of making every possible preparation to ensure the rapid and correct assembly of troops concerned is emphasised.
(b). All "A" Coy dispositions to be complete by ZERO minus 90 minutes.
(c). The assembly to be covered by patrols.
(d), General idea of dispositions as in sketch below:

X X X

Bombers. O.......Infantry.at.five.yards.interval..............O Bombers.

Bombers.. O.........ditto................O. Bombers.

xxxxxxx bearers.

6. The time for the advance of the Infantry will be given by the start of the barrage, i.e. ZERO TIME.
NOTE. The rolling barrage to begin at ZERO time is intended to fall on a line approximately through FOLLY TRENCH and EASTWARDS i.e. about 150 yards in advance of the assembly position.
It is important this this distance at least (150 yards) be kept between that assembled troops and the barrage at the moment the barrage is first laid on as the actual line is liable to an error of 75 yards from the line of FOLLY TRENCH upon which the first barrage is supposed to fall.
The barrage willremain on the FOLLY TRENCH line until ZERO plus 4 minutes, during which time the infantry must advance as close to barrage as possible.
At ZERO plus four minutes the barrage leaps 100 yards and remains fixed for a further 4 minutes during which time the infantry advances so as to get close up.
NOTE Further details as to barrage programme on Artillery programme being received.

7. Party will withdraw from enemy trench not later than 30 minutes after time of entry. The signal to confirm time for withdrawal will be given by O.C. Enterprise by the firing of numerous Very Lights towards out own lines and close to the ground.

8. "A" Coy will be relieved by "C" Coy in the course of Battalion relief probably on night of 11/12th.

Battalion Order 82 (continued)

9. The Battalion Bombing Officer will detail four complete groups as outlined on attached appendix. He will be responsible for equipping and organising these four groups and will report with them to O.C. "A" Coy before 5 p.m. on 10th inst. He will arrange all questions of supply of bombs direct with Bde Bombing Officer.

10. A small enterprise having got for its objective FOLLY TRENCH will be carried out by 6th Warwicks commencing at same ZERO time.
FOLLY TRENCH JUNCTION with SIXTEEN ROAD will be secured and held by this party to cover our withdrawal from GRANDCOURT TRENCH.
Communication with O.C. 6th WARWICKS party should be established by "A" Coy sometime before ZERO time.

11. Details of equipment are left to discretion of O.C. "A" Coy butit should follow generally table in attached appendix.

12. The necessity of securing the flanks of the raiding party both whilst in the enemy trench and during withdrawal is emphasised.

13. MEDICAL ARRANGEMENTS. The M.O. and one orderly will be in advanced Coy. Headquarters at midnight 10th. Casualties would be kept there if found impossible to evacuate them to Aid Post.

14. Reports to RIGHT BATTALION HEADQUARTERS.

sgd. W.E.Phillips. Major. for Lt,Col,

Commdg. 2/8. R.WARWICK.R.

APPENDIX TO ORDER 82. 9th JANuary 1917.

1. EQUIPMENT - BOMBERS.

DETAILS.	Rifles Bayts.	S.A.A.	REVLR.	Belts Bayts.	Mills.	No.23
1st Bayt man.	1	20 rds.			2	
1st thrower.			1	1	4	
Carrier.			1	1	12	
Leader.			1	1	4	
2nd Bayt man.	1	20 rds			2	
2nd Thrower.			1	1	6	
2nd Carrier.			1	1	12	
Rifle Grenadier.	1	24 rds.				12
2nd ditto	1	24 "				

DRESS. Steel Helmets. Gas Helmets in ALERT position. Ordinary haversacks slung from leather braces to be used to carry Bombs, carriers carrying two haversacks.

It is not intended that every man should carry Mills Bombs but there will be a certain number of Bombers surplus to the number required for the organised bombing groups and it is suggested that these surplus bombers should each carry two Mills.. (40 are available).

2. INFANTRY. Rifles. Bayonets fixed before moving to assembly position covered if necessary by sandbags.
Gas Helmets in Alert position.
10 rounds in magazine. 40 rounds carried in pocket.
Steel Helmets.
Boots and puttees will be worn. Not gum boots.
Each man will carry a wire cutter.

12 to 24 men will be detailed to carry "P" Bombs and MSK Bombs for use against dugouts.
The four snipers employed with Bombers will be equipped under orders of O.C "A" Coy.

MATERIAL.				
Mills No.23.	264.		Very Pistols.	3
Mills No.5.	80.		Cartridges.	24
"P" Bombs.	24			
"MSK" Bombs.	12			
Rods for 23	192			
Blanks ditto	192.			

NOTE. The Bombing Officer is responsible that the above and any additional stores required are actually in possession before 12 noon on the 10th inst.

sgd. W.E.PHILLIPS. Major. for Lt.Col.

2/8. R.WARWICK.R.

SUPPLY ARRANGEMENTS TO ACCOMPANY B.O. 82.

1. "B" Coy will be available to assist in carrying etc. and will supply men as required by O.C. "A" Coy.

2. 115 rations will be sent via tramway to RIFLE DUMP tomorrow where they will be taken over by an Officer of "B" Coy with party to carry them to LEFT COY HEADQUARTERS in the front line, this officer will be responsible that all rations reach these Headquarters and are personally handed over to O.C. "A" Coy.
12 petrol tins of water will be sent up and handed over to Officer of "B" Coy who will dump them with rations.
A ration of fresh meat and vegetables will be sent of O.C. "B" Coy by the Quartermaster. O.C. "B" Coy will arrange for cooking and sending forward in food containers to reach LEFT COY HDQRS sometime before 4 a.m. on the morning of the 11th. (this food is intended for consumption during the day of the 11th).
The Quartermaster will arrange to send up alcohol or fat cookers with the 115 rations mentioned above.

3. Wire Cutters, Very Pistols etc. will reach TULLOCHS CORNER at 10 a.m. on the 10th. O.C. "B" Coy will arrange to convey these to O.C. "A" Coy.

4. Extra haversacks to complete Bombers equipment will be drawn from "A" Coy.

5. Quartermaster will arrange to send (larger size) Service Dress Tunics for use of Officers.

6. O.C. "B" Coy will give every assistance in his power to "A" Coy and will detail any of his Officers for duty with "A" Coy as required.

sgd. W.H.PHILLIPS, Major for Lt.Col.

Comdg. 2/6. R.WARWICKS

A F T E R O R D E R.

1. The strictest precautions will be taken by O.C. "A" Coy to ensure that every possible means of identification from the person of all ranks participating in the raid.
2. Every man will be given a written slip showing Regimental number, rank and Name but NOT Regiment.
3. Arrangements to be made to facilitate rapid checking off of party to return to our trenches.

ARTILLERY PROGRAMME TO ACCOMPANY ORDER 82.

1. The rolling barrage will open on a front parallel to GRANDCOURT TRENCH and about 250 yards in front of it, between R.16.a.0.8. and R.12.c.9.9. This barrage opens at ZERO time.
NOTE. It must not be forgotten that the signal to advance will be the opening of the barrage (for instance if barrage should be three minutes late in opening Infantry will not advance at ZERO time but rather ZERO time will be indicated by the opening of the barrage when the Infantry will advance).

ZERO. (a). Barrage opens as above.
(b). Infantry advances to close up with barrage.

ZERO plus 4 minutes. Barrage advances and will roll 100 yards towards GRANDCOURT TRENCH. (b). Infantry advances to close barrage.

ZERO plus 8 minutes. (a). Barrage lifts 100 yards further towards GRANDCOURT TRENCH.
(b). Infantry advance to close up with barrage.

ZERO plus 12 minutes. (a). Barrage lifts to GRANDCOURT TRENCH and there joins the fixed barrage.
(b). Infan try advances to close up with barrage.

ZERO plus 17 minutes. (a). The barrage lifts to GRANDCOURT TRENCH and there joins b fixed barrage.
(b). Infantry enter trench.

THIS PROGRAMME IS SUBJECT TO SLIGHT ALTERATION WHICH WILL BE COMMUNICATED TO YOU AS SOON AS RECEIVED.

S E C R E T. C.4/6.

182nd Inf.Bde.

Herewith copy of the report on the operation carried out by "A" Coy 2/8 Warwicks, and a party of the 2/6 WARWICKs on morning of January 11th.

The G.O.C. 61st Division is well satisfied at the manner in which Capt. Whatmore 2/8 Warwicks and Lieut GRIFFITHS 2/6 WARWICKS carried out their tasks and commanded their men. He considers that the plan was ably conceived, and that, but for an unfortunate accident due to the fire of one battery, it would have been successful.

The G.O.C. congratulates all ranks on their behaviour under the circumstances.

A copy of this letter, and of the report, will be forwarded to Os.C. 2/6 and 2/8 Warwicks for communication to the Officers and men concerned.

13-1-17. sgd. H.WARE. Lieut.Col.

Comdg. 2/8. WARWICKS.

To 8th Warwicks.

The Brigade Commander has much pleasure in forwarding this complimentary report.

15-1-17. sgd. J.R.HEELIS. Major. B.M.

182nd Inf.Bde.

S E C R E T.   C.4/6.

4th Corps.

1. I beg to enclose the report by G.O.C. 182nd Inf.Bde on the attempted raid on the morning of Jan.11th by "A" Coy 2/8. Warwicks, supported by a party of 2/6 Warwicks, together with copies of Divisional, Brigade and Battalion Orders issued for the operation.

2. Both parties deployed successfully on the line arranged and the capture of the enemy patrol at 6-30 a.m. did not effect the arrangements.

3. At ZERO, both parties were thrown into confusion by our guns, on both sides of SIXTEEN ROAD, firing short, one Officer and 13 men being killed and wounded.

4. I agree with G.O.C. 182nd Bde that the preliminary arrangements were carefully planned and well carried out: the men were anxious to advance, and I feel confident that the enterprise would have been successful if the accident of the guns firing short had not occurred.

As it was, I consider that Capt.WHATMORE acted wisely in abandoning the operation. Our barrage, having started about 300 yards short, would have halted in front of GRANDCOURT TRENCH instead of behind it.

5. I am of opinion that Lieut, STEPHENS also acted with judgment u under trying circumstances.

6. Further enquiries are being made with respect to the short barrage.

12-1-17.

General.

Comndg. 61st Division.

REPORT ON RAID ON ENEMY ON MORNING JAN.11th 1917.

Ref. Map Sheet.

ASSEMBLY. The preparations for assembly proceeded without a hitch.
CAPT. WHATMORE and 2/LT. KITCHEN took out a covering party and laid tapes marking assembly position, according to pre-arranged plan, based on reconnaissance of previous night. The lines taped out were as follows:-

1st LINE. R.16.c.7.9½. and thence to a point 250 yards due E.

2nd LINE. Parallel to and 30 yards in rear of 1st line.

The taping was completed at 1.30 a.m.
Troops left Hdqrs dugout in the Ravine at 4-45 a.m. and were led to assembly positions. These positions were completed at 5-45 a.m. as under:-

Bombers———————— 2 Platoons ————————Bombers.

30 yards distance.

Bombers————————2 Platoons ————————Bombers.

Provision to secure right flank during withdrawal was made by the inclusion of four snipers with the Right rear Bombing group.
Touch was obtained with the Platoon of the 8th Warwicks in position on the left of SIXTEEN ROAD and this touch was maintained until ZERO hour.
At 6-30 a.m. an enemy patrol approached our RIGHT Covering party. This patrol numbered 8, and of these one was killed and six captured. Nothing was seen of the other man.
At ZERO hour the rolling barrage came down in front of the 1st assembly line. The first salvoes seemed to be more or less in the expected line, bursts being almost overhead the men in the 1st Assembly line. A certain portion of the immediate subsequent salvoes were short, bullets falling among the first and second line, and several casualties were suffered at this time. This being totally unexpected caused some confusion.
Shells fell in rear of our posts in CROSS TRENCH, and one man forming part of the garrison of one of these posts were killed by one of our own shells.
On the left flank near SIXTEEN ROAD, the raiding party appeared to be completely caught in a portion of our barrage, shells falling well in their neighbourhood and in the area about point 66.
(At about 2 a.m. on the morning of the 11th CAPT. WHATMORE reported to Artillery Liaison Officer at RIGHT Battn. Hdqrs that shells suspected to be a Howitzer, had been falling about point 66 at 12-30 a.m. at which time he had been taping his assembly position.)
All our barrage seemed definitely to clear to the front of the original assembly line about 15 minutes after ZERO, but the confusion caused by the unexpected dropping of a portion of the barrage on our own troops during these 15 minutes was such as to render impossible the pursuit of the original plan, and attempts were made to collect casualties, all of which were found and brought in.
The casualties suffered were all inflicted by our own barrage and within the period between Zero and Zero plus 15.
No enemy barrage was laid down to the East of SIXTEEN ROAD before ZERO plus 30 minutes.

CASUALTIES.	Wounded.	Officers.	1	(2/Lt. KITCHEN).
		Other ranks.	13.	
PRISONERS.	Wounded.	2		
	Unwounded.	4.		

Sheet 2.

As far as the Infantry were concerned, all arrangements worked as well as could be desired. All necessary preparations were complete well before Zero hour. The men were all in most excellent spirits and eager for the enterprise: but it seemed the sudden and unexpected opening of a certain portion of our own barrage upon them rendered it impossible to pursue the original plan.

1. CAPT. WHATMORE saw shells burst in rear of CROSS TRENCH. He was in the 2nd assembly line (this would be at least 180 yards from the line on which the 1st barrage was supposed to open) and 2 men were hit by shrapnel beside him. There is also his report as to firing near point 66 whilst taping of assembly position was in progress.

2. CAPT. MUNGLE was at the entrance to LEFT COY HDQRS DUGOUT and shrapnel bullets hit the dugout entrance.

3. 2/LT. CLAYDON confirms the shells in rear of CROSS TRENCH and in area about Point 66.

4. 2/LT. PROSSER was in front of our own shell bursts near SIXTEEN ROAD.

5. All the above Officers are convinced that the majority of shells falling short were shrapnel, except in the case of the Left where H.E. did certainly fall.

Jan. 11th. 1917. sgd. W.E. PHILLIPS. Major.

Commdg. 2/8. WARWICKS.

2/6.WARWICKS.

REPORT ON RAID ON FOLLY ON MORNING OF JAN.11th.1917.

The Raiding Party of 34 o.r. under 2/Lt. STEPHENS reached the assembly point at R.16.a.9.7. at 6-30 a.m. without incident and immediately got into touch with the left of the raiding party of 2/8 WARWICKS.

2/Lt Stephens also personally spoke to CAPT.[illegible] O.C. 2/8.WARWICKS Raiding Party.

At 6-35 a.m. our barrage opened directly on a line of assembly and also on DEXTER TRENCH from R.16.a.6.6. westwards for about 200 yards. Our Artillery had been previously warned that between 12-20 a.m. and 12-40 a.m. they had been firing on DEXTER TRENCH.

The whole party assembled in a large shell hole and took cover as best they could from the intense fire.

A similar intense barrage was directed from our own guns on the raiding party of the 2/8 Warwicks and they were seen to withdraw at 6-40 a.m. as a result.

At 6-45 a.m. a verbal message was received by 2/Lt.STEPHENS from his N.C.O. specially posted to keep touch with 2/8 WARWICKS that they had withdrawn.

At 6-49 a.m. the barrage referred to above lifted about 100 yards, and on orders from 2/Lt.Stephens the party prepared to advance, but before they could move forward our barrage which had been previously directed on DEXTER TRENCH lifted on to the assembly point (R.16.a.9.7) and the party was againxx forced to take cover. This barrage lasted four minutes.

Taking into consideration that the party of the 2/8.WARWICKS had been forced to retire, 2/Lt.Stephens decided to go forward himself with a small party. Four N.C.Os and two men immediately volunteered and followed him. This small party advanced to LONE TREE (R.16.a.7.1). On nearing this tree two figures were seen and were thought to be snipers, but on being bayonetted proved to be dummies constructed of wood and canvas with German Steel Helmets on top.

2/Lt.Stephens left one N.C.O. and the two privates at this point (R.16.a.7.1) to investigate and guard the old trench running from R.16.a.7½1 to R.16.a.9½.0.

Forward of LONE TREE the ground was found to be in a much better condition and 2/Lt.Stephens and the three N.C.Os moved forward at the double and entered FOLLY TRENCH at R.16.a.7.3. and 6-55 a.m. and worked westwards along the trench for about 120 yards. The trench was found to be unoccupied, about 4 feet deep, without duckboards, revetment, or dugouts, and dry with the exception of a few shallow pools. Footprints denoting recent occupation were observed, but no evidence of any work was seen. There was no wire in front of the trench.

They then retraced their steps along the trench and examined the remaining portion between the point of entry and SIXTEEN ROAD. While doing this the enemy opened a heavy barrage on FOLLY TRENCH and the party withdrew, rushing through the barrage.

They returned along SIXTEEN ROAD and picked up the N.C.O. and two men left to guard the small trench by LONE TREE referred to above at about 7-5 a.m. The N.C.O. reports that this trench was very much traversed, fairly dry, without dugouts, duckboards, or revetment, and that there was no wire of signs of occupation. This party then withdrew towards our lines, and rejoined the remainder of the raiding party at R.16.a.7.9. at about 7-10 a.m. and again encountered our own barrage running east and west through point R.16.a.8.1. The whole party had to pass through an enemy barrage about 70 yards NORTH of DEXTER TRENCH, but returned safely to our own trenches at about 7-15 a.m. with the exception of two stretcher bearers who stayed out to attend to a man of the 2/8 WARWICKS who had been severely wounded in the leg. A telephone message received at 11.40 a.m. states that these men have returned.

* *

The following method of negotiating barrages was employed and found most successful.

The burst of the shells was observed and after four had dropped approximately on the same spot, a small party of men rushed through the barrage over this spot.

Three barrages were successfully negotiated in this manner without casualties.

Jan.11th.1917. sgd. C.R.WHITFIELD, Lieut,Col.
Comdg. 2/6 WARWICKS.

App 3.

2/8th Bn. The Royal Warwick. Rgt.

Battalion Order No.

dated 14-1-17.

1. 2/8th Warwicks will be relieved by 6th Northants. Regt. in the line on the night of 15/16th, in accordance with the following table:-

2/8 R WAR R.	Relieved by 6 NORTHANTS	
C	B	LEFT FRONT.
D	A	RIGHT "
B	C	REGINA.
A	D	HESSIAN.

2. SIGNALLERS will be relieved under the arrangements of the Battn. Signalling Sergt.

3. LEWIS GUNNERS under the arrangements of LT. CHIDGEY.

4. All GUIDES will parade at BN. HDQTRS at 3·30pm under following arrangements:-

C. Coy 4 for Coy. Hqtrs 1 for REX TRENCH
D. Coy 4 for Coy. Hdqtrs. 1 for DW. platoon.
B. Coy. 1 for each platoon & post as required.
A. Coy. -do- -do-

Guides for posts will be at their respective Company Hdqtrs.
The above allotment of Guides is subject to alteration to meet arrangements between Company Cmdrs concerned, as is convenient.

5. The following will remain in the line until after dark on the 16th inst.
1 Battn. Signaller at Btn. Hdqtrs
2 Battn. Runners at Btn. Hdqtrs.
1 Officer per Company.
(names of Officers to be wired to Btn. Hdqtrs immediately)

6. LEWIS GUNNERS. On relief each team will bring out guns, spare parts and 5 buckets of empty magazines and any other L/G equipment on charge of Battn.
A limber will wait for guns etc. at TULLOCH'S CORNER, and will convey to rendezvous, near AVELUY, where buses will be. All guns go with teams on buses.
Company Cmdrs. will ensure that all Lewis Gunners are acquainted with above order.

7. On Relief the Battn. will proceed to LA VICOGNE by 'bus from Aveluy.

8. On Relief Companies will proceed to AVELUY via MOUQUET FARM - NAB ROAD - CRUCIFIX CORNER. At Crucifix Corner tea or soup will be available. It is uncertain where the buses will be in AVELUY, but Guides will be at CRUCIFIX CORNER.

9. GUM BOOTS. Ankle boots and putties will be worn. Gum boots will be dumped at head of NAB ROAD

10. TRENCH STORES. All stores will be carefully handed over and a receipt obtained. Macintosh Capes and HEDGING GLOVES will be handed over. This does not include the Macintosh Capes issued by Battalion

11. PETROL TINS. Special parties are carrying in water for incoming Units' consumption. Every effort will be made to return all empty tins to RIFLE DUMP before 9·30 am to-morrow. All FOOD CONTAINERS must be sent to Battn. Hdqtrs before noon to-morrow.

12. POLICE. Policeman will be posted at RIFLE DUMP and at junction of R.D. track with T.C. track to direct incoming units.

13. INFORMATION. Everything possible will be done to place all available information in hands of incoming units.

14. ACKNOWLEDGE.

14-1-17.

W. G. Phillips Major.
Cmdg. 2/8th R War. R.

2/8 R. War. R.

Batalion Order No 84
of 14.1.17.

(15) All cooks are to proceed to TULLOCH'S CORNER with their dixies immediately tea is finished. They are to carry their dixies with them; these will be taken on to the buses. It is intended to provide soup at CRUCIFIX CORNER

(16). Officers' mess cart will be at TULLOCH'S CORNER at 9 p.m. for the conveyance of Officers' Mess Stores.

sd. W. C. Phillips
Maj.
Comdg 2/8 Warwicks

Sheet 1. 2/8. R. WARWICK. REGT. App 4
Battn. Order 84. 11-1-17

Ref. Map. LENS - ABBEVILLE. Sheet 1/100000

1. The Battn. will move on 17th inst. to billets at CANDAS.
2. Starting point - Cross roads 1/8 mile WEST RUBEMPRE CHURCH. time 11-30 am
3. The Battn. will march closed up. Order of March. - Headquarters. B. C D. A. Coys.
Lewis Gunners will march with their Companies.
4. The Battn. will fall in facing WEST. Head of column to be 200 yards WEST of Headquarters Mess (Billet No. 19). The whole to be ready to move by 11-20 am. Steps must be taken to avoid congestion on the road on which Coys are falling in.
5. Dress. Full marching Order - Steel Helmets will be carried on pack. Rations will be carried in the pack.
6. Haversack rations will be carried.
7. Billeting Parties - Lt. R.H. Parsons and Billeting Party will meet Staff Captain at CANDAS CHURCH on 17th inst. at 11 am.

Sheet. 2.

8. Lewis Guns will be carried on limbers. They will be loaded in ROSS LANE by 10-30 am. They will be wrapped in the No. 13 blankets which in consequence will not be loaded with remainder of Coy Blankets.

9. Blankets. Officers kits, mens blankets & Mess Baskets, as laid down in Standing Orders for the move.

Sick Parade — 8 am

10. Transport, baggage wagons and Cookers will march in rear of Battalion

11. Company Commanders are responsible that billets are left clean.

12. Supply wagons will proceed direct to CANDAS & guides will be sent to conduct them to stores meeting them outside billets.

[illegible]
Lieut & Adjt
1/6 R War R

Issued 10.30. pm.

App VI

[illegible]

1. The Battalion will march [illegible] 17th [illegible] CANCHY.

2. Order of march – [illegible] D.A.B.C [illegible] with their Coys. [illegible] of [illegible] Coys.

3. Halting place – CRAMONT church. [illegible] CONTEVILLE – CRAMONT road [illegible] 8.55 a.m. [illegible] form up [illegible] side of road. [illegible] 9.50 a.m.

4. [illegible]

5. Billeting party [illegible] CANCHY church at 10 a.m.

6. [illegible]

7. Transport including baggage wagons, [illegible] of battalion.

15-1-17.

[illegible]
Lt & Adjt.
[illegible]

SECRET.

App. V

2/8th Bn. Royal Warwickshire Regt.

Battalion Order 85
dated 17 January 1917.

1. The Battalion will move tomorrow 18th inst. to billets at CRAMONT.
2. Order of march HQ, C. D. A. B. Cookers will move with their companies. Interval of 200 yds will be maintained between Coys.
3. Starting Point. Cross roads at Orderly Room (junction of RUE de VALHEUREUX and RUE du FOUR). Battalion will fall in facing N.W. with head of column at starting point, ready to move at 7.55 a.m. Companies will fall in two deep at side of road and will be on the road no longer than necessary before starting time.
4. Dress, Full marching order — steel helmets on pack — Leather jerkins should be worn.
5. Billeting Party. LT. B.H. PARSONS & C/Q.M.S. will meet Staff Capt. at CRAMONT CHURCH at 10. a.m.
6. Blankets etc. as laid down in Standing Orders.
7. Transport, including Baggage wagons, will move in rear of Battalion.

17.1.17.
Published at 7 p.m.

(sd.) W. S. Farmer
Capt & Adjt
2/8 Warwicks

Instructions regarding War Diaries and Intelligence Summaries are contained in F. S. Regs., Part II. and the Staff Manual respectively. Title pages will be prepared in manuscript.

WAR DIARY
or
INTELLIGENCE SUMMARY.
(Erase heading not required.)

Army Form C. 2118.

10.H.

Place	Date	Hour	Summary of Events and Information	Remarks and references to Appendices
	1917			
CANCHY	Feb. 1	9 am to 11 am	Training continued. Use of the entrenching tool – working tasks – rapid wiring	
		8 pm to 10 pm	Detailing of working parties – construction of trenches by night	WH
"	2	9 am – 5 pm	Training continued – Phys exercises – Rapid changes of formation – Passing of messages	
		8-10 pm	Rapid wiring – patrol work at night	WH
"	3	9 am to 1 pm	Battalion attack – Visit from B.G.C. – Scheme attached	App. I WH
"	4	10 a.m.	C. of E. service in Recreation Room	
			2/Lt F.N. PHIPPS & 1 O.R. proceeded on Course to IV Corps Infantry School ST RICQUIER. 2Lt [illegible] ENTWISTLE proceeded on Course to IV Corps Sniping School ST RIQUIER	
			Guard of 1 N.C.O. 3 [illegible] sent to [illegible] Dump at Cross Roads between CAPENNES – [illegible]	WH
	5	9 am	Battalion moved by march route to BUIGNY L'ABBE – Shortage of water – carted water from ST RIQUIER	App. II
		6 pm	2 LT K.C.F. WATSON & 2 N.C.Os proceeded on L.G. Course at [illegible] H.Q. LONG	WH
BUIGNY L'ABBE	6	9-1 pm	Training continued – R.E.s repaired well. Specialist training continued under Specialist Officers	
		6 pm	2 LT PROSSER, Bombing Cpl & 1 Bomber per Coy (39 All ranks) to Bde Bombing Course at MONFLIERS	
	7	9-1 pm 2-4 pm	Training continued – Batt. drill – changing formations – Batt attack as part of a Brigade	WH
	8	9-11 am	Training continued – Tactical schemes under Coy Commanders	WH
		11-1 pm	Map reading for section commanders & [illegible] – 8-10 pm Night attack – forming up [illegible]	WH

T2134. Wt. W708–776. 500000. 4/15. Sir J. C. & S.

Instructions regarding War Diaries and Intelligence Summaries are contained in F. S. Regs., Part II. and the Staff Manual respectively. Title pages will be prepared in manuscript.

WAR DIARY
or
INTELLIGENCE SUMMARY.
(*Erase heading not required.*)

Army Form C. 2118.

Place	Date	Hour	Summary of Events and Information	Remarks and references to Appendices
	1917			
BUIGNY L'ABBE	Feby 8	10 a.	MAJOR W.E. PHILLIPS sat as Pres. of Court Martial at 2/6 R WAR. R. Headquarters	WP
	9	9 a. – 12.30 pm	Movement through woods – Tactical exercise for Coys – 2.30 – 4.30 pm Outposts. Knowledge of Signals &c.	
			Advanced orders for move received	WP
	10	10 am	2LT G GILDERTHORPE reported for duty	
		9 am – 12.30 pm	Training continued – Tactical exercises by Coys. Batt Attack including reorganised to meet counter attack. 2LT ENTWISTLE returned from Sniping Course ST RIQUIER	
		2.30 – 4.30 pm	Demonstration of result of 1 weeks intensive training of a platoon – 700 yds N. of BUIGNY L'ABBE Church. All officers & N.C.O.s commanding platoons & their understudies attended.	WP
	11	10 a.	Nonconformist Service in School. – 3 pm Voluntary C of E Service.	
		10.30 a.	2LT TONKS & 2 OR proceeded to Divl. School ST RIQUIER – 2LT K.L.P. WATSON returned from LG School, LONG. Sgt Instr. DREW reported for Musketry Instruction to Batt. – Bry orders for move recd.	WP
	12	9 am	Training continued – Rapid stepping out from line of march – Batt. drill under C.O. – Spec. training	
			2/LT F.A. LEIGH and draft of 67 O.R. arrived – all fully trained. Batt. orders for move of transport published	App III WP
	13	11.30 a.	Batt. attack – witnessed by G.O.C. Division, and B.G.C. – Training under C.O. Coys in afternoon.	App IV
			Brigade orders for move to "C" Staging Area received. Batt orders for move published.	App V WP

T2134. Wt. W708–776. 500000. 4/15. Sir J. C. & S.

Instructions regarding War Diaries and Intelligence Summaries are contained in F. S. Regs., Part II. and the Staff Manual respectively. Title pages will be prepared in manuscript.

WAR DIARY
or
INTELLIGENCE SUMMARY.
(Erase heading not required.)

Army Form C. 2118.

Place	Date	Hour	Summary of Events and Information	Remarks and references to Appendices
	1917 Jany			
BUIGNY L'ABBE	13		Transport moved by march to ST SAVEUR	WM
	14		Transport moved by march to AUBIGNY – Batt training continued.	WM
	15		Transport moved to MARCELCAVE – 9.15am Batt moved by march route to PONT REMY – 11.45am Batt. proceeded by train to MARCELCAVE – arriving 2.45 pm. Billets good.	WM
MARCELCAVE	16	9am	Batt training continued. A Coy L.G. teams [illegible] course under Batt L.G.O. – 2Lt PROSSER Batt Bombing Off. & 1 Bombing Sgt [illegible] for Bde Bombing School – Training of Bombers proceeded with under Bombing Corpl – 2 OR [illegible] 5.30pm [illegible] 3 Candidates for Commissions interviewed by B.G.C. – 2Lt HODGSON retd from leave	WM
	17	9am	Training contd under Coy Comdrs Specialists as on 16th – B Coy L.G. teams under Batt L.G.O.	WM
	18	11 am	Brigade Orders for move received. Batt. Orders published. Capt S.E. BROCK to Camp 102 as Town Major	
		9am	Training contd under Coy Comdrs C Coy L.G. teams under Batt L.G.O. Voluntary Church Service at 6.30pm. 1 O.R. retd from 1st Q. Mobile Workshops – 3 Coy Comdrs proceeded to view new line	WM
	19	9.20am	Batt moved by march route to Camp 101 – V.30 b. – arrived 10.45am – huts clean but bare of furniture – no latrines or cookhouses – camp dirty. Sgt GREENAWAY and Cpl GWYNNE to England for commissions 2.30pm CO attended conference at B.H.Q.	App VI WM
Camp No 101 near CAYEUX	20		Weather bad – ground very deep in mud – Cleaning up of Camp –	WM
	21		Cleaning up & inspections – Weather still bad. 2Lts A.A. ROGERS and A.L. PESKETT reported for duty –	WM

T.134. Wt. W708–776. 500000. 4/15. Sir J. C. & S.

Instructions regarding War Diaries and Intelligence Summaries are contained in F. S. Regs., Part II. and the Staff Manual respectively. Title pages will be prepared in manuscript.

WAR DIARY
or
INTELLIGENCE SUMMARY.
(Erase heading not required.)

Army Form C. 2118.

Place	Date	Hour	Summary of Events and Information	Remarks and references to Appendices
CAMP N° 101	1917 Jany 21		and are posted to B & D Coys respectively	[illegible]
"	22	9am	Training continued. L.G. Teams under Batt. L.G.O. Officers available attended Brigade Bombing School. Brigade Orders for move to FRAMERVILLE received. 2 Runners sent to B.H.Q.	[illegible]
"	23	9am	Training contd. L.G. teams under Batt. L.G.O. Bombing Squads preliminary training under Cpl HUGHES. Orders for move to FRAMERVILLE recd & Batt Orders for move published.	[illegible] App. VIII
"	24	9am	Training contd – L.G. teams – & Bombing squads as for 23rd inst. Pte STEEL R. to England for Commission. 38 O.R. & 1 Officer returned from Brig Bombing School. Pte MOORE to O.C. Transportation Depot BOULOGNE. Capt BROCK returned from Camp 102. C.O. reconnoitred line with Major PHILLIPS.	[illegible]
"	25		2 N.C.O.s to Gas Course HARBONNIERES – L/Cpl WALKER to same School as Instructor. 2Lt F.A. LEIGH, 2Lt A.A. ROGERS & 3 N.C.O.s to Div. School MARCELCAVE. L/Cpl HAYES to O.C. Transportation Depot BOULOGNE.	
		1.30pm	Batt moved by march route to Billets at FRAMERVILLE – arrived 5pm. Billets good.	[illegible]
FRAMERVILLE	26		Cleaning up. Batt training contd. – for tactical drill. CAPT S.E. BROCK to HARBONNIERES as Town Major. Pte HOWELL to England for Commission. C.O. reconnoitred line.	[illegible]
"	~~27~~	8.30a	Working party of 1 Officer & 60 O.R. for work on roads near HARBONNIERES under C.R.E. 2 O.R. returned from 29 I.B.D.	[illegible]

T2134. Wt. W708–776. 500000. 4/15. Sir J. C. & S.

Instructions regarding War Diaries and Intelligence Summaries are contained in F. S. Regs., Part II. and the Staff Manual respectively. Title pages will be prepared in manuscript.

WAR DIARY
or
INTELLIGENCE SUMMARY.
(Erase heading not required.)

Army Form C. 2118.

Place	Date	Hour	Summary of Events and Information	Remarks and references to Appendices
	1917			
FRAMERVILLE	Feby 27	9.30a	Training contd – 2 new L.G. teams under Bett L.G.O. – 2 O.R. to Transportation Officer BOULOGNE. Working party of 1 Officer & 60 O.R. for work on roads under C.R.E. Capt W. MACKAY attached to A/306 Batt. R.F.A. for three days. C.O. acted as President of Court of Enquiry in regard to Trench Feet – held at VAUVILLERS.	WH
"	28		Training contd. L.G. teams, Bombing squads & backward Signallers under Specialist Officers. Working party of 1 Officer & 60 O.R. for work on roads under C.R.E. C.O. visited line. Pte FERRINGTON returned from employment at Div Cinema. No 20302 Pte WEST to England to be released for Munitions.	WH

Ed. C. Cadman
Lieut. Col.,
Comdg. 2/8 R. War. R.

T2134. Wt. W708-776. 500000. 4/15. Sir J. C. & S.

[illegible] 1. APP 1.

2/8TH BATTALION THE ROYAL WARWICKSHIRE REGIMENT.

BATTALION ORDERS BY LT.COL. R.C. CADMAN. COMMANDING.
February 2nd 1917.

Ref. Map CANCHY 1/5000.
ST.RIQUIER 1/20000.

1. The 61st Division will resume the attack tomorrow Feb.3rd.

2. The Battalion will be the assaulting Battalion on the right of the 182nd Bde frontage.
Left Flank Unit X Warwicks.
Right .. .. A Battalion of 51st Division.

3. OBJECTIVES. The Battalion will assault, capture and consolidate three objectives
1. FIRST OBJECTIVE. Brown Line (Fritz Trench)
2. Second .. Blue Line (Tirpitz Trench)
3. Third. .. Red Line. (Lamotte Trench)

4. ALLOTMENT OF COMPANY OBJECTIVES.
"A" Coy. The Lamotte - Domvast road inclusive to a point 100 yards South of that road
1st. Objective)
2nd.)

"B" Coy. From a point 100 yards South of the LAMOTTE - DOMVAST
1st Objective) ROAD, inclusive to a point 200 yards South of that
2nd ..) road.

"C" Coy. From a point 200 yards South of the LAMOTTE - DOMVAST
1st Objective) ROAD, inclusive to a point 300 yards South of that
2nd ..) road.

"D" Coy. Acts as Battalion reserve prepared to support any
1st. Objective) portion of Battalion front.
2nd ..)

3rd Objective. From the LAMOTTE - DOMVAST ROAD inclusive to a point on the Red line 200 yards South of that road.

5. METHOD OF ATTACK.
Companies in front line ("C" "B" "A" Coys) will attack on a frontage of two Platoons in two waves at 50 yards distance.
Third Platoon with mopping up party from the Y Warwicks will provide the third wave moving 60 yards in rear of the second wave.
Fourth Platoon will form Company reserve and will move in shallow column 80 yards in rear of the third wave.

6. ASSEMBLY.
BRUM TRENCH. 1st and 2nd Waves. (Two Platoons each of "C" "B" "A")
CRUCIFIX TRENCH. Detachments from 182nd M.G.Coy. and 182.L.T.M.B.
WARWICK TRENCH. 3rd & 4th Waves. (Two Platoons each of "C" "B" "A")
VILLA TRENCH. Battalion Reserve. ("D" Coy)

7. BATTALION HEADQUARTERS, ADVANCED BRIGADE HEADQUARTERS, and Brigade Dumps, Prisoners Cage, Bearer Posts, Brigade Runners Posts, and Battle Stops etc. will be in the positions shown on the attached map.

8. TIMETABLE.
1st. --

BATTALION ORDER DATED [illegible] MAY 2nd 1917,

1st.	ZERO	"A" "B" "C" Coys move with barrage and will capture and consolidate 1st Objective. "D" Coy moves from VILLA to BRUM TRENCH.
2nd.	ZERO plus 25.	"A" "B" "C" Coys having reorganised move from 1st Objective with barrage to the assault of 2nd Objective which they will capture and consolidate. "D" Coy moves from BRUM TRENCH to a position immediately in rear of 2nd Objective.
3rd.	ZERO plus 39.	"D" Coy moves to a position in advance of 2nd Objective preparatory to assaulting 3rd Objective.
4th.	ZERO plus 49.	"D" Coy will advance with barrage and will capture and consolidate 3rd Objective.

9. CONSOLIDATION.
The first step in consolidation will be the construction of the strong points shown on the attached map. Garrisons for Nos.4 & 6 will be found by "A" Coy.

10. Details as to dress, equipment, use of rockets, aeroplane flares, etc. will be as arranged at conference with Commanding Officer today.

11. ACKNOWLEDGE.

sgd. W.S. FARMER Lieut & Adjutant.

2/8th R.WARWICK.REGT.

Issued at 6.30 pm.

Copies to (1) A Coy
(2) B "
(3) C "
(4) D "
(5) 182 M.G "
(6) 182 T M B
(7) File
(8) War Diary

2/8. WARWICKS.

Sheet 1.

APP. 2.

2ND 8TH BATTALION THE ROYAL WARWICKSHIRE REGIMENT.

BATTALION ORDER No. 90. by LT. COL. E. C. CADMAN. COMMDG. 4-2-17.

1. The Battalion will move tomorrow 5th inst to BUIGNY L'ABBE.
2. ROUTE:-. CROSS ROADS AT U in NEUILLY L'HOPITAL - LE PLESSIAL - ABBEVILLE - BELLANCOURT.
3. ORDER OF MARCH. H.Q. "A" "B" "C" "D" Coy. (200 yds between coys) Cookers will march in rear of their Coys. Baggage wagons will march with Transport in rear of "D" Coy. Supply wagons will move direct to Battalion billets after refilling and will be met by guides outside Battalion billeting area, approximate time will be notified to Billeting Officer by Staff Captain.
4. LEWIS GUN HANDCARTS. These will be drawn by Coys from Lewis Gun Officer today as follows:-- "A" 2. "B" 2. "C" 1. "D" 1. They will be used for carrying Lewis Guns on the march.
5. STARTING POINT. The Battalion will fall in facing South on the main road, head of column outside Battalion Orderly Room. The Battalion will be ready to move at 8-30 a.m.
6. DRESS. Full marching Order. Steel Helmets will be carried on the pack.
7. Billeting Party will meet Staff Captain at cross roads ¼ mile west of VAUCHELLES les QUESNOY at 10 a.m. today. They will remain in the new billeting area and will take rations for the 5th inst. Party will consist of Lt. B. K. Parsons and 5 C.Q.M.S's.
8. Attention is directed to Standing Orders for the move.
9. Kits. Blankets. etc. as per Standing Orders.

issued at 9 a.m.

sgd. W. S. FARMER. Lieut & Adjt.
2/8. R. WARWICK. REGT.

App 111

THE 8TH BATTALION THE ROYAL WARWICKSHIRE REGIMENT.

BATTALION ORDER No.96 by LT.COL.E.C.CADMAN. COMDG, 12-2-17.

Ref. 1/100000. LENS - AMIENS - ABBEVILLE.

1. The Transport of the Battalion will move to "C" Staging area as follows:-

DATE.	TO	STARTING POINT.	TIME.	ROUTE.
13-2-16.	ST.SAVEUR.	Cross roads 600 yards S.E. of T in BELLANCOURT.	9-11 a.m.	BELLANCOURT - AILLY FLIXECOURT - ST. SAVEUR.
14-2-16.	AUBIGNY.	Cross roads in ARGOEUVES.	10-10 a.m.	

2. All Officers chargers with grooms, Coy Cookers with 1 Cook per Coy, 8 Signallers with Cycles, Water Carts with 1 R.A.M.C. water duty man, will proceed with the Transport. Lewis Gun Handcarts will not proceed with the Transport ~~and guns will be retained to be carried in limbers.~~
On 13th Supply wagons will move independently after refilling.

3. Distances of 200 yards will be maintained between Transport of Units on the road.

4. Lieut. CHADWICK, 2/7th.Warwicks will be in charge of the Transport of the Brigade Group.

5. On 13th inst. column will halt between 12-30 p.m. and 1-15 p.m. to water and feed.

6. Transport Officer will detail 1 Billeting N.C.O. mounted on a bicycle to report to Billeting Officer, Brigade Group at FLIXECOURT STATION (main entrance) at 10 a.m. on 13th inst. and on subsequent days as he may direct.

7. Fuel for Transport on 13th inst will be with 307th Bde R.F.A. at R.P. on ST SAVEUR - LA CHAUSSEE ROAD 1½ miles W.N.W. of ST.SAVEUR. On 14th inst. it will be at POUILLY opposite Church.
Rations for 14th, 15th & 16th for Transport personnel and horses will be drawn at ST.SAVEUR CHURCH on arrival.

sgd. W.S.FARMER. Lieut & Adjt.

2/8. R.WARWICK.REGT.

App IV

2nd 6th [illegible] REGIMENT.

[illegible] ORDER No. [illegible] by Lt.Col. [illegible] Comdg. 10-2-17.

Ref.Map. [illegible]

1. The attack against enemy second line system will be commenced on Feb.13th.
1[illegible].Brigade will attack enemy positions S and E of BUIGNY L'ABBE.
BRIGADE FRONTAGE between a line joining L of BELLANCOURT and B of BUIGNY L'ABBE and a line drawn parallel to this through Y of BUIGNY.

2. The Battalion will be assaulting Battalion right of Brigade frontage BATTALION FRONTAGE - from right of Brigade frontage to a point 300 yards N.W. of same.

FLANKS.	RIGHT.	—	7th DIVISION.
	LEFT.	—	R WARWICKS.

3. Bombardment commenced at 9 a.m. Feb.10th and Infantry advance with creeping barrage will be at Zero time on 13th.

4. The Battalion will assault, capture and consolidate three objectives as follows:—

1st Objective...	POSEN TRENCH.	YELLOW LINE.
2nd "	[illegible] TRENCH.	BLUE LINE.
3rd "	[illegible] TRENCH.	RED LINE.

5. ALLOTMENT OF FRONTAGES.

"C" Coy.	1st Objective.	from a point 100 yards North of GORSE COPSE to a point 200 yards North of GORSE COPSE.
	2nd Objective.	from a point 80 yards South of [illegible] FARM to a point 20 yards North of same.
"A" Coy.	1st Objective.	From a point 200 yards North of GORSE COPSE to a point 300 yards North of same.
	2nd Objective.	From a point 20 yards North of [illegible] FARM to a point 100 yards North of same.
"B" Coy.	1st Objective.	From a point 300 yards North of GORSE COPSE to a point 400 yards North of same.
	2nd Objective.	From a point 100 yards North of [illegible] FARM to a point 200 yards North of same.
"D" Coy.	1st Objective) 2nd Objective.)	Battalion Reserve.
	3rd Objective.	From the L of BUIGNY L'ABBE to a point 300 yards N.E. of same.

6. METHOD OF ATTACK. Companies in front line "C" "A" "B" Coys. will attack on a frontage of two platoons in two waves at 30 yards distance. Third Platoon with mopping up party from the Y [illegible] will provide the third wave, moving 60 yards in rear of second wave.
Fourth Platoon will form Company Reserve and will move in shallow column 60 yards in rear of third wave.

7. ASSEMBLY.

BROAD STREET.	1st and 2nd Waves.	(2 Platoons each "B" "A" "C" Coy)
HILL STREET.	3rd and 4th Waves.	(2 .... .. "B" "A" "C" ")
[illegible] ROAD.	4 Platoons "D" Coy	(Battalion Reserve).

8. [illegible]

Sheet 2.

8. INFANTRY TIME-TABLE.

ZERO. (1). "B" "A" "C" Coys move with barrage and will capture and consolidate 1st objective.
(2). "D" Coy moves to HILL [illegible].

ZERO plus 23 min. (1). "B" "A" "C" Coys having reorganised move with barrage from 1st objective to assault 2nd objective which they will capture and consolidate.
(2). "D" Coy move to a position immediately in rear of 2nd Objective.

ZERO plus 45 min. (2). "D" Coy moves to a position in advance of 2nd Objective preparatory to assaulting 3rd Objective.

ZERO plus 55 min. "D" Coy will advance with barrage and will capture and consolidate 3rd Objective.

9. ARTILLERY TIME-TABLE.

0.	Barrage is laid down on a line 150 yards in front of our front line.
0.1. - 0.07.	Barrage creeps at the rate of 50 yards per minute and halts 100 yards beyond 1st objective.
0.7. - 0.10.	Barrage slackens during consolidation and remains in front of 1st objective.
0.10. - 0. 23.	Barrage quickens and troops pre are for the assault on 2nd Objective.
0.23 - 0.33.	Barrage creeps at the rate of 50 yards per minute and halts beyond 2nd Objective.
0.33 - 0.45.	Barrage slackens and remains in front o[illegible] 2nd objective
0.45. - 0.55.	Barrage quickens and troops prepare for assault on 3rd Objective.
0.55. - 0.67.	Barrage creeps at the rate of 50 yards per minute and halts beyond 3rd Objective
- 0.90.	Barrage lifts to form protective barrage 300 yards in advance of 3rd Objective.

10. ACTION OF RESERVE COY.
It is intended that the Reserve Coy remain under orders of the Battalion Commander until ZERO plus 45, at which time if it has not already been called upon by him to perform some special task it will be committed to the attack (ZERO plus 55) under orders of O.C.Coy.
It is impressed upon O.C. Reserve Coy that he should endeavour to keep in touch with the situation on the whole of the Battalion front as until ZERO plus 45 he is liable to be diverted to any portion of the front in event of serious opposition being encountered.
From ZERO until ZERO plus 45 movements are automatic as in time-table.

ZERO from [illegible] ROAD to HILL [illegible].
ZERO plus 23. from HILL [illegible] to a position in rear of 2nd objective.
ZERO plus 45. to position in advance of 2nd objective preparatory to assault on 3rd objective at ZERO plus 55.

11. [illegible]
Two guns will be in dugouts near Battalion Headquarters at ZERO.
On capture of first objective these two guns will move forward to report to RIGHT and CENTRE Coys.
O.C. RIGHT and CENTRE Coys will be prepared to utilize these guns should resistance be encountered in the area about [illegible] C.2.
Carrying parties will dump near [illegible] in 1st objective.

Sheet 5.

12. LEWIS GUNS.
Four guns will be in dugouts near Battalion Headquarters. These guns will be pushed to the front and used to secure captured line during consolidation.

13. CONSOLIDATION.
Strong points will be constructed by R.E. parties in accordance with attached sketch. Parties for No. 7 and 8 will move from our lines as soon as 1st objective is gained. Party for No.10. will move from 1st objective as soon as 2nd objective is captured.
Strong points will when completed be garrisoned by Companies in whose area they are situated.

14. DRESS AND EQUIPMENT.
As laid down in Battalion Standing Orders for Fighting Order.

DISTINGUISHING ARMLETS. Scouts. Dark Blue.
Runners. Red.
Signallers. Light Blue.

15. COMMUNICATIONS.
Contact aeroplane will be in the air from ZERO until ZERO plus 1½ hours.
Flares will be lit on attaining each objective.

16. DUMPS.
Advanced Dumps - - -
Brigade Dumps. - - -
Battalion Bombing Officer is responsible for supply of ammunition, bombs etc to advanced Battalion Dump as above.
Battalion Transport Officer will be responsible for supply of rations etc.

17. S.O.S. ------ 1 RED - 1 GREEN.

18. PRISONERS.
Prisoners will be passed back to Battalion Headquarters.

19. MEDICAL ARRANGEMENTS.
No.6. Dugout near Battalion Headquarters.

20. R.S.M. will detail Control Posts.

UP trench. CHAPEL ALLEY.
DOWN " CENTRAL BOYAU.

21. Officers going into action will not exceed numbers notified to Coys by the Adjutant.

22. SYNCHRONISATION OF TIME.
Watches will be synchronised by arrangements with Signal Officer at 3 hours before ZERO.

23. Battalion Headquarters. No.5 Dugout junction CHAPEL ALLEY -- HILL CENTRE.

24. ACKNOWLEDGE.

sgd. W.S.FARMER. Lieut & Adjt.
2/6. R.WARWICK.REGT.

Issued at 7-40 p.m.

Copies 1/4. Companies.
5. 182. T.M.B.
6. 182 M.G.C.
7. File.
8/20. Spare.

[illegible] 18-[illegible]-37.

Ref: Map [illegible] 1/10,000 & [illegible]

The enemy holds a second line system running NORTH and SOUTH generally following the line of the [illegible] - [illegible] ROAD and the [illegible] - [illegible] ROAD with strong points commanding intervening ground.

The entrenched line following the line of the [illegible] - [illegible] ROAD is reported in fairly good condition but enemy troops are more or less disorganised, having been forced back on to this second line system three days previously.

Our line runs approximately from S of VAUCHELLES SOUTH EAST through E of [illegible] then SOUTH EAST to the [illegible] - [illegible] ROAD.

The first objective is carried with slight loss, and after reorganisation the attacking Companies advance to assault the second objective. The left of the Battalion attack gains the second objective. The Centre Coy meets with unexpected opposition from a small strong point at "X" 300 yards in front of [illegible] LINE. This holds up the CENTRE and RIGHT of the CENTRE COY, this leaves the RIGHT Coy's left flank in the air.

Elements of the RIGHT COY reach the second objective and are forced to clear by bombing along the trench towards the left owing to the CENTRE COY being held up. After 35 minutes fighting the advance point at "X" is cleared up and the CENTRE COY is able to make good their frontage of the [illegible] LINE.

It has become apparent from reports of RIGHT and CENTRE Coys that serious opposition is being made about [illegible] FARM. Later a report reaches Battalion Headquarters that a hostile bombing party from this point has penetrated our newly gained line.

It is now decided that vigorous action must be taken to secure [illegible] FARM in order to protect the Battalion's RIGHT flank which is becoming seriously threatened from this point.

The Reserve Coy still under the Battalion Commander is detailed to launch an attack across the open on this point.

The Battalion Commander having absorbed his Reserve Coy, which normally would carry the third objective in the attack is forced to ask Brigade for new troops to be allotted to carry that objective.

Sheet 1. App V

2ND 8TH BATTALION THE ROYAL WARWICKSHIRE REGIMENT.

BATTALION ORDER No.97 by LT.COL. E.C.CADMAN. COMDG. 13-8-17.

1. The Battalion will move on the 15th inst to "C" Staging Area by train from PONT REMY to MARCELCAVE. The train journey is estimated to take four hours.

2. STARTING POINT. The Battalion will fall in facing SOUTH on the main street. Head of column opposite the CAFE DES CINQ ROUTES.
The Battalion will be ready to move at 8-30 a.m.

3. ORDER OF MARCH - H.Q. "B" "C" "D" "A" Companies.

4. DRESS. Full marching order, Jerkins will be worn, Steel Helmets on pack - Ground Sheet on banderole - waterproof cape in pack.

5. Kits, Blankets etc. as per Standing Orders.
Pailliasses will be emptied of straw and will be rolled with blankets. Straw from pailliasses will be made into a tidy heap in each billet and the Billitor will be informed that it remains the property of the British Army.
Lorries will move with the Battalion and will be unloaded by party detailed by the 2/6th.WARWICKS.

6. ENTRAINING. The train will consist of 44 covered trucks, - each holding 50 men - or an equivalent number of coaches.
O.C.Coys are responsible that there is no delay in entraining their Companies.
Lieut.Col. C.S.Whitfield, 2/6th.WARWICKS will be in command of the train.

7. LEWIS GUN HANDCARTS - BICYCLES. These will march to PONT REMY in rear of Battalion. Two flats are provided on the train on which these will be loaded. It may be necessary to take the wheels off the handcarts and they should be looked to to see that this can be done easily.

8. MARCHING OUT STATE. Companies will render to the Orderly Room by 8 pm on the 14th inst. a marching out state, showing separately Officers and Other Ranks proceeding with the Battalion.

9. RATIONS. Rations for 15th inst. will be carried on the man.
Rations for the 16th will be drawn by Quartermaster at PONT REMY STATION and loaded by him on train. On arrival at MARCELCAVE they will be unloaded by Quartermaster and dumped under a Guard until fetched by Battalion Transport.

10. BILLETS. Billets must be left clean and any claims for damage settled. before leaving the village.

sgd. W.S.FARMER. Lieut & Adjt.

2/8th. WARWICKS.

Issued at 9 p.m.

Copies Nos. 1/4. Coys.
5. Quartermaster.
6. Sig. and L.G.Officer.
7. R.S.M.
8. File.
9. War Diary.
10. C.O.

[illegible] G.C.59 S

NOTES ON TAKING OVER FROM 106th DIV. F.

1. The country is flat - overlooked from high ground about CHAULNES on the right - devastated by shell fire in front of VERMANDOVILLERS - DENIECOURT (both inclusive), these places being one degree less destroyed than POZIERES. But the country is not nearly so badly cut up by shell fire. The soil is clay - no chalk.

2. The 106th Div. has been 1 month in the line, little work possible the last three weeks owing to frost.

3. C.T's are very deep and rather narrow and likely to fall in when it thaws. Mostly duckboarded but not revetted.

4. No deep dugouts in front line, but a fair number of German dugouts elsewhere.

5. Front not covered by wire. The French are putting out Chevaux-de-frises - exact state of wire doubtful.

6. It is possible with care to get up to the front line by day, but reliefs carrying etc. are done by night.

7. No mining.

8. The French attitude has been purely defensive. A little sniping, 6 M.G.'s in position but never used offensively, only in retaliation. Their guns seem to fire about 600 rounds a day however. Casualties have averaged 5 or 6 a day in the Division.

9. There are three Regiments in front area, each with two Battalions holding the front, and 1 in Reserve. Each Battalion has two Companies in front and support line, and one Company in support, except the Battalion on the right which has only 1 Coy in front. Battalions are 10 days in front line and 5 in reserve. The trench strength of a Company is about 150.

10. The Germans are also on the defensive. They snipe a little, and only fire their Trench Mortars very rarely. They have lately been showing curiosity regarding reliefs; one or two raids have been made, patrols have been active, and since 5th aeroplanes have been very numerous. German Artillery has been fairly active. They do not appear to shell back areas very much. VERMANDOVILLERS is said not to be shelled. Back areas are bombed at night by aeroplanes, and [illegible] has been bombed the last six nights.

11-2-17. Sgd. [illegible] Lieut.Col.

To
A.[illegible]

Company Commanders are responsible that all ranks under their Command are familiar with the distinguishing marks of FRENCH Officers so that they may be treated with the respect due to their rank.

The undermentioned list shows different badges of rank.

[illegible]   sgd. W.S.[illegible]. Lieut & Adjt.
O/C. [illegible].

GENERAL.... 3 small gold stars.
GENERAL (de [illegible]). 2 ....
COLONEL... 5 gold bars.
Lieut-Colonel. 3 gold and 2 silver bars.
Major. 4 gold bars.
Captain. 3 gold bars.
Lieutenant. 2 gold bars.
Sous-Lieutenant. 1 gold bar.

All on lower part of sleeve.

App VI

[illegible]

[illegible] Order No. 60 by [illegible]. [illegible]

Ref. Map. [illegible] 1/[illegible]

1. The Battalion will move tomorrow [illegible] inst. to Camp [illegible] ([illegible]).

2. Order of march — H.Q. "A" "B" "C" "D" Coys. Transport.
Lewis Gun Limbers will march in rear of their Coys.
Distance of 100 yards will be maintained between Companies.

3. STARTING POINT. The Battalion will pass the Starting POINT on the [illegible] ROAD — head of column to be at cross roads [illegible].
The Battalion will be ready to move at [illegible] a.m.

4. DRESS. Full marching order — Leather jerkins will be worn. Steel helmets on pack. Great coat on bandolier. Waterproof cape in pack.

5. [illegible] Blankets etc. as per Standing Orders.

6. Coys will take steps to adjust and settle any claims that are made by proprietors of billets in their area, and will forward to the Orderly Room by 9 a.m. tomorrow the usual certificate for each billet that no claim is outstanding.

Sgd. [illegible], Lieut & Adjt.
[illegible]

Copies 1/4. Coys.
5. Quartermaster.
6. O.C.
7. File
8. War Diary.
9. [illegible]
10. [illegible]

THE 8th BATTALION THE ROYAL WARWICKSHIRE REGIMENT.

BATTALION ORDER 59 by Lt.Col. [illegible], Commdg.
Friday 23rd Feb.1917.

1. The Battalion will move to FRAMERVILLE on the 25th inst. and will relieve 2/4. GLOSTERS in support there.

2. Order of March:-- H.Q. "C" "D" "A" "B" Coys.
Coys will march independently at 200 yards distance.
Headquarters will pass Orderly Room on the [illegible] ROAD at 1-30 pm.
Cookers and Lewis Gun Handcarts will move in rear of their Coys.

3. DRESS: Full marching order. Jerkins will be worn. Steel Helmets on packs. Ground sheet on bandolier. Waterproof caps in pack.

4. Kits, blankets etc. as per Standing Orders.

5. Huts must be left clean and tidy.

Sgd. W.S.PARKER. Lieut & Adjt.
2/8 WARWICKS.

THE [illegible] BATTALION THE ROYAL [illegible] REGIMENT.

AFTER ORDER. to B.O.88. 24-2-17.

1. BLANKETS & PACKS. Packs containing surplus kit not required in the line [illegible] and one blanket per man will not be taken to [illegible], but will be stacked at Billet [illegible] [illegible]. These blankets and packs will be stacked at Battalion Quartermaster's stores by 9 a.m. tomorrow. The remaining blankets will be loaded at the time laid down in Standing Orders.

Kit required will be carried in the haversack.

2. DRESS. Coats will be rolled on the back. Steel helmets will be worn.

Sgd. [illegible] Lieut & Adjt.
[illegible]

11 H. 10

Confidential.

Vol XI

War Diary of:-

2/8th Battalion The Royal Warwickshire Regiment

Volume XI.

Period:-

From March 1/17.

To March 31/17.

Instructions regarding War Diaries and Intelligence Summaries are contained in F. S. Regs., Part II. and the Staff Manual respectively. Title pages will be prepared in manuscript.

WAR DIARY
or
INTELLIGENCE SUMMARY.
(Erase heading not required.)

Army Form C. 2118.

Place	Date	Hour	Summary of Events and Information	Remarks and references to Appendices
FRAMERVILLE	1917 March 1		Batt training continued – Specialists under Specialist Officers – C.O. & Coy Officers visited line to reconnoitre. Brigade orders for move received. 2 LT F N PHIPPS returned from [illegible].	WR
	2.		Specialist Officers visited line. Batt training contd.	
			Advanced party of 1 Officer per Coy & 1 N.C.O. per Platoon went into line	WR
	3		Batt relieved 2/7 R WAR R in CHAULNES Subsector. Relief complete 11.20 pm. Weather dry – slight frost. Disposition A & B Coys in Front line, D & C Coys in Support [illegible]	WR
CHAULNES			2 LTS LEIGH & PERKETT returned from Course.	
	4	5 am	Right Front Coy withdrawn to support line	
		8.30 am	Heavy shelling reported on KRATZ Wood. 11 am – 3 pm H.A. bombarded KRATZ Wood.	
		6 pm	Right Front Coy returned to line – Enemy's reply weak – Patrols out from C & D Coys. 2 LT CLAYDON to Divl School for Bn. [illegible] Course & 3 OR. Enemy planes over our lines flying very low. 5 am Rockets sent up as test	WR
	5		Artillery quiet – Special [illegible] – Patrols out from C & D Coys – latter being fired on. 2 LT LEIGH & 14 OR to [illegible] Corps L T M School. Sgt GREEN to 4 Army Musketry School as Instructor	WR

T2134. Wt. W708–776. 500000. 4/15. Sir J. C. & S.

Instructions regarding War Diaries and Intelligence Summaries are contained in F. S. Regs., Part II. and the Staff Manual respectively. Title pages will be prepared in manuscript.

WAR DIARY
or
INTELLIGENCE SUMMARY.
(Erase heading not required.)

Army Form C. 2118.

Place	Date	Hour	Summary of Events and Information	Remarks and references to Appendices
	1917 Mch			
CHAULNES	6		Artillery fire normal – night quiet – Patrols out from D Coy. Night too bright for patrolling work. 2LT CLAYDON to IV Army Musketry School as instructor. Capt S.E. BROCK assumed duties as IV Army Corps Agricultural Officer. Orders for move rec'd.	WH
	7		Artillery fire normal – some aerial torpedoes on PRESSOIRE. Enemy work party on ridge seen & dispersed by Artillery. 2/5 GLOS relieved B & C Coys. Orders for move issued	WH
	8		Day exceptionally quiet. A little snow & frost at night. HQ & A & D Coys of the Batt relieved by 2/4 GLOSTERS & marched to FRAMERVILLE. Relief complete 8.30 pm. 2LT H.L. PECKETT & 5 O.R to Divl Sharpshooting School. 1 O.R to Divl School of Cookery	WH
FRAMERVILLE	9		Weather cold – some snow. Cleaning up – Bathing under Batt arrangements. 6 O.R to Divl HQ for Railway work. Auth B 244/17	WH
"	10		Cleaning up – Inspections – Bathing under Batt arrangements – refitting – 6 O.R to DEMUIN for work on Decauville Railways	WH
"	11	9 am	Coy training. Coy in the attack – Rapid loading, bombing. Bayonet Fighting. LT. B.K. PARSONS 2LT GILDERTHORPE and 3 O.R. on Divl Course	WH
"	12	9 am	Coy training contd. Rapid extension – tactical exercise. 1 O.R. released for munitions. 1 O.R to	WH

Instructions regarding War Diaries and Intelligence Summaries are contained in F. S. Regs., Part II. and the Staff Manual respectively. Title pages will be prepared in manuscript.

WAR DIARY
or
INTELLIGENCE SUMMARY.
(Erase heading not required.)

Army Form C. 2118.

Place	Date	Hour	Summary of Events and Information	Remarks and references to Appendices
1917	1917 Mch			
FRAMER-VILLE	12		Transportation Depot. F.G.C.M. at HARBONNIERES on No 5491 Pte. FISHER E. negligently (?) wounding comrade. CO & Coy commanders reconnoitred line	
"	13		Batt training – Batt attack. rapid loading (?). Brigade orders received	
"	14		Coy training – Tactical schemes under O.C. Coys. 11 O.R. to C.R.E. for work on dugouts. Sentence of F.G.C.M. on Pte FISHER E (No 5491) 3 months imprisonment, commuted to 3 months F.P. No 1 – promulgated & extracts taken. Batt orders for move into line published. Advance party proceeded to line	
"	15		2 O.R. to C.R.E. for work on tramway. Batt relieved 2/1 BUCKS in the right subsector ABLAINCOURT	

Instructions regarding War Diaries and Intelligence Summaries are contained in F. S. Regs., Part II. and the Staff Manual respectively. Title Pages will be prepared in manuscript.

WAR DIARY
or
INTELLIGENCE SUMMARY
(Erase heading not required.)

Army Form C. 2118.

Place	Date	Hour	Summary of Events and Information	Remarks and references to Appendices
RIGHT Subsector ABLAINCOURT (Sprits)	1917 March 15		Relieved 2/1 BUCKS in the line – relief complete 11.15 pm. Night clear and relief easy. Patrols out from each front line Coy – reported sounds of enemy in his trenches at various points. Artillery fire, rifle fire & Very Lights normal – Disposition:- B Coy Rt Front; C Coy Centre; D Coy Left. A Coy Support. – Fires seen all round during the night	W.H.
Do.	16		Day quiet – conditions normal at night – Patrol from B Coy reconnoitred junction of BORET and GAVAIL. Patrol of D Coy reconnoitred SEBASTOPOL ALLEY – both on instructions from Brigade – They were both fired on, and enemy appeared to be holding posts at both points	W.H.
Do.	17	11 am	Warning received from Brigade that enemy retiring on next Divisional front. 11.5. Warned front line Coys and instructed 'C' Coy to send out patrols. 11.20 am. Instructed B & D Coys to send out patrols. 12 noon. Recd report from patrols – no signs of enemy. 12.5. Issued orders to front Coys to go over – conforming to movements of 6th R WAR R. on the left. 12.15 pm. 6th WARWICKS going over – Instructions received from Brigade that posts to be established in enemy front line – Coys instructed to do so & push on patrols beyond. 2 pm Coys report posts established. 2.15 pm. C.O. left to make personal reconnaissance. 2.40 pm. C Coy report patrols 1 mile east to B. ST GEORGES – in touch on right & left. 3.10 pm C Coy report patrols in MARCHLEPOT – Queried this. 3.30 pm. This confirmed. 3.45 pm. B Coy report posts on line T.28 A.1.5. 4.30 pm B Coy report patrols reached HYENCOURT LE GRAND without opposition except some long distance sniping – Other Coys reached within 200 yds of Railway. 5 pm. On instructions from Brigade ordered patrols to be withdrawn at dusk. D Coy report posts at T 32 [illegible] 4.0. C at T.26 a. 4.4. B at T.25 a. 2.4. – in touch on right & left. – Instructions received to advance tomorrow	W.H.
B 2 A 9.9	18	7 am	Instructions received to move at 9 am – 9 am Coys moved forward. ~~Moved to Advanced H.Q. [illegible]~~ W.H.	
		9 am	Coys moved forward, and established line on Railway. Patrols pushed forward to LICOURT PERTAIN Road. 5 pm. Coys report all clear to that point. Moved Batt H.Q to B 2 A 9.9. 4.30 pm. Enemy shelled POTTE. 8 pm. Posts established on LICOURT – PERTAIN Road – Report good trench system near – also wells in PERTAIN – 1 O.R to L.G. School B at LE TOUQUET – 2 O.R to Bde Courses at BOYES. Div. Training Centre at MARCELCAVE cancelled. Fatigue party from R.E returned. Lt B.K. PARSONS and 2Lt GILDERTHORPE returned from courses –	W.H.
	19	7 am	Instructions received to be ready to move at 9 am.	
		9 am	Coys advanced to take up position on line MORCHAIN – LICOURT.	
		6 pm	Batt H.Q moved to C.14.a. 2.4. Coys taken up positions as follows A Coy C.15 a central – B C.15 central C. C.7. D 2.6 D C.14 a. Patrols report no sign of enemy to Canal – PARGNY clear – Canal passable for infantry in file – River SOMME impassable – all bridges being destroyed. Fires burning all round. Q.M. Stores moved to DENIECOURT	W.H.

Army Form C. 2118.

Instructions regarding War Diaries and Intelligence Summaries are contained in F. S. Regs., Part II. and the Staff Manual respectively. Title Pages will be prepared in manuscript.

WAR DIARY
or
INTELLIGENCE SUMMARY
(Erase heading not required.)

Place	Date	Hour	Summary of Events and Information	Remarks and references to Appendices
C.14 A.2.4	1917 Mch 20		Patrols out along river - reconnoitred, but found no signs of enemy: all villages destroyed but possible to billet a Batt. in ruined houses at PARGNY - Orders received that no move today	W.B.
Do.	21		Patrols out again along river - reconnoitred FALVY. No signs of enemy. One civilian DUVAL ARISTIDE found at PARGNY having come from NESLE - Examined him and obtained services of interpreter, who certified him harmless. Work on roads where blown up at MORCHAIN and PARGNY - Erected billets for Battn.	W.B.
Do.	22		Patrols again report no sign of enemy. Sent DUVAL ARISTIDE, French civilian, back to NESLE. Work on roads. Part of transport moved to MORCHAIN. 1 Coy & H.Q. billeted in improvised billets.	W.B.
Do.	23		Working party of 100 O.R. (2 Coys) worked under R.E. on roads & bridge at PARGNY - 1 Coy working of road water between MORCHAIN & PARGNY, and 1 Coy billeted in improvised billets. Batt moved to FALVY on instructions received from Brigade - covered by screen of outposts. Dispositions when completed. Rt front Coy B Coy F6a1.2. Lt front Coy A Coy. W29 B.5.0. Batt HQ C5 a.7.7. D Coy. C5a 3.9. C. Coy. (support) PARGNY. Ref. map ROSIERES 1/40000. Posts established covering FALVY Bridgehead. Patrols report no sign of enemy. FALVY destroyed. Batt billeted in cellars &c - work clearing out these & improving accommodation. 1 N.C.O. & 1 [illegible] O.R. from Divl. Signal School. LT J.J. SLATER reported from 1/8 R.WAR.R. for duty.	W.B.
FALVY Do.	24		Situation unchanged. Work 1 Coy at FALVY Bridge under R.E. 2 Coys digging & wiring posts under R.E. 1 Coy working on roads &c. Pte PARKER B Coy for work in munitions left for England. 5 O.R. returned from Divl. Signalling School	
Do.	25		Situation unchanged. Work 2 Coys at FALVY Bridges under R.E. 2 Coys digging and wiring posts at bridgeheads. H.Q. details worked putting village in state of defence. 1 Officer & 4 O.R. returned from Sharpshooting Course. 2 LT PESKETT to Hosp.	W.B.
Do.	26.		Situation unchanged. Work as yesterday. 2LTS F. SMITH & W.S. GUNTER reported for duty - posted to D & C Coys respectively - Advance Orders for move received.	W.B.
Do.	27		Situation unchanged. 150 O.R. worked at Bridge under R.E. Orders for move received. Batt Orders published. 2LT WHITELEY C.T. reported for duty from Hosp. 7.45 pm Batt marched to billets at FOURQUET, arrived 9.35 pm. Billets poor.	W.B.

2449 Wt. W14957/M90 750,000 1/16 J.B.C. & A. Forms/C.2118/12.

Instructions regarding War Diaries and Intelligence Summaries are contained in F. S. Regs., Part II. and the Staff Manual respectively. Title pages will be prepared in manuscript.

WAR DIARY
or
INTELLIGENCE SUMMARY.
(Erase heading not required.)

Army Form C. 2118.

Place	Date	Hour	Summary of Events and Information	Remarks and references to Appendices
	1917 MCH			
FOUCQUES	28		Cpl THOMSON left for England for Commission. 2 Lt HODGSON to 1st ARMY Course. 1 Officer & 40 O.R working party at TERTRY Crater. Billeting party proceeded to billet Batt. at MERAUCOURT in accordance with B.O. 89. B.O. received that Batt. will not move tonight – arranged for 40 O.R. being billeted at BHQ. C.O. went to conference at BHQ. 9pm. C.O. had conference with Coy Commanders.	
Do	29	5.30am	C.O. 2nd in Command & Coy Commanders reconnoitred SOYECOURT area. B.O. received that Batt moves to MERAUCOURT area tonight. 2pm Batt marched to MERAUCOURT & billeted there. Billets very bad. B.O. received as to attack on SOYECOURT.	W.R. W.R.
Do	30	2pm	Batt marched off from MONTIECOURT – arrived VRAIGNES Wood 4pm. 6pm Coys moved up to position behind POEUILLY. 7pm Coys in position. 7.15pm Coys moved to the attack with barrage. 7.40pm Barrage lifted. 7.50pm First two Coys entered SOYECOURT – no opposition – two prisoners. 8.15pm Communication to two Coys by telephone. (Batt H.Q. in BRULIE Wood) 8.45pm R.E & M.Gs advanced. 9pm C Coy report enemy gun firing from MONTELLE Copse – arranged with artillery to shell same till 10pm. 10pm Patrol of C Coy attacked MONTELLE Copse, and found gun position empty with tracks leading east & one freshly killed horse. Sniping from MONTEL & MONTALU Copses. Considerable shelling of village & consolidation proceeding. Posts 250 yds in front of village 11pm Prisoners received & sent to B.H.Q. Posts now	App. 1 W.R.

Army Form C. 2118.

WAR DIARY
or
INTELLIGENCE SUMMARY.
(Erase heading not required.)

Instructions regarding War Diaries and Intelligence Summaries are contained in F. S. Regs., Part II. and the Staff Manual respectively. Title pages will be prepared in manuscript.

Place	Date	Hour	Summary of Events and Information	Remarks and references to Appendices
	1917 MAR			
FOUILLOY	28		Cpl THOMSON left for England for commission. 2 Lt HODGSON to 1st ARMY Course. 10 offrs & 40 OR [illegible] party at TERTRY [illegible]. Billeting party proceeded to [illegible] at MERAUCOURT in accordance with BO 89. BO received that Batt will not move tonight – accommodation for 400 OR being billeted at [illegible]. BHQ. CO went to conference at BHQ. 9pm CO held conference with Coy Commanders.	
do	29	5.30am	CO 2nd in Command & Coy Commanders reconnoitred [illegible] area. BO received that Batt will move to MERAUCOURT over night. 2pm Batt proceeded to MERAUCOURT & billeted there. Billets very bad. Batt received orders to attack on [illegible].	WR
				WR
do	30	2pm	Batt marched off from MERAUCOURT & reached VRAIGNES at 6pm. 6pm Coys moved up to position behind POEUILLY. 7pm Coys in position. 7.15pm Coys moved to the attack with barrage. 7.40pm Barrage lifted. 7.50pm First two Coys entered [illegible] – no opposition – two prisoners. 8.15pm Communication to two Coys by telephone (Batt HQ in BRULE Wood). 8.45pm RF & MGs advanced. 9pm C Coy reported enemy [illegible] from [illegible] arranged with artillery [illegible] 10pm [illegible] attacked MONTIGNY Copse [illegible] found [illegible] partly finished [illegible] from MONTIGNY & MONTAIN Copse. Considerable shelling [illegible] 250 yds [illegible] 11pm Prisoners [illegible] Posts now	WR

T2134. Wt. W708–776. 500000. 4/15. Sir J. C. & S.

Instructions regarding War Diaries and Intelligence Summaries are contained in F. S. Regs., Part II. and the Staff Manual respectively. Title pages will be prepared in manuscript.

WAR DIARY
or
INTELLIGENCE SUMMARY.
(Erase heading not required.)

Army Form C. 2118.

Place	Date	Hour	Summary of Events and Information	Remarks and references to Appendices
	1917 MCH			
SOYECOURT	30	(contd)	Batt HQ moved to SOYECOURT (Q 24 b 6 8). Casualties 5 killed & wounded. Night quiet. Patrols out saw no sign of enemy.	WB
Do	31		Situation quiet during morning. Party of enemy seen digging in at R 10 c & R 9 b. Fired on by 60 pdr. & dispersed. Returned again later & again fired on. Village heavily shelled from 12.50 pm to 3.30 pm. 4 O.R. wounded. 2 Coys withdrawn from SOYECOURT - one to Q 24 central & one to SAILORS WOOD	WB

W. G. Phillips, Major
Comdg 3/8 R. War. R.

T2134. Wt. W708-776. 500000. 4/15. Sir J. C. & S.

2ND BN. [illegible]

BATTALION ORDER 111 by LT.COL. [illegible]
30th APRIL 1917.

1. The Battalion will attack, capture and consolidate the village of [illegible]. There will be no supporting Infantry on either flank.
2. The intention is to assault the village on its [illegible] face. Approximately from the road running through [illegible].24.d.4.9. to [illegible].24.b.7.3. to the road [illegible].19.a.5.0. inclusive then swinging into the village and working through to its Northern and Eastern extremities.
3. The Battalion will assemble in the valley (low ground) about 500 yards in rear of [illegible] ([illegible].28.d).
Assembly will be completed by 5-30 p.m. All Commanders will remember that the precautions necessary to avoid observation will render the process of assembly a lengthy one.
4. ALLOTMENT OF FRONTAGE.

The village will be divided into two areas, EAST and WEST area by a line running from [illegible].18.d.3.0. to [illegible].24.b.9.[illegible].
The LEFT attacking Company will be responsible for the WEST area.
The RIGHT attacking Coy will be responsible for the EAST area.
The outer flanks of each of the attacking Coys will be inclusive of the outer edges of the village.

5. METHOD OF ATTACK.
Two Companies in the front line ("B" and "C" Coys) will attack on a frontage of two platoons at 4[illegible] yards distance. The third platoon will provide the third wave moving 6[illegible] yards in rear of second wave. The fourth Platoon will form Company Reserve and will move in shallow column 60 yards in rear of third wave.
The advance of the first wave will be preceded by a screen of skirmishers widely extended thrown forward by each of the two front Coys.
In all other respects the formation will be such as laid down in the [illegible] PATTERN ATTACK.

6. DISTRIBUTION.
LEFT FRONT COY — "B" Coy.
RIGHT " " — "[illegible]" "
SUPPORT COY. — "[illegible]" "
BATTN. RESERVE. — "[illegible]" "

7. INFANTRY TIME-TABLE.

5-30 p.m. — Infantry assemble in formations as in 5 above, considerably closed up to facilitate passage through village.
6 p.m. — Bombardment commences, Infantry moves forward through village and extends its formation.
6-15 p.m. — Battn. leaves eastern edge of [illegible] village and moves forward to the assault.
[illegible] GUNS WILL BE FIRING ON [illegible].24.c.7.3. (North of [illegible] WOOD) until 6-55 p.m.
7 p.m. — Bombardment lifts beyond [illegible] and Infantry assault. A barrage will remain beyond the North end of the village during consolidation.

8. ACTION OF SUPPORT COY.
O.C. SUPPORT Coy will, moving off with remainder of Battalion at ZERO hour will detach one platoon to which is attached one Vickers gun section with orders to clear up the Northern end of [illegible] WOOD, to establish a Vickers gun post at a suitable point to support the advance of the assaulting Companies and to command enemy's line of retreat on roads leading from south-eastern exit of the village. This post will remain in position until ordered to withdraw by Battalion Commander.

9. ACTION OF RESERVE COY.
Reserve Coy will move up with remainder of Battalion and unless required in urgent support of the assaulting Coys will stop short of [illegible], on capture of village in default of further order in the meantime will move forward [illegible] into Western edge of village and will be kept intact as long as possible in event of enemy counter attack.

10. CONSOLIDATION.
On capture of village "[illegible]" "B" "C" Coys will proceed to consolidate. Barricades will be made at all exits and posts to give flanking fire will be dug to the North and South of village.
One section of R.E. will be held in readiness at Battn. H'Qrs and will move forward on capture of village.
During consolidation Battle Patrols will be pushed well to the front.

12 H 14

2/8th BATTALION
ORDERLY ROOM
1 MAY 1916
No. 591/17.
THE ROYAL WARWICKSHIRE REGT

Confidential

Vol 12

War Diary

of

2/8 Bn. The Royal Warwickshire Regt

for period

April 1st 1917 to April 30th 1917

Volume XII

*Instructions regarding War Diaries and Intelligence Summaries are contained in F. S. Regs., Part II. and the Staff Manual respectively. Title pages will be prepared in manuscript.

Army Form C. 2118.

WAR DIARY or INTELLIGENCE SUMMARY.

(Erase heading not required.)

Place	Date	Hour	Summary of Events and Information	Remarks and references to Appendices
	1917 Apl.			
SOYECOURT	1	2 am	Warning received that Brigade will be relieved today. 10 am C.O. & reconnoitring Officers of 2/1 BUCKS arrived. 2.15 pm Relief complete. No hostile shelling. Our batteries fired all morning on ridge in front. Batt marched to TERTRY – MERAUCOURT area. Batt HQ at TERTRY (W26.1.6)	WR
TERTRY	2	12.5 am	Orders received from Brigade that Batt. to be prepared to move at 9 am. Sent for 1st line Transport from FOUCAUCOURT. Working parties for today cancelled. 8 pm order received that Batt may stand down but will be prepared to move on an hours notice. 8 O.R. (casuals) reported from Base.	WR
D°	3	9 am	3.30 pm All Coys working on road TERTRY Crater exclusive to Crater at Q 30 D 5 1 inclusive. C.O. & 2 Coy Commanders reconnoitred new line taken up by Division	WR
D°	4	9 am	– 3.30 pm. All Coys working on road & craters as yesterday. Weather very bad – snow & sleet all day. Warning order received that Brigade will probably go into line on 7th inst	WR
D°	5	9 am	– 3.30 pm 2 Coys working on crater Q 29 d. – 2 Coys road Q 29 c 0.5 – Q 30 c 1.5. W5 c 1.9. 3 limbers provided for work	WR
D°	6	9 am	– 3.30 pm Work as yesterday – Orders for move received – Time to be notified later. 2 Lt. A.E. TONKS + 1 O.R. proceeded on leave.	WR
D°	7	9 am	– 12 noon – Work 3 Coys on Crater Q 29 d. 1 Coy on Crater at Q 26 d. Capt LEFROY reported from Course in England. 2.30 pm Orders for move published. 5 pm Batt marched to billets at	WR

T2134. Wt. W708–776. 500000. 4/15. Sir J. C. & S.

Instructions regarding War Diaries and Intelligence Summaries are contained in F. S. Regs. Part II. and the Staff Manual respectively. Title pages will be prepared in manuscript.

WAR DIARY
or
INTELLIGENCE SUMMARY.
(Erase heading not required.)

Army Form C. 2118.

Place	Date	Hour	Summary of Events and Information	Remarks and references to Appendices
VILLEVEQUE	1917 Apl 7		VILLEVEQUE - arrived 7 pm - Batt billeted in improvised shelters & bivouacs. 9 pm 60 pr gun fell into crater at VILLEVEQUE and blocked road. A Coy worked till 11 pm making new road to allow of transport passing.	[illegible]
Do	8	8 am	to 1 pm 1 Coy working at crater VILLEVEQUE and one Coy at crater MARTEVILLE.	
		1 pm	to 6 pm 1 Coy Do and one Coy Do	
		1.30 pm	Orders received in advance that one Coy to support 6th R.War.R. tonight. 3 p.m. Orders received.	
		4 pm	Enemy aeroplane attacked kite balloon VILLEVEQUE, & was itself brought down by M.G. fire from one of our planes. Lt & QM HODGKINS returned from England	
		9 pm	Orders received that another Coy will also move up. 10.30 pm D Coy moved off	[illegible]
Do	9	2 am	A Coy left to support attack. 2 platoon bombing squads of B Coy reported to B.R.6 to fuse bombs. 7 O.R. returned from the up - Casualties - 2 O.R. wounded	
			Orders received to relieve 2/6 R.WAR.R in the line. Batt Orders issued. Batt moved 5.30 pm Relief complete 10.40 pm. Dug new posts in front of line & wired same. Got touch with flank unit on right. Arranged light signals through Brigade with left flank unit	[illegible]
Left Sub Sect Line	10	3 am	Considerable shelling on left front Coy - got artillery retaliation. Shelling ceased 4.30 am.	
		3 pm	Our artillery active. Retaliation 4.2 in front line - 2 4.2s + 77 mm on MAISSEMY	[illegible]

T2134. Wt. W708-776. 500000. 4/15. Sir J. C. & S.

Instructions regarding War Diaries and Intelligence Summaries are contained in F. S. Regs., Part II. and the Staff Manual respectively. Title pages will be prepared in manuscript.

WAR DIARY
or
INTELLIGENCE SUMMARY.
(Erase heading not required.)

Army Form C. 2118.

Place	Date	Hour	Summary of Events and Information	Remarks and references to Appendices
Left Sub Sect BERTHAUCOURT	1917 Apl 10	6 pm	Burst of M.G fire from BERTHAUCOURT	[illegible]
"	11		Orders for relief received. Batt orders issued. Day quiet – considerable shelling in the night in evening, some shells in VILLECHOLLES – Road. Batt relieved by 23 MANCHESTERS. Relief complete 10 pm. On relief Batt marched to VILLECHOLLES	[illegible]
VILLECHOLLES	12	12.40 pm	Batt relieved in support by 20th LANCS. FUSILIERS. On relief Batt marched to VAUX (1 Coy & Batt HQ) and ETREILLERS (3 Coys). Billets non existent – weather stormy, constructed shelters, but great scarcity of material for covering roofs.	[illegible]
VAUX	13	"	Billet improvements. Divisional orders for work received. 3 pm orders received that Batt will work under orders of 32 Divn. 8 pm 1 Officer & 40 O.R. of A Coy worked on road near SAVY. 2Lt. S.E. PARSONS & 6 O.R. returned from Corps P.T. & B.F. Course.	[illegible]
"	14	"	8 Officers & 320 O.R. working under orders of 32 Divn on roads – 3 Coys 6 hrs [illegible] each [illegible] 8 am to 4.30 pm. 5 limbers working with parties. L/Cpl SHORT left for Commission. Lt. T.S. MORRIS reported from 1/8 R.WAR.R. for duty. 4 O.R. returned from [illegible] salvage [illegible] 8 O.R. from Hospital	[illegible]
"	15		8 Officers & 320 O.R. working as yesterday – 4 limbers. Capt MORTON reported from Hosp. for duty. 4 new reserve L.G. teams started training. Short Coy parades – after work.	[illegible]

T.134. Wt. W708–776. 500000. 4/15. Sir J. C. & S.

Instructions regarding War Diaries and Intelligence Summaries are contained in F. S. Regs., Part II. and the Staff Manual respectively. Title pages will be prepared in manuscript.

WAR DIARY
or
INTELLIGENCE SUMMARY.
(Erase heading not required.)

Army Form C. 2118.

Place	Date	Hour	Summary of Events and Information	Remarks and references to Appendices
	1917 Apl			
VAUX	16	8am	9 Officers and 320 O.R. – work on roads T[illegible] – 1 hours training	WW
Do	17	8am	9 Officers and 320 O.R. – work on roads T[illegible] 2Lt T.H. BUCKINGHAM, & Draft of 5 O.R. casuals reported from Base. 1 O.R. to Corps Musketry Course. Training for separate [illegible] – Bayonet fighting	WW
Do	18		Advance orders received from Brig. – Batt Advance Orders published – no working parties – Inspections refitting [illegible] – A Coy & H.Q. bathed at [illegible] baths	App. I WW
Do	19		C.O. Coy Commanders & R.S.M. visited line. R.S.M. killed. 2Lt ROGERS & 1 O.R. proceeded on leave – 2Lt TONKS & 2Lt CHIDGEY reported from leave & Hosp respectively. Brigade orders for relief received	WW
Do	20		Draft of 5 O.R. (casuals) reported from Base – Batt orders issued – Advance party of	App. II
		7.45pm	1 Officer 4 NCOs 1 Signaller & 1 Runner per Coy with 1 NCO 2 signallers & 4 runners from HQ proceeded to line	WW
Do	21		Batt marched out at 7.30pm to relieve 15 H.L.I. in Right Subsector. Capt T.E. LEEROY assumed command of Batt in line. Capt WHATMORE acting Second in Command remained at Q.M. Stores. Casualties 2/Lt H.T. BUCKINGHAM wounded (shell shock) 1 O.R. killed 4 O.R. wounded – relief complete 1.20am on 22/4/17. Heavy shelling in parts & near Batt H.Q. (S 17 a 0 3). Disposition [illegible] Coys in front line (less 2 platoons reserve)	WW

T2134. Wt. W708—776. 500000. 4/15. Sir J. C. & S.

Instructions regarding War Diaries and Intelligence Summaries are contained in F. S. Regs., Part II. and the Staff Manual respectively. Title pages will be prepared in manuscript.

WAR DIARY
or
INTELLIGENCE SUMMARY.
(Erase heading not required.)

Army Form C. 2118.

Place	Date	Hour	Summary of Events and Information	Remarks and references to Appendices
Map 62B SW S 17 a 0.3	22		Hostile artillery quiet throughout the day. Much aerial activity. L.G. fired on one hostile plane – no casualties. Night quiet. Tunnelling Coy part worked on dugouts. Work wiring posts & deepening trenches. MAJOR PHILLIPS took over command of Batt in line.	WR
D°	23		Enemy artillery active throughout day – particularly on posts, BOIS DES ROSES and on batteries. No casualties – Night – hostile artillery very active of left & centre Coy. Retaliation asked for through Artillery Brigade – Delay of 50 minutes in getting same. Got heavy guns to fire on application of Inf. Brigade. Result satisfactory. Hostile fire ceased. Work wiring	WR
D°	24		Quiet after 5.30 am. Several aeroplane fights. Our guns fired salvos on zones arranged from 8pm to 10.10pm. Brigade Order for relief received. Batt orders published. Batt relieved by 2/6 R.War.Regt. Night dark – relief complete 3.30 am on 25/4/17	App. III
SAVY	25		Batt rested – improved billets and cleaned up. Draft of 6 O.R. (casuals) received. Capt T.E. LEFROY left to act as Instructor at IV Corps School of Instruction. Party of 1 off & 40 O.R. carrying material to front line (Outpost H.Q.) for Tunnelling Coy at 8 pm	WR
D°	26		Working parties 7 Officers and 250 men on roads, billet improvements, and carrying timber and wire to front line. No hostile shelling in immediate neighbourhood. 2 Lt WHITELEY returned from leave	WR
D°	27.		Brigade orders for relief of 2/7 R.War.R. in BROWN LINE received 9am. Batt orders published 11.40 a.	App. IV

Instructions regarding War Diaries and Intelligence Summaries are contained in F. S. Regs., Part II. and the Staff Manual respectively. Title pages will be prepared in manuscript.

WAR DIARY
or
INTELLIGENCE SUMMARY.
(Erase heading not required.)

Army Form C. 2118.

Place	Date	Hour	Summary of Events and Information	Remarks and references to Appendices
SAVY	1917 Apl 27		Working parties as follows – 5 officers 160 O.R. 2 LT GUNTER & 2 O.R. to IV Corps Signalling School	
			2 LT SMITH and 1 O.R. to Lewis Gun School LE TOUQUET	
			Batt relieved 2/7 R. War R in right subsection BROWN LINE – Relief complete 10.35 pm	
			Hostile artillery active at intervals throughout the night – Our artillery bombarded enemy trenches	
			at 4.20 am on 28th in support of enterprise by Left Bde.	WP
BROWN LINE S20 a 4.8 (Map 62 B S.W.)	28		C.O. returned from leave. Enemy artillery active between 6 & 10 pm – especially on batteries.	
			French Ammunition dump on right blown up. Much aerial activity – German planes seeming to	
			have upper hand. Work – digging switch line with 320 yds of triple fence wire & 70 yds cross wire erected	WP
Do	29		Major PHILLIPS returned to Q.M. Stores. Orders received that left boundary will be line drawn from	
			S21 b 5.8 to S20 central. Left post took over this additional line from 5 R WAR R at 8.30 pm	
			1 O.R. returned from leave. 2 LT PROSSER and 1 O.R. to Divl. Bombing School. Considerable hostile shelling	
			with 5.9s on batteries in HOLNON Wood during the day. Normal night shelling. Our guns quiet. Many	
			German planes up during day. Worked at night on digging & wiring switch line	WP
Do	30		Day quiet – hostile artillery activity below normal – 2/5 R War R on our left relieved by	
			2/6 R War R – Work as last night – during day started deep dugout at Batt H.Q.	WP

Ed. C. Coleman
Lieut. Col.
Comdg. 2/8. R. War. R.

T2134. Wt. W708–776. 500000. 4/15. Sir J. C. & S.

SECRET

Appx I

2ND 8TH BATTALION THE ROYAL WARWICKSHIRE REGIMENT.

ADVANCE ORDER BY MAJOR W.E.PHILLIPS. COMMDG. 18-4-17.

1. The Battalion will probably relieve 15th Battn.H.L.I. in the Outpost Line RIGHT Sector on the night 21/22nd inst.

2. 6th WARWICKS will be on the main line of defence with Headquarters at S.20.a.7.5. 7th WARWICKS will be in support at SAVY WOOD and 5th WARWICKS will be in Reserve at SAVY.

3. DISPOSITIONS.

No.1. Outpost Coy. ("A" Coy at S.17.a.0.3)with posts at
S.23.a.0.7. -- 1 Platoon.
S.17.c.6.6. -- ½ Platoon.
S.17.c.4.3. -- 1 Section.
S.17.b.2.0. -- 1 Section.

2. Outpost Coy. in BOIS DES ROSES with posts at
"D" Coy.
S.12.c.6.7. -- ½ Platoon.
S.11.d.4.3½ -- 1 Section.
S.17.b.4.4. -- ½ Platoon.

3 Outpost Coy. "C" COY.
in S.6.c.5.2. with posts at:-
S.12.a.7.6. -- 1 Platoon.
S. 6.d.0.3. -- 1 Section.
Detached post at GEPY FARM - 1 Platoon
2 Platoons BY NIGHT

No.4.Coy. in Reserve ("B" Coy) at S.17.a.0.3. with detached post at S.22.b.9.2. and keeping liasson with the French on railway at S.29.a.3.6.

4. Company Commanders, Signalling Officer and R.S.M. will visit the line tomorrow 19th inst. They will meet the Commanding Officer at cross roads X.27.d. at 9-30 a.m. Guides will be provided at Headquarters of 14th Inf.Bde SAVY at 10 a.m.
Lieut.J.J.SLATER will attend and will reconnoitre the line for "D" Coy.

Ref. Map 62.B. 1/40000 and
62.B.S.W. 1/20000

sgd. W.S.FARMER. Lieut.&.Adjt.
2/8.R.WARWICK.REGT.

SECRET.

App. II

2ND 8TH BATTALION THE ROYAL WARWICKSHIRE REGIMENT.

BATTALION ORDER 118 by MAJOR W.E.PHILLIPS. COMMDG.
FRIDAY 20th APRIL 1917.

1. The Battalion will relieve 15th H.L.I. on Outposts on the night 21/22nd April. Relief will be according to following table:-

2/8.WAR.			H.L.I.
No.1.Outpost Coy.	RIGHT.	"A"	"C" Coy
2 ..	.. BOIS DES ROSES.	"D"	"D" "
3. ..	.. CEPY FARM.	"C"	"A" "
LEFT SUPPORT COY.		"B"	"B" "

2. GUIDES. One Guide per Coy in charge of an Officer of H.L.I. will be at Headqrs 14th Inf.Bde. on the ETREILLERS - SAVY Road X.28.d. at 7-45pm

3. ROUTE FOR INGOING COYS. The ETREILLERS - SAVY HALTE ROAD as far as S.E.corner of SAVY WOOD in S.20.d., thence North to railway in S.20.b. thence East across country to Batt.H.Q. keeping Quarry on the Right.

4. ORDER OF MARCH. "C" "B" "D" "A" Coys. Leading Coy will not march off before 7-30 p.m. Coys will move East of ETREILLERS by Platoons at 100 yards intervals.

5. DRESS. Fighting Order. Jerkins will be worn. 20 men per Coy will carry shovels and 5 per Coy picks. These will be carried as laid down in Battalion Standing Orders.

6. SURPLUS KIT. Valises with surplus kit will be stacked by Coys at Q.M. Stores by 5 p.m. on 21st.

7. LEWIS GUNS. 32 Magazines per gun will be taken into the line. These and the Lewis Guns will be carried on one limber per Coy which will be detailed by the Transport Officer to report to each Coy Hdqrs by 7 p.m.

8. RATIONS. For consumption on the 22nd will be carried on the man. All water bottles will be filled.

9. STORES &C. Only such tools, S.A.A. and Grenades as are surplus to outgoing Battalion establishment will be taken over and it is known that the quantity of these available will be small. All 1/10000 and 1/20000 Maps, Air Photos and Defence Schemes will be taken over. Copies of receipts will be sent to Battn.H.Q. by 10 p.m. on 22nd inst.

10. ADVANCE PARTY. 1 Officer 4 N.C.O's. 1 Runner and 1 Signaller per Coy. 1 N.C.O., 2 Signallers and 4 Runners from Headquarters will be sent in advance of Battalion tonight 20/21st inst. Guides will be at H.Q. 14th Inf.Bde X.28.d. at 7-45 p.m. These will carry rations for two days and fat cookers.

11. Relief complete will be notified to Battn.H.Q. by telephone. Code word "MOTHER".

12. ACKNOWLEDGE.

sgd. W.S.FARMER. Lt.&.Adjt.
2/8.WARWICKS.

issued at 11-30 a.m.

Coys. 1/4. Coys.
5. C.O.
6. Q.M. & T.O.
7. File
8. War Diary.

App 11.

SUPPLY ARRANGEMENTS TO ACCOMPANY BATTALION ORDER 118.

1. Quartermaster's Stores and Transport will remain at VAUX.
2. RATIONS.
   Rations for consumption on the 22nd will be carried on the man, being drawn from Q.M.Stores early on the 21st under arrangements between Q.M. and C.Q.M.S's.
   Rations for 23rd and ensuing daysx will go up on Pack animals via SAVY - SAVY WOOD - thence overground to Battalion Headquarters where they will be dumped.
   Coys will find their own Ration and water parties, who will carry from Battalion Hdqrs.
   Rations will consist of, amongst other things, Bacon semi-cooked or boiled. Fresh Meat - small issue for messes. Bread and biscuits to be packed in double sandbags.
   No Hot Food Containers being available it will be impossible to provide Hot Food from the rear, and the only source of supply will be the Tommy's Cookers which the men must use themselves.
3. WATER.
   For consumption on the 22nd will be carried in the water bottles.
   The Sergeant Master Cook will arrange that water carts are available on the 21st for filling bottles.
   It is reported that there is a well or pump near CEPY FARM.
   Water in petrol tins will come up nightly with rations and will be dumped with them at Battalion H.Q.
   There is a very great shortage of petrol tins (forty only being in possession) and water bottles should be filled from petrol tins as soon as the latter arive. Petrol tins being sent back to H.Q.atonce.
4. FUEL.
   Fat Cookers for the 22nd will be carried on the man.
   It is hoped to be able to maintain a supply of these Cookers nightly and they will be supplemented by Charcoal and Coke.
5. COOKERS.
   Cookers will remain with Transport and one Cook per Coy will report to Sergt.Master Cook at VAUX at 7 p.m. on the 21st. These men will remain behind with Cookers and will be rationed and accommodated by the Transport Officer.
6. AMMUNITION.
   The Bombing Officer will arrange for the following to be dumped at Battn.H.Q. on the night of relief.

12000 rounds S.A.A.	1 Box 1"Very Lights WHITE
2 dox 1" Very Lights RED	2 doz 1½" Very Lights GREEN.
S.O.S. Grenades.	1" and 1½" Very Pistol.
10 boxes of Bombs.	

   NOTE: All other ranks including Bombers armed with a rifle will carry 120 rounds S.A,A.
7. BOMBS.
   Coy Bombing Squads will carry Bombs in accordance with instructions issued to them by Battalion Bombing Officer.
8. TOOLS.
   The only tools available for work in the line will be the 80 shovels and 20 picks carried in by Coys.
9. BOMB STORE. is at SAVY X.29.d.5.5. R.E.DUMP AT SAVY RAILWAY CROSSING X.29.b. Advanced Dressing Station - SAVY X.29.d.

sgd. W.S.FARMER. Lt.&.Adjt.
2/8.WARWICKS.

20th APRIL 1917.

App 11.

2ND 6TH BATTALION THE ROYAL WARWICKSHIRE REGIMENT.

AMENDMENT TO BATTALION ORDER 118. dated 28-4-17.

1. Relief table in para.1. of B.O.118 is amended and will read as follows:-

2/6.WARWICKS.		15th H.L.I.
No.1. Outpost Coy."RIGHT"	"A"	"C" Coy
2. .. .. BOIS DES ROSES	"D"	"D" "
3. .. .. LEFT	"C"	"A" "
Battn.Reserve.	"B"	"B" "

Sgd. [illegible].FARMER. Lt.&.Adjt.
2/6.WARWICKS.

Appx

COMMANDING OFFICER'S TRENCH NOTES. 20-4-17.

1. SITUATION. The Outposts are only moderately well dug in in fact they are all under direct observation. Movement during daylight will be absolutely forbidden if for no other reason than that it discloses our dispositions to the enemy.
NOTE. Similar orders have been recently issued but have been tacitly disregarded by runners and ration parties etc., The present orders must be obeyed to the letter, only movement being urgent messages and linesmen.
Hostile artillery has been active and making good shooting upon certain centres of movement. It is therefore important that adequate cover against artillery fire be obtained as soon as possible, and it is to be impressed on all ranks that this is infinitely more important than mere protection against weather.
To minimise casualties it is important that men avoid congregating in unprotected localities in any numbers, either by day or night. All Units should be kept as dispersed as ~~xxxxxxx~~ the tactical situation permits, and no more than four to six men should be grouped together unless under effective cover.
Coy Commanders will make the above the subject of a brief talk to all ranks before going in.

2. COMMUNICATION. is reported to be unsatisfactory, but telephonic communication has been maintained more or less constantly with all Coys except No.3.
Wherevers possible telephonic communication will be supplemented by visual and lamp stations.
In order to provide against disconnection of the No.3. Coy, an observation post will be established within close view of CEFY FARM. (if CEFY FARM should be abandoned before the Battalion goes into the line the functions of this Observation Post remain unchanged). This post will be manned by an intelligent N.C.O. and 2 Signallers and will be provided with a telephone. It will serve to keep constant observation on the area about CEFY FARM and will be established by O.C. LEFT SUPPORT COY (or O.C. No.3. Coy) on the night 21/22nd.
The use of Runners will be confined except in urgent cases to the hours of darkness.

3. INTELLIGENCE.
At present there is no very effective system within the Battalion for the collection of intelligence, and a special effort must be made to organise and improve this most vital service. 2/Lt.CHIDGEY will be the Officer responsible for Intelligence and one Officer per Coy will be made responsible by Coy Commander for the careful recording and communication of all items of Intelligence effecting the Coy.
Items of Intelligence fall under two main heads:- (1) Those which are of value when collected and communicated at regular periods of 24 hours. (2). Those which cease to be of value unless communicated atonce. Such items should be communicated by wire atonce.

4. REPORTS. Tactical Progress Reports to reach Headquarters by 6 a.m. daily and to contain intimation of any change of dispositions. Situation Report by wire to reach Batt.H.Q. by 5 a.m. and 5 p.m.
Returns as follows are required from Coys as soon as possible after relief Trench Stores taken over; Trench Shelters taken over; Dispositions, including Vickers Guns.

5. PATROLS. The three Coys on Outpost will send out patrols nightly with the object of obtaining information as to the enemy's dispositions. The attention of Coy.Commanders is drawn to recent IV Corps Intelligence and 1/20000 CHISY Sheet showing latest trenches, copies of both the above have been sent round to Coys.
Attention is also called to 32 Div. Intelligence , extracts from,.
Patrol Reports must invariably be forwarded with T.P.Report and should be signed by Patrol Leader as well as Coy Commander. A precis of patrol report will be wired immediately patrol returns.

6. WORK. To continue deepening and improving ~~xxxxxxxx~~ existing trenches with a view to providing cover against hostile artillery fire.
Strengthening existing wire in the Outpost line.

7. All ranks should be reminded of the need for encouragement of the offensive use of rifle and L.G. fire. In the past there has been a tendency to delay or even to avoid the opening of fire due to some unfounded fear of disclosing position occupiedby us. An enemy battery in T.20. was recent engaged by a gun at CEFY FARM and a M.G. firing from the Barracks was also was engaged.

8. Owing to the difference in the squaring of the maps in use, all map references will be referred to 62.B.S.W. unless otherwise stated.

Sgd. W.E.PHILLIPS. Major for Lt.Col.
Commdg. 2/8.R.WARWICK.REGT.

App 41

2/8th Battn R Warwicks Regt

Battalion Order No. 119. by Major W. E. Phillips Commanding Tuesday Apr 24/17

1. The Batt. will be relieved in the line tonight 24/25th inst. by the 2/6th R War. R according to the following table:–

2/8th R War. R.	2/6th R War. R
'C' Coy.	'C' Coy
H.Q.	H.Q.
'A' Coy	'D' Coy
'B' "	'B' "
'D' "	'A' "

2. Guides. Two guides per Coy. who have reconnoitred the road from BROWN LINE, will report to Batt. H.Q. at 7 pm.

3. On relief the Batt will march to billets at SAVY. C.Q.M.Sgts have proceeded in advance to take over billets. Route will be at O.C. Coys discretion

4. Stores. All Trench Shelters & surplus S.A.A. will be handed over & receipts taken. S.O.S Grenades, & filled Lewis Gun Magazines will be brought out. Tools & petrol tins will also be brought out. It is important that these should be carefully collected & checked, with a view to ensuring that none are left behind. Receipts for stores handed over will be sent to Batt. O.R. by 10 am. on the 25th inst.

5. Coys. will report relief complete by telephone – Code word – ST QUENTIN.

6. ACKNOWLEDGE

W Mathews
Lt & Adjt
2/8 Warwicks

SECRET

War Diary
App IV

2ND 8TH BATTALION THE ROYAL WARWICKSHIRE REGIMENT.

BATTALION ORDER 180 by MAJOR W.E.PHILLIPS. COMMDG.
Friday 27th April 1917.

1. The Battalion will relieve 2/7.WARWICKS in the BROWN LINE - RIGHT Sub-Sector tonight 27/28th inst.

2. DISPOSITIONS.

RIGHT FRONT COY.	"A" Coy
LEFT " "	"D" "
RIGHT SUPPORT	"C" "
LEFT "	"B" "

3. GUIDES. Coys will make their own arrangements for guides from their their advance parties.

4. ORDER OF MARCH. Coys will move independently by Platoons at 100 yards interval, leaving SAVY immediately after dark.

5. TOOLS. Each Coy will carry on the man 20 shovels and 5 picks, these to be drawn from the R.S.M. at Battalion Headquarters before 5 p.m.

6. STORES. All Trench shelters will be taken over and any surplus stores. S.O.S. Grenades will be drawn from R.S.M. before 5 p.m.and these and the usual number of Very Lights will be carried into the line by Companies.

7. DRESS. Fighting Order. Valises with surplus kit will be labelled and stacked at Coy Headquarters by 5 p.m. and will be taken to Q.M. Stores by empty Ration limbers. Officers kits, Mess Baskets etc. will be collected by Transport Officer at 7 p.m.

8. RATIONS. Rations for the 28th will be carried on the man, being drawn by C.Q.M.S's at SAVY before 5 p.m. Rations for "D" "C" and "B" Coys and Headquarters will be carried by limber to S.20.d.2.2. on subsequent days. Rations for "A" Coy will be carried by Pack Mules through S.26.d. - S.27.c. to about S.27.central.

9. WATER. Water for 28th will be carried in water bottle.

10. Code word for relief complete. "SHUFFLE".

11. ACKNOWLEDGE.

sgd. W.S.FARMER. Lt.&.Adjt.
2/8.WARWICKS.

issued at 11-40 a.m.

Copies 1/4 Coys.
5. Q.M.
6. R.S.M.
7. 2/7.WARWICKS.
8. C.O.
9. File
10. War Diary.

War Diary of:- Confidential.

2/8th Battalion The Royal Warwickshire Regt.

Vol 13

Volume XIII

13 H 23

Period:-
May 1/1917 to:-
May 31/1917.

Instructions regarding War Diaries and Intelligence Summaries are contained in F. S. Regs., Part II. and the Staff Manual respectively. Title pages will be prepared in manuscript.

WAR DIARY
or
INTELLIGENCE SUMMARY.
(Erase heading not required.)

Army Form C. 2118.

Place	Date	Hour	Summary of Events and Information	Remarks and references to Appendices
	1917			
BROWN LINE S20a5.5 ref 62BSW	May 1	8am-8.30pm	Heavy shelling by enemy with 4.2s and 5.9s on batteries in S20a - rest of day quiet. BM visited line. 1 O.R. retd from Tramway fatigue. Our guns quiet. Work digging and wiring BROWN LINE	W.R.
Do.	2		Artillery quiet throughout the day. Work at night on digging & wiring trench for BROWN LINE	W.R.
Do.	3		Hostile artillery very quiet throughout the day. Some shelling at night. Orders for relief received and Batt orders published. 2 LT HODGSON returned from IV Army Course. 2 LT LLEWELLYN BEVAN and LLOYD reported for duty. Draft of 4 O.R. (casuals) from Base. Batt relieved 2/5 R.WAR.R in outpost line. relief complete 11.55pm.	W.R.
Outpost line SAVY Sector	4		Day quiet - much aeroplane activity. Some shells at night - CAPT MORTON (W.R.) killed - 2 O.R. wounded. G.S.O.2 Divn & BM visited left Coy posts at night. Capt MUNSHE and 1 O.R. proceeded on leave. 2 LT ROGERS returned from leave. 3 Patrols out at night - Work wiring in front of line of posts.	W.R.
	5		Day quiet - hostile aeroplane brought down in enemy's lines at 4.30 pm. 2 Patrols out at night. Work dugouts at Batt HQ and left Coy HQ - wiring in front of outpost line. G.S.O. II Divn visited round right Coy posts. Bde orders for relief received. Heavy rain at night.	W.R.
	6		Day quiet. Batt orders for relief published. 13 O.R. (casuals) from Base. Batt relieved by 2/6 R.War.R. Relief complete 11.55pm - Batt marched to billets at SAVY. Billets poor.	W.R.

T.2134. Wt. W708-776. 500000. 4/15. Sir J. C. & S.

Instructions regarding War Diaries and Intelligence Summaries are contained in F. S. Regs., Part II. and the Staff Manual respectively. Title pages will be prepared in manuscript.

WAR DIARY
or
INTELLIGENCE SUMMARY.
(*Erase heading not required.*)

Army Form C. 2118.

Place	Date	Hour	Summary of Events and Information	Remarks and references to Appendices
	1917 May			
SAVY	7		Weather fine – 170 men on working parties with R.E. – remainder of Batt cleaning up & refitting. Improved billets – Bathing in improvised baths – no clean clothes available.	W.P.
do	8		Weather wet. 150 men on working parties with R.E. remainder refitting, bathing – and cleaning roads & improving village – Brigade orders for relief received.	W.P.
do	9		Weather fine – 2 Coys (200 men) working on Dotted Brown Line West of SAVY – Batt relieved 2/7 R WAR R. in BROWN LINE – Relief complete 10.45 pm. Work on BROWN LINE after relief –	App I W.P.
SAVY WOOD (BROWN LINE)	10		Day quiet – Bombardment by British & French Artillery 3 – 3.15 pm. Little retaliation – Work 9.30 pm – 3 am. carrying to front line, wiring in front line & repairs & improvements to BROWN LINE. Major PHILLIPS, Lt S E PARSONS & 2 O.R. proceeded on leave.	W.P.
	11		Enemy artillery active on batteries in SAVY WOOD from 7.30 – 11 am. quiet after – Draft of 46 O.R. reported. Work as last night.	W.P.
	12		Capt WHATMORE retd from leave – Day quiet – Work at night in BROWN LINE – Preliminary orders received from Brigade as to relief of Divn. Heavy showers.	W.P.
	13		Day quiet – weather fine – thunderstorm at night. Sgt CALDER to Corps R.F. Course – Night exceptionally quiet – few shells in SAVY Wood between 2 & 3 am. BO for relief recd.	W.P. App II

T2134. Wt. W708–776. 500000. 4/15. Sir J. C. & S.

Instructions regarding War Diaries and Intelligence Summaries are contained in F. S. Regs., Part II. and the Staff Manual respectively. Title pages will be prepared in manuscript.

WAR DIARY
or
INTELLIGENCE SUMMARY.
(Erase heading not required.)

Army Form C. 2118.

Place	Date	Hour	Summary of Events and Information	Remarks and references to Appendices
SAVY Wood (BROWN LINE)	1917 May 14		Day quiet – no artillery fire from enemy & no aircraft up. French advance parties arrived and went round line. Batt relieved by 1½ Coys 3rd Batt 131 French Inf Regt & ½ Coy 1st Batt 131st French Inf. Regt – Relief complete 10.45 pm. On relief Batt marched to GERMAINE – Billets good. Lt T. S. MORRIS to Hosp.	W.R.
GERMAINE	15		Batt. marched to billets at NESLE – arrived 8.30 p.m. C.O. inspected new draft.	W.R. App III
NESLE	16		Rest and refitting. Draft 5 O.R. (casuals)	W.R. App IV
"	17		Draft 6 O.R (casuals) Batt entrained at NESLE Station 7.15 am. Train to LONGEAU – arrived 10 am – marched to FLESSELLES – arrived 3.45 pm Capt T. MUNGLE returned from leave	W.R.
FLESSELLES	18		Cleaning up – Brigade Commander inspected Draft of 46 O.R. Lt B.K. PARSONS & 3 O.R. on leave.	
Do	~~19~~		L/Sgt WILLSHER to England for Commission. 1 O.R retd from leave	W.R.
Do	19		Cleaning up. C.O. inspected A & B Coys – These Coys also practised attack & gas helmet drill	W.R. App V
Do	20		C.O. inspected C & D Coys – Practice attack by Coys. Gas mask drill – G.O.C. presented medals – Brigade parade. 5.30 pm. 6.30 pm. C of E parade service.	W.R.
Do	21	5 am	Batt. marched to billets at LONGUEVILLETTE. arrived 10.30 am. Billets good – weather showery	W.R.
LONGUEVILLETTE	22		Cleaning up & rest. 11.30 am B.G.C. inspected Batt. in full marching order	W.R. App VI

T2134. Wt. W708–776. 500000. 4/15. Sir J. C. & S.

Instructions regarding War Diaries and Intelligence Summaries are contained in F. S. Regs., Part II. and the Staff Manual respectively. Title pages will be prepared in manuscript.

WAR DIARY
or
INTELLIGENCE SUMMARY.
(*Erase heading not required.*)

Army Form C. 2118.

Place	Date	Hour	Summary of Events and Information	Remarks and references to Appendices
	1917 May			
LONGUE-VILLETTE	23	am. 5.35	Batt marched to billets at IVERGNY - arrived 11 am. Billets for men good - Officers billets scarce. Weather fine.	[initials]
	24th	8.15 am	Batt proceeded by buses to BERNEVILLE arrived BERNEVILLE 12.40 pm. Billets good. Lieut. W.S. FARMER proceeded on leave	App VII [initials]
BERNEVILLE	25th		Cleaning up etc. 3 O.R. proceeded on leave. Training programme submitted to Brigade. Lieut. S.E. PARSONS returned from leave	[initials]
	26th		Parades as per training programme (App) 2nd Lieuts. J.W. WOOLDRIDGE + T.A. SCOTT reported for duty. Draft of 8 O.R. received from base.	App VIII [initials]
	27th		Training as per programme. 2.30 pm Tank demonstration at training area in R.18 WAILLY. 2nd Lieut. J.W. JESSOP reported for duty.	[initials]
	28th		Training as per programme.	[initials]
	29th		Training as per programme. Draft of 4 O.R. received from base.	[initials] App IX
	30th		Training as per programme - battalion practised the attack from trenches.	[initials]
	31st.		Brigade practised the attack from trenches with contact aeroplanes. 4 pm. Demonstration of gas + smoke clouds on training area R.18 WAILLY. Inspection of billets, transport and horse lines by B.G.C. 182nd INF. BDE.	App X [initials]

T. A. Calver [signature]
Lieut. Col.,
Comdg. 2/8 R. War. R

T2134. Wt. W708-776. 500000. 4/15. Sir J. C. & S.

2ND 8TH BATTALION THE ROYAL WARWICKSHIRE REGIMENT.

BATTALION ORDER 124 by LT.COL.E.C.CADMAN. COMMDG. 9-5-17. I

1. The Battalion will relieve 2/7.WARWICKS in the BROWN LINE RIGHT SUB-SECTOR tonight 9/10th inst.

2. DISPOSITIONS.

				2/7.WARWICKS.
RIGHT FRONT COY.	(SWITCH LINE)	"A" Coy.	relieves	"A" Coy
LEFT " "	(BROWN LINE)	"D" "	..	"D" "
RIGHT SUPPORT COY.	do	"B" "	..	"C" "
RESERVE COY.		"C" "	..	"B" "

3. GUIDES.
No guides will be provided by the outgoing Battalion.

4. ORDER OF MARCH.
Coys will move independantly by Platoons at 200 yards interval leaving SAVY immediately after dark.

5. ADVANCE PARTY. Advance party not to exceed 3 per Coy will proceed in advance to take over from outgoing Coys. The party will ~~report~~ leave not later than 7 p.m.

6. STORES. S.O.S. Grenades and the usual number of Very Lights will be carried into the line by Coys. All other stores will be handed over here to incoming Battalion and will be taken over in the new line on relief. Handing over states will be sent to the Orderly Room by 9 a.m. tomorrow.

7. DRESS:- Fighting Order. Valises with surplus kit will be labelled and stacked at Coy Headquarters by 4 p.m. and will be taken to Q.M. Stores by returning Ration limbers. Officers kits, Mess Baskets etc. will be collected by Transport Officer at 7-30 p.m.

8. RATIONS. Rations for the 10th will be carried on the man. Rations for subsequent days will be brought up as follows:- for "A" and "B" Coy by packmule to "A" Coys old ration dump at S.27.central. For "C" and "D" Coy and Headquarters by limber to old ration dump at S.20.d.2.2.

9. WATER. Water for 10th inst will be carried in water bottles. For subsequent days one water cart will be near Headquarters in S.20.a. and one near "C" Coys Headquarters in S.20.d.

10. WORK. Work in progress will be explained to Coy Commanders by Coys whom they relieve and "A" and "D" Coys will be prepared to carry on with work tonight.

11. Relief complete will be reported atonce by telephone. Code word "LANDON".

12. ACKNOWLEDGE.

sgd. W.S.FARMER. Lieut.&.Adjt.
2/8.WARWICKS.

Copies 1/4. Coys.
5. C.O.
6. 2/7.WARWICKS.
8. R.S.M.
9. Quartermaster.
10 File
11. War Diary.

II

2/8 Bn Royal Warwickshire Regiment.

Battalion Order No 125

d/ 14-5-1917

1 The Battalion will be relieved by the 3rd Battn. 121 French Regt on the night of 14/15th inst

2 <u>Guides</u> - 2 guides per Company will report to 2/LT. CHIDGEY at Battn. H.Q at 7.30 p.m.

3 <u>Billets</u> - On relief the Battalion will march to billets at GERMAINE. Each company, on being relieved, will march independently as follows - by platoons at 200x distance East of ETREILLERS, and by Companies at 200x distance West of ETREILLERS

4 <u>Billeting party</u> - 2/LT PROSSER and C/Q.M. Sergeants will proceed in advance tomorrow to billet the Battalion.

5 <u>Lewis Guns</u> - Lewis Gun drums will be brought out filled. Any drums fired will be refilled from spare ammunition in time.

6 <u>Transport</u>. - 1 limber for Lewis Guns will be at 'C' Coys H.Q for 'C' and 'D' Coys. One limber will be at crossroads on road in S. 26 d. for 'A' and 'B' Coys. In addition to Lewis Guns these limbers will be available to carry L/G drums and dixies. Medical cart will be at 'C' Coys H.Q at 10 p.m.

2 pack mules will be at 'B' Coys ration dump at dusk for 'A' and 'B' Companies empty petrol tins. 'C' & 'D' Coys' empty tins will be placed in water cart at 'C' Coys H.Q at dusk

7 <u>Hot Tea</u> will be served at VAUX Cross Roads as Battalion comes out. Cookers will be at billets, GERMAINE on arrival. Officers' valises will also be there

8 <u>Handing over</u>, Receipts for stores and documents handed over in accordance with attached 'Handing over Arrangements' will be sent to Battn. H.Q. by 10 a.m. on 15th inst.

9 Relief complete will be notified to Battn H.Q by telephone Code word - VICTORY

10 Acknowledge

Copies to
1-4 Coys.
5 182 Bde
6 C.O
7 War Diary
8 File.

[signature]
Lieut & Adjt
2/8 Warwicks

2/8th Bn. Royal Warwickshire Regiment.

Battalion Order No. 126
by Lt. Col. C. C. Cadman. Commdg.

Maps Reference. { St Quentin 1/100000
Amiens 1/100000

1. The Battalion will march tomorrow 15th inst. from GERMAINE to NESLE.

2. Route - FORESTE - DOUILLY - MATIGNY - BUNY - VOYENNES - NESLE

3. The Battalion will fall in, facing west on the GERMAINE - FORESTE road, head of column just short of road junction S of G in GERMAINE, the whole ready to move at 3.50 p.m. O.C. Coys will take precautions to keep road clear for passing traffic

4. Order of march. H.Q. 'C' 'D' 'A' 'B' Transport. Distance of 200 yards will be preserved between Companies, also between rear Company & transport. Cookers will march with Companies

5. Billeting parties will proceed in advance under Battalion arrangements

6. Officers' Valises, Mess Baskets etc. as per standing orders.

7. Company Commanders will take every step possible that their Companies turn out as clean and smart as possible on marching off.

8. Acknowledge.

Copies to:-
1-4. Coys.
5. C.O.
6. Q.M.
7. File
8. War Diary

[signature]
Lieut & Adjt
2/8 Warwicks

2ND. 8TH. BATTALION THE ROYAL WARWICKSHIRE REGIMENT.

IV

BATTALION ORDER No. 127, by Lieut. Col. E.C. CADMAN
dated 16-3-1917. Commanding.

1. MOVE. The Battalion will entrain tomorrow, the 17th. inst., and will proceed to LONGUEAU.

2. PARADE Battalion will parade in the Square, facing North, ready to move at 6 a.m. Order:- H.Q. "A" "B" "C" "D" Coys.

3. DRESS. Full Marching Order. Steel helmets on pack. Water bottles will be filled.

4. STORES. Camp Kettles will be drawn from the Q.M. Stores today by Companies. These, Coy Mess Baskets and Lewis Guns (in chests) will be carried to the Station under Company arrangements to arrive there by 5-30 a.m.: and ~~hand~~ whole handed over to Sgt. CROSS.
Officers' valises and Mess Boxes will be stacked outside Companies' H.Q.'s by 8-30 p.m. tonight, and will be collected by Baggage wagons. These will move with Transport, and will not be returned to Officers before 19th. inst.

5. RATIONS. Rations for tomorrow will be carried on the man, with the exception of tea, sugar and milk ration which will be prepared when opportunity occurs.

6. COOKS. One cook per company will report to the Quartemaster by 10 p.m. tonight, and will accompany cooker on march.

7. STATE Companies will render to the Orderly Room by 10 p.m. tonight entraining state showing Officers and other ranks proceeding by rail tomorrow.

8. LOADING PARTY. O.C. "D" Company will detail a loading party of 1 Officer and 10 other ranks to be at the station by 5-30 a.m.
The Officer will report to the Adjutant today for further instructions.

9. ENTRAINING PARTY. C/QMS Walker will report to the R.T.O. NESLE at 5-30 a.m. tomorrow. He will proceed with the 2nd. train, leaving 4-15 p.m.
Detraining party will be found by the 184 Inf. Bde.

10. O.C. TRAIN. The senior Officer on the train will be O.C. Train.

11. ACKNOWLEDGE

Issued at 1-0 p.m.
16-5-17.

Lieut. & Adjt.,
2/8 Warwicks.

Copies to

1-4. Coys.
5. Q.M.
6. C.O.
7. R.S.M.
8. War Diary.
9. File.
10. Spare.

V

SECRET.

2ND 8TH BATTALION THE ROYAL WARWICKSHIRE REGIMENT.

BATTALION ORDER 128 by LT.COL.E.C.CADMAN. COMMDG. 20-6-17

Reference Map LENS 1/100000.

1. The Battalion will march tomorrow to billets at LONGUEVILLETTE.

2. ROUTE. HAVERNAS - CANAPLES - MONTRELET - FIENVILLERS.

3. STARTING POINT. TIME &c. The Battalion will fall in facing North on RUE DE L'EGLISE. Head of column just South of cross roads West of E in FLESSELLES.
The Battalion will be ready to move by 5 a.m. There will not be more than 10 yards distance between Coys.

4. ORDER OF MARCH. H.Q. "D" "A" "B" "C" Coys, Transport. Cookers will march with Transport.

5. DRESS. Full Marching Order - Steel Helmets will be worn in accordance with Army Order.

6. BAGGAGE. Mess Baskets etc. will be ready in accordance with Standing Orders and will be called for by baggage wagons at Coy Headquarters. Camp Kettles will be handed in to Q.M.Stores by 10 p.m. tonight.

7. RATIONS. The days rations will be carried on Cookers. O.C.Coys will ensure that all men have hot tea before marching off. This will be prepared on Cookers. Breakfasts will be cooked on the march and there will be a halt from 5.50 to 6.30 a.m. for breakfast.

8. 2/Lieut.H.T.CHIDGEY will remain behind for two hours to collect claims. He will also inspect billets and forward report to Battalion H.Q. on arrival.

9. C.Q.M.S's will fall in with Battalion with cycles and will proceed in advance when Battalion moves off, in order to assist in Billeting the Battalion.

sgd. W.S.FARMER. Lieut.&.Adjt.
2/8.R.WARWICK.REGT.

VI

SECRET.

2ND 8TH BATTALION THE ROYAL WARWICKSHIRE REGIMENT.

BATTALION ORDER No.129 by LT.COL.E.C.CADMAN. COMMDG.
Tuesday 22nd May 1917.

Ref. Map LENS 1/100000.

1. The Battalion will march tomorrow to billets at IVERGNY.
ROUTE:- BRETELLE - DOULLENS - BOUQUEMAISON - LE SOUICH.

2. The Battalion will fall in facing East in the main street, head of column opposite "D" Coy's headquarters, and will be ready to move at 5-35 a.m.
Order of March :- H.Q. "C" "D" "A" "B" Coys.

3. There will be not more than 10 yards distance between Coys. Cookers will march with Transport.

4. DRESS:- Full Marching Order with Steel Helmets.

5. BAGGAGE. Officers Valises, Mess Baskets etc. to be ready in accordance with Standing Orders. They will be called for by Transport at Coy Headquarters.

6. Camp Kettles will be carried on Cookers.

7. Day's Rations will be carried on Cookers. Breakfast before leaving.

8. 2/Lt.H.T.CHIDGEY will remain behind for two hours to collect claims. He will also inspect billets and forward report to Orderly Room on arrival.

9. C.Q.M.S's will fall in with cycles with the Battalion, and will proceed in advance when the Battalion moves off. in order to assist in the Billeting of the Battalion.

sgd. W.G.PALMER, Lieut.& Adjt.
2/8.R.WARWICK.REGT.

Copies 1/4. Coys
5. C.O.
6. Headquarters.
7. Quartermaster & T.O.
8. R.S.M.
9. File
10. War Diary.

VII

2/8th BATTALION, THE ROYAL WARWICKSHIRE REGIMENT.

BATTALION ORDER 130 by LT.COL. [illegible] COMDG. [illegible]

The Battalion will move tomorrow [illegible] inst. by bus [illegible] to BERNEVILLE.

The Battalion will fall in, ready to move at 7 a.m. in fours, facing North, on the IVERGNY - LE SOUICH ROAD, head [illegible] yards South of Battalion Headquarters. Order of march [illegible] Coys. H.Q.

The Battalion will travel in closed lorries, each lorry holding 20 men. Officers will ride with their Platoons. Coy Commanders will attend at Headquarter Mess at 6-15 p.m. tonight to receive instructions regarding the move.

On de-bussing at BAC DU SUD on the DOULLENS - ARRAS ROAD, the Battalion will march by Coys to BERNEVILLE via BEAUMETZ-LES-LOGES. Interval of 100 yards will be maintained between Coys.

DRESS. Full Marching Order. Steel helmets will be worn.

RATIONS. Breakfast before moving. Remainder of day's rations except meat for dinner will be carried on the men. Meat for dinners and Camp Kettles will be taken to new area on first lorry and will be prepared in time for arrival of Battalion. Q.M. will arrange for one cook per Coy to travel on this lorry and one Cooker per Coy will go with Transport.

BAGGAGE. Officers valises will be stacked at Coy Headquarters at [illegible] and Mess baskets etc. at 6-30 a.m.

2/Lieut. [illegible] will remain behind after evacuation of billets to inspect same and collect claims. He will obtain certificate from Area [illegible] that the latter is satisfied with the condition in which billets, horse standings etc have been left.

C.Q.M.S's will travel with their Coys.

10. TRANSPORT.
The Transport will proceed by road. Starting Point - Cross Roads 600 yards N.E. of second N in [illegible] on the IVERGNY - [illegible] ST LEGER road. Time of passing Starting Point - 10-5 a.m. in rear of 2/7 WARWICKS.
ROUTE: [illegible] ST LEGER - [illegible] - SAULTY - LARBRET - BAC DU SUD - BEAUMETZ - BERNEVILLE.
Distance of 100 yards will be maintained between Transport of Units.

11. ACKNOWLEDGE.

Sgd. W.S.FARMER. Lieut.& Adjt.
2/8.WARWICKS.

Copies 1/4. Coys.
5. C.O.
6. [illegible] & T.O.
7. [illegible]
8. H.Q.Mess.
9. Headquarters.
10. File.
11. War Diary.

VIII

[illegible] Battn Royal Warwickshire Regiment

Specialist Training [illegible]

Specialists	May 26th	May 27	May 28th	May [illegible]	[illegible]
Signallers	6 - 7am 8 - 11am 9 - 10pm	8 - 11am. C & D Coys 4.30 - 7.30pm A & B	8-11 [illegible] A & B Coys [illegible] for training 4.30 - 7.30pm [illegible] C & D Coys [illegible] their Coys	[illegible]	[illegible]
Lewis Gunners	8 - 11am 4.30 - 6.30pm	8 - 11am C & D Coys 4.30 - 7.30pm A & B	8 - 11am C & D Coys 4.30 - 7.30pm [illegible] A & B Coys	8 - 11am [illegible] [illegible]	[illegible]
Rifle Grenadiers	8 - 11am 4.30 - 6.30pm	8 - 11am C & D Coys 4.30 - 7.30pm [illegible]	8 - 11am C & D Coys 4.30 - 7.30pm A & B Coys	8 - 11am [illegible] [illegible]	[illegible]
Scouts & Snipers	8 - 11am 4.30 - 6.30pm	8 - 11am C & D Coys 4.30 - 7.30pm [illegible]	8 - 11am A & B Coys 4.30 - 7.30pm A & B Coys	8 - 11am [illegible] 4.30 - [illegible]	[illegible]

[illegible] Lewis Gunners, referred to [illegible] [illegible] dated [illegible]

2ND 8TH BATTALION THE ROYAL WARWICKSHIRE REGIMENT.

APPENDIX TO TRAINING PROGRAMME.

(a). The undermentioned exercises must be carried out daily:-

(1). Rapid Loading ---- 10 minutes.

(2). Rapid Firing ---- 10 minutes.

(3). Bomb Throwing for all men ---- 10 minutes.

(4). Rapidly occupying a position and firing from it under orders of Section Leaders. 10 minutes.

(5). Gas Drill. ---- 5 minutes.

(b). Platoon training will include:-

(1). Reorganisation after casualties.

(2). Training to form any wave of the normal trench to trench attack.

(3). The method of combining Rifle Grenadiers, Lewis Guns etc. in the Attack.

(4). All points emphasised in S.S.143 (Training of a Platoon for the offensive).

(c). There are 32 targets on Range.

All men in the Battalion must fire 10 rounds deliberate and 10 rounds rapid.

All Specialists will be with their Coy's when they are on the Range.

sgd. E.J.CAIMAN. Lieut.Col.

Commdg. 2/8.R.WARWICK.REGT.

28th MAY 1917.

SECRET. IX

2ND 8TH BATTALION THE ROYAL WARWICKSHIRE REGIMENT.

BATTALION ORDER XXX BY LT.COL.E.C.CAIMAN. COMMDG.
Wednesday 30th May 1917.

1. The enemy are reported to be about to withdraw from the trenches immediately in front of the line held by the 61st Division and Divisions on either flank.

2. It is the intention of the G.O.C.VI Corps to anticipate the enemy and to attack and capture the system of trenches held by them.

3. The 61st Division has been ordered the capture the hostile system of trenches between R.29.c.6.0. (exclusive) and R.29.b.8.1. (inclusive and to be prepared to exploit success by following up and maintaining touch with the enemy.

4. The 182nd Infantry Brigade is allotted the task of assaulting and securing the four lines of trenches known as first, second, third, and fourth objectives, the right of the attack running parallel to and 50 yards West of the WAILLY - FICHEUX road and the left to include MAUDE LANE. The front to be attacked by the Bde is approximately 400 yards.

5. 2/8.R.WARWICKS will be on the right of the Brigade front and will attack
with its right on line R.29.d.1½.5½. inclusive - MARGARET LANE inclusive
- Junc. of MARGARET LANE with MAIDENHEAD TRENCH inclusive. Its left
will be on the line R.29.d.4½.8½. - thence parallel to WAILLY - FICHEUX
road, but 150 yards east of it to R.35.b.0.7½. exclusive.

FLANK UNITS. RIGHT ---------- 9th Division.
LEFT. ---------- 2/5.WARWICKS.

6. OBJECTIVES.
There are four objectives for the Brigade, the leading Battalions will capture the first three and the Battalion in Support will then pass through them in order to assault the fourth objective.

7. The Battalion will assault, capture and consolidate the first three objectives shown on sketch attached.

8. ALLOTMENT OF FRONTAGES.

		RIGHT.	LEFT.
"A" Coy.	1st Objective.	R.29.d.1½.5½.	WAILLY - FICHEUX RD inclusive.
~~xxx~~ "	2nd Objective.	Junc. of MARGARET LANE with 2nd objective inclusive.	ditto.
	3rd Objective.	Junc. of MARGARET LANE. and 3rd Objective.	ditto.
"B" Coy.	1st Objective.	WAILLY - FICHEUX RD inclusive.	R.29.d.4½.8½.
	2nd Objective.	ditto.	R.29.d.5½.5
	3rd.Objective.	ditto.	R.29.d.6½.5.
"C" Coy.	RIGHT SUPPORT COY.		
"D" "	LEFT SUPPORT COY.		

9. METHOD OF ATTACK.
Coys in front line ("A" & "B") will each attack on a Platoon frontage
the first wave consisting of two lines. Mopping Up parties will be
provided from 2/7.WARWICKS and will operate in rear of first wave.
The second wave also consisting of two lines will be formed by the
second platoon of each assaulting Coy.

Distance between lines of	first wave.	30 yards.
....	Moppers Up.	30 "
....	2nd wave.	30 "
....	1st wave & Moppers Up.	20 "
....	Moppers Up & 2nd wave.	30 yards.

10. ASSEMBLY.

First Assembly trench.	....	First Wave and Moppers Up.
Second Assembly trench.	....	Second Wave.
Third Assembly trench.	....	Third and fourth waves.

11. TIMETABLE & BARRAGE.

The Artillery barrage will lift at ZERO on to the support line where it will remain for 5 minutes. At ZERO plus 6 it will lift and creep back 50 yards to the minutes on to the third line where it will remain till ZERO plus 21 and then creep back on to the fourth line where it will remain till ZERO plus 60.

At ZERO plus 60 the barrage will creep back and stand on a line 300 yard in advance of the fourth objective till ZERO plus 90 after which it will gradually die down.

Special Artillery fire will be directed against strong points R.29.d.5.5 and R.29.d.8½.9.

12. ACTION OF INFANTRY.

(a). The leading wave of assaulting Coys must be in position ready to assault at ZERO. They must therefore leave their assembly trenches before ZERO, the time depending on the distance they have to go.

(b). The two assaulting Coys will assault all three objectives.

(c). The first line of Moppers Up will remain in the ~~second~~ 1st objective and clear that.

The second line of the Moppers Up will remain in the 2nd objective and clear that.

The assaulting Coys will be responsible for clearing the third objective.

(d). The third wave of support Coy will go to 2nd objective and remain there.

The fourth wave of Support Coy will go to first objective and stay there.

13. LIGHT TRENCH MORTARS.

Four L.T.M's will move forward into first objective as soonas it is captured.

Two L.T.M's will be at disposal of Battalion and will be in dugouts near Battalion Headquarters. When Battalion Headquarters move these guns will move with them.

A runner from the L.T.M's will report to Battalion Headquarters one hour before ZERO.

14. MACHINE GUNS.

The M.G.Section attached to the Battalion will assemble in third Assembly trench, and will move forward to each objective after it is captured to secure the line during consolidation.

15. CONSOLIDATION.

(a). As the Support Battalion is going through the third objective there will be no need to put out an Outpost Line.

Patrols should be sent out with instructions to withdraw after the fourth objection has been taken.

(b). The actual enemy trench forming the first and second objectives will beconsolidated, but a new trench will be dug 60 to 100 yards beyond the enemy trench forming the third objective.

(c). R.E.parties have been detailed to dig strong points and O.C.Coys will render all the help they can by placing fatigue parties at their disposal, if the tactical situation permits it.

16. O.C;Coys must do everything in their power to assist Battalions and Coys on their flanks if they are held up.

18. (a). MOPPERS UP. Half a Coy 2/7.WARWICKS will be attached to each of the assaulting Coys and will come under the orders of the Coys to which they are attached.

18.(b).CARRYING PARTIES. O.C.LEFT SUPPORT & RIGHT SUPPORT COYS will each detail half a platoon for carrying up bombs, S.A.A. etc to third objective. They will leave the assembly trenches with their Coys and will draw their stores from Battalion Dump which has been established in third assembly trench.

19.COMMUNICATIONS.
(a).Battalion Headquarters will be in 3rd Assembly trench. After 2nd objective has been taken it will move forward to original German front line at about R.29.d.2.6.
(b).A separate sheet is attached showing what communications will be established, stating routes for and relays of runners.
(c).Contact patrol aeroplane will fly over at 11-20 a.m. and will call for flares. These will be lighted by leading line of Infantry only.
(d).Aeroplane call for flares is a very light fired from Aeroplane.

20.DRESS & EQUIPMENT. FIGHTING ORDER.

21.DUMPS. Brigade Dump of R.E.material, Bombs, S.A.A., rations, water, Very Lights and flares will be formed at R.29.b.2.5.
Battalion Dumps will be formed as under:-
(1). Battalion Headquarters.
(2). 3rd Assembly Trench.

22.S.O.S.Rockets will be carried by all Coys.

23.PRISONERS.
Prisoners will be passed back to Battalion Headquarters.

24.The Regimental Aid Post will be at original Battalion Headquarters in 3rd Assembly trench.

25.Coys will be in position by 10-30 a.m.

26.Watches will be synchronised by 10-30 a.m.

27.ZERO will be notified later.

28.ACKNOWLEDGE.

sgd. E.C.CADMAN. Lieut.Col.

Comdg. 2/8.R.WARWICK.REGT.

issued at 9-30 p.m.

Copies No.1/4. Coys.
5. C.O.
6. L.T.M.B.
7. M.G.Co.
8. Brigade.
9. Bn.Headquarters.
10. File.
11. War Diary.

COMMUNICATIONS IN BATTALION ATTACK.

30-5-17.

RUNNERS.

	Carry messages. From.	To
Battn.Runners.	Battn.H.Q.	Bde.H.Q. and 1st Objective.
Coy runners of Coy in 1st Objective.	Coy.H.Q.	Battn.H.Q. and 2nd Objective
Coy runners of Coy in 2nd Objective.	Coy.H.Q.	1st Objective and 3rd Objective.
Coy runners of Coy in 3rd Objective.	Coy.H.Q.	2nd Objective and 4th Objective.

Alternate routes will be chosen and used in the event of existing ones being severely shelled.

To assist runners in finding Coy Headquarters a signal shutter should be fixed with the RED surface showing somewhre near Coy Headquarters.

2. TELEPHONES.

Battalion Signallers will run out a line following the second wave and establish stations in each objective. This line will be supplemented by a second one as soonas possible.

3. VISUAL.

All Coys willcarry shutters which willbe used where the ground permits for sending code messages. If necessary messages can be transmitted from one objective to another until they reach Battalion H.Q.

At Battalion Headquarters an aeroplane shutter and ground strip will be used for sending messages to contact patrol aeroplane.

4. CODE.

Short of Ammunition.	-------	MM
Short of Bombs.	-------	YY
Lengthen Barrage.	-------	HH
Held up by Machine Guns.	-------	XX
Held up by wire.	-------	ZZ
In all the above map references should be sent.		
1st Objective taken.	-------	FOT
2nd.	-------	SOT
3rd.	-------	TOT
4th.	-------	DOT
Casualties slight.	-------	CS
..... heavy.	-------	CH
Prisoners taken.	-------	PT

In the last three if the code letters are followed by a number this will denote the numbers in each case.

Brigade in Attack

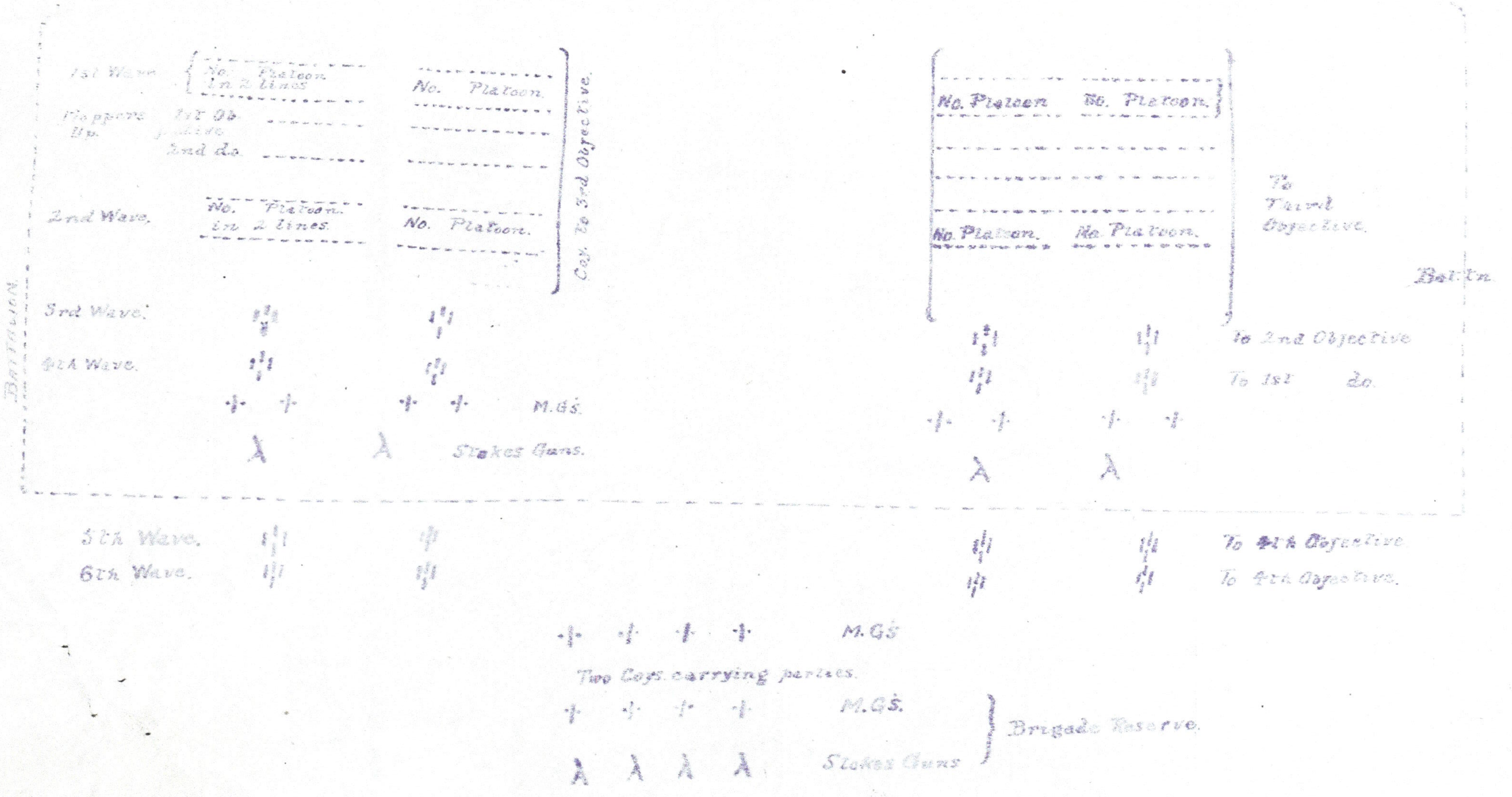

Battalion

1st Wave. No. Platoon in 2 lines — No. Platoon.

Moppers Up. 1st Objective — 2nd do.

2nd Wave. No. Platoon in 2 lines. — No. Platoon.

Coy. to 3rd Objective.

3rd Wave.

4th Wave.

M.G's.

Stokes Guns.

No. Platoon — No. Platoon.

No. Platoon. — No. Platoon.

To Third Objective.

Batt'n.

To 2nd Objective

To 1st do.

5th Wave. — To 4th Objective

6th Wave. — To 4th Objective.

M.G's

Two Coys. carrying parties.

M.G's.

Stokes Guns

Brigade Reserve.

TRAINING SCHEME FOR TRENCH ATTACK.

SECRET.

Ref. 1/20000 Sheet ARRAS S.E.
and attached sketch. May 22nd..1917.

1. The enemy are reported to be about to withdraw from the trenches immediately in front of the line held by the 61st Division and Divisions on either flank.

2. It is the intention of the G.O.C. VI Corps to anticipate the enemy and to attack and capture the system of trenches held by them.

3. The 61st Division has been ordered to capture the hostile system of trenches between R.23.c.6.0. exclusive, and R.22.b.3.8. inclusive, and to be prepared to exploit success by following up and maintaining touch with the enemy.

[illegible] BATTN. [illegible] ROYAL WARWICKSHIRE REGIMENT.

BATTALION ORDER No.000. by Lt.Col. [illegible]
20th MAY 1917.

1. The 182 INF.BDE has been ordered to capture the four lines of trenches comprised in the area shown on the attached sketch (taken from aeroplane photographs). The right of the attack running parallel to and 50 yards East of the WAILLY - FICHEUX road and the left to include [illegible] LANE at R.29.b.8.1. inclusive.

2. There will be two assaulting Battalions. The 2/6th R.WARWICKS will be on [illegible] and will be on the left of the Brigade front.
The right boundary will be a point 150 yards East of the WAILLY - FICHEUX road at R.29.[illegible].0[illegible]. and left will be at R.29.b.8.1. to include [illegible] LANE.
FLANK UNITS.
Right ------ 2/7th Battn.R.WAR.R.
Left ------ [illegible] Divisions.

3. OBJECTIVES.
There are four objectives for the Brigade, the leading Battalions will capture the first three and the Battalion in support will then pass through them in order to assault the fourth objective.

4. The Battalion will assault, capture and consolidate the three objectives as shown in sketch attached.

5. ALLOTMENT OF OBJECTIVES.

"A" Coy.	1st Objective.	From right of Battalion at R.29.d.[illegible].0[illegible]. to a point R.29.d.[illegible].8.
"B" Coy.	1st Objective.	From R.29.d.6.8. to left of Battalion front at R.29.b.8.1. inclusive.
"C" Coy.	1st Objective.	RIGHT SUPPORT.
"D"	1st Objective.	LEFT SUPPORT.
	2nd & 3rd Objectives.	No map references or sketches are available to show frontages allotted to Coys for second and third objectives, but it is presumed that these are more or less parallel to first objective.

6. METHOD OF ATTACK.
Coys in front line ("A" and "B") will each attack on a [illegible] platoon frontage the first wave consisting of two lines. Mopping up parties will be provided from Support Coys and will operate in rear of first wave. The second wave also consisting of two lines will be formed by the second Platoons of each assaulting Coy.
Distance between lines of first wave .... 50 yards.
.... Mopping Up .... [illegible]
.... second wave .... [illegible]
.... [illegible] ...... 50 [illegible]
.... between [illegible] and second [illegible] ...... [illegible]

7. [illegible].
First [illegible] trench .... First Wave and Mopping Up.
Second [illegible] .... Second Wave.
Third [illegible] .... Third and Fourth Waves.

8. ARTILLERY BARRAGE.
[illegible] barrage will lift at ZERO on to the [illegible] where it will remain for five minutes. At ZERO plus 5 it will lift and creep back 75 yards to the minute on to the [illegible] line where it will remain till ZERO plus [illegible] and then creep back on to the fourth line where it will remain till ZERO plus [illegible].
Special Artillery fire will be directed against the strong points R.29.d.5.5. and R.29.[illegible].6.[illegible].

9. ACTION OF INFANTRY.
(a). The leading wave of assaulting Coys must be in position ready to assault at ZERO. They must therefore leave their assembly trenches before ZERO, the time depending on the distance they have to go.
(b). The two assaulting Coys will assault all three objectives
(c). The first line of the Moppers Up will remain in the 1st objective to clean up.
The second line of the Moppers Up will remain in the second objective and clean that.
The assaulting Coys will be responsible for clearing the third objective.
(d). The third wave of SUPPORT COY will go to second objective and remain there.
The fourth wave of SUPPORT COY will go to first objective and stay there.

10. LIGHT TRENCH MORTARS.
Four L.T.M's will move forward into first objective as soon as it is captured.
Two L.T.M's will be at disposal of Battalion and will be in dugouts near Battalion Headquarters. When Battalion Headquarters moves these guns will move with them.
A runner from the L.T.M's will report to Battalion Headquarters one hour before ZERO.

11. MACHINE GUNS.
The M.G.Section attached to the Battalion will assemble in third assembly trench, and will move forward to each objective after it is captured to secure the line during consolidation.

12. CONSOLIDATION.
(a). As the Support Battalion is going through the third objective there will be no need to put out an Outpost Line.
Patrols should be sent out with instructions to withdraw after the fourth objective has been taken.
(b). The actual enemy trench forming the first and second objective will be consolidated, but a new trench will be dug 80 to 100 yards beyond the enemy trench forming the third objective.
(c). R.E.Parties have been detailed to dig strong points and O.C. Coys will render all the help they can by placing fatigue parties at their disposal, if the tactical situation permits it.

13. On reaching third objective flares will be lighted.

14. O.C. Left assault and O.C. Left Support Coys must do everything in their power to assist Battalion on left should it be held up.

15. FATIGUE PARTIES ETC.
(a). MOPPERS UP. O.C.Left SUPPORT Coy and O.C. Right SUPPORT Coy will each detail half a platoon to act as Moppers Up to assaulting Coys in front of them. They will march to the assembly trenches with the Coys to which they are attached for the Attack.
(b). CARRYING PARTIES. O.C.LEFT SUPPORT and RIGHT SUPPORT COYS will each detail half a Platoon, for carrying up Bombs, S.A.A. etc., to Third Objective. They will leave the assembly trenches with their Coys and will draw their stores from Battalion Dump which has been established in third assembly trench.

16. COMMUNICATION.
(a). Battalion Headquarters will be in our front line at about R.29.b.4.2. After second Objective is taken they will move forward to enemy front line.
(b). A separate sheet is attached showing what communications will be established, and stating routes for and relays of runners.

17. DRESS & EQUIPMENT. FIGHTING ORDER.

18. DUMPS. Brigade Dumps of R.E.material, Bombs, S.A.A. water, rations, Very Lights and Flares will be formed as follows:-
Adv. Dump. R.29.b.2.5.
Battn. Dumps will be formed as under:-

9. ACTION OF INFANTRY.
(a). The leading wave of assaulting Coys must be in position ready to assault at ZERO. They must therefore leave their assembly trenches before ZERO, the time depending on the distance they have to go.
(b). The two assaulting Coys will assault all three objectives
(c). The first line of the Moppers Up will remain in the 1st objective to clean up.
The second line of the Moppers Up will remain in the second objective and clean that.
The assaulting Coys will be responsible for clearing the third objective.
(d). The third wave of SUPPORT COY will go to second objective and remain there.
The fourth wave of SUPPORT COY will go to first objective and stay there.

10. LIGHT TRENCH MORTARS.
Four L.T.M's will move forward into first objective as soon as it is captured.
Two L.T.M's will be at disposal of Battalion and will be in dugouts near Battalion Headquarters. When Battalion Headquarters moves these guns will move with them.
A runner from the L.T.M's will report to Battalion Headquarters one hour before ZERO.

11. MACHINE GUNS.
The M.G.Section attached to the Battalion will assemble in third assembly trench, and will move forward to each objective after it is captured to secure the line during consolidation.

12. CONSOLIDATION.
(a). As the Support Battalion is going through the third objective there will be no need to put out an Outpost Line.
Patrols should be sent out with instructions to withdraw after the fourth objective has been taken.
(b). The actual enemy trench forming the first and second objective will be consolidated, but a new trench will be dug 60 to 100 yards beyond the enemy trench forming the third objective.
(d). R.E.Parties have been detailed to dig strong points and O.C. Coys will render all the help they can by placing fatigue parties at their disposal, if the tactical situation permits it.

13. On reaching third objective flares will be lighted.

14. O.C. Left assault and O.C. Left Support Coys must do everything in their power to assist Battalion on left should it be held up.

15. FATIGUE PARTIES ETC.
(a). MOPPERS UP. O.C.Left SUPPORT Coy and O.C. Right SUPPORT Coy will each detail half a platoon to act as Moppers Up to assaulting Coys in front of them. They will march to the assembly trenches with the Coys to which they are attached for the Attack.
(b). CARRYING PARTIES. O.C.LEFT SUPPORT and RIGHT SUPPORT COYS will each detail half a Platoon for carrying up Bombs, S.A.A. etc., to Third Objective. They will leave the assembly trenches with their Coys and will draw their stores from Battalion Dump which has been established in third assembly trench.

16. COMMUNICATION.
(a). Battalion Headquarters will be in the front line at about R.29.b.4.2½ After second Objective is taken they will move forward to enemy front line.
(b). A separate sheet is attached showing what communications will be established, and stating routes for and relays of runners.

17. DRESS & EQUIPMENT. FIGHTING ORDER.

18. DUMPS. Brigade Dumps of R.E.material, Bombs, S.A.A. water, rations, Very Lights and Flares will be formed as follows:-
Adv. Dump. R.29.b.2.5.
Battn. Dumps will be formed as under:-

18. MINES (Contd).
    1. Battalion Headquarters.
    2. 3rd Assembly Trench.
    3.

19. S.O.S. Rockets will be carried by all Coys.

20. PRISONERS.
    Prisoners will be passed back to Battalion Headquarters.

21. MEDICAL ARRANGEMENTS.
    The Regimental Aid Post will be at Battalion Headquarters in R.29.b.4.2.

22. Coys will be in position by 12 noon. ZERO will be notified later. Watches will be synchronised at 11-35 a.m.

23. ACKNOWLEDGE.

Issued at 2-30 p.m.

(Sgd.) E.C. CALMAN. Lieut.Colonel.
Commdg. 2/8.R.WARWICK.REGT.

Copies 1/4. Coys.
5. C.O.
6. Brigade.
7. T.M.B.
8. M.G.Coy
9. Headquarters. 2/8.
10. War Diary.
11. File.

COMMUNICATIONS IN BATTALION ATTACKS

SECRET.

1. RUNNERS.

	(Carry Messages)	
	From	To
Battn Runners	Battn.H.Q.	Bde.H.Q. & 1st Objective.
Coy Runners of Coy in First Objective.	Coy.Hdqrs.	Battn.H.Q. & 2nd Objective.
Coy Runners of Coy in Second Objective.	Coy.Hdqrs.	1st Objective and 3rd Objective.
Coy Runners of Coy in 3rd Objective.	Coy Hdqrs.	2nd Objective and 4th Objective.

Alternate routes will be chosen and used in the event of existing ones being severely shelled.

To assist runners in finding Coy Headquarters a Signal shutter should be fixed with the RED surface showing somewhere near Coy Headquarters.

2. TELEPHONE.

Battalion Signallers will run out a line following the second wave and establish stations in each objective, this line will be supplemented by a second one as soon as possible.

3. VISUAL.

All Companies will carry shutters which will be used where the ground permits for sending code messages. If necessary messages can be transmitted from one objective to another until they reach Battalion Headquarters.

At Battalion Headquarters an aeroplane shutter and ground strip will be used for sending messages to contact patrol aeroplane.

4. CODE.

Short of Ammunition.	------	NN
Short of Bombs.	------	YY
Lengthen barrage.	------	HH
Held up by Machine Guns.	------	XX
Held up by wire.	------	ZZ

In all the above map references should be sent.

1st Objective taken.	------	FOT
2nd	------	SOT
3rd	------	TOT
4th	------	FOT
Casualties slight.	------	CS
..... heavy.	------	CH
Prisoners taken	------	PT

* In the last three if the code letters are followed by a number this will denote the numbers in each case.

14 H 12

Confidential

Vol 14

War Diary of:-

2/8th Battalion The Royal Warwickshire Regt.

Volume XIV

Period:-

June 1/17 to:-

June 30/17

* 2/8th BATTALION *
ORDERLY ROOM
1 - JUL 1917
No. 801/17
THE ROYAL WARWICKSHIRE REGT.

Instructions regarding War Diaries and Intelligence Summaries are contained in F. S. Regs., Part II. and the Staff Manual respectively. Title pages will be prepared in manuscript.

WAR DIARY
or
~~INTELLIGENCE SUMMARY.~~
(Erase heading not required.)

Army Form C. 2118.

Place	Date	Hour	Summary of Events and Information	Remarks and references to Appendices
	1917			
BERNEVILLE	1st June	9am	Battalion moved to barracks (SCHRAMM BARRACKS) in ARRAS. Battalion arrived 11-40 am.	App. I
			Barrack rooms and officers billets very dirty. Transport moved to ACHICOURT	[illegible]
ARRAS	2nd June		Cleaning up barrack-rooms and billets. Cleaning up equipment etc } Inspection	
			by Company Commanders. Hostile aircraft dropped bombs on town of ARRAS (night)	[illegible]
ARRAS	3rd June		Rest Day. Church parade service at ST. GEORGES SOLDIERS CLUB at 11.30 am.	
			Companies bathed between 4 pm and 8 pm. Further night bombing by hostile aircraft.	[illegible]
ARRAS	4th June		Training as per Training Programme. Lt. B.K. PARSONS returned from leave.	[illegible]
ARRAS	5th June		Half battalion inoculated. Remainder training according to training programme.	
			Lt. Col. Cadman awarded D.S.O. (London Gazette 4th June 1917)	[illegible]
ARRAS	6th June		Remainder of Battalion inoculated. Captain R.B. GIBBINS rejoined from 2/7th R. War. R.	[illegible]
ARRAS	7th June		Working party of 100 supplied to RE for work at RITZ DUMP.	
			Captain T.E. LEFROY rejoined from IV CORPS SCHOOL. Attached 2/7th R. War. R.	[illegible]
ARRAS	8th June		Training according to Training Programme. 2nd. LIEUT. CHIDGEY proceeded on	App II
			leave.	[illegible]
ARRAS	9 June		Training according to Programme. Lt. FORMER and 2 O.R. returned from leave	[illegible]
ARRAS	10 June		Rest day. Church parade. 66 [illegible] all officers in musketry at 2 pm 2Lt GUNTER & 1 O.R. from Corps Signalling School	[illegible]

T2134. Wt. W708–776. 500000. 4/15. Sir J. C. & S.

WAR DIARY
or
INTELLIGENCE SUMMARY.
(Erase heading not required.)

Army Form C. 2118.

Instructions regarding War Diaries and Intelligence Summaries are contained in F. S. Regs., Part II. and the Staff Manual respectively. Title pages will be prepared in manuscript.

Place	Date	Hour	Summary of Events and Information	Remarks and references to Appendices
	1917 June			
DUISANS	11	6.30am	Batt marched to huts at DUISANS - huts in bad condition and sanitary state unsatisfactory	App 3
			2 Lt GILDERTHORPE and Sgt RAY to Bde Bombing School as Instructors - 2 Rifle Grenade Sections	
			to Bde Bombing School for 4 day course	WR.
Do	12	10am.	C.O. attended Divisional Exercise. Training per Programme - B.G.C. inspected Batt at	
			3.45pm. Draft of 3 O.R. from Base (casuals)	WR.
Do.	13		Platoon & Coy Training. 11.30 am B.G.C. returned to offices on command - 2 Lt PHIPPS & 1 O.R. to	
			VI Corps Inf School	WR.
Do.	14		Platoon & Coy Training - Bde Bombing Course commenced - 18 O.R. (Rifle Bombers)	WR.
Do.	15	6-7am	& 9-11 am Platoon & Coy Training - 5 pm Batt marched to Field Firing Range ACHICOURT and bivouaced	App 4
			there for the night	WR.
Do.	16	6 am	Field Firing - 5 pm Batt returned to camp - 6 O.R. returned from Traffic Control ARRAS	WR.
Do.	17	9.30am	Batt Church Parade - [16th 2 Lt TOSLAND proceeded on leave	WR.
Do.	18	6 am	Training as per programme -	WR.
Do.	19		Brigade Horse Show & sports at WAGONLIEU. L/Sgt WARD to VI Corps Bombing Course	WR.
Do.	20		Draft of 8 O.R. (casuals) New Rifle Bombing Squad to Bde Bombing Course -	
		6 am	Training as per programme - Platoon & Coy work.	WR.

T.2134. Wt. W708-776. 500000. 4/15. Sir J. C. & S.

Instructions regarding War Diaries and Intelligence Summaries are contained in F. S. Regs., Part II. and the Staff Manual respectively. Title pages will be prepared in manuscript.

WAR DIARY
or
INTELLIGENCE SUMMARY.
(Erase heading not required.)

Army Form C. 2118.

Place	Date	Hour	Summary of Events and Information	Remarks and references to Appendices
	1917			
DUISANS Camp No 3	June 21	6am	Coy & Platoon training per programme. Sgt FINNEMORE to 3rd Army Corps School, ALBERT	
		10.30a	C.O. held Staff ride for Coy Commanders. 11 am Batt bathed. Bde orders for transport received	W.R. App 5
Do	22	6am	Coy & Platoon training per programme. C.O. visited VI Corps School with B.G.C. 2/Lt CHIDGEY &	
		10 R.	from leave. Lecture to all officers by Major PENBERTHY on Scouts in the attack. Bde orders for Batt move to FONTAINE received.	W.R.
		3.30a	Transport moved by route march to REBREUVIETTE.	W.R.
Do	23	7.30a	Batt embussed and proceeded to ERQUIERES - from there by march route to FONTAINE arriving 11.30am. Billets good. 2Lt CLAYDON & 1 O.R. proceeded on leave. 4 Cpl IMRIE on VI Corps L.G. Course.	App. VI W.R.
FONTAINE	24	-	Sunday. rest day - 8am. C.O. went by motor car with Staff Capt to inspect billets at DUISANS	
		11am	C.O's Conference with B.G.C. at VACQUERIETTE	W.R.
Do	25		Specialist training - Remainder training under Coy arrangements - 2 Rifle grenade sections to Bde Bombing School - 1 O.R. from leave (extension). LT MIDDLETON reported from Div.	W.R.
Do	26		Specialist training - Coy training - 2/Lt WOOLDRIDGE & 26 O.R. to Bde Sniping School - 2Lt TEDCOP & 4 O.R. to Bde. P & B.T. Course. Com Officer held Conference, all Officers.	

Instructions regarding War Diaries and Intelligence Summaries are contained in F. S. Regs., Part II. and the Staff Manual respectively. Title pages will be prepared in manuscript.

WAR DIARY
or
INTELLIGENCE SUMMARY.
(Erase heading not required.)

Army Form C. 2118.

Place	Date	Hour	Summary of Events and Information	Remarks and references to Appendices
	1917			
FONTAINE L'ETALON	June 27		Specialist training – Remainder under C.O. Coy. –	
		10am	Tactical Exercise without troops for all Officers under C.O.	W.P.
D°	28		Specialist training – Coy Training – 11am Batt Parade under C.O. – 2Lt TOLLAND retd from leave – Draft of 6 O.R. – Canals	W.P.
D°	29	9am-12noon 5-7pm	C.O's inspection of "B" Coy in all branches of training – Other Coys – Coy & platoon training	W.P.
D°	30	9-12noon 5-7pm	C.O's inspection of "A" Coy in all branches of training – Other Coys – Coy & platoon training	
			2Lt WATSON & 1 O.R. on leave – Capt T. MUNGLE to Coy Commanders L.G. Course LE TOUQUET	
			1 O.R. to 3rd Army T.M. School. 18 O.R. from Rifle Bombing Course	W.P.

G. C. Cadman [signature]
Lieut. Col.,
Comdg. 2/8 R. War. R.

T2134. Wt. W708–776. 500000. 4/15. Sir J. C. & S.

App. I

[illegible] BATTALION [illegible] REGIMENT.

BATTALION ORDER [illegible] by [illegible]

1. The Battalion will move to [illegible] (North) [illegible]

2. ROUTE: [illegible] ROAD - [illegible]

3. Billeting Parties will proceed in advance of the Battalion to ARRAS (North) by bicycles leaving [illegible] and [illegible] report at ARRAS to 2/Lieut. [illegible]

4. The Battalion will parade in mass [illegible] at [illegible] a.m. [illegible] North East end of [illegible], on North [illegible] side of the [illegible].

5. DRESS. Full Marching Order - Steel Helmets will be worn.

6. The following distances will be maintained on the march: 250 yards between Battalions. 100 yards between Coys and other Units, [illegible] last Coy and transport.
[illegible] East of ARRAS a distance of 200 yards will always be maintained between Platoons and [illegible]

7. TRANSPORT will be drawn up on the [illegible] ROAD, clear of the village and will [illegible] Battalion [illegible]

8. ORDER OF MARCH: H.Q. "D" "A" "B" "C" Coys. Transport.

9. 2/Lt. [illegible] will remain behind to [illegible]
[illegible] will [illegible] certificates will be rendered to [illegible] in the usual manner.

10. O.C. "D" Coy will detail a fatigue party of [illegible] to report to an Officer of the [illegible]

11. The G.O.C. has decided that [illegible] will [illegible] from the left shoulder [illegible] on the right side of the [illegible].

Issued at [illegible]

[illegible] 2/Lt. & A/Adjt.
[illegible]

Copies 1/4. Coys.
5. C.O.
6. Headquarters.
7. R.Q.M.
8. Files.
9. War Diary.

APP 11

2/8th Bn. Royal Warwickshire Regiment.

Training Programme.

A. General Training

Coy.	[illegible] 4th.		[illegible] 5th		[illegible] 6th	
	Time		Time		Time	
"A"	a.m. 7–9 9–11	Range. Musketry.	a.m. 8–11 p.m. 4.30–6.30	Platoon Training Musketry.	a.m. 8–11. p.m. 6.30–8.30	Musketry, Bayonet fighting etc. Range.
"B"	9–11. p.m. 4.30–6.30	Range Musketry.		As for "A" Coy.	a.m. 8–11. p.m. 4.30–6.30	Musketry, Bayonet fighting etc. Range
"C"	a.m. 9–11 p.m. 4.30–6.30	Musketry Range	a.m. 9–11. p.m. 5–8.	Musketry. Platoon Training	a.m. 9–11. p.m. 4.30–7.30	Range. Musketry, Bayonet fighting etc.
"D"	9–11. p.m. 6.30–8.30	Musketry. Range.		As for "C" Coy.	7–9 p.m. 4.30–7.30	Range. Musketry, Bayonet fighting etc.

Lectures for N.C.O.'s on Map Reading, Disc[illegible]ine etc. to be arranged by Company Comma[illegible]rs. One hour at Coy. Cmdr's disposal.

B. Specialist Training

Specialist	June 4th.	June 5th.	June 6th.	Specialist.	All days.
SIGNALLERS.	a.m. 8–11 p.m. 5–7	a.m. 8–11 p.m. 5–7	a.m. 8–11 p.m. 5–7.	BOMBERS.	1 section per Company under Brigade arrangements.
LEWIS GUNNERS.	a.m. 8–11 p.m. 5–7	a.m. 8–11 p.m. 5–7	a.m. 8–11 p.m. 5–7.	SCOUTS.	These will be trained under Company arrangements.

(1) Lewis Gunners above are those who have already started a course. The L.G. Officer hopes to complete their training, including firing, [illegible] 6th inst.

(2) Signa[illegible] Company includ[illegible] 4 runners.

C. Appendix

(1) Musketry The greater part of time available for training has been devoted to musketry. As the Brigade will ~~practically~~ probably remain where it is for 10 days, it is hoped to put everyone through an elem[illegible]ry course.

(2) Bayonet fighting S.M. Macdonald will be available on 6th inst.

June. 3. 1917.

Lieut. Col.
Cmdg. 2/8 R. War. R.

APP. 2

2nd 8th Battalion The Royal Warwickshire Regt
General Training

June 8th	June 9th	June 10th	June 11th
"A" Coy. 8-11 am Platoon Training Musketry 5-7 pm On 50x Range "B" Coy. 7-9 am On 200x Range 4.30-7.30 pm Musketry + Platoon Trng "C" Coy. 9-11 am On 200x Range. 4.30-7 pm Musketry + Platoon Trng. "D" Coy. 8-10.30 am On 50x Range 4.30 to 7 pm Musketry + Platoon Training.	"A" Coy. 7-9 am On 50x Range. 4.30-7.30 pm Musketry + Platoon Trng "B" Coy. 9-11 am On 50x Range. 4.30-7.30 pm Musketry + Platoon Trng. "C" Coy. 8-11 am Musketry + Platoon Trng 4.30-6.30 pm On 50x Range. "D" Coy. 8-11 am Musketry + Platoon Trng 6-30-8.30 pm On 50x Range	"A" Coy. 8-10.30 am. On 50x Range 4.30-7 pm. Musketry + Platoon Trng "B" Coy. 9-11 am On 50x Range 4.30-7 pm Musketry + Platoon Trng. "C" Coy. 7-9 am On 50x Range 4.30-7.30 pm Musketry + Platoon Trng "D" Coy. 8-11 am. Platoon Training Musketry 5-7 pm. On. 50x Range	"C" Coy. 8-10.30 am. On 50x Range 4.30-7 pm Musketry Platoon Training "B" Coy 9-11 am On 50x Range 4.30-7 pm. Musketry Platoon Training "A" Coy. 7-9 am On 50x Range 4.30-7.30 pm Musketry + Platoon Training "D" Coy. 8-11 am. Platoon Training Musketry 5-7 pm On 50x Range
June 12th	**June 13th.**	**June 14th**	
"A" Coy. 8-10.30 am On 50x Range. 4.30-7 pm. Musketry + Platoon Trng. "B" Coy. 9-11 am. On 200x Range. 4.30-7 pm. Musketry + Platoon Trng "C" Coy. 7-9 am On 200x Range. 4.30-7.30 pm Musketry + Platoon Trng. "D" Coy. 8-11 am. Platoon Trng. Musketry 5-7 pm On 50x Range	"A" Coy. 9-11 am. On. 50x Range. 4.30-7.30 pm. Musketry + Platoon Trng. "B" Coy. 7-9 am. On 50x Range. 4.30-7.30 pm. Musketry + Platoon Trng. "C" Coy. 8-11 am. Musketry + Platoon Trng. 6.30-8.30 pm On. 50x Range "D" Coy. 8-11 am Musketry + Platoon Trng 4.30-6.30 pm On. 50x Range	"A" Coy. 7-9 am On 50x Range. 4.30-7.30 pm Musketry + Platoon Trng. "B" Coy. 9-11 am On 50x Range. 4.30-7.30 pm Musketry + Platoon Trng. "C" Coy. 8-11 am. Musketry + Platoon Trng. 4.30-6.30 pm. On 50x Range. "D" Coy. 8-11 am Musketry + Platoon Trng 6-30-8.30 pm. On 50x Range	

(1) Platoon training includes. Fire Control + Fire Discipline. Attention will also be given to Platoons in Attack as laid down in F.S.R.
(2) Lectures by Company Commanders. – suggested subjects "Map Reading", "The Attack" &c.
(3) The C.O will lecture on "Military Etiquette" at a date to be notified later.
(4) During the week the B.G.C. hopes to be able to lecture to all Officers on "Command".

6th June 1917.

Sgd E. C. Cadman Lieut Col.
Commdg 2/8 R. WAR R.

2ND 8TH BATTALION THE ROYAL WARWICKSHIRE REGIMENT.

BATTALION ORDER 134 by LT.COL.E.C.CADMAN. D.S.O. Commdg.
10th June 1917.

APP. B

1. The Battalion will march tomorrow to Huts at DUISANS.

2. ROUTE: ARRAS - ST.POL ROAD,

3. ORDER OF MARCH. H.Q. "D" "A" "B" "C" Coys.
A distance of 200 yards will be maintained between Platoons till out of ARRAS and thereafter 100 yards between Coys.

4. TIME. The Battalion will fal in in mass facing West in Barrack Square at 6-25 a.m.
DRESS: Full Marching Order - Steel Helmets will be worn.

5. TRANSPORT. Transport will move separately and will pass cross roads 500 yards N.E. of T in ACHICOURT on ACHICOURT - ARRAS ROAD at 6-45 a.m. and will march by route DAINVILLE - WAGNONLIEU to DUISANS.
Cookers, Watercarts, and Medical Cart will proceed with Transport.

6. A/Transport Officer will arrange to send horses to remove these at 5-45 a.m.

7. Officers Kits, Mess Baskets etc. will be collected in accordance with Battalion Standing Orders.

8. REAR PARTY. O.C."A" Coy will detail 1 Officer to remain behind. The Officer will report to the Adjutant for instructions before the Battalion moves off.

9. ACKNOWLEDGE.

sgd. W.S.FARMER. Lt.&.Adjt.
2/8.R.WARWICK.REGT.

Copies	1/4.	Coys.
	5.	C.O.
	6.	H.Q.
	7.	H.Q.Mess.
	8.	Q.M.&.T.O.
	9.	File.
	10.	War Diary.

APP IV

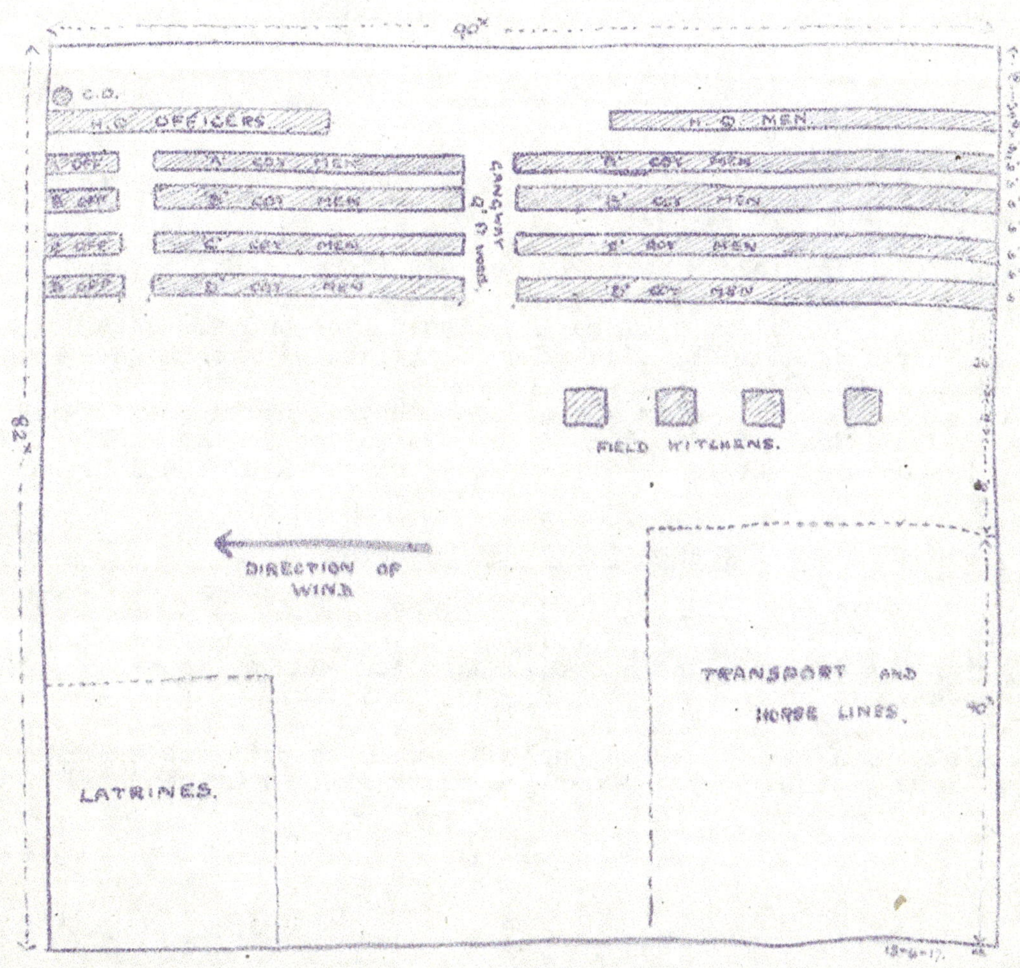

PLAN OF BIVOUAC. Scale: 1" represents 10x.

Note. Each bivouac is approximately 8' x 6'. About 26 shelters per Coy. will be needed: 1 foot [illegible] space between each bivouac will be allowed.

TACTICAL SCHEME FOR COY COMMANDERS OF THE 2/8. BATTALION.

THE ROYAL WARWICKSHIRE REGIMENT.

APP V

Ref. Map. 51c. 1/40000.

1. 182nd Inf.Bde. is moving as advance guard of the 61st Division and is advancing along road running from DUISANS to L.14.d.[illegible].0.
Other troops are on either flank.

2. The B.G.C. decides that the main body will rest at DUISANS and that Outposts are to be put out.

3. The boundaries of the Brigade are as under:-
RIGHT. Line drawn from wood in L.26.d. to L.13.central both inclusive.
LEFT. DAINVILLE - WAGNONLIEU - DUISANS road inclusive.

Company Commanders will bear in mind the following points when making their decisions.

(I). It will take **2** hours to get additional artillery and substancial reinforcements into action.
(2). One Battalion will be in Outpost Line and two Battalions in the BROWN LINE. The other Battalion of the Brigade will be at DUISANS.
(3). Four Machine Guns are at the disposal of Outpost Battalion and four at disposal of each Battalion in the BROWN LINE.
(4). One Brigade of Artillery is at disposal of 182nd Brigade.

QUESTIONS TO BE ANSWERED.

1. Where would you select the BROWN LINE?
2. Where would you select the OUTPOST LINE?
3. After the Outpost Line has been selected and Coy frontages allotted where would you select your Picquet positions?

As much information as possible will be put into sketches which will be sent in to the Orderly Room by all Coy Commanders.

20-6-17.

APP VI

2ND 8TH BATTALION THE ROYAL WARWICKSHIRE REGIMENT.

BATTALION ORDER 134 BY LT.COL.E.C.CADMAN. D.S.O. COMMANDING.
22nd JUNE 1917.

1. The Battalion will proceed by Motor Bus to ERQUIERES tomorrow, and thence by march route to FONTAINE.

2. Battalion will fall in in mass on Battalion Parade Ground ready to move at 6.40 a.m.
DRESS: Full marching order. Steel Helmets on pack.

3. The Battalion will be carried on 28 Motor Lorries, each holding 20 men, the lorries being in groups of six with interval of 25 yards between each group. Head of group of lorries carrying Battalion will be at L.7.c.2.9.
2/Lt.CHIDGEY will proceed in advance of the Battalion to the embussing place and will direct the embussing. Two men per Coy will report to 2/LT.CHIDGEY at Battalion Headquarters at 6.30 a.m. to act as markers. These men will not return to the Camp again.

4. LEWIS GUNS. Lewis Guns in chests will be carried in rear of each Coy, they will be dumped at ERQUIERES on arrival and a guard placed over them. "B" Coy will provide the Guard and the Corporal in charge will report to the R.S.M. after de-bussing for instructions.

5. RATIONS. Rations for 23rd will be carried on the man. Water Bottles will be filled before starting.

6. ACKNOWLEDGE.

7. Officers' valises will be handed in at Q.M.Stores by 6 a.m.

sgd. W.S.FARMER. Lt.&.Adjt.
2/8 WARWICKS.

Copies 1/4. Coys.
5. C.O.
6. Headquarters.
7. R.S.M.
8. File
9. War Diary.
10. Quartermaster.

15H 15

Confidential.

War Diary of:

2/8th Batt: The Royal Warwickshire Regt.

Volume XV

W 15
31 JUL 1917
93/17.

Period:
July 1/17.
to July 31/17.

Instructions regarding War Diaries and Intelligence Summaries are contained in F. S. Regs., Part II. and the Staff Manual respectively. Title pages will be prepared in manuscript.

WAR DIARY
or
INTELLIGENCE SUMMARY.
(Erase heading not required.)

Army Form C. 2118.

Place	Date	Hour	Summary of Events and Information	Remarks and references to Appendices
FONTAINE L'ETALON	1917 July 1		Sunday – Brigade Church parade cancelled owing to rain. R.C. service in morning – C of E voluntary service 6pm – 18 O.R. from Bde Bombing Course	WR
Do	2	9am	All day inspection of B Coy by C.O. in all branches of training – Other Coys preparation for Platoon training Competition – Scouts under 2Lt WOOLDRIDGE – 4 O.R. to Bde Signal Course – 1 Off & 4 O.R. to Bde P. & B.T. Course	WR
Do	3	9am	All day inspection of D Coy by C.O. 10am F.G.C.M. on Sgt CARTWRIGHT F. 6pm Lecture to N.C.Os by C.R.E. at VALQUERIETTE. Other Coys Platoon Training. Cinema opened	WR
Do	4	9am	Batt in wood fighting – C.O. inspected Band, Drivers & Transport – 5pm Coy training. Draft of 26 O.R. arrived – 2Lt PROSSER retd from VI Corps Bombing School – L/Cpl WARD for VI Corps Bombing Course	WR
Do	5		2 O.R. to Divl Signal Course	
		9am	Inter Platoon Competition – Won by B Coy for All branches of training. Won by A Coy for Coy H.Q.	App I WR
Do	6		Major WHATMORE proceeded to England to Batt Commanders Course, Aldershot	
		9am	Coy training 11am B Coy represented Batt at Brigade Coy Open Fighting Competition	
		5.30pm	Interplatoon Cross country race – Brigade Major – 10 per Platoon	WR

T2134. Wt. W708—776. 500000. 4/15. Sir J. C. & S.

Instructions regarding War Diaries and Intelligence Summaries are contained in F. S. Regs., Part II. and the Staff Manual respectively. Title pages will be prepared in manuscript.

WAR DIARY
or
INTELLIGENCE SUMMARY.
(Erase heading not required.)

Army Form C. 2118.

Place	Date	Hour	Summary of Events and Information	Remarks and references to Appendices
	1917			
FONTAINE	July 7	6.30 am	Batt parade – Batt marched to WAIL – 9.15 am Batt wood fighting in presence of B.G.C. LT. MIDDLETON & 4 O.R. from Bde P.T. & B.T. Course – C.O. Pres. of F.G.C.M. at QUOEUX	W.B.
Do	8	11.10 a	Bde. parade church service at ERQUIERES. 2.30 pm Bde Sports at ERQUIERES. 6.30 pm B.G.C. conference with all officers – Draft of 50 O.R. arrived. Draft of 26 inspected by B.G.C.	W.B.
Do	9	9 am	Batt marched to WAIL. 9 am Tactical scheme there under B.G.C. 8 pm Divisional Follies performed in CHATEAU grounds – 15 O.R. transferred to 251 Employment Coy Labour Corps	W.B.
Do	10		Divisional Sports – Holiday – Capt MUNGLE returned from L.G. Course – Capt. DONALD MACKINTOSH, Non C of S Chaplain arrived	W.B.
Do	11	6 am	Running drill – 9 am Coy training. Drafts of 50 & 26 attached to Coys & fully trained – Draft of 17 O.R. arrived (1 casual) 9 pm – 11 pm Night operations taking up outpost line by night. 2LT PHIPPS from II Corps Infantry School.	W.B.
Do	12	6 am	Running Drill 9 am – 11 am. 5–7 pm Platoon & Coy training – musketry & firing on range.	W.B.
Do	13	6 am	Running Drill 9–11 a. 5–7 pm Coys trench to trench attack & Open Fighting – 2 pm Junior Officers & CSMs compass work & reconnaissance under Batt Intel Officer – 2LT PROSSER & 10 R proceeded on leave. 3 pm C.O. attended Bde Conference. 2LT WATSON returns from leave	W.B.
Do	14	11 am	Each Coy in turn – Open Fighting scheme at WAIL Training Area under C.O. – Capt S.E. PARSONS	W.B.

T2134. Wt. W708–776. 500000. 4/15. Sir J. C. & S.

Army Form C. 2118.

Instructions regarding War Diaries and Intelligence Summaries are contained in F. S. Regs., Part II. and the Staff Manual respectively. Title pages will be prepared in manuscript.

WAR DIARY
or
INTELLIGENCE SUMMARY.
(Erase heading not required.)

Place	Date	Hour	Summary of Events and Information	Remarks and references to Appendices
FONTAINE L'ETALON	1917 July 14		on F.G.C.M. at QUOENX - LT PHIPPS and 2 LT CHIDGEY attended for instruction - LT MIDDLETON to Hosp. - 2 LT LLOYD & 4 O.R from Bde P & B.T. Course. LT PHIPPS & 9 O.R on leave	W.M.
Do	15		Sunday - Church parade 10am on 7th R. War R. Range near QUOENX - 2 LT KITCHIN & draft of 104 O.R. (1 casual) reported from Base - Sgt WATTS to 3rd Army Musketry School - 2 LT JESSOP & 5 O.R to Bde Scouting Course. 2 LT BEVAN & 4 O.R to Bde P & B.T. Course	W.M.
Do	16	6a	Running Drill - 9-11 am - 5-7 pm Coy training - Specialist training of new drafts	
		10am	B.G.C. inspected draft received yesterday - Sgt FINNIEMORE retd from 3rd Army Cooking School, ALBERT. 4 O.R per platoon on Tunnelling Course under R.E. at FONTAINE - 1 O.R retd from leave - 5 O.R. from Bde employ.	W.M.
Do	17	5.45a	Batt marched to WAIL Training Area & took part in Bde Trench to Trench Attack 2 LT HODGSON retd from leave - 5-7 pm Coy Training & Specialist training	App. 2 W.M.
Do	18	6am	Running Drill 9-11 am - 5-7 pm Coy & Platoon training - Divnl. Horse Races at WILLEMAN	W.M.
Do	19	6a	Running Drill - 9-11 am - 5-7 pm Coy training - Training of reserve specialists - 3pm Bde stage of Stretcher Bearers Comp. won by Batt team at WAIL	W.M.

T2134. Wt. W708-776. 500000. 4/15. Sir J. C. & S.

Instructions regarding War Diaries and Intelligence Summaries are contained in F. S. Regs., Part II. and the Staff Manual respectively. Title pages will be prepared in manuscript.

WAR DIARY
or
INTELLIGENCE SUMMARY.
(Erase heading not required.)

Army Form C. 2118.

Place	Date	Hour	Summary of Events and Information	Remarks and references to Appendices
FONTAINE L'ETALON	1917 July 20	9am	Inspection of Batt. by B.G.C. – 2pm Batt Sports & Concert at night	WB
Do	21	8.30am	Batt marched to WAIL and practised Trench Attack – 5-7pm Coy training. 2LT GILDERTHORP and 9 O.R. proceeded on leave. Advance orders for move received – 2LT JESSOP & 8 O.R. returned from Bde Scouting Course & 2LT BEVAN and 4 O.R. from Bde L.T.M. B.T. Course – Draft of 34 (plus 2 casuals) OR arrived	App. 3 WB
Do	22	Sunday	Church parade 9.30am – Lecture on Esprit de Corps by Capt MACKINTOSH, CF. at 5.30pm	WB
Do	23	6am	Running Drill – 9-11am 5-7pm Coy training – All Coys practised Wood to Wood attack with smoke barrage – All new drafts through live bombs – Bde Orders for move recd	WB
Do	24	6.5am	Batt marched to BONNIERES – arriving 10.30am – Day very hot – Billets good –	App 4
BONNIERES			C.O. visited Training Schools ETAPLES under Bde arrangements	WB
Do	25	3.20pm	Batt marched to FREVENT (less A (Coy)) and entrained 6.20pm. Arrived BAVINCHOVE Station CASSEL 9.50pm – Marched to billets RUBROUCK area. Arrived 4am. Billets good but very scattered – A Coy left behind	App. 5 WB
RUBROUCK	26	A Coy	entrained 2.20am – arrived RUBROUCK 4pm – Day spent resting – 2LT PROSSER returned from leave	WB
Do	27	9.30am	Latest draft had gas appliances inspected by Bde Gas N.C.O. Training of new specialists – Other training under Coy arrangements – Draft of 101 O.R. reported 11.30pm. 1 OR retd from leave	WB

T2134. Wt. W708—776. 500000. 4/15. Sir J. C. & S.

Instructions regarding War Diaries and Intelligence Summaries are contained in F. S. Regs., Part II. and the Staff Manual respectively. Title pages will be prepared in manuscript.

WAR DIARY
or
INTELLIGENCE SUMMARY.
(Erase heading not required.)

Army Form C. 2118.

Place	Date	Hour	Summary of Events and Information	Remarks and references to Appendices
ROUBROUCK (HOFLAND)	1917 July 28	6-7 am	9-12 noon – 5-7 pm – Coy training – 2pm C.O.s inspection of new draft. 1 O.R. transferred to R.F.C. 6 O.R. returned from leave. Coys reorganised to 4 Platoons each.	WM.
Do.	29		Sunday – Church parade cancelled owing to rain – Non Conf. Service in Barn at H.Q. 1 Off & 3 O.R. per Coy – at V Army Musketry School. 2LT SUTTON reported for duty. 3 O.R. from leave	WM.
Do.	30	6-7 am	9-12 noon – Coy training & Specialists – 11 am new drafts ~~for appl~~ inspected by R.F.C. – 5 pm C.O. inspected Batt & put Coys through Platoon Test of organization. Each Coy did 1 hours intensive digging – Training of 8 additional & 52 reserve Stretcher Bearers.	WM.
Do.	31	6-7 am	9-12 noon 5-7 pm Coy training – Specialists as yesterday – 9.30 am new drafts for appliances inspected – Batt bathed at Divnl Baths ERKELSBRUGGE. C.O. proceeded on leave – LT PHIPPS retd from leave.	WM.

[signature], Capt.
Comdg 2/8 R. War. R.

T2134. Wt. W708–776. 506000. 4/15. Sir J. C. & S.

App I

SUPPLEMENT TO BATTALION ORDERS BY LT.COL.E.C.CADMAN.D.S.O.

BATTALION PLATOON COMPETITION.

---

1. The Competition will take place tomorrow. The Platoon selected from each Company will parade at the M of AN^cn M^in. at 8-30 a.m.

2. The following Officers will attend as Judges:-
   (a). Lewis Gun Officer - for event 5.
   (b). Bombing Officer & SGT.RAY. for events 3 and 4.
   (c). 2nd in Command. for event 7.
   (d). One Subaltern per Coy for event 2. These will report to CAPT.SLATER who will be O.C.Firing Point.
   The Commanding Officer will judge events 1 and 6 himself.

3. Each syndicate of judges will award points as they think fit for the events for which they are judging and will send in results to Orderly Room by 3 p.m. The different maxima will then be reduced to a standard one for each event. Result will be announced as soon as possible.

4. TIMETABLE.

"A" COY. TIME.	EVENT.	"B" COY. TIME.	EVENT.
9 - 9-30.	1.	9 - 9-30.	4.
9-30 to 10.	4.	9-30 - 10.	1.
10 - 11.	2.	10 - 11 .	5.
11 - 12.	5.	11 - 12.	2.
12 - 12-30.	3.	12 - 12-30.	6 & 7.
12-30 - 1 pm.	6 & 7.	12-30 - 1 pm.	3

"C" COY. TIME.	EVENT.	"D" COY. TIME.	EVENT.
9 - 10.	2.	9 - 10.	5.
10 - 10-30.	1	10 - 10-30.	4
10-30 - 11.	4	10-30 - 11.	1
11 - 11-30.	6 & 7.	11 - 11-30.	3
11-30 - 12.	3	11-30 - 12.	6 & 7.
12 - 1. pm.	5	12 - 1 pm.	2

---

5. COMPANY HEADQUARTER CONTEST.
   (a). The Signalling Contest will take place at the same place and at the same time. The Signalling Officer will make his own arrangements. He will send in results to the Orderly Room as soon as possible after the conclusion of the Competition.
   (b). "A" Coy's Cookhouse will be inspected at 5-15 p.m. followed "B" "C" & "D" Coys. Utensils will be laid out for inspection. The Quartermaster will report to the Commanding Officer at 5.p.m. to assist in judging.

4-7-17.

sgd. W,S.FARMER. Lieut.&.Adjt.
2/8.WARWICKS.

BATTALION PLATOON COMPETITION.

1. TURN-OUT. Platoons will be inspected in Fighting Order. Points will be deducted for bad condition, fitting and dirtiness of each article of clothing and equipment.

2. MUSKETRY. (a). Each man will fire 5 rounds application at a range of 100 yards.
(b). Each man will fire 10 rounds rapid. Position - lying - rifle to be unloaded and pouch buttoned until order 'Rapid Fire' is given. Loading by 5 rounds from pouch. Time - 1 minute.
(c). One fire Order per Section given by Section Leader.

3. RIFLE BOMBERS. Every man in Platoon Rifle Bombing Section will fire three rifle Grenades at a target 150 yards Range.

Bull's Eye.	.....	10 yards circle.
Inner.	.....	15 ....
Outer.	.....	20 ....

4. BOMBERS, Every man of Platoon will throw two Dummy Bombs at an objective:-
(a). 20 yards.
(b). 30 yards.
(c). 40 yards.

5. LEWIS GUNNERS. Each team of six will fire:-
(a). Ten rounds at 100 yards Range.
(b). Each team will also strip and assemble their gun. Points will be given for speed and when the gun is stripped it will be subjected to a minute inspection.
(c). Each Platoon will furnish a team comprised entirely of Reserves who will be put through one or two simple tests.

6. BOX RESPIRATOR DRILL. Platoon will be timed in putting on Helmet from the "ALERT" position. In awarding points the general efficiency of the whole Platoon will be taken into account.

7. TACTICS. Each Section Commander will be given a simple situation and asked how he would deal with it.

NOTES:. (a). Nominal rolls of Platoons will be forwarded to Orderly Room by 9 p.m. on Wednesday July 4th.
(b). Every man on the strength of the Platoon, with the exception of those on Battalion employ, will take part in the Competition.
(c). There will be a prize of three francs per head for the winning platoon.

2nd JULY 1917.

BATTALION PLATOON COMPETITION.

1. COMPANY HEADQUARTERS CONTEST.

SIGNALLERS.

SIGNALLERS.	(1). FLAG DRILL.	Points will be given for smartness and general knowledge.
	(2). LINE RUNNING.	Run out 200 yards of wire, fix telephone at each end and send message. Points given for speed in fixing up stations and accuracy of message sent.
	(3). PICKING UP UNKNOWN STATIONS. (SHUTTER).	Points will be given for speed with which communication is established.
	(4). LAMP READING.	Points given for accuracy and filling in of message form.
COOKS.	The Field-Kitchen and Cookhouse of each Company will be inspected.	

A prize of three francs per head will be awarded to the winning Company Headquarters.

2-7-17.

App II

2nd 8TH BATTALION THE ROYAL WARWICKSHIRE REGIMENT.

BATTALION No.AAA by LT.COL.[illegible] D.S.O. Commanding.
16th JUNE 1917.

1. The Battalion will attack tomorrow: [illegible] in accordance with 182.Bde. Order No.000., copy of which is attached.

2. "A" "B" & "D" Coys will act as Moppers Up to the first and second objectives.
"C" Coy. will act as Brigade Reserve.

3. Companies will be formed up in the Assembly Trenches as follows:-

2 Coys. 2/6.WAR.			2 Coys. 2/7.WAR.		
1 Plat.	Coy.H.Q. Entrn.L.G.Sec.	1.Plat.	Bn.L.G.Sec.	1 Plt.	Bn.L.G. Sec.
1 ..	1 Platn.	1 Platn.	1.Platn.	1 Plt.	1 Plt

"C" Coy. will be formed up behind the 6th Wave (2/8.WARWICKS)

4. Companies will be in position ready to advance at 8.a.m.
At ZERO "A" "B" & "D" Coys will advance behind first wave. The first line of "A" "B" & "D" Coys will remain in the RED LINE on reaching same and act as Moppers Up there. The second line of "A" "B" & "D" Coys will go into the YELLOW LINE behind the first wave and will remain in the YELLOW Line and Act as Moppers Up.

5. At ZERO plus 40 "C" Coy will move up following 6th wave (2/8.WAR) and will occupy and secure our original front line were they will act as Brigade Reserve.

6. DRESS. As in Routine Orders.

sgd. W.B.PALMER. Lieut.& Adjt.
2/8.R.WAR.R.

Issued at 8 p.m.

BRIGADE ATTACK.

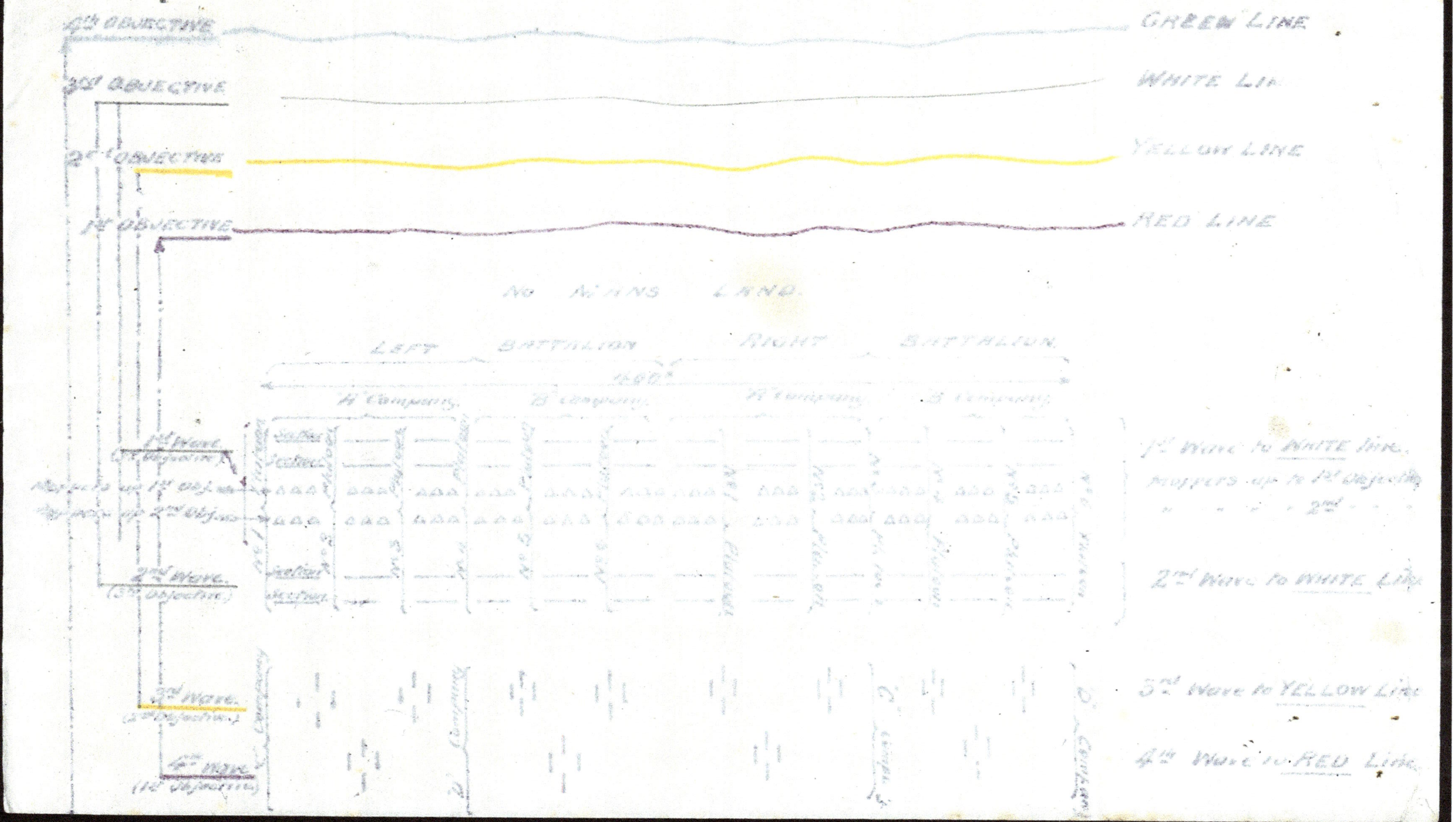

4th OBJECTIVE — GREEN LINE

3rd OBJECTIVE — WHITE LINE

2nd OBJECTIVE — YELLOW LINE

1st OBJECTIVE — RED LINE

NO MANS LAND

LEFT BATTALION — RIGHT BATTALION

400×

"A" Company — "B" Company — "A" Company — "B" Company

No 1 Platoon — No 2 Platoon — No 3 Platoon — No 4 Platoon — No 5 Platoon — No 6 Platoon — No 1 Platoon — No 2 Platoon — No 3 Platoon — No 4 Platoon — No 5 Platoon — No 6 Platoon

Section / Section — Section / Section

1st Wave (1st Objective)

Moppers up 1st Obj.

Moppers up 2nd Obj.

2nd Wave (3rd Objective)

3rd Wave (2nd Objective)

4th Wave (1st Objective)

"C" Company — "D" Company — "C" Company — "D" Company

1st Wave to WHITE Line.

Moppers up to 1st Objective

" " " " 2nd "

2nd Wave to WHITE Line

3rd Wave to YELLOW Line

4th Wave to RED Line

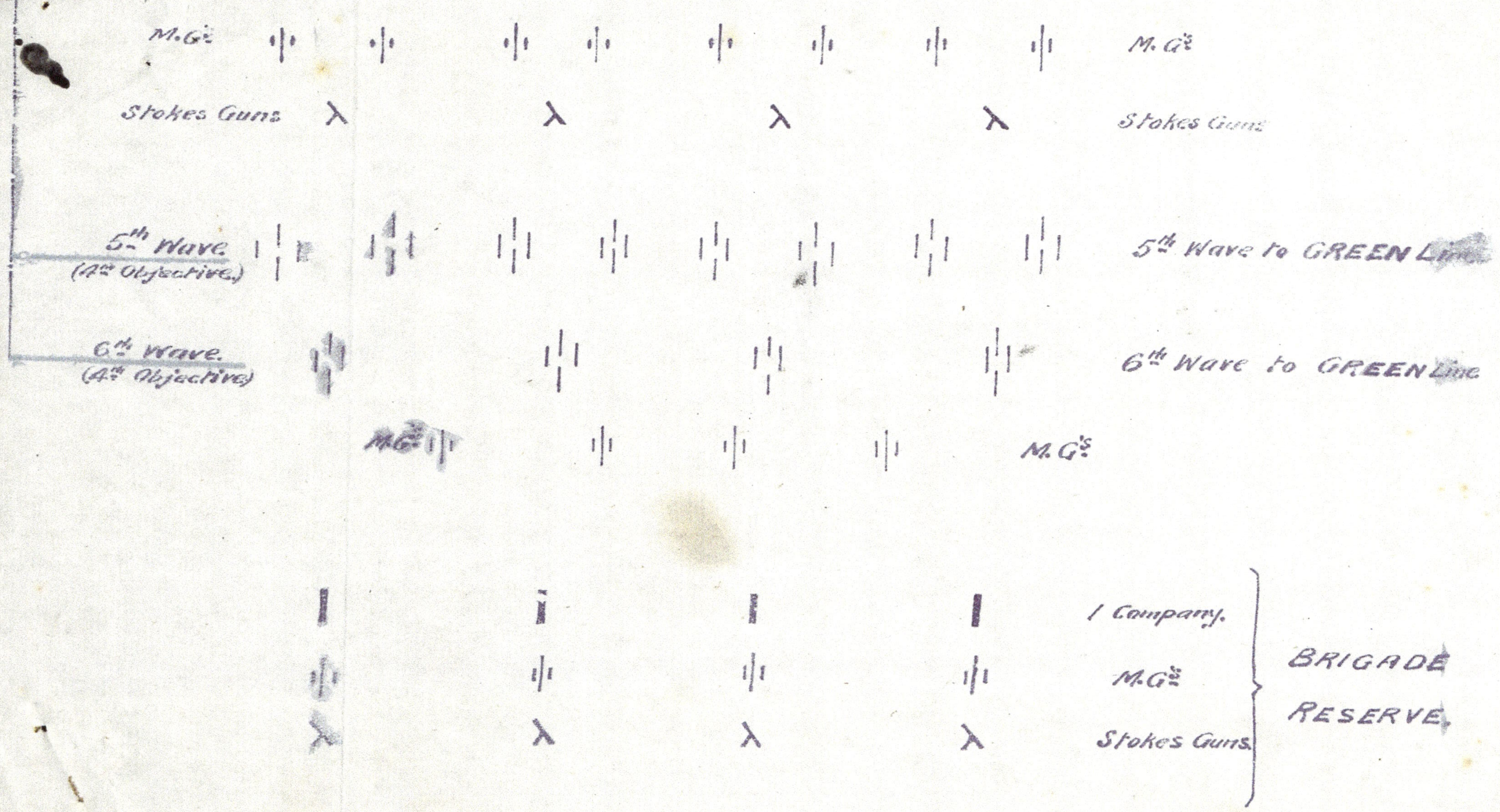

M.G.s

Stokes Guns

M.G.s

Stokes Guns

5th Wave
(4th Objective)

5th Wave to GREEN Line

6th Wave.
(4th Objective)

6th Wave to GREEN Line

M.G.s

M.G.s

1 Company.

M.G.s

Stokes Guns.

BRIGADE RESERVE.

App 3

2ND 8TH BATTALION THE ROYAL WARWICKSHIRE REGIMENT.

SECRET.

BATTALION ORDER 0000. by LT.COL.E.C.CADMAN.D.S.O. Commdg.
30th JULY 1917.

Ref. Map. No.61.M.64. (1/5000).

1. It is the intention of the G.O.C. VI Corps to attack and capture the system of trenches held by the enemy.

2. The 61st Division has been ordered to capture the hostile system of trenches opposite, and to be prepared to exploit the success by following up and maintaining touch with theenemy.

3. The 182nd Inf.Bde is allotted the task of assaulting and securing the four lines of trenches known as RED, YELLOW, WHITE and GREEN Lines. The front to be attacked is approximately 400 yards.

4. The 2/8.R.WAR.R. will attack on a front of 400 yards.
X.Batt.R.WAR.R. will be in support in the first instance and after the capture of the WHITE LINE by the 2/8.R.WAR.R. will pass through them and secure the GREEN LINE.
The Y Batt.R.WAR.R. will detail 3 Coys as MOPPERS UP for the 1st and 2nd Objective. The remaining Coy will follow X Batt.R.WAR.R. and secure our original front line, where it will be in Bde Reserve.
O.C.182.M.G.Coy. will detail one Section to follow leading and support Battalions, and O.C.182.L.T.M.B. will detail 4 guns to move forward into RED LINE, these will act as ordered in Bde Orders.

5. ZERO time will be notified later.

6. Preliminary bombardment and wirecutting by the Artillery will be carried out on days preceding Z day and up to ZERO.

7. The Artillery barrage will lift at ZERO from NO MAN'S LAND and creep back at 50 yards a minute to the YELLOW LINE where it will remain for five minutes. At ZERO plus 6 it will lift and creep back 50 yards to the minute on to the WHITE LINE where it will remain till ZERO plus 60 . At ZERO plus 60 the barrage will creep back and stand on a line 300 yards in advance of the 4th Objective (i.e. GREEN LINE)till ZERO plus 90, after which it will gradually die down.

8. At ZERO Infantry assault will commence and will be carried through by 2/8.R.WAR.R. to the 3rd Objective. X Batt.R.WAR.R. will leave their forming up trench at ZERO plus 40, and on the capture of the 3rd objective will pass through the 2/8.R.WAR.R. and will form up to continue the attack on the 4th objective.
The 3rd Wave will push on to the 2nd Objective, and the 4th wave to the 1st Objective.
The attached plan shows the disposition of the Battalion with Moppers Up.

9. DRESS, COMMUNICATIONS ETC: as in Brigade Orders.

10. Synchronisation of Watches. Watches will be synchronised at 8 a.m. under arrangements to be made by the Battalion Signalling Officer.

11. ACKNOWLEDGE.

sgd. W.S.FARMER. Lieut.& Adjt.
2/8.R.WAR.R.

issued at 8-45 a.m.

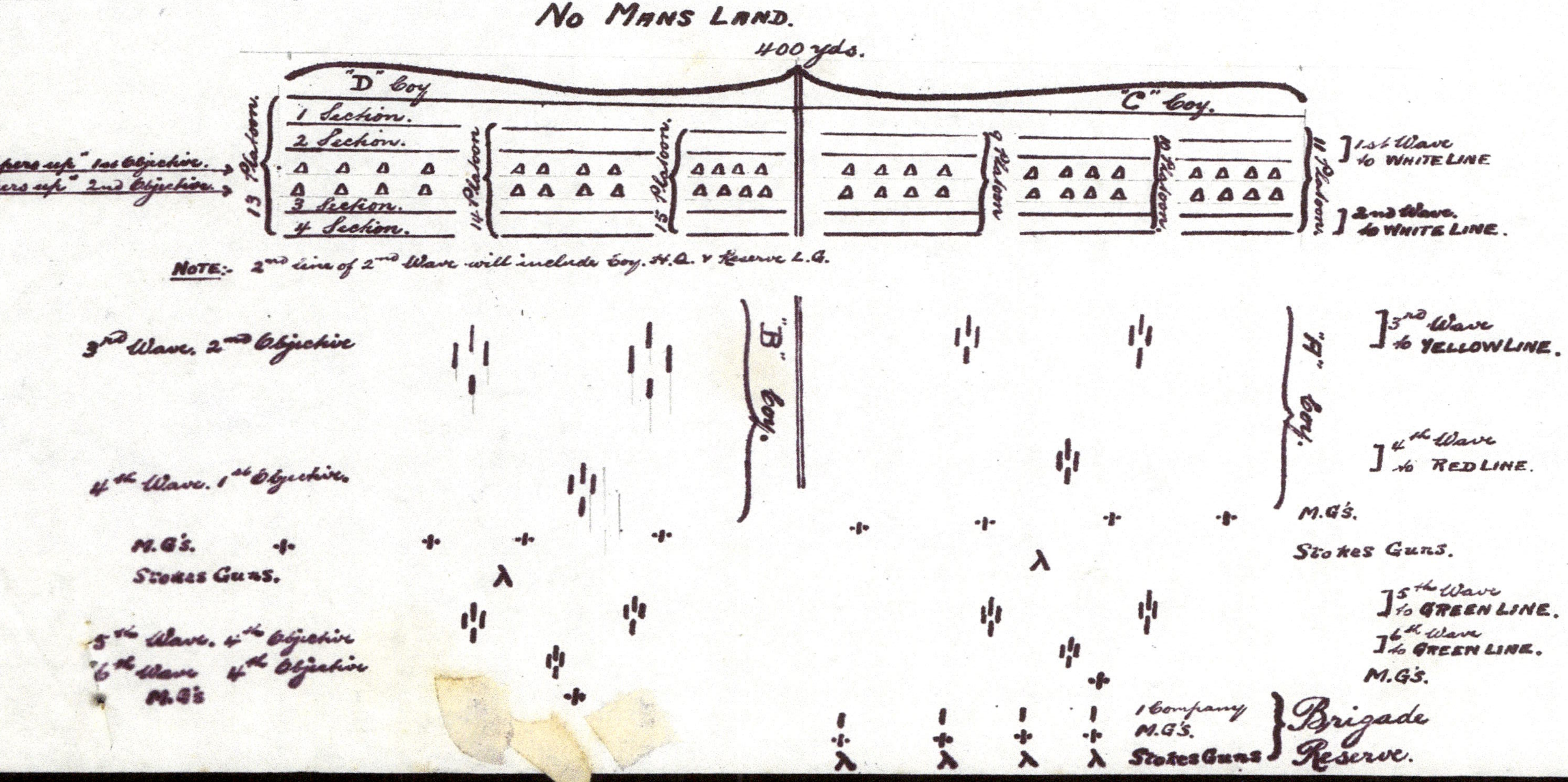

NO MANS LAND.
400 yds.
"D" Coy
"C" Coy.
1 Section.
2 Section.
3 Section.
4 Section.
13 Platoon.
14 Platoon
15 Platoon.
9 Platoon
10 Platoon.
11 Platoon.
"Moppers up" 1st Objective.
"Moppers up" 2nd Objective.
1st Wave to WHITE LINE
2nd Wave. to WHITE LINE.
NOTE:- 2nd line of 2nd Wave will include Coy. H.Q. & Reserve L.G.
"B" Coy.
"A" Coy.
3rd Wave. 2nd Objective
3rd Wave to YELLOW LINE.
4th Wave. 1st Objective.
4th Wave to RED LINE.
M.G's.
Stokes Guns.
M.G's.
Stokes Guns.
5th Wave. 4th Objective
6th Wave 4th Objective
M.G's
5th Wave to GREEN LINE.
6th Wave to GREEN LINE.
M.G's.
1 Company
M.G's.
Stokes Guns
Brigade Reserve.

App 4

2 ND 8TH BATTALION THE ROYAL WARWICKSHIRE REGIMENT.
156
BATTALION ORDERS/BY LT.COL. E.C.CARMAN.D.S.O. Commanding.
23rd JULY 1917.

1. The Battalion will march tomorrow to billets at DO[illegible].

2. ROUTE: QUOEUX - HARAVESNES - BACHIMONT - ROUGEFAY - VACQUERIE-le-BOUCQ - FORTEL.

3. The Battalion will fall in, in line, on South side of QUOEUX ROAD - head of column ½ mile East of FONTAINE CHURCH, ready to move at 6-5 a.m.
Transport including Cookers will march in rear of the Battalion.
A distance of 10 yards will be maintained between Coys, and 20 yards between Battalions.

4. DRESS: Marching Order. Steel Helmets on pack. Water Bottles will be filled before leaving.

5. Valises, Mess Baskets, etc., as in Standing Orders.

6. All known claims will be settled by Coys before the Battalion leaves.
2/LT.CHIDGEY will remain behind for two hours to settle any others.

7. Company Commanders are again reminded of the necessity of personally satisfying themselves before leaving that not only the billets but their surroundings are left scrupulously clean.

sgd. W.S.FARMER. Lieut.& Adjt.
2/8 R.WAR.R.

Copy No. 1. C.O.
2. H.Q.Mess.
3/6 Coys.
7. Q.M.& T.O.
8. H.Q.Details.
9. File
10. War Diary.

App 5

2ND [illegible] BATTALION [illegible] ROYAL [illegible] REGIMENT.

BATTALION ORDER 102 by Lt.Col. [illegible] D.S.O. Commanding.
24th JUNE 1917.

1. The Battalion will proceed by march route to [illegible] tomorrow and from there by train to CASSEL.

2. The Battalion, less "A" Coy and Transport, will fall in, in line, facing North in the main street - head of column opposite [illegible] (Billet No.17) - Order of March. H.Q. "B" "C" "D" Coy. Whole ready to move at 1-00 p.m.

DRESS:- Marching Order - Steel Helmets on packs.

No one will fall out on the march.

3. Transport & Q.M. Stores, less "A" Coy's Cooker and Mess, will fall in as shown ready to move at 1-00 p.m. One Cook per Coy will march with Cooker.

4. "A" Coy with Cooker and Mess will fall in as shown ready to move at 11-00 p.m.

5. Trains will depart as follows:-
Battalion less "A" Coy. 6-00 p.m. on 24th.
"A" Coy and Cooker. 2-00 a.m. on 25th.

6. Men will have teas before leaving, and dixies will be loaded on "A" Coy's Cooker and brought on by that Company.

7. Water bottles will be filled by 12 noon, and water carts will be loaded on train filled.

8. Officers Kits will be ready outside Coy.H.Q. by 12 noon and Mess Baskets by 12-45 p.m.

9. Billets will be left clean and the usual certificates in regard to claims will be handed in to the Battalion Orderly Room by 12 noon.

sgd. W.G.[illegible] Lieut.& Adjt.
2/[illegible]

Copy No. 1/4. Coys.
5. C.O.
6. [illegible]
7. [illegible]
8. [illegible]
9. File.
10. War Diary.

16H" Confidential

War Diary of:-

Vol 16

2/8th Battalion The Royal Warwickshire Regt.

Volume XVI

Period:-

Aug. 1/17.
to Aug. 31/17.

Instructions regarding War Diaries and Intelligence Summaries are contained in F. S. Regs., Part II. and the Staff Manual respectively. Title pages will be prepared in manuscript.

WAR DIARY
or
INTELLIGENCE SUMMARY.
(Erase heading not required.)

Army Form C. 2118.

Place	Date	Hour	Summary of Events and Information	Remarks and references to Appendices
HOFLAND near ROUBROUCK	1917 Augt 1		Draft 10 O R received 11pm on 31/7/17 – Day very wet. Batt practice attack cancelled by order of Bde. Specialist training in billets. 3.30pm C.O. attended Conference at Bde	WB
Do	2		Very wet – Batt attack again postponed – Training in billets – 2LT WOODBRIDGE and Batt scouts searched country for 3 escaped German prisoners (1st) 2LT PHIPPS rejd from leave	WB
Do	3		Very wet – Batt attack again postponed – training in billets – GOC Divn inspected A Coy & put them through various tests – 2LT GILDERTHORP & 3 O R rejd from leave – 2LT W.H. BOWERS (A Coy) & 2LT G.J. WAREHAM (D Coy) reported for duty	WB
Do	4	9.30am	C.O. inspected B Coy in all branches of training – 5pm C.O. inspected C Coy. Batt practice attack cancelled owing to rain. C.O. attended Bde Conference at 3.30pm. Further training in billets – Reserve S.Bs under M.O. 2 OR to Corps Amphibian & Pontoon Bridging School. 2LT BEVAN – 1 OR to I Corps Inf. School	WB
Do	5	10am	Church Parades (C of E. – & Pres.) Training of reserve men for Pack work – Cpl. BOUCKER to I Army Sanitation School.	WB
Do	6	7.20am	Batt paraded for Bde Practice Attack at LEURDAM – Zero 10 am – Finished 1pm. Conference of all officers with Corps Commander afterwards – 5pm C.O. attended Conference at Bde HQ – Draft of 12 O R – (10 casuals)	WB
Do	7		Coy training – 10am C.O. inspected D Coy in all branches of training – 2pm C.O. went over	WB

T2134. Wt. W708–776. 500000. 4/15. Sir J. C. & S.

Instructions regarding War Diaries and Intelligence Summaries are contained in F. S. Regs., Part II. and the Staff Manual respectively. Title pages will be prepared in manuscript.

WAR DIARY
or
INTELLIGENCE SUMMARY.
(Erase heading not required.)

Army Form C. 2118.

Place	Date	Hour	Summary of Events and Information	Remarks and references to Appendices
RUBROUCK	1917 Aug 7		ground on which practice attack took place - with all officers, & made comments on manner in which attack carried out. L G O. & 24 O.R. attended L.G. School for firing practice - 18 O.R. trained reserve L.T.M.B personnel attended Refresher Course	WR
Do	8		Coy training in morning - Route march 5pm. S.Bs & Reserve Signallers classes contd 5.45pm C.O. Adjt & 3 Coy Commanders attended lecture by B.G. STOCKWELL 164 Inf Bde on Recent Operations near YPRES	WR.
Do	9	7.15a	Batt marched to BROXEELE training area & took part in Bde Practice attack - Corps Commander was present. Draft of 4 O.R. received. Heavy rain in afternoon - 2 OR for leave	WR
Do	10	9am	Batt Route March - 11 miles - 5pm All Coys practised attacking strong points. Bde G visited Coys - Draft of 3 O.R. - 2Lt KITCHIN & Sgt CALDER to II Army Inf School 4 O.R for leave	WR.
Do	11	9am	Batt Route March - 10 miles - Coy training during rest of day - 16 packloaders reported to transport for instruction - 8 Reserve S Bs to 2/2 F.A for instruction - 8 O.R to 182 M.G. Coy as carriers - 10 O R proceeded on leave	WR
Do	12	10am	C of E Church Parade - 10.30am Joint Bde. Hon C of E Service - Day of rest	WR
Do	13	9am	Batt Route March. 7 miles. 4-7pm Coy training including platoon attacks on strong points	WR

T2134. Wt. W708–776. 500000. 4/15. Sir J. C. & S.

Instructions regarding War Diaries and Intelligence Summaries are contained in F. S. Regs., Part II. and the Staff Manual respectively. Title pages will be prepared in manuscript.

WAR DIARY
or
INTELLIGENCE SUMMARY.
(Erase heading not required.)

Army Form C. 2118.

Place	Date	Hour	Summary of Events and Information	Remarks and references to Appendices
10	1917 Augt			
RUBROUCK	13 cont		C.O. retd from leave - Capt B.K. PARSONS, 2Lt A.L. CLAYDON & 4 O.R to Divnl. Depot, MERCKEGHEM	WR
Do.	14	9a	12 noon - Coy training 10 am. C.O attended conference at Bde HQ. M.O retd from leave - C.O inspected A Coy in all branches of training - 4-7pm. Route march	WR.
Do			Bde orders for move received - 1 O.R to M.G.C. to replace casualty 1 O.R to Base unfit	WR.
Do	15	10.30am	B.G.C. inspected A Coy equipped as for attack - 9am-12 noon - Coy training -	WR.
Do	16	9am	Batt. proceeded by march route to ARNEKE - arrived 10.30 am. Entrained there - left 1pm. arrived HOPOUTRE 5.45pm - marched via POPERINGHE to Camp B. BRANDHOEK area. arrived 7.20pm - Batt in huts & tents, accommodation good - 2Lt WHITELEY for leave.	WR
Camp B BRANDHOEK	17	9am	Inspections and parades for gas drill, rapid loading, bayonet fighting & [illegible] to training ground available - 1 O.R. Killed by bombing raid at Bde HQ.	WR.
Do.	18	9a	Parades as yesterday - 2 men to Point Duty under A.P.M. 1 OR to leave	WR
Do	19		Sunday - Church parade 10 am 2 Coys firing on 25 yds range allotted by Bde. 2nd Coy stopped by order of Area Commandant - 3 OR to Water Duty under Division - Capt TONKS and 1 O.R proceeded on leave	WR
Do	20		Parades as for 18th - 5 O.R proceeded on Traffic Control - Coy Commanders & 2Lt CHIDGEY proceeded to WIELTJE to reconnoitre route.	WR

Instructions regarding War Diaries and Intelligence Summaries are contained in F. S. Regs., Part II. and the Staff Manual respectively. Title pages will be prepared in manuscript.

WAR DIARY
or
INTELLIGENCE SUMMARY.
(Erase heading not required.)

Army Form C. 2118.

Place	Date	Hour	Summary of Events and Information	Remarks and references to Appendices
B Camp BRANDHOEK No 1 Area	1917 Aug 21	3 am	1 Officer & 50 reserve S.Bs to Main Corps Dressing Station, WIELTJE Mine Dugout – 15 Officers & 10 Motor Cyclists proceeded to Demonstration in attacking Strong Points – at place 10 miles N.W. of ST OMER. – 2 Coys fired on 25x range – 3 Coys bathed at Corps Baths POPERINGHE – All Coys taken over model constructed under Batt arrangements of German lines – objectives & next attacks – weather fine. Some shelling in neighbourhood	WH
			Casualties 1 O.R wounded – 8pm 32 O.R. carrying party at Brigade. 5.30pm C.O. attended Bde Conference	WH
Do	22	9am	Company training. 6am. 1 Officer & 50 emergency S.Bs to Corps Walking Wounded Station – 2 LT WHITELEY & 2 O.R. to Anti Aircraft L.G. Course at 25 Squadron R.F.C. C.O. held Conference of Coy Commanders – All Coys went over model of German lines	WH
Do	23		Coy training – All Coys went over model – also Coy runners & Batt runners & Signallers	WH
Do	24		Coy training – 2 Coys firing on 25 yds range – 1 Coy & Batt HQ bathed at POPERINGHE Batt & Coy runners & signallers went over model trenches. Bde orders for move rec'd C.O. attended Conference at Bde HQ – Conference with Coy Commanders afterwards	WH
Do	25	3 am	1 Off & 50 O.R reported at Main Dressing Station as emergency stretcher bearers 9.15am Batt marched to Camp at YPRES N. (H 11 c. 5 9 – Sheet 28) 8 tents & trench shelters – 2 LT WHITELEY & 2 OR retd from leave – Day quiet – no hostile shelling –	WH

T2134. Wt. W708—776. 500000. 4/15. Sir J. C. & S.

Instructions regarding War Diaries and Intelligence Summaries are contained in F. S. Regs., Part II. and the Staff Manual respectively. Title pages will be prepared in manuscript.

WAR DIARY
or
INTELLIGENCE SUMMARY.
(Erase heading not required.)

Army Form C. 2118.

Place	Date	Hour	Summary of Events and Information	Remarks and references to Appendices
Camp. YPRES N	1917 Aug 26		4 N.C.O.s to XIX Corps L G & Bombing School – 2a 1 Off & 50 O R to Main Dressing Station as emergency stretcher bearers – 21 O.R to 2/3 S.M. F.A to clean HQ Canal Bank – 10 am Voluntary Service C of E. – 10.30 pm – 2 Off & 52 O R to C.28 b 0.3 carrying Gas Drums 2 Off & 52 O.R. to same place carrying Gas Drums. 7 pm. These parties cancelled.	WA
Do	27	9 am	C.O. had Conference with B.G.C. at WIELTJE and reconnoitred line – warning order from Bde that Batt would move up on night of 28th & attack on morning of 29th – 4 Off & 4 OR went up to reconnoitre – weather too bad to see much – Capt T.T. SLATER & 1 O.R proceeded on leave. 1 O R to 182 M.G.Coy to replace casualty. Working parties 100 O.R. 2 O.R. wounded	WA
Do	28	7 am	Order as to proceeding to line cancelled. Coy Commanders reconnoitred line – Observation very poor	WA
Do	29		Warning order that Bde will relieve 183 Bde in line tomorrow night – parties from each Coy reconnoitred line. Working parties 4 Officers 250 O.R. 8 pm Orders for relief received	WA
Do	30	9 am	C.O. attended Conference at Bde HQ – 1 O.R retd from leave – Batt relieves 7th R War R in left support – Dispositions Batt HQ & 2 Coys in CALL RESERVE, (C 23 c 7.6 Map Sheet Nº 28) 2 Coys in ADMIRAL TRENCH – Relief complete 9.30 pm Casualties – O.R 2. Hostile shelling slight	WA
CALL RESERVE TRENCH	31		Day quiet – some hostile shelling near RAT FARM. Our guns active – casualties nil – work cleaning up trenches & providing cover for garrison	WA

Ed. C. Cadman
Lt. Col.
Cmdg. 2/8 R War R

T2134. Wt. W708–776. 500000. 4/15. Sir J. C. & S.

2nd 8TH BATTALION THE ROYAL WARWICKSHIRE REGIMENT.

BATTALION ORDER ZZZ by CAPT.J.MUNGLE.M.C. COMMANDING.
1st AUGUST 1917.

1. OBJECTIVE OF DIVISION.	The 61st Division will on Z day attack the enemy on the front shewn on Map A attached. It will establish itself on the RED LINE covered by a line of Outposts on the DOTTED RED LINE. The 182.Bde will form the RIGHT attack and 183.Bde the LEFT Attack. The 184,Bde. will be in Divisional Reserve. On the right of the 61st Division is the A Inf.Bde of X Divisions on the Left K Inf.Bde of Y Division. The attack will be preceded by a two days' bombardment.
2. OBJECTIVES & BOUNDARIES OF 182.INF.BDE.	Objectives and boundaries are shewn on Map A attached:- 1st OBJECTIVE. Occupation of GREEN LINE and forming an Outpost Line in front of it on or about DOTTED GREEN LINE. 2nd OBJECTIVE. Occupation of RED LINE and consolidation of a defensive position. The actual line to be consolidated is the best from a tactical point of view. 3 rd OBJECTIVE. Occupation of DOTTED RED LINE as an Outpost position.
3. FLANKS, FRONTAGES AND METHOD OF ATTACK.	The 2/8.R.WAR.R. will attack on the right and the 2/7th R.WAR.R. on the left (see May A attached). Each Battn. will have a frontage of about 400 yards and will deploy two Coys on a two platoon frontage (see diagram 1 attd). The objectives of these two Battalions are the occupation of the GREEN LINE, with an Outpost Line on or abour the DOTTED GREEN LINE and the occupation of the RED LINE and its consolidation as a defensive position (see para.2. - 2rd OBJECTIVE). Ist and 2nd Waves proceed to GREEN LINE, 3rd & 4th Waves to RED LINE. The 2/5th.R.WAR.R. will in the first instance be in support of the assaulting Battalions and will follow them - this Battalion will, after the capture of the RED LINE, pass through the two leading Battalions and establish outposts on the DOTTED RED LINE. The 2/6th.R.WAR.R. will be in Brigade Reserve.

4. DISPOSITION OF COYS.

"B" COY.	RIGHT FRONT COY.	)	1st & 2nd Waves.
"A" "	LEFT	)	
"D" "	RIGHT SUPPORT COY.	)	3rd & 4th Waves.
"C" "	LEFT	)	

5. ALLOTMENT OF FRONTAGES TO COYS. These are shewn on Map A attached.

6. MACHINE GUNS. O.C.182.M.G.Coy. will detail 1 section to follow each assaulting Battalion and the Support Battalion.
The remaining Section will be in Bde Reserve.
These Sections will come under the orders of the O.C. Battalions concerned as soon as the Attack commences.
They will form yp in the trenches occupied by the last waves of these Battalions.
2 M.G.Officers will be detailed to go forward with the leading wave (one Officer with each Battn.) to reconnoitre positions for the guns coming up behind.
These Officers will be accompanied by 2 Orderlies to act as guides to the guns if necessary.

7. TRENCH MORTARS. 2 Guns will follow 4th Wave and will be available under orders of O.C. "C" & "D" Coys to assist in advance to RED LINE. They will assemble in same trenches as 4th wave.

8. MOPPERS UP. The 2/6th.R.WAR.R. will detail 2 Coys, as "MOPPERS UP" for the German 2nd and 3rd lines, i.e., HUN TRENCH and the line of strong posts.
The "MOPPERS UP" will follow closely the leading wave of the waves for which they are Mopping Up.
Each man will carry 5 bombs. H.Q. of these Coys will move forward with the 2nd line of the 4th wave and will be established in the dugout known to exist in HUN TRENCH where the inter-Battalion boundary crosses that trench.
When each Platoon mopping up in the line of strong posts has done its job and the RED LINE has been consolidated it will withdraw to HUN TRENCH.
When the situation is satisfactory the two Coys will be withdrawn to the original British Front Line.
O.Cs "MOPPERS UP COYS" informing the Battalions in the RED and GREEN LINES that they are withdrawing.
"MOPPERS UP" will wear the distinguishing white band as laid down in Section XXXII para.2. of SS.135.

9. ASSEMBLY. The 1st Wave and "Moppers Up" for HUN TRENCH will assemble in the British Front Line.
The 2nd wave will assemble in trenches dug about 150 yards behind the front line.
The 3rd & 4th Waves and their Moppers Up will assemble in trenches dug about 150 yards in rear of the 2nd Wave.
The Supporting Battalion i.e. 2/5.R.WAR.R. will assemble in the open about 200 yards in rear of the 4th wave of assaulting Battalions, taking advantage of all natural cover.
The Reserve Battalion i.e. 2/6th.R.WAR.R. will assemble in the orchard at B.27.a.5.8. (map 27.N.W.).
the Section of the M.G.Coy is reserve will also assemble at this point.

10. TIME. All troops will be in position ready to advance at ZERO minus 1 hour 15 min.

11. ARTILLERY BARRAGE. The 18 pdr barrage will regulate the pace of the advance It will remain 6 minutes on the enemy front line.
Between front line and GREEN LINE the pace will be 100 yards in two minutes. After reaching GREEN LINE the pace will be 100 yards in 4 minutes throughout.
The barrage will halt for 30 minutes 200 yards beyond DOTTED GREEN LINE and for 30 minutes beyond RED LINE.
It will finally haltm at ZERO plus 3 hours ~~12 min~~. 300 yards beyond the DOTTED RED LINE 'final objective).

12. CONTACT PATROL AEROPLANE. Contact Patrol Aeroplanes of the 15th Squadron R.F.C. will fly over the front during the attack on each objective, and the Infantry will show their position by lighting flares when called for by aeroplanes by AAA on KLAXON Horn or VERY LIGHT.

13. STRONG POINTS. As soon as the RED LINE is definitely reported in our possession a line of strong points will be constructed on the general line 300 yards in rear of the RED LINE near the following points:-

(1). About B.25.c.8.0.
(2). N.E. of CLYTHIL FARM.

13. STRONG POINTS. O.C. Reserve Battalion i.e. 2/6.R.WAR.R. will detail two working and carrying parties of 2 Officers and 100 o.r. one to each of the strong points mentioned above.
These parties will assemble with their Battalion and at ZERO will follow the Supporting Battalion as far as the trench where the 2nd wave of the assaulting Battalions assembled.
A R.E. ~~Officer~~ party under an Officer has been detailed to go forward when the situation allows (receiving orders from R.E. LIAISON Officer at Bde H.Q. when to go) to reconnoitre positions for the strong points.
He will be accompanied by a M.G. Officer detailed by O.C. 182.M.G. Coy and will be responsible for sending guides to bring the Infantry working parties forward.
The M.G. Officer detailed for this duty will report at advanced Bde Headquarters at ZERO - 15 minutes.
1 Section of a Field Coy has been detailed to assist in this work. As soon as the strong points are completed an Officer of the working party will inform O's.C. Battalions in the GREEN LINE of this.
Each Battalion will then send forward a garrison of 2 Sections for each strong point and O.C. 182.M.G. Coy will place 1 Machine Gun in each post, being informed when to do so by the Machine Gun Officer who assisted in selecting the Strong Points.
When the garrison of the strong points is in position the Infantry working parties will withdraw to the old British Front Line.
O.C. "B" Coy will be prepared, when ordered to do so, to find the two Sections to garrison strong point at B.25.c.8.0.

14. LIAISON. In order to ensure close touch with Units on left and right:-
(a). O.C. "B" Coy will detail a special party of 1 Officer and 4 o.r. to meet party of left Battalion of A Inf. Bde at:-
(I). X Roads B.26.c.0.1.
(2). H.1.a.5.9.

(b). O.C. "A" Coy will detail special party of 1 N.C.O. and three o.r. to meet party of 2/7.R.WAR.R. at:-
(I). Bend in the road at H.2.a.1.7.
(2). H.1.b.0.3.
Both above parties will move with 2nd Wave as far as GREEN LINE and with 4th Wave as far as RED LINE.
O.C. "A" Coy will arrange for the N.C.O. in charge of his Liaison Party meeting the N.C.O. in charge of 2/7.R.WAR.R. before ZERO day.

Liaison Party

15. SYNCHRONISATION OF WATCHES. Watches will be synchronised from Brigade H.Q. at 12-15 p.m. and 8-15 p.m. on X and Y days.

16. HEADQUARTERS. (1). Advanced Bde H.Q. will open at ZERO - 1 hour 15 min. at the farm at B.26.d.5.7.

(2). The Brigade forward station will be established at H.2.a.1.1. after the taking of the RED LINE.

(3). Battalion forward Command Posts will be established:-

(a). By Right Assaulting Battalion in the dugout in HUN TRENCH at H.1.b.8.9.

(b). By Left Assaulting Battalion at the corner of the orchard at H.1.b.8.2.

(c). By Outpost Battalion in RED LINE at H.1.a.45.00

~~(d).~~

16. HEADQUARTERS. (d). By Reserve Battalion in BRITISH FRONT LINE at E of LEURDAN.

Battalion H.Q. will be at B.26.d.5.8. till ZERO plus. 2 hours. Thereafter at H.1.b.8.9.

17. DRESS &c. Instructions regarding Fighting Kit, &Flares, Rockets, etc. as in separate Bde.instructions.

18. REPORTS. Situation reports will be rendered to Batt.H.Q. every 30 minutes after ZERO and all material information will be sent when received.

19. ZERO hour will be notified later.

ACKNOWLEDGE.

sgd. W.S.FARMER. Lieut.&.Adjt.
2/8.R.WAR.R.

issued. at 9-30 p.m.

2/7TH BATTALION THE ROYAL WARWICKSHIRE REGIMENT.

BATTALION ORDER 168 BY [illegible]
15th AUGUST 1917.

1. The Battalion will move from [illegible] AREA to [illegible] AREA No.1. tomorrow 16th inst.
The Battalion will march to [illegible]; ROUTE: [illegible]. And will entrain there for [illegible].

The Battalion will fall in, in line, facing N.E. on the S.E. side of the road running N.E. and S.W. through [illegible] c. and d. in the following order H.Q. "B" "A" "C" & "D" Coys. Head of column 100 yards W of the cross roads at [illegible] the whole ready to move at 8-55 a.m.

DRESS; Full Marching Order, Steel Helmets will be worn.

2. RATIONS. Haversack Rations will be carried on the men. Water Bottles will be filled.

3. DISTANCES. The Battalion will march closed up to [illegible]. In march from [illegible] to the new area, the Battalion will march closed up W. of the [illegible] - [illegible] - [illegible] ROAD and 200 yards between Coys East of that road.

4. BILLETS. The usual certificates regarding damage to Billets will be obtained and returned to the Orderly Room by 8 p.m. tonight.

Company Billets will be inspected by an Officer, and will be left scrupulously clean. O.C. Coys will also take steps to see that no rubbish is left lying on the ground used for training, and in particular that no ammunition etc. is left lying about.

sgd. [illegible] Lieut. & Adjt.
2/7 R.War.R.

Issued at 8 p.m.

[illegible] BATTALION [illegible]

BATTALION ORDER [illegible] BY [illegible]
[illegible]

1. The Battalion will relieve the [illegible] in [illegible] tonight [illegible]

2. DISPOSITIONS.

[illegible]	RIGHT FRONT COY.	[illegible]
[illegible]	LEFT " "	ditto.
[illegible]	RIGHT SUPPORT COY.	[illegible]
[illegible]	LEFT " "	ditto.

3. [illegible]

4. Lewis Guns will be carried in limbers as far as possible.

5. [illegible]

6. Coys will make their own arrangements for guides.

7. ACKNOWLEDGE.

Sgd. [illegible], Lieut.[illegible]
[illegible]

Confidential

War Diary of:-

1/8th Battalion The Royal Warwickshire Regt.

Volume XVII

Period:-

Sept. 1/17 to
Sept. 30/17.

2nd 8th Battalion The Royal Warwickshire Regt

War Diary

Vol 17

Volume XVII

17 H 23

Period 1st to 30th September 1917

Instructions regarding War Diaries and Intelligence Summaries are contained in F. S. Regs., Part II. and the Staff Manual respectively. Title pages will be prepared in manuscript.

WAR DIARY
or
INTELLIGENCE SUMMARY.

(*Erase heading not required.*)

Army Form C. 2118.

Hour, Date, Place		Summary of Events and Information	Remarks and references to Appendices
CALL RESERVE C 23 c 8.6 - Map Sheet 28	1917 Sept 1	Weather showery - day quiet - some hostile shelling on Batt H.Q. and Reserve Coys in ADMIRALS TRENCH - Warning order as to relieving 2/7 Batt in Front Line received. Casualties - Wounded O.R. 2 - Accidentally wounded O.R. 1. Officers went up to reconnoitre	WM
"	" 2	Orders for relief tonight received. Batt orders issued. 8.30 pm. Batt moved off to relieve 2/7 R War R. - Dispositions. A Coy Right front Co including Platoon in HINDU COTT. 3 Plat. C Coy left front Coy 3 Plat. B Coy Support in CAPRICORN TRENCH - Relief complete 11.15 pm night quiet	WM
CAPRICORN KEEP C 18 d 6.6.	" 3	7 am. Artillery put down smoke barrage & front line Coys lit smoke candles. Enemy at once put down heavy barrage on CAPRICORN KEEP & Trench - 10 pm Heavy enemy barrage on same points during attack by 6 R War R on Hill 35 - barrage lasted 1½ hours. Very heavy artillery fire on both sides throughout the night. Casualties 4 O.R. killed 4 wounded.	WM.
"	" 4	3.30 am. Gas discharged on our front by R.E. special Coy. - Enemy replied immediately with heavy barrage on usual points. 4 pm. Bde orders received to attack & capture AISNE FARM & trenches. 2 platoons of C Coy detailed. 8.45 pm. 1 Plat of B Coy moved up to POND - 10.30 pm. attacking platoons assembled at Batt H.Q. 11 pm attack launched from N & N.W. Party came under fire from both flanks & after getting to within 30 yds of AISNE were forced to withdraw as both flanks were being enfiladed by party about twice their strength. Party withdrew in good order & crawled back to point of assembly. - Moon was very bright & there was no opportunity for surprise. Casualties O.R. 4 K. 1 W.	WM
"	" 5	Day quiet as far as hostile shelling concerned. Our heavies fire continued on Hill 35 and other points near GALLIPOLI. 6.35 pm. Smoke barrage by artillery brought heavy reply from enemy guns on CAPRICORN & other	

(73989) W4141—463. 400,000. 9/14. H.&J.Ltd. Forms/C. 2118/10.

Instructions regarding War Diaries and Intelligence Summaries are contained in F. S. Regs., Part II. and the Staff Manual respectively. Title pages will be prepared in manuscript.

WAR DIARY
or
INTELLIGENCE SUMMARY.
(*Erase heading not required.*)

Army Form C. 2118.

Hour, Date, Place			Summary of Events and Information	Remarks and references to Appendices
Batt HQ CAPRICORN KEEP C 18 d. 6 6 (Sheet 28) Left Front Batt	1917 Sept 5		points - 4 pm. Bde orders received that AISNE FARM to be attacked again by us at 8.35 pm taking advantage of barrage put down for operations on our right. Same platoons of C Coy again detailed. Difficulty experienced in getting them withdrawn from front posts in daylight to enable them to attack at 8 pm. Party assembled at Batt HQ. 8.30 pm. - attacked 8.45 pm under 2 Lt WATSON. They crept up to within 30 yds of objective without being observed & then reorganised. On advancing they came under heavy MG & rifle fire. One enemy MG. was put out of action but 4 remained. Party charged & took concrete post, but were under heavy fire & bombing from trenches flanking the position & were eventually forced to withdraw - Casualties in operation 18 OR. 8 pm. 1 Platoon support Coy moved up to POND. 11.30 pm attacking party returned. 12.30 pm. Bde orders that relief to be carried out. Platoon of support Co withdrawn from POND. 2.30 am. Batt relieved by 2/4 R War R - Casualties for day 1 Off. & 23 O.R.	WB
Left Support Batt HQ. C 23 c 8 6 CALL FARM	6th	6pm	A Coy came under orders of 6.6 R War R. moved to Right Support. Batt heavily shelled all day - 2 platoons moved up at 11 pm & came under orders of 6 6 R War R. to support attack on Hill 35 - Casualties 2 O.R. Night very quiet	WB
Do.	7th	11am	Bde orders recd that Batt to be relieved tomorrow. Day exceptionally quiet. Working parties 150 O.R. reclaiming dugouts &c. Casualties 10 O.R. B Coy & 2 detached platoons of B. H. Coy returned from right support.	WB
Do.	8th		Day very quiet. Notice received of attack on left at dusk - Ascertained that barrage would not start till 9.45 pm. Relief of front Batt postponed, but our relief to proceed. Batt relieved by 2/4 GLOSTERS. Relief complete 7.20 pm. Batt entrained at C 27 c. 7. 4 (map Sheet 28) Detrained G 6 a (central) - marched to B Camp BRANDHOEK No 1 Area. arriving 11.30 pm. Casualties 4 O.R.	WB

(73989) W4141—463. 400,000. 9/14. H.&J.Ltd. Forms/C. 2118/10.

Instructions regarding War Diaries and Intelligence Summaries are contained in F. S. Regs., Part II. and the Staff Manual respectively. Title pages will be prepared in manuscript.

WAR DIARY
or
INTELLIGENCE SUMMARY.
(Erase heading not required.)

Army Form C. 2118.

Hour, Date, Place	Summary of Events and Information	Remarks and references to Appendices
Battn H.Q. Brandhoek ? Area B Camp. Sept 9th 1917	1 Officer & 1 Sgt Instructor & 28 O.R proceeded to 19th Corps Musketry school Mercheghem. 16 O.R were attached to 476 Field Coy R.E. for duty. Battalion bathing from 1pm – 5pm at 19 Corps Baths POPERINGHE. C of E church parade at 6.15 pm. The remainder of the day cleaning up.	R.L.P
Do Sept 10th 1917	1 Rifle Bombing section from A Coy & 2nd Lt GILDERTHORPE on Brigade Bombing Course. Parades under Coy arrangements, re-organization & intense rifle inspections. 1 O.R wounded.	R.L.P
Do Sept 11th 1917	1 officer & 50 O.R reported to VLAMERTINGHE MILL for stretcher bearing. Parades as for the 10th. Bn personnel which had been left out of the line bathed at VLAMERTINGHE baths from 9-30–11-30 am.	R.L.P
Sept 12th 1917	2ND Lt BOWERS & 32 O.R were gassed at WIELTJE whilst employed as stretcher bearers. Parades under Coy arrangements. 6 O.R reported from 182 M.G. Coy & fifteen O.R from 476 Field Coy.	R.L.P

(73989) W4141—463. 400,000. 9/14. H.&J.Ltd. Forms/C. 2118/10.

Army Form C. 2118.

Instructions regarding War Diaries and Intelligence Summaries are contained in F. S. Regs., Part II. and the Staff Manual respectively. Title pages will be prepared in manuscript.

WAR DIARY
or
INTELLIGENCE SUMMARY.
(*Erase heading not required.*)

Hour, Date, Place	Summary of Events and Information	Remarks and references to Appendices
Brandhoek No1 Area B. Camp. Sept 13 1917	Parades under Coy arrangements. 1 W.C.O & 25 O.R reported VLAMERTINGHE MILL for stretcher bearing. Movement orders received. 5 O.R. reported from traffic control duties.	A.L.P
WATOU No1 Area ESK CAMP Sept 14 1917	Battalion moved to billets at WATOU, starting at 9.6 am. Took over the camp from 12th Royal Scots at 12.0 noon.	A.L.P
WATOU No1 Area ESK CAMP Sept 15 1917	Parades under Coy arrangements, specialists under specialist officers; 2ND LTS HARRIS, TYLER, JONES, PITT, PARROTT & RICHARDS & 8 O.R reported from the Divisional Depot. Cpt B.K. PARSONS & 3 O.R rejoined the Battn from the Divisional Depot	A.L.P
WATOU No1 Area ESK CAMP Sept 16 1917	Church of England Church Parade at 10 am & Non-Conformist parade at 11 am (Brigade): Movement orders were received. 2ND LT ~~[illegible]~~ WOOLDRIDGE + 1 O.R proceeded to EECKE to billet the battalion.	A.L.P

(73989) W4141—463. 400,000. 9/14. H.&J.Ltd. Forms/C. 2118/10.

Instructions regarding War Diaries and Intelligence Summaries are contained in F. S. Regs., Part II. and the Staff Manual respectively. Title pages will be prepared in manuscript.

WAR DIARY
or
INTELLIGENCE SUMMARY.

(*Erase heading not required.*)

Army Form C. 2118.

Hour, Date, Place	Summary of Events and Information	Remarks and references to Appendices
No 3 CAMP EECKE Q 19 a 47 (Sheet 27) SEPT 17th 1917	BATTn marched to billets at EECKE starting at 7.23am & took over the camp at 11.15 am. 2nd Lt GUNTER & 3 O.R proceeded to the BERNEVILLE AREA under Brigade arrangements to billet the Battalion Movement orders for the 19th were received.	A.L.P
Ditto SEPT ~~17th~~ 18th 1917	Parades under Coy arrangements; a conference was held at Brigade Hdqs for O.C. Units. C Coy reported at CAESTRE STATION to help with the entraining of the Brigade.	A.L.P
Ditto Sept 19th 1917	Battn marched to CAESTRE where they entrained for ARRAS, time of departure 7.40 pm. B Coy proceeded by an earlier train. C Coy rejoined the Battn at CAESTRE STATION	A.L.P
Camp ~~at~~ DAINVILLE L 28 a 4.2 Sept 20th	Battn detrained at ARRAS at 3.0am & marched to billets in a camp just outside DAINVILLE (Sheet 51C) at L 28 a 4.2. There was a Brigade conference at BERNEVILLE for Commanding Officers at 3.0 pm.	A.L.P
Ditto Sept 21st	Parades under Coy arrangements, particular attention to rifle inspections, movements orders received late at night 2nd Lt GILDERTHORPE & 4 O.R proceeded to Lancaster Camp (H11 c 1.1.) reference sheet 51B. 26 O.R proceeded to FAMPOUX for tunnelling. Capt R.K. PARSONS & 2 joined Depot Bn. & 12 Officers & 18 O.R reconnoitred the line	A.L.P

(73989) W4141—463. 400,000. 9/14. H.&J.Ltd. Forms/C. 2118/10.

Instructions regarding War Diaries and Intelligence Summaries are contained in F. S. Regs., Part II. and the Staff Manual respectively. Title pages will be prepared in manuscript.

WAR DIARY
or
INTELLIGENCE SUMMARY.
(Erase heading not required.)

Army Form C. 2118.

Place	Date	Hour	Summary of Events and Information	Remarks and references to Appendices
Lancaster Camp. H11C1.1.	Sept 1917	22	Battn marched to billets at Lancaster Camp at 10.35. took over the camp at 12.30 pm. Officers conference at 2 pm. Lt WOOLDRIDGE & 3 O.R for H.Q & 1 officer & 3 O.R per coy went into the line to take over. Relief orders were received. 2 O.R went on Traffic Control	A.L.P
CHEMICAL WORKS SECTOR H18 b 6 8	Sept	23	1 N.C.O & 3 men joined the Div Burial Party. 2 officers & 46 O.R joined the Brigade School at B10 b40. Col CADMAN assumed command of the 182 BRIGADE & Major MUNGLE took command of the Bn. At 1.30 pm advance party left for the line. Bn relieved 7th Lincolns in the CHEMICAL WORKS sector. Relief complete 10.35. Remainder of night quiet.	A.L.P
	Sept	24	At 4.30 am till 5.15 am enemy put down a heavy barrage on our front line & posts with 5.9's & T.M's. A raid was attempted on the Bn on our right but was repulsed. Remainder of the day quiet wind slightly dangerous. Gas alert ordered at 9 pm. CHEMICAL WORKS & FAMPOUX shelled intermittently with 5.9's. Capt Gibbins & 2nd Lt SMITH returned from leave. Casualties 2 killed & 3 O.R wounded.	A.L.P

T2134. Wt. W708–776. 500000. 4/15. Sir J. C. & S.

Instructions regarding War Diaries and Intelligence Summaries are contained in F. S. Regs., Part II. and the Staff Manual respectively. Title pages will be prepared in manuscript.

WAR DIARY
or
INTELLIGENCE SUMMARY.
(Erase heading not required.)

Army Form C. 2118.

Place	Date	Hour	Summary of Events and Information	Remarks and references to Appendices
Ditto ~~Sept~~	Sept 25 1917		A patrol went out from each coy about 10.0 pm, one or two enemy wiring parties were encountered & dispersed. Active wiring was also carried out between 9 pm & midnight. 1 O.R despatched to England for mining. Col CADMAN resumed command of the Bn & BRIGADIER GEN EVANS D.S.O took command of the brigade. Corps Commander visited Bn Hdqs about 2.30 pm. Weather fine. Casualties 2 O.R. wounded	A.C.P.
Ditto	Sept 26	–	A patrol went out from each coy about 10.0 pm & reconnoitred the enemy's wire, no enemy patrols encountered, good progress was made with the wiring especially near the railway cutting. Enemy artillery quiet during the day, one or two Trench Mortar 'strafes' by the enemy were immediately silenced by our artillery. Working parties from 6am – 1.15 pm improving front line & posts. Weather fine wind favourable & mild. Casualties nil.	A.C.P.
Ditto	Sept 27	–	The usual patrols & wiring took place during the evening, no enemy patrols were encountered. Enemy artillery active during the morning. Working parties as for the 26th. Enemy's T. M. silenced by Stokes. 1 O.R to Div. Depot. 2 O.R. to 182 LTMB. Weather fine. Wind mild & favourable. Casualties 1.O.R wounded.	A.C.P.

T2134. Wt. W708–776. 500000. 4/15. Sir J. C. & S.

Instructions regarding War Diaries and Intelligence Summaries are contained in F. S. Regs., Part II. and the Staff Manual respectively. Title pages will be prepared in manuscript.

WAR DIARY
or
INTELLIGENCE SUMMARY.
(Erase heading not required.)

Army Form C. 2118.

Place	Date	Hour	Summary of Events and Information	Remarks and references to Appendices
Ditto	Sept 28 1917		Very little activity in the morning, between 2-30 pm & 6-30 pm enemy's TM positions, front & support lines were "strafed" by our Corps Heavies & Divisional Artillery, very little retaliation. Wiring & patrolling were successfully carried out during the night, work on trenches made headway under R.E supervision 1 O.R to Div^l Cinema; 1 OR to LTM. Casualties 1 killed & 2 O.R wounded. Weather fine wind fine & favourable.	A.L.P.
	Sept 29		Relief orders received. H.T.M's & 19 T.M's bombarded enemy's ~~to~~ line between 2-30 & 4-30 pm, Bn relieved in line by 2/7 R.War.R. at 9.35 pm enemy put down 2 barrages during relief one at 6.50 & the other at 7.30. Bn moved to support line in NORTHUMBERLAND AVENUE, A & B Coy moved to CADIZ & COLT RESERVE respectively. Casualties nil. Work as for previous day. Weather fine wind mild & favourable.	A.L.P.
H11a6.2	Sept 30 1917		Various parties under R.E supervision, at 1 a.m a hostile barrage was put down which covered a raid attempted by enemy on our left front. R.E working parties were used in the evening. Capt GIBBINS, 2nd Lts ROGERS, WAREHAM & LLOYD & 5 O.R went on Army & Corps Courses	A.L.P.

T2134. Wt. W708—776. 500000. 4/15. Sir J. C. & S.

Army Form C. 2118.

Instructions regarding War Diaries and Intelligence Summaries are contained in F. S. Regs., Part II. and the Staff Manual respectively. Title pages will be prepared in manuscript.

WAR DIARY
or
INTELLIGENCE SUMMARY.
(Erase heading not required.)

Place	Date	Hour	Summary of Events and Information	Remarks and references to Appendices
Ditto	Sept 30 1917		2nd Lt RICHARDS went to 1/8 R.WAR.R. Lt WATSON & 40 O.R returned from brigade school; 30 O.R went to Brigade school. 2 E.A. [enemy aircraft] were brought down between 12.15 & 12.30 pm. Weather fine.	[illegible initials]

Ed. C. Cadman, Lieut Col
Commdg 2/8. R Warwick Regt.

T2134. Wt. W708—776. 500000. 4/15. Sir J. C. & S.

2/8th Bn. Royal Warwickshire Regt

Battalion Order, dated 2-9-1917

1. The Battalion will relieve the 2/7 R. WAR. R in left front section tonight, 2/3rd inst.

2/8 R. War. R.	2/7 R War R	Position
"A" Coy	"A" Coy	Right front Coy, including HINDU COTT
3 platoons "C" Coy	"D" Coy	Left front Coy FORT HILL AREA
1 platoon, "C" Coy will remain in support in new shelters to be erected in CALL SUPPORT TR.		
3 platoons "B" Coy	"B" Coy	CAPRICORN TR. area
1 platoon "B" Coy will remain in support in new shelters to be erected in CALL SUPPORT TR.		
"D" Coy	"C" Coy 2/8 R. WAR. R.	in left of CALL RESERVE TR.

2. GUIDES. 4 Guides for "A" Coy and 3 per each of "B" and "C" Coys will report at Battn. H.Q., CALL RESERVE TRENCH at 8.30 p.m. & will guide platoons to posts etc. Companies will leave in the following order, "A", "C" "B", the first Coy leaving as soon as possible after dark, but not before 9 pm. "B" and "D" Coys will not move up from their present positions before 8.15 pm.

… movement will be by platoons at 200x interval.

4. All air photos, L.G. drums and trench stores will be taken over. 2/7 R.WAR.R. will hand over 38 L.G. drums per gun in good condition, and Coys will leave for them in their present trenches a similar number of drums. O.C. Coys will send in to Battn. H.Q. by 8.30 p.m. a list of all trench stores they are handing over, unless they have already obtained a receipt for these from a representative of 2/7 R.WAR.R. O.C. Coys will also send in to Battn H.Q. by 9 p.m. tomorrow a list of the trench stores etc taken over by them from 2/7 R.WAR.R. in the front line.

5. Coys will report relief complete as soon as possible. If telephones are available, the code word BRQTLL may be used.

6. Acknowledge.

2/9/17.

(Sd) W.S.FRAME
Lt&Adj
2/8 Warwicks

2/7 R War R

Battⁿ Order No. 5.9.17

1. 2/7th R. War. R. will relieve 2/6th R War R in front line left section on the right of 5th/6th unit.

2. On relief 2/6th R War R will withdraw to the accommodation occupied by 2/7 R War R and will be in left support.

3. Dispositions & reliefs are as follows

2/6th R War R	2/7 R War R
A Coy	Right Front Coy
2 Platoon C Coy	Left front Coy
3 Platoon B Coy	Support in Farm area in support
D Coy & 1 Platoon B Coy & 1 Platoon C Coy	Hill Farm area

4. Guides. 11 Guides from A Coy & 2 from each of B & C Coys 2/6th R War R will report to H.Q. 2/7th R War R Hill Farm by 8.15 pm & will guide platoons to the posts

5. The actual time for commencement of relief will depend on the result of operations taking place this evening & whole unit will be ready to relieve at 12 midnight. 2/7th R War R will not commence to move up till code word "SPEY" is received from Bde. H.Q.

5. In the event of relief being impossible owing to hostile barrage the Batt. may have to remain in the line another 24 hrs, in which case two Rations may be consumed. In view of this contingency water supply should be conserved as much as possible.

6. All air photos, L.G. Drums & trench stores will be handed over – receipt that Coys will hand over to relieving Coys of 1/7th R. War. R. the same number of drums which they actually took over on relief themselves. The result will be that each Batt[n] will have back its own drums. Receipts in duplicate will be obtained and one copy sent to Batt. H.Q. by 6 pm the day after relief.

7. All movement will be by platoons at 200 yds interval. Completion of relief will be reported to Batt. H.Q. by telephone or runner, by code word "TAY".

8. Acknowledge.

Lt. & Adjt.

1/8th R. Warwickshire Regt.
Batt. Order No. 167. Sept. 8/17.

1. The Battalion will be relieved tonight 8/9th inst. in left support by 1/4th Gloucesters, & will proceed to camp at G.6.d.4.6. (BRANDHOEK, Area No 1) by train.
2. All air photos, sketch maps, gas rattles & trench stores will be handed over, & receipts obtained & sent to Orderly Room by 12 noon, tomorrow. Lewis Gun magazines will not be handed over.
3. 4 Guides per Coy. & 2 for Batt. HQ will be at junction of OXFORD ROAD & main road at 7 pm.
4. A train will be at C.27.c.7.4. at 9.30 pm. to carry personnel to BRANDHOEK area – detraining at H1a5.2 ~~[illegible]~~ central. Arrangements have been made for guides at detraining point. Coys. will if necessary reconnoitre route to entraining place.
5. In event of train not being large enough there are odd trucks returning empty throughout the night & men can travel by them.

(2)

Batt. Order 167. Contd

6 All movement will be by platoons at 200x distance.

7. Relief complete will be intimated to Batt. H.Q. by telephone by code word "NESS."

8. Acknowledge.

Lt & Adjt.
2/8 Warwicks.

After order,

2/4 Glosters are ~~very~~ weak – mostly 2 plats per Coy & Relief of Coys will be as follows:–

2/8 WAR	2/4 GLOS.
D Coy	B Coy (3 plats) & C Coy (2 plat)
B & C Coys	A Coy (2 platoons)
A Coy	D Coy 2 platoons

War Diary

[illegible] BATTALION [illegible]

[illegible] ORDER 140 by [illegible] 13th SEPT 1917.

1. The Battalion will move to [illegible] CAMP [illegible] (SHEET No. [illegible]) tomorrow 14th inst.

2. ORDER OF MARCH: H.Q., "A", [illegible], "B" "C" "D" Coys.
STARTING POINT: [illegible] road crossing road at [illegible].
Headquarters will pass Starting Point at 9-0 a.m.
A distance of 300 yards will be maintained between Coys and transport [illegible] of [illegible] and 500 yards between Battalions [illegible] of [illegible].

Transport will fall in in rear of Battalion at [illegible].

ROUTE: [illegible] - Cross Roads [illegible] - Cross Roads [illegible] - Road Junction [illegible] - Cross roads [illegible] - Level Crossing [illegible] - Cross roads [illegible].

3. DRESS: Full Marching Order - Steel Helmets will be worn.

4. Officers Valises and Mess Baskets as per Standing Orders.

5. No halts will take place on the main [illegible] - [illegible] ROAD.

6. [illegible] will precede the Battalion at a sufficient distance to give warning to Traffic Control Posts of the approach of the column.

7. O.C.Coys are held responsible that the huts and the vicinity of huts are left in a clean and sanitary condition.

8. ACKNOWLEDGE.

Sgd. [illegible], Lieut.& Adjt.
[illegible]

Issued at 6 p.m.

[illegible] BATTALION [illegible]

[illegible] ORDER [illegible] by [illegible] Commanding.
[illegible] 1917.

1. The Battalion will move to [illegible] CAMP [illegible] No.1 [illegible] tomorrow [illegible] inst.

2. [illegible] Coys.
[illegible] ROUTE [illegible] No.1 [illegible] road of [illegible]
Headquarters will pass starting point at [illegible] a.m.
A distance of [illegible] yards will be maintained between Coys and Transport [illegible] and [illegible] yards between Battalions [illegible]

Transport will fall in in rear of Battalion at [illegible]

ROUTE: No.1 [illegible]
[illegible]
[illegible]

3. DRESS: Full Marching Order [illegible] will be worn.

4. Officers Valises and Mess Baskets as per Standing Orders.

5. No halts will take place on the main [illegible] Road.

6. 2/Lt. [illegible], will precede the Battalion at a sufficient distance to give warning to Traffic Control Posts of the approach of the column.

7. O.C.Coys are held responsible that the [illegible] and the [illegible] of [illegible] are left in a clean and sanitary condition.

8. ACKNOWLEDGE.

Sgd. [illegible] Capt. & Adjt. [illegible]
[illegible]

Issued at 6 p.m.

SECRET.

COPY No. 10

2ND 8TH BATTALION THE ROYAL WARWICKSHIRE REGIMENT.

BATTALION ORDER NO 170 by Lt.COL. [illegible] COMMANDING.
[illegible] 1917.

Ref.Map. Sheet [illegible] 1/40000.

1. The Battalion will move by march route to [illegible] AREA on [illegible] inst.

2. The Battalion will fall in, in column, head of column at Road entrance to Camp, ready to move at 7.45 a.m.

ORDER OF MARCH: H.Q., "B" [illegible] "C" "D" "A" Coys, Transport.

ROUTE: Road Junction [illegible] [illegible] [illegible] [illegible].

3. DRESS: Full Marching Order - Steel Helmets.

4. The Battalion will march [illegible] of Brigade Headquarters, a distance of 200 yards being maintained.

5. Officers Kits, Mess Baskets etc as per Standing Orders.

6. Officers Commanding Companies are held responsible that the Camp is left in a thoroughly clean and sanitary condition.

7. Billeting [illegible] and [illegible] will be rendered immediately on arrival in new area.

8. ACKNOWLEDGE.

sgd. A.[illegible] Lieut. & Adjt.
2/8.R.War.R.

Copies No.1. C.O.
2/5. Coys.
6. Q.M.&T.O.
7. [illegible]
8. [illegible]
9. File.
10. War Diary.

War Diary

2ND 8TH BATTALION THE ROYAL WARWICKSHIRE REGIMENT.

BATTALION ORDER 171 by LT. COL. E. C. CADMAN. D. S. O. COMMANDING.

18th SEPT. 1917.

1. The Battalion will move by march route and train to billets in the BERNEVILLE AREA on the 19th inst.

2. H.Q. DRUMS "A" & "D" Coys will fall in in fours, head of column at Q.19.b.10.4 , ready to move at 4-30 p.m. facing S.E. DRESS: Full Marching Order. ~~Sd Caps~~ Steel Helmets. Water Bottles will be filled.

3. Officers Valises and Mess Baskets will be dumped outside Company Headquarters at 2 p.m. Transport Officer will arrange to collect these.

4. Unconsumed portions of rations for the 19th and breakfast ration for the 20th will be carried on the man.

5. The train will leave CAESTRE STATION at 7-5 p.m. Transport will arrive at CAESTRE STATION three hours before the departure of the train.

6. Baggage & Supply Wagons will entrain with Transport.

7. Transport Officer will provide a horse holder for each horse, also drag ropes for use as breast lines in the covered trucks. Railway authorities provide lashing for the vehicles.
No fused Bombs or Grenades are to be carried on the train.
Water Carts will be full on entrainment.

8. No lights will be lit in any train after dark. The fires of Cookers will be drawn before entrainment

9. Coys will render to the Orderly Room by 10 a.m. tomorrow Entraining State showing numbers of Officers and other ranks proceeding by train.

10. "C" Coy will join Battalion at the Station and entrain with the Battalion.

11. O.C. Coys will ensure that the Camp is left in a clean and sanitary condition.

sgd. A. L. PROSSER. Lieut. & Adjt.
2/8. R. WAR. R.

Copies No. 1. C.O.
2/4. "A" "C" & "D" Coys.
5. H.Q. Mess.
6. Q.M. & T.O.
7. R.S.M.
8. File.
9. War Diary.

2ND 8TH BATTALION THE ROYAL WARWICKSHIRE REGIMENT.

BATTALION ORDER 175 by Lt.COL. [illegible], D.S.O. COMDG.
22nd [illegible].1917.

1. RELIEF. The Battalion will relieve the 7th Lincs in the [illegible] SECTION of the line ([illegible]) on the night of 23/24th.

2. DISPOSITIONS.

	2/8 R.WAR.R.	–	7th LINCS.
RIGHT FRONT COY.	"D"	to relieve	"D"
CENTRE " "	"B"	do	"B"
LEFT " "	"C"	do	"C"
RESERVE COY.	"A"	do	"A"

3. GUIDES. ADVANCE PARTY. Guides will be at [illegible] BRIDGE at 3 p.m. to guide Batt. Signallers and Snipers to Batt. H.Q. and Coy. H.Qs. [illegible] 4 Lewis Gun teams to the front line.
MAIN PARTY. 4 Guides per Coy and 2 for Batt. H.Q. will be found by 7th Lincs. and will meet the Battalion at the western end of [illegible].

4. ROUTES. Railway Bridge [illegible] – [illegible] TRACK – [illegible]
"D" COY. – [illegible] RD – STATION CROSS RDS – [illegible]
"B" COY. – [illegible] RD – STATION CROSS RDS – CROOK ALLEY.
"C" COY. – [illegible] RD – STATION CROSS RDS – CALICO – [illegible].
"A" COY. – For "C" [illegible] POINT – as for "C"
For "B" [illegible] POINT – [illegible] RD – CALICO.
For remainder of Coy. – [illegible] – CADIZ [illegible].
H.Q. COY. 1 guide for personnel.
1 guide to await C.O. of relieving Battn.

5. ORDER OF MARCH. "D" "B" "C" "A" Headquarters.
Coys will move independently by Platoons at 200 yards interval. Leading Platoon to pass junction of [illegible] and [illegible] LANE at 7.15 p.m. and will therefore leave the Camp at 6 p.m.

6. ADVANCE PARTY. 1 Officer and 1 N.C.O. and [illegible] for Batt. H.Q. will leave at 1.30 p.m. and proceed in advance to take over from out-going Coys. The party will proceed with that mentioned in para. 3 (a).

7. STORES. All maps, aeroplane photos, defence schemes, instructions for a forward move, work programmes etc. will be taken over and receipts given.
Handing over receipts will be sent to the Orderly Room by 9 a.m. tomorrow.

8. DRESS. Full Marching Order, minus Greatcoat and Haversacks. The latter will be placed in sandbags, labelled and taken to Q.M. Stores by returning ration limbers.
Officers Kits, Mess Baskets etc will be collected by Transport at 5 p.m.

9. RATIONS. Rations for the 24th will be carried on the man.

10. WATER. Water Bottles will be filled before starting for consumption on ~~[illegible]~~ 24th.

11. TRANSPORT. 1 Limber will accompany each Coy and the Mess Cart Battalion Headquarters and will report at Batt. H.Q. at 5 p.m.

12. Relief complete will be reported at once by telephone or runner to Batt. H.Q. Code word "[illegible]"

13. O.C. Coys will ensure that the Camp is left in a clean and sanitary condition.

14. ACKNOWLEDGE.

sgd. A. [illegible], Lieut. & A/Adjt.
2/8 R.WAR.R.

W.P.

2ND 8TH BATTALION THE ROYAL WARWICKSHIRE REGIMENT.

BATTALION ORDER 122 by Lt.COL. [illegible] C.B.E.? D.S.O. COMMANDING.
21st SEPT. 1917.

1. The Battalion will move tomorrow by march route to LANCASTER CAMP at G.11.c.1.1.

2. Order of march: H.Q. "C" DRUMS, "D" "A" "B" Coy. Transport.
DRESS: Full Marching Order - Steel Helmets.

3. Headquarters will pass starting point cross roads L.30.d.5.5. at 10-25 a.m.

4. ROUTE: L.29.d.2.2. - Road Junc. G.25.b.3.3. - X Cross G.29.a.[illegible].4. - forked roads G.20.b.1.7. - G.21.a.35.05. - G.16.c.5.6. - ROND POINT (G.21.b.4.7) - ST. NICHOLAS.

5. A distance of 200 yards will be maintained between Coys and 400 yards between Battalions.

6. Transport will be divided into two halves, a distance of 200 yards being maintained between the rear Coy and head of Transport and between the two halves of Transport.

7. ACKNOWLEDGE.

sgd. A.L. PROSSER. Lieut. & A/Adjt.
2/8.R.WAR.R.

Officers Kits & Mess Baskets as per Standing Orders.

War Diary

2/8th Battn Royal Warwickshire Regt
Battalion Order 174 by Lt Col C C [illegible] DSO
Commanding 25th Sept 1917

Ref Map FAMPOUX 1/10000

1 Relief The Battalion will be relieved tomorrow night 27/28th Sept by 2/7 R WAR R in accordance with following table

2/7 R WAR R	2/8 R WAR R	DISPOSITIONS
C COY	A COY	CADIZ RES
D	D	RIGHT FRONT
B	B	CENTRE COY
A	C	LEFT FRONT

On relief by 2/7 R WAR R "A" Coy will relieve D Coy 2/5 R WAR R in CADIZ RES and B Coy will relieve B Coy 2/5 R WAR R in CULT RES. C & D Coy & HQ will relieve A & C Coy & HQ respectively of 2/5 R WAR R in Support [illegible] in H 11 a & c [illegible]

2 Advance Parties & Guides Advance Parties of 2/7 R WAR R will be at junction of road and CAMEL TRENCH H 18 a 5.6 at 3pm and 1 guide for four Gun teams, Coy Signallers, Battalion Signallers, Stretcher Bearers will be found to meet them.

1 Guide per Platoon will be at junction of road and CAMEL TRENCH at [blank] to meet incoming Battalion.

A Coy will send 1 guide for garrisons of "C" & "D" Strong points.
Front Coys will arrange to have 1 guide per post at Coy Hqrs to await arrival of relieving Battalion

3 Routes

RIGHT FRONT COY	CAMEL AVENUE - CHICK ALLEY CINEMA TR - CHEMICAL TR
CENTRE COY	CAMEL AVENUE - CHICK ALLEY CINEMA TR - CLOD TR
LEFT FRONT COY	CAMEL AV - CALL - CASH
RESERVE	CAMEL - CADIZ

[illegible]

[illegible] [illegible]

[illegible] [illegible]

[illegible]

Remarks [illegible]

[illegible]

[illegible]

[illegible]

18 H 15 1190/17

Vol 18

Confidential

War

Diary of

2/8th. Bn. The Royal Warwickshire Regiment.

for period from

1st. October. 1917 31st October 1917

VOLUME 18.

Instructions regarding War Diaries and Intelligence Summaries are contained in F. S. Regs., Part II. and the Staff Manual respectively. Title pages will be prepared in manuscript.

WAR DIARY
or
INTELLIGENCE SUMMARY.
(*Erase heading not required.*)

Army Form C. 2118.

Place	Date	Hour	Summary of Events and Information	Remarks and references to Appendices
	H 11 a 6 2 (Fampoux) Oct 1st 1917		During the day all available men in the Battalion were employed on R.E. working parties. 2nd Lt. STEPHENS joined the Battn. Weather fine wind dangerous.	O.L.P
	Ditto Oct 2nd		During the day all available men in the Battalion were employed on R.E. working parties, weather fine wind mild.	O.L.P
	Oct 3rd		During the day all available men were employed for work under R.E. supervision weather fine. 2nd Lt. Jessop & 1 O.R. went on a course at 3rd Army School.	O.L.P
	Oct 4th		Men were again employed throughout the Bn. on R.E. working parties. Relief orders were received. Weather wet.	O.L.P
	Oct 5th		Coy Commanders reconnoitred the line. Men were again employed on R.E. working parties, relief was started at 8-0 pm & was complete at 11-20 pm. sector (Chemical Works), casualties nil, weather unsettled.	O.L.P. App 1
	Oct 6th		Day very quiet, 100 O.R working on trenches under R.E. supervision. Hostile shelling practically nil; casualties 1 O.R. killed, weather wet.	O.L.P

T2134. Wt. W708–776. 500000. 4/15. Sir J. C. & S.

Army Form C. 2118.

WAR DIARY
or
INTELLIGENCE SUMMARY.
(Erase heading not required.)

Instructions regarding War Diaries and Intelligence Summaries are contained in F. S. Regs., Part II. and the Staff Manual respectively. Title pages will be prepared in manuscript.

Place	Date	Hour	Summary of Events and Information	Remarks and references to Appendices
Cadiz Reserve	Oct 7	'17	Very little activity by the enemy; we carried out the usual destructive fire on his M.G. & T.M. emplacements. 100 O.R were employed on cleaning & improving the line under R.E. supervision. Casualties nil, weather wet. 2nd Lt. Walker & 5 platoon went on a course to the Brigade School	A.L.P.
ditto	8	'17	Enemy very quiet except for M.G. fire at night; our operations were the same as for the previous day the enemy's T.M's & M.G. emplacements were subject to concentrated artillery fire. 100 O.R were employed under R.E. supervision improving the lateral C.T's. Casualties nil, weather wet. Col Cadman went to Albert on a gas course.	A.L.P.
—	9	'17	Nothing exceptional took place, our T.M's carried out several bombardments on the enemy's T.M. emplacements. 1 O.R L/Cpl Hughes proceeded to 5th Corps Schools. Casualties nil.	A.L.P.
—	10	'17	At 9am there was a smoke & 18 pounder barrage on enemy's front & support lines, which was taken lying down by the enemy, weather unsettled. Casualties 1 O.R killed. 2 wounded.	APP2 A.L.P.

D. D. & L., London, E.C. (A7883) Wt. W609/M1672 350,000 4/17 Sch. 52a Forms/C/2118/14

Instructions regarding War Diaries and Intelligence Summaries are contained in F. S. Regs., Part II. and the Staff Manual respectively. Title pages will be prepared in manuscript.

WAR DIARY
or
INTELLIGENCE SUMMARY.
(Erase heading not required.)

Army Form C. 2118.

Place	Date	Hour	Summary of Events and Information	Remarks and references to Appendices
Cadiz Reserve	Oct 11	17	Enemy very inactive during the day. Relief orders were received at 9.15 pm the 2/7 R. War. R had relieved the 2/8 R. War. R in the line, the latter moved to support at H 11 a 6 4. Weather unsettled casualties nil.	[illegible]
H 11 a 6 4	Oct 12	—	All the battalion were employed during the day on R.E. working parties. Col Cadman returned from his course. Weather wet casualties nil.	[illegible]
H 11 a 6 4	Oct 13		Battalion was employed on R.E. working parties during the day. 2nd Lt. A.C. DEVERELL reported for duty from Corps Course. 2nd Lt. LLOYD & 4 O.R. returned from Courses. Casualties nil. Weather fine.	[illegible]
Ditto	Oct 14	—	Battalion was employed on R.E. working parties during the day. Casualties nil weather fine.	[illegible]
—	Oct 15	—	Battalion was employed on R.E. working parties during the day. Enemy's artillery quiet. Casualties nil weather [illegible]	App 3
—	Oct 16		Relief orders received. The Bn was relieved by [illegible] & moved to Levis Barracks Arras. Casualties nil, weather fine.	[illegible]
Levis Barracks Arras	Oct 17		The Battalion spent the day cleaning up & holding kit inspections.	[illegible]

D. D. & L., London, E.C. (A;883) Wt. W809/M1672 350,000 1/17 Sch. 52a Forms/C/2118/14

Instructions regarding War Diaries and Intelligence Summaries are contained in F. S. Regs., Part II, and the Staff Manual respectively. Title pages will be prepared in manuscript.

WAR DIARY
or
INTELLIGENCE SUMMARY.
(Erase heading not required.)

Army Form C. 2118.

Place	Date	Hour	Summary of Events and Information	Remarks and references to Appendices
Levis Barracks Arras.	Oct 18	17	Parades for the day included close order drill, musketry, P.T. & B.F. & Gas Drill. Specialist training was carried out. A Coy had the Moat Range. 2nd Lts. JESSOP & WAREHAM & 3 O.R returned from courses. 2nd Lt DUCKWORTH & 5 O.R reported from the Div. Depot Bn.	[illegible]
ditto	Oct 19	–	Parades for the day included close order drill musketry etc. specialist training was carried out. B. Coy had the 50 yds range at G 10 c.	[illegible]
—	Oct 20	–	Parades for the day included close order drill, P.T & B.F, musketry & gas drill. Specialist training was continued. 2nd Lt TYLER & 6 O.R went to 3rd Army Rest Camp. C. Coy had the 50 yds range at G 10 c.	[illegible]
—	Oct 21	–	There was a church parade in the morning at St George's Club for C of E. B Coy were allotted the Moat Range. 2nd Lts SMITH & HARR[illegible] & 4 O.R went to the XVII Corps School at HAUTES-AVESNES.	[illegible]
—	-22	–	Parades for the day included musketry, close order drill & P.T & B.F. Specialist training was continued. D Coy were allotted the range at G 10. c.	[illegible]

D. D. & L., London, E.C. (A7883) Wt. W807/M1672 350,000 1/17 Sch. 52a Forms/C/2118/14

Instructions regarding War Diaries and Intelligence Summaries are contained in F. S. Regs., Part II. and the Staff Manual respectively. Title pages will be prepared in manuscript.

WAR DIARY
or
INTELLIGENCE SUMMARY.
(Erase heading not required.)

Army Form C. 2118.

Place	Date	Hour	Summary of Events and Information	Remarks and references to Appendices
Levis Barracks Arras	Oct 23 '17		During the day the Bn carried out parades under Coy Commanders. 1 O.R went to 3rd Army Officers Mess Cook Course. 2nd Lt WHITELEY returned from Hospital.	R.P.
	Oct 24		In the morning parades were carried out & PT & BF, Musketry, Close Order Drill & Arm Drill were practised. C Coy had the Mont Range & the Lewis gunners of B & C Coys used the Lewis Gun Range at the Mont.	R.P.
	Oct 25		In the morning parades were carried out, PT & BF Musketry Close Order Drill & Arm Drill were practised. D B Coy were allotted the Range. Col CADMAN went to Camiers to see Machine Gun Barrage demonstration.	R.P.
	Oct 26		In the morning there was a concentration march to Etrun, one company was employed on working parties. 1 O.R went to England for a commission.	R.P.
	Oct 27		There were bathing parades during the town, parades under Coy arrangements.	App IV R.P.

D. D. & L., London, E.C. (A7833) Wt. W803/M1672 350,000 4/17 Sch. 52a Forms/C/2118/14

Instructions regarding War Diaries and Intelligence Summaries are contained in F. S. Regs., Part II. and the Staff Manual respectively. Title pages will be prepared in manuscript.

WAR DIARY
or
INTELLIGENCE SUMMARY.
(Erase heading not required.)

Army Form C. 2118.

Place	Date	Hour	Summary of Events and Information	Remarks and references to Appendices
LEVIS BARRACKS ARRAS	28/10/17		Cleaning up of Barracks – Voluntary Church Parades. – 1 O.R. to Eng: Commission	
		12 noon onwards	Battalion relieved the 2/5 GLOSTERS in the GREENLAND HILL SECTOR	
			Dispositions. 'D' Company RIGHT company 'A' " CENTRE " 'B' " LEFT " 'C' " RESERVE "	App.
RIGHT BN GREENLAND HILL SECTOR	"	8.50 p.m.	Relief complete – 8.50 p.m.	
		11.0 p.m.	Patrol under 2/Lt. LUNT went out to investigate gaps in the enemy's wire at I 2 c. 05.70 and I.1 b. 70.56. Light – bright moonlight. Patrol work difficult	
"	29/10/17	3.0 a.m.	Situation quiet. Wind S – slight.	
			Day quiet – some shelling of front line – Communications temporarily broken.	
		10.0 p.m.	Patrols went out to investigate gaps in enemy's wire. In spite of bright moonlight, good results obtained – Night quiet.	
			CAPT. W.R. SCOTT returned from leave – to be act. Bde Staff Captain	
"	30/10/17	3.0 a.m.	Battalion on our right carried out raid on enemy trenches.	
		5.0 a.m.	Situation normal. – Wind S.S.E. – slight.	
			Day quiet – Work by night on support trenches – Cleaning up; burial of bodies. Ground in vicinity of trenches cleared.	
		10.0 pm	Patrol under 2/Lt JONES went out to report on condition of enemy wire	
"	31/10/17		Enemy aircraft fairly active in the early morning – Situation normal – Work on support trenches continued 12.20 p.m. One of our machines brought down by E.A	
		4.30 pm	Trench gas shelling on CAULDRON and CONRAD support (SOROC)	
		10.30 pm	Patrols sent out by D Coy and 'A' Coy under 2/Lt. KITCHIN.	

Ed. C. Cadman
Lt. Col.,
Cmdg 2/8 R. War. R.

D. D. & L., London, E.C. (A7883) Wt. W80/M1672 350,000 3/17 Sch. 52a Forms/C/2118/14

SECRET

2/8th Batt. R. Warwickshire Regt.

Batt. Order No. 175 by Lt. Col. E. C. Cadman D.S.O. Commanding. Oct. 5/17. 1

Reference Map - FAMPOUX - GREENLAND HILL. 1/10,000.

INFORMATION

1 The Batt. will relieve the 2/7th R. War. R. in the CHEMICAL WORKS Sector on the night of Oct. 5/6th.

INSTRUCTIONS

1 TABLE OF RELIEF

2/7th R. War. R.	2/8 R. War. R.	Disposition
D	C	RIGHT COY.
A.	D	LEFT COY.
B	A.	CENTRE COY.
C	B.	RESERVE.

2 ROUTES. Coys. will relieve by the following routes, time shown being the time Coys. will pass junction of CADIZ & CAMEL.

COY	ROUTE	TIME
RIGHT COY	CAMEL AVE. - CROOK ALLEY - CINEMA CHEMICAL TRENCH	8. 0 pm
LEFT COY	CAMEL AVE. - CALICO - CASH TRENCH	8.45 pm
CENTRE COY	CAMEL AVE - CROOK ALLEY - CINEMA - COLD ALLEY	9.15 pm
RESERVE COY	CAMEL - CADIZ	10. 0. pm
BATT. H.Q.	CAMEL - CADIZ	10.15 pm

3. GUIDES

1 Guide per Platoon of 2/7 R. War. R. will be at junction of CADIZ & CAMEL at 7.45 pm. to meet incoming Coys. Coys. will move by platoons with 200x distance between platoons.

4 ADVANCE PARTY

One representative per Lewis Gun team, one Signaller per Coy, 2 Batt. Signallers, 2 Snipers from Batt. H.Q. will proceed ahead of Batt. Coy. Commanders will make their own arrangements.

5. All maps, aeroplane photos, defence schemes, trench stores, etc. will be taken over & receipts given. Receipts will also be forwarded in duplicate to Batt. H.Q. by 12 noon Oct. 6th. Disposition maps will be sent to reach Batt. H.Q. at that time.

6. RATIONS Rations for consumption on Oct 6. & until further orders, will be dumped at QUARRY DUMP at 7.45 pm. On Oct. 5. C.Q.M.S's have been instructed to stay with their Coy. rations until Coys. can send for them.

Camp Kettles & Petrol tins of A & B Coys. will be put on returning ration limbers at 7.45 pm. at junction of COLT RESERVE TRENCH & the QUARRY. Those of C & D Coys. & Batt. H.Q. will be put at TANK DUMP by 7.30 pm & Transport Officer will arrange to collect them.

7. Code word for relief complete "SOFITA."

8. Acknowledge.

[illegible]
Lt. & Adj.
2/8 R. Warwicks.

2

1/8 R. Warwicks Regt.

Battalion Order No. 176. by Major W. R. L. Whatmore Commanding. Oct: 10/17

Reference Map:- FAMPOUX - GREENLAND HILL 1/10,000

1. INFORMATION. The Batt. will be relieved by 1/7 R. War. R. on night of Oct: 11/12.

2. INSTRUCTIONS. (a) Table of relief

1/8 R. War. R.	1/7 R. War. R.	Disposition.
'C' Coy.	'C' Coy.	RIGHT COY.
'D' "	'A' "	LEFT "
'A' "	'B' "	CENTRE "
'B' "	'D' "	RESERVE

(b) Coys. will relieve by the following routes, time shown being time Coys. will pass junction of CADIZ & CAMEL

COY.	ROUTE	TIME.
RIGHT COY.	CAMEL - CROOK - CINEMA - CHEMICAL	7.0 pm.
LEFT COY.	CAMEL - CALICO - CASH:	7.20 pm.
CENTRE COY.	CAMEL - CROOK - CINEMA - COLD	7.40 pm.
RESERVE	CAMEL - CADIZ	8.0 pm.
BATTN. H.Q.	CAMEL - CADIZ.	8.15 pm.

(c) GUIDES.
One guide per platoon & one per 'C' & 'D' Strong Points will report to Batt. H.Q. at 6.30 pm. 2/Lt. Gildesthorp will be in charge of these guides, & will see all relieving Companies in.

(d) ADVANCE PARTY.
Advance party of 1/7 R. War. R. will not exceed one representative per L. Guns Team, one signaller per Coy. 2 signallers & 2 observers for Batt. H.Q. No guides are wanted for these parties.

(e) All maps, aeroplane photographs, defence schemes S.O.S. grenades & trench stores etc. will be handed over & receipts forwarded to Batt. H.Q. by 12 noon Oct: 12.

(f.) On relief by 1/7 R. War. R. Coys. will move as under.

COY.	DISPOSITION.	Occupied now by.
'A' Coy.	HERON TRENCH.	'C' Coy. 1/7 R. War. R.
'B' "	HERON TRENCH	'B' "
'C' "	COLT RESERVE.	'D' "
'D' "	3 plns. CADIZ 1 " LEMON.	'A'

One Officer per Coy. & 1 N.C.O. per platoon will take over from Coys. of 1/7 R. War. R. in support by 3.0 pm. Coys. will make their own arrangements about guides.

(g.) RATIONS.
Rations for 'C' & 'D' Coys. will be dumped nightly where COLT RESERVE crosses road leading to QUARRY at 6.45 pm.
Rations for 'A' & 'B' Coys. & H.Q. will be dumped at TANK DUMP at H.11.a.6.2. at 6.45 pm.

Sheet 2.

Battalion Order No. 176. Contd.

(g) RATIONS (Contd.)
On night of Oct. 11/12th, C.Q.M.S. have been instructed to stay with their Coy. Rations until Coys. can send for them.
Camp Kettles for all Coys. will be brought up tomorrow, Oct. 11th.

(h) CODE WORD.
Relief complete - SKIBOO.

These orders will be acknowledged.

A. J. [illegible]
Lt. & Adj.
1/8 Warwicks.

Copies to.
1. CO
2-5. Coys.
6. 1/7 R.War.R.
7. H.Q. Files.
8. File & War Diary

SECRET.

Copy. no. 10.

3

2/8th Bn. Royal Warwickshire Rgt.

Battalion Order no. 17, dated 15-10-17
by LT. COL. E. C. CADMAN. D.S.O. Commanding.

Reference Map Sheets:
FAMPOUX (1/20,000)
GREENLAND HILL (1/20,000)
51 B.N.W. (1/20,000)

15: 10: 1917.

INFORMATION. 1. The Battalion will be relieved by 2/6 GLOS. RGT. on OCTOBER. 16th 1917.

INSTRUCTIONS. 2. (a) Table of RELIEF.

2/8 R. WAR. R.	2/6 GLOS. R.	DISPOSITION
"A" Company.	"C" Company.	HERON
"B" "	"B" "	HERON
"C" "	"A" "	COLT.
"D" "	"D" "	CADIZ.

(b) Relieving Companies will come in by routes as under:–

2/6 GLOS.	ROUTE.
"C" COMPANY	CAM VALLEY – CASSEL.
"B" "	–do– –do–
"A" "	H.15.d.0.5. – along road – FAMPOUX –
"D" "	Jn of road & COLT RESERVE – COLT.

(c) GUIDES.

Guides of "A" and "B" Coys, 2/8 R. WAR. R. will meet incoming platoons at end of CASTLE LANE at H.16.a.4.7. at 2.15 p.m. Relief to be complete by 4.0 p.m.

Guides of "C" and "D" Coys will meet incoming platoons at 5.45 p.m. on road at H.15.d.0.5.

2/Lt. TOSLAND will be in charge of the guides

(d.) ADVANCE PARTY.

Previous to relief, Advance parties of 2/6 GLOS. R. will take over from Signallers, etc.

(e). All maps, aeroplane photos, defence schemes etc. will be handed over, and receipts in duplicate will be sent to Battn. H.Q. by 10.30 A.M. 17th inst.

(f). On relief by 2/6 GLOS. R., Companies will move independently to billets in LEVIS BARRACKS, ARRAS. C/Q.M. Sgts have been instructed to meet Coys at G.16.d.3.6. – FEBRUARY CIRCUS (opposite JOCK's ENTERTAINMENT).

Coys will move by platoons with 200x distance, of ARRAS – LENS railway.

(g) TRANSPORT.

SHEET. 2.

(g) TRANSPORT.

2 limbers, one each for "A" and "B" Coys, will be ready by CAM VALLEY at 7.0 p.m. for Lewis Guns, Camp Kettles etc.

2 limbers, one each for "C" and "D" Coys, will be at junction of road and COLT RESERVE at 7.0 p.m.

Mess Cart will be at CASTLE LANE, CAM VALLEY at 12 noon, and at Batn. H.Q. at 6.45 p.m.

Officers' Chargers will come up with their Coy. limbers.

H.Q. chargers will be at H.Q. at 6.45 p.m.

(h) The Q.M. will arrange to provide hot tea or cocoa for "C" and "D" Companies and H.Q. at about 9.0 p.m. at FEBRUARY [illegible].

Tea will be provided for "A" and "B" Coys on arrival at Billets at about 10 p.m.

(i) Code Word – Relief complete – PISTOL SHOT.

(j) ACKNOWLEDGE.

Copies issued to:-

(1). C.O.
2.–5. Companies
6. [illegible] (2/6 [illegible])
7. 2/5 GLOS. R.
8. Transport Off. & Quartermaster.
9. R.S.M.
10. War Diary.
11. File.

[signature]
Lieut + Adjt
2/8 Warwicks

SECRET.

2ND 8TH BATTALION THE ROYAL WARWICKSHIRE REGIMENT.

TRENCH NOTES.

4.

Reference Map. No.[illegible]/4. 1/10000. 4-10-17. 27-10-17.

1. BOUNDARIES. FRONT LINE.- Left I.1.d.60.46.
Right. I.7.[illegible].30.

2. TRENCHES. Trenches consist of FRONT & SUPPORT LINE - LINE OF STRONG POSTS - and RESERVE LINE.
The only strong post on Battalion front is [illegible] at I.7.b.[illegible].4.
Battalion Headquarters is in CHILI at H.6.d.[illegible].

3. DISPOSITIONS. LEFT COY. "B" Coy.
CENTRE. "A" "
RIGHT. "D" "
RESERVE. "C" "
The dispositions of the present Battalion are not good and there is plenty of room for improvement. Coy Commanders will submit any changes they think necessary to Battalion H.Qrs for approval.

4. DIVISIONAL POLICY.
(a). Patrolling to be constant.
(b). All work to be undertaken with the advice of the R.E's if it is possible to obtain it.
(c). Work Policy will be issued later.

5. FLANK UNITS. RIGHT ---- [illegible] Inf.Bde.
LEFT ---- 2/[illegible].R.WAR.R.
Mixed Posts will be established with Battalions on either flank and O.C.Coys will ascertain position of Headquarters of Coys on their flanks.

6. DEFENCE SCHEME. Defence Scheme will be issued as soon as it becomes available.

7. S.O.S.
(a). S.O.S.Signal. Grenade bursting into TWO RED & TWO WHITE LIGHTS simultaneously.
(b). S.O.S.GAS. Grenade bursting into GOLDEN RAIN.

8. COMMUNICATIONS.
(a) Telephone. Coy Commanders are reminded that they must not ring up Batt.H.Qrs unless the matter is urgent.
(b). Visual.
(c). Runners. RELAY POSTS will be established at junction of CHILI and [illegible] TRENCH at I.7.a.9.6 Battalion Runners will meet Coy Runners at [illegible] p.m. [illegible] p.m. and 6-30 p.m. If Coy Runners are required at any special time they will be informed by Code Word "[illegible]" followed by the time.

9. REPORTS.
(a). Situation Report twice daily to reach Batt.H.Q. at 5 a.m. and 5 p.m.
(b). TACTICAL PROGRESS REPORT to reach Batt.H.Q. at 8-30 a.m. daily.
(c). CASUALTY REPORT. to reach Batt.H.Q. at 12 noon daily.

10. GUM BOOTS. Any losses in Gum Boots will be charged against the men concerned.

11. LEWIS GUNS. Coy Commanders will make every effort to preserve their Lewis Gun Teams, either by frequent [illegible] reliefs or by using only three of a team at one time in a post.

12. HEALTH OF MEN.
(a). TRENCH FEET. It is important that the orders issued on the Prevention of Trench Feet are strictly adhered to. Providing everything has been done as far as supervision is concerned all men who get Trench

Post will be tried by Field General Court Martial.
(b). HOT FOOD. More use is to be made of Charcoal issued to Front Line Coys. The issue of fresh meat is not sufficient to ensure an ample supply of fat cookers, and it is therefore essential that they are used economically and only where necessary.

12. MEDICAL. Regimental Aid Post in CALF [illegible] at N.12.b.8[illegible].8[illegible]. Advanced Dressing Station at N.11.a.6[illegible].8[illegible].

13. OBSERVATION POST. Battalion Observation Post is in CHILI at N.7.a.8[illegible].6[illegible]. Coy Commanders may use this if they desire to.

14. ARTILLERY. The Battery covering Battalion front is C/[illegible].

sgd. [illegible] Lieut.Col.

Comdg. 2/[illegible]

issued at

COPY No......

2ND 8TH BATTALION THE ROYAL WARWICKSHIRE REGIMENT.

OPERATION ORDER No.178. 27th OCTOBER 1917.

Ref.Map. [illegible] 1/10000.

INFORMATION. 1. The Battalion will relieve 2/8.[illegible] in the [illegible] on the night 28/29th inst.

INSTRUCTIONS. 2. (a). TABLE OF RELIEF.

2/8.R.WAR.R.	2/8.[illegible]	DISPOSITION
"C"	"D"	RIGHT COY.
"A"	"A"	CENTRE COY.
"B"	"B"	LEFT COY.
"D"	"C"	RESERVE.

(b). ROUTE. [illegible] BARRACKS – CROSS ROADS at [illegible] – GAP VALLEY at [illegible] – overland to [illegible] AVENUE.

(c). TIME. "C" Coy will meet their guides at 5 p.m. at junction of [illegible] LANE and [illegible] AVENUE at [illegible] 11.a.60.40.
"B" "A" & "D" Coys will move off in order named with ten minutes interval between Coys, leading Coy to leave [illegible] BARRACKS at 5-45 p.m.

(d). GUIDES. 1 guide per Platoon for "B" "A" & "D" Coys will be at junction of GAP VALLEY & ROAD at [illegible] at 6-45 p.m.
Guides for "C" Coy as above.

(e). ADVANCE PARTIES. The following will parade at Battalion Headquarters at 9-45 a.m. and will go into the line in advance of the Battalion:-
(1). 1 Officer per Coy, and 1 N.C.O. per Platoon.
(2). 2/Lt. [illegible] & Battalion Observers.
(3). 4 Battalion Runners.
(4). Lt. [illegible] and all Batt. & Coy Signallers.
(5). 1 man per Lewis Gun Team.

(f). All trench maps, Aeroplane Photographs, Defence Schemes Documents relating to the Sector, Trench Stores etc will be taken over and receipts obtained and forwarded to Batt.H.Q. by 12 noon on 29th inst.
Disposition Maps will be sent to reach Batt.H.qrs at the same hour.

(g). TRANSPORT. 1 Limber will report to O.C."C" Coy at 11.30 a.m.
1 Limber for each for "B" "A" & "D" Coys will report to O.C.Coys at 1 p.m.
1 limber will report to Lt. [illegible] at 8-15 a.m.
Mess Cart will report at H.Q.Mess at 2 p.m.
M.O. will issue his own orders to Maltese Cart.
Cookers will move with "B" "A" & "D" Coys who will have tea en route.

(h). CODE WORD for relief complete "[illegible]"

(i). These orders will be acknowledged.

Sgd. [illegible] Lieut.Col.

Comdg. 2/8.R.WAR.R.

Copy No.

2ND 8TH BATTALION THE ROYAL WARWICKSHIRE REGIMENT.

SUPPLY ARRANGEMENTS. 27-10-17.

---

1. TRANSPORT & STORES. Transport and Q.M. Stores will remain at ST.NICHOLAS. That part of the Q.M. Stores which is at present at LEWIS BARRACKS will move to ST.NICHOLAS any time after 1 p.m. 28-10-17.

2. RATIONS. Rations for consumption on the 29th will be carried on the man, being drawn from Q.M. Stores early on the 28th. Rations for the 30th and ensuing days will be brought up on limbers to TANK DUMP at H.11.a.60.80. whence they will be pushed on light railway to dump at I.1.c.50.30. where Ration Parties from Coys will meet C.Q.M.S's.
Rations for Battalion Headquarters will be loaded on the last truck and will be intercepted by Headquarter Ration Party at H.6.d.0.5.
Rations will arrive at Railhead at 6 p.m.
No hot food containers being available, it will be impossible to send up hot food from the rear.
The Battalion at present occupying the line uses dixies in the front line. If Coy Commanders think this advisable they will report it to Battalion Headquarters before 10 a.m. on the 29th inst. and dixies will be brought up with their rations the same night.

3. WATER Water for consumption on the 30th will be carried in the water bottle. There is an ample supply of water in tanks at junction of CHILI and CHALK RESERVE at H.12.b.70.50.
Petrol tins will be taken over by relieving Coys. Coy Commanders will reportif they have not sufficient.

4. FUEL. Fat Cookers for the 30th will be carried on the man. The subsequent issue of fuel will depend on reports received.

5. COOKERS. Cookers will join the remainder of the Transport. 1 Cook per Coy will remain behind with the cookers. These men will report to the Quartermaster ~~at 4 p.m. on 29th inst.~~ on return of Cookers on the 28th.

6. AMMUNITION. Bombing Officer will arrange to fill up Battalion and Coy Dumps to new establishment if this has not already been done.

7. CANTEEN. The Quartermaster will arrange to move Canteen Stores to ST.NICHOLAS. Battalion Canteen will be opened in the line on the morning of the 30th inst.

sgd. W.R.T.WHATMORE, Major.
2/8.R.WAR.R.

19H 13 Confidential

War Diary of:-

1/8th Batt. R. Warwickshire Regt.

Volume XVIII

Period:-

Nov: 1/17.

to Nov. 30/17.

Army Form C. 2121
(In pads of 100)

"A" Form
MESSAGES AND SIGNALS.

No. of Message..............

Prefix..............Code..................m.

Office of Origin and Service Instructions

Words.	Charge.

Sent

At......................m.

To.........................

By.........................

This message is on a/c of:

.................................*Service.*

....

(Signature of "Franking Officer.")

Recd. at............m.

Date.......................

From.......................

By.........................

TO

Sender's Number.	Day of Month.	In reply to Number.	AAA
*			

From

Place

Time

The above may be forwarded as now corrected.

....

Censor.

(Z)

....

Signature of Addressor or person authorised to telegraph in his name.

* This line should be erased if not required.

(7981) Wt. W492/M1647 130,000 Pads 5/17 D. D. & L. E1187

Army Form C. 2118.

Vol 19

WAR DIARY
or
INTELLIGENCE SUMMARY.
(Erase heading not required.)

Instructions regarding War Diaries and Intelligence Summaries are contained in F. S. Regs., Part II. and the Staff Manual respectively. Title pages will be prepared in manuscript.

Place	Date	Hour	Summary of Events and Information	Remarks and references to Appendices
RIGHT BN GREENLAND HILL SECTOR	1/11/17	9 a.m -12 noon	Heavy shelling of support lines with 5.9's and 4.2's — some gas shells. Enemy aircraft quiet. Casualties. Killed O.R. 1 Wounded O.R. 1	[initials]
		10.30 pm	Patrols sent out by 'D' 'A' 'B' Coys under 2/Lt. JONES. Situation normal	
-do-	2/11/17		LT. COL. E.C. CADMAN. D.S.O. proceeded on leave; Major W.R.T. WHATMORE assumed command	
		9 a.m - 5 pm	Intermittent shelling of front and support lines, especially CHILI and CAULDRON. Enemy aircraft very quiet.	
		10.30 pm	Patrols of 'A' and 'B' Coys went out under 2/Lieuts WALKER and LUNT. Casualties 1 O.R. (Sgt LESTER missing)	
			Orders for relief received.	[initials]
-do-	3/11/17	9 a.m - 5 p.m	Enemy artillery fairly quiet — Situation normal. Casualties - NIL.	
RIGHT ~~LEFT~~ SUPPORT, GREENLAND HILL SECTOR		5 p.m	Battalion relieved by 2/7 R. WAR. R — became Support Battalion on the left sector, Right sub-sector. Relief complete 7.30 p.m.	
			Night quiet. Working parties found in accordance with Brigade instructions	[initials]
		3 pm	Platoon of B Company proceeded to Brigade School, in relief of platoon already there. — SGT TURNER & 1 O.R. to Divisional Depot Bn. — Casualties NIL	

D. D. & L., London, E.C.
(A7883) Wt. W809/M1672 350,000 4/17 Sch. 52a Forms C/2118/14

Instructions regarding War Diaries and Intelligence Summaries are contained in F. S. Regs., Part II. and the Staff Manual respectively. Title pages will be prepared in manuscript.

WAR DIARY
or
INTELLIGENCE SUMMARY.
(Erase heading not required.)

Army Form C. 2118.

Place	Date	Hour	Summary of Events and Information	Remarks and references to Appendices
LEFT SUPPORT GREENLAND HILL SECTOR	4/11/17	During the day	Working Parties in accordance with Brigade schedule	
		9.30 – 3.30	'A' 'C' 'D' Companies & H.Q. bathed at Advanced Divisional Baths, ATHIES LOCK	
		3 pm.	2/LT. DEVERILL & 2/LT. DAVIES attached for 3 days to Batteries, 306 Bde R.F.A.	
		4.30 – 10.0 pm.	Enemy artillery very active in reply to our Bombardment of the enemy lines at 4.30 pm.	
			Casualties – NIL.	
-do-	5/11/17		Working parties as for the 4th.	
		9 am – 10 pm	Enemy artillery and aircraft very quiet. Situation normal. Casualties NIL.	
			SGT J. HALL sent as Instructor to XVII Corps Schools	
-do-	6/11/17		Working parties as for previous day	
		9 am – 10 pm	Enemy Artillery quiet – situation normal – casualties NIL	
			2/LT. C.H.B. KITCHIN proceeded on Company Leader's L.G. Course, G.H.Q. S.A. Sch. Le TOUQUET — 3 O.R. sent to 182 T.M. Battery.	
			Instructions re disposal of Pte. DUNN sentenced to 3 yrs P.S. received from APM 61D.	
-do-	7/11/17		15 O.R. proceed to Brigade School on Course for training of N.C.O's.	
		2 pm	Pte M. DUNN, sentenced to 3 years P.S., committed to prison.	
		9 pm – 10 pm	Enemy Artillery fairly active. Situation normal – Casualties NIL	

Instructions regarding War Diaries and Intelligence Summaries are contained in F. S. Regs., Part II. and the Staff Manual respectively. Title pages will be prepared in manuscript.

WAR DIARY
or
~~INTELLIGENCE SUMMARY.~~

(Erase heading not required.)

Army Form C. 2118.

Place	Date	Hour	Summary of Events and Information	Remarks and references to Appendices
LEFT SUPPORT GREENLAND HILL SECTOR	8/11/17		Enemy artillery active on support line – Enemy aircraft abnormally active. One E.A. brought down in enemy lines – Casualties Nil – Orders for relief received	
		8 am – 10 pm	Working Parties found, as per Brigade schedule. Work on CONRAD finished	
			Lieut A.L. TOSLAND proceeded on leave: LT. WOOLDRIDGE returned from leave.	[initials]
	9/11/17	8 am	Morning working parties found as usual. After 9 p.m. parties for work on strong points. – Enemy artillery quiet.	
LEFT BATTN. GREENLAND HILL SECTOR.		5 pm	Battn. relieved 2/7 R. WAR R. in the front line. Relief complete 7 pm. Casualties Nil. Dispositions: C. Coy. Right Front Coy; B' Coy. Left Front Coy; A " Centre -do-; 'D' " Reserve Coy.	[initials]
		11.0 pm	Patrols sent out by A. B. C Coys, to investigate state of enemy's wire	
-do-	10/11/17	During day.	Enemy artillery unusually quiet – Weather very bad – Casualties Nil	
			1 platoon of 'D' Company ~~proceeded~~ proceeded to Bde School in relief of platoon of 'B' Coy	
			CAPT. A.E. TONKS proceeded on 3rd Army Infantry Course	[initials]
-do-	11/11/17	5.0 am – 7.0 am	Enemy artillery quiet – rather more aerial activity than usual – day very fine – Casualties Nil – 1 OR to 3rd Army Inf. Sch.; 1 OR to 3rd Army Sniping School.	[initials]
	12/11/17		2/LT. A DEVERILL & 1 N.C.O. proceeded on 4 days R.E. Course	
		3.0 am	Slight gas cloud drifted over lines – Casualties 4 OR (very slight) – Enemy artillery	[initials]

D. D. & L., London, E.C. (A7883) Wt. W803/M1672 350,000 4/17 Sch. 52a Forms/C/2118/14

WAR DIARY
or
INTELLIGENCE SUMMARY.
(Erase heading not required.)

Army Form C. 2118.

Instructions regarding War Diaries and Intelligence Summaries are contained in F. S. Regs., Part II. and the Staff Manual respectively. Title pages will be prepared in manuscript.

Place	Date	Hour	Summary of Events and Information	Remarks and references to Appendices
RIGHT BN GREENLAND HILL SECTOR	12/11/17	(cont)	quiet – Casualties Wounded O.R. 1 – 2 'Lovat's Scouts' attached for instruction	
		10.0 p.m.	Patrols from 'B' & 'C' Coys to investigate state of enemy wire. – Work on strong posts	
-do-	13/11/17	during day	Enemy artillery very quiet – Casualties NIL	
			LT F.N. PHIPPS, 2/LT WAREHAM proceeded on leave.	
-do-	14/11/17	during day	Artillery quiet. – Day clear, more air work, principally ours – No casualties.	
			Usual patrols & working parties at night. – Orders for relief prepared	
-do-	15/11/17		In reply to our midday bombardment, much enemy shelling of C.T.'s, particularly CHILI AV.	
			Casualties Killed 1 O.R. Wounded 1 OR	
		12.0 noon	Advance parties from 2/7. R. War. R. arrived to take over line	
		5.0 p.m.	Battalion relieved by 2/7 R. WAR. R. – Relief complete 7.0 p.m. Casualties NIL	
RT SUPPORT BN GREENLAND HILL			Night quiet. – Working parties for carrying R.E. material & for work on strong points found	
			MAJOR W.E. PHILLIPS reported for duty from England, taken on strength, and assumed command of Battn, vice A/MAJOR W.R.T. WHATMORE (LT COL E.C. CADMAN on leave)	
			2/LT. G. GILDERTHORP returned from hospital (C.R.S)	
-do-	16/11/17		Working parties found according to Brigade schedule – Day quiet – Casualties NIL	

D. D. & L., London, E.C. (A7833) Wt. W80/M1672 350,000 4/17 Sch. 52a Forms/C/2118/14

Instructions regarding War Diaries and Intelligence Summaries are contained in F. S. Regs., Part II. and the Staff Manual respectively. Title pages will be prepared in manuscript.

WAR DIARY
or
INTELLIGENCE SUMMARY.
(Erase heading not required.)

Army Form C. 2118.

Place	Date	Hour	Summary of Events and Information	Remarks and references to Appendices
RT. SUPPT BATTN. GREENLAND HILL	16/11/17		2LT. WOOLDRIDGE and 2/LT. SCUTT attached to 307 Bde R.F.A. for 3 days	
	17/11/17		Working parties found according to Bde schedule – Day fairly quiet – Casualties Wounded O.R. 1	JJS
		11-12 2-4	Forward Divisional Baths at ATHIES LOCK allotted to Bdes 'A' 'C' & HQ bathed	
		3.0 pm	1 platoon of 'C' Coy relieved that of 'D' Coy at the Brigade School.	
			1 platoon of 'C' Coy attached to RE's for working parties	JJS
"	18/11/17		Working parties found according to Bde schedule – Casualties Nil	
		3.0 pm	Smoke discharged along Divisional Front – Fairly heavy artillery retaliation – C.T's damaged – Special working party at night to clear C.T's	JJS
			1 O.R. to 'B' Lewis Gun Course, G.H.Q. Small Arms School, LE TOUQUET	
"	19/11/17	am 2.0	2/7. R. War R raided enemy trenches – Slight enemy retaliation – 1 man to England (comm)	
			Working Parties found according to Bde Schedule. Casualties NIL	
			2/LT. C.H.B. KITCHIN admitted to hospital. Orders for relief received.	JJS
"	20/11/17	3.0 am	Gas projected on right Brigade against dug-outs in Railway cutting	
		6.15 am	Smoke barrage along Divisional front – Enemy retaliation fairly heavy on support lines.	
		During day.	Enemy unusually quiet – no artillery; no M.G. activity – slight shelling of back	

D. D. & L., London, E.C. (A7833) Wt. W803/M1672 350,000 4/17 Sch. 52a Forms/C/2118/14

Instructions regarding War Diaries and Intelligence Summaries are contained in F. S. Regs., Part II. and the Staff Manual respectively. Title pages will be prepared in manuscript.

WAR DIARY
or
INTELLIGENCE SUMMARY.
(Erase heading not required.)

Army Form C. 2118.

Place	Date	Hour	Summary of Events and Information	Remarks and references to Appendices
RIGHT SUPPT GREENLAND HILL SECTOR.	20/11/17 (cont)		area about 11 pm — Casualties NIL.	
			Working parties found according to Brigade schedule — advance party of 2/7 WORC RGT	[initials]
			visited the lines — Precautions in event of enemy withdrawal taken.	
	21/11/17.		Enemy artillery very quiet. — Working parties found as usual during the morning	
			Casualties NIL	
		4.0 pm	Battalion relieved by the 2/7 WORC. RGT. Relief complete 5.30 pm. Battalion	[initials]
LEVIS BARRACKS ARRAS.			proceeded into reserve at LEVIS BARRACKS ARRAS	
	22/11/17.		25. O.R. arrived from Div. Dep. Batn. Day spent in cleaning up & kit inspections. — Working parties of 55 OR. found	[initials]
-do-	23/11/17		LT COL. E.C. CADMAN returned from leave and re-assumed command of Battalion.	
			LT. W.R.T. WHATMORE relinquishes acting rank of MAJOR and assumed duties of	
			adjutant — CAPT. S.E. PARSONS to Hospital. LT. A.L. PROSSER assumed command	
			of 'D' Company. — CAPT. J.J. SLATER re-assumes duties as O.C. 'C' Coy	
			Majority of Battalion on working parties — remainder Coy Training	
			15 men per Company commenced a course of Instruction in Lewis Gun.	
			2/LT R.O. LUNT & 1 O.R to G.H.Q. School for Training of Instructors in Recreational	
			Training — 1 O.R to England (Commission) 1 OR to Base (perm. unfit)	[initials]

D. D. & L., London, E.C. (A7833) Wt. W803/M1672 350,000 1/17 Sch. 52a. Forms/C/2118/14

Instructions regarding War Diaries and Intelligence Summaries are contained in F. S. Regs., Part II, and the Staff Manual respectively. Title pages will be prepared in manuscript.

WAR DIARY
or
INTELLIGENCE SUMMARY.
(Erase heading not required.)

Army Form C. 2118.

Place	Date	Hour	Summary of Events and Information	Remarks and references to Appendices
LEVIS BARR. ARRAS.	24/11/17		Working parties, amounting to 150 O.R. found by Battalion — Remainder, Company training, firing on Range — Training of new Lewis Gunners (continued)	[illegible]
"	25/11/17		Battalion Bathed — Disinfector at Disposal of Battn — Inspection of Arms by Divisional Armourer Sergt: reported to be in good condition. Training of new Lewis Gunners continued. — W. Party of 30 OR found.	[illegible]
"	26/11/17		Company Training & training of Specialists continued — Working parties, amounting to 150 O.R. found —	[illegible]
"	27/11/17		Company Training continued	
		4.0 pm.	Warning Order for move to DAINVILLE about 10.30 a.m. 28th received	
			Men on Courses returned from Bde. School: 49 OR at Tunnelling returned	[illegible]
"	28/11/17	2.0 am.	Orders for move to WANQUETIN received — Battalion Orders published	[illegible] App
WANQUETIN		10.30 a	Battalion moved by route march to WANQUETIN — arrived 2.30 p.m. — Billets good	
"			7 O.R's received from Divisional Depot Battn — 2/LT. WHITELEY proceeded on leave	[illegible]
"	29/11/17		Inspection of Transport by Commanding Officer	

Army Form C. 2118.

WAR DIARY
or
INTELLIGENCE SUMMARY.
(Erase heading not required.)

Instructions regarding War Diaries and Intelligence Summaries are contained in F. S. Regs., Part II. and the Staff Manual respectively. Title pages will be prepared in manuscript.

Place	Date	Hour	Summary of Events and Information	Remarks and references to Appendices
WANQUETIN	30/11/17	12 noon.	Battalion paraded at 12 noon & marched to BEAUMETZ. Entrained at 3.30 pm. Detrained at BAPAUME. at 7.0 pm.	
		9. pm.	Embussed at BAPAUME. proceeded to METZ EN COUTURE arriving at midnight	[illegible]

Ed. C. [illegible] Lt Col.
Cdg. 1/8 Warwicks.

D. D. & L., London, E.C.
(A7883) Wt. W809/M1672 350,000 4/17 Sch. 52a Forms/C/2118/14

SECRET. Copy No.

2/8th Battn. Royal Warwickshire Regiment.

Battalion Order. No. 180.

Ref. FAMPOUX – GREENLAND HILL (1/10000).
SKETCH. No A/4. 4·10·17.

8-11-1917.

INFORMATION. 1. The Battalion will be relieved by the 2/7 R.WAR.R. in the GREENLAND HILL SECTOR on night of 3/4th November.

INSTRUCTIONS. 2. (a) TABLE OF RELIEF.

2/8 R.WAR.R.	2/7 R.WAR.R	Present position of 2/7 R.WAR.R. Coy. H.Q.
'D' Company	'X' Company	H.11. b.45.55.
'A' "	'Z' "	H.11. b.60.60.
'B' "	'W' "	H.11. a.90.30.
'C' "	'Y' "	H.11. b.20.40.

(b) ROUTE AND TIME. Time shown is that at which leading platoon of incoming companies will reach junction of CHILI AV. and CALF RESERVE

2/7 R.WAR.R.	ROUTE	TIME
'X' Coy.	HUSSAR – CHILI.	5·30 p.m.
'Z' "	– do –	5·40 p.m.
'W' "	– do –	5·50 p.m.
'Y' "	– do –	~~—~~ p.m 6.0pm

(c) GUIDES.

One Guard per platoon will meet incoming coys. The guides will report to LT. A.L. TOSLAND at junction of CHILI and CALF RESERVE at 5.20 p.m.

(d) ADVANCE PARTY.

2/7 R.WAR.R. will send in the undermentioned advance parties:–

(1) 1 officer per Coy, and 1 N.C.O. per platoon.
(2) 1 man per L.G. team.
(3) All Battn. and Coy. signallers.
(4) Battalion Observers.

(e) All trench maps, aeroplane photographs, defence schemes, Documents relating to the sector, trench stores etc. will be taken over, and receipts obtained and forwarded to Battn. H.Q. by 12 noon on 4th inst.

(f). On relief, Coys will take over from the coys of 2/7 R.WAR.R., which relieve them.

1 officer per Coy and 1 N.C.O. per platoon will take over from corresponding Coys before 2·0 p.m. on ~~5th~~ 3rd inst.

(g) CODEWORD for relief complete – DASHWOOD.
" " Coys on reaching support billets – BUCKSKIN.

(h) Acknowledge.

REPORTS. 3. Battalion Headquarters will be at H.11. b.60.80.

Copies to:–

1. C.O.
2. All Coys.
2/7 R.War.R.
Q.M & T.O.
8. R.S.M.
9. War Diary
10. File.

W. R. T. Ka[illegible]
Commanding. 2/8 R. War.

SECRET. Copy. No.

2/8th Bn. Royal Warwickshire Regiment.

Battalion Order. No. 181.
dated 8.11.1917.

Ref. Map. FAMPOUX – GREENLAND HILL

INFORMATION. 1. The Battalion will relieve the 2/7 R. WAR. R. in the GREENLAND HILL sector on the night of the 9/10th inst.

INSTRUCTIONS. 2. (a) Table of Relief.

2/7 R.WAR.R.	2/8 R.WAR.R.	DISPOSITIONS
"W" Company.	"B" Company.	LEFT COY.
"Z" "	"A" "	CENTRE "
"X" "	"C" "	RIGHT "
"Y" "	"D" "	RESERVE "

(b) Route. HUZZAR – CHILI AVENUE.

(c) Time. Companies will move off in the following order:- "B" "A" "C" and "D", ten minutes interval between companies, leading coy to pass junction of CHILI AV – HUZZAR at 5 pm.

(d) The following will parade at Bn. H.Q. at 2.30 p.m., and will go into the line in advance of the Battalion.
① 1 Officer per Coy. & 1 N.C.O. per platoon.
② 2/Lt. GUNTER and Bn & Coy signallers.
③ 1 man per Lewis Gun team.

(e) Guides. 1 Guide per platoon for all Coys will be at the junction of CALF RESERVE & CHILI AV. at 3.15 p.m.

(f) Battalion Observers. LT. WOOLDRIDGE and Batn. Observers will take over from 2/7 R.WAR.R. by 12 noon.

(g) All trench maps, aeroplane photographs, Defence schemes & Documents relating to Trench System, Trench stores etc., will be taken over, and receipts obtained, and forwarded to Bn. H.Q. by 12 noon 10th inst. Disposition maps to reach Bn. H.Q. at the same hour.

(h) Code word for relief complete – MISSED POST

(i) ACKNOWLEDGE.

(sd.) W.R.T. WHATMORE,
Major,
Comdg. 2/8 R. War. R.

Copies to:-
1. C.O.
2. Adjt.
3-6. Coys.
7. 2/7 R.War.R.
8. Q.M. [illegible]
9. M.O.
10. War Diary
11. File.

SUPPLY ARRANGEMENTS.

Rations will be brought up to CUBA DUMP. C/QM. Sgts have been instructed to await there the arrival of Company Ration parties.

SECRET. Copy No.

2/8th Bn. Royal Warwickshire Regiment.

Battalion Order. No. 182

Reference: FAMPOUX – GREENLAND HILL. (1/10000) November 14. 1917

INFORMATION. 1. The Battalion will be relieved by the 2/7 R. WAR. R. in the GREENLAND HILL SECTOR on the night of the 15/16 November.

INSTRUCTIONS. 2. a) TABLE OF RELIEF

2/8 R. WAR. R.	2/7 R. WAR. R.	Position of 2/8 Coy H.Q's
'B' COMPANY	'Y' COMPANY.	same as occupied last time
'A' "	'Z' "	– do –
'C' "	'X' "	– do –
'D' "	'W' "	– do –

b) ROUTE AND TIME.
Time shown is that at which leading platoon of incoming Coys will reach junction of CHILI AV. – CALF RES.

2/7 R. WAR. R.	ROUTE	TIME
'Y' COMPANY.	HUSSAR — CHILI	~~5.30~~ p.m. 5.0
'Z' "	– do –	~~5.40~~ p.m. 5.10
'X' "	– do –	~~5.50~~ p.m. 5.20
'W' "	– do –	~~6.00~~ p.m. 5.30

c) GUIDES. One guide per platoon will meet incoming Companies. The guides will report to 2/LT. GUNTER at junction of CALF and CHILI at 5.20 p.m.

d) ADVANCE PARTY. The 2/7 R. WAR. R. will send in the undermentioned advance parties:-

(1) 1 Officer per Coy + 1 N.C.O. per platoon.
(2) 1 man per L.G. team.
(3) All Battn and Company Signallers.
(4) Battalion observers.

e) All Trench maps, aeroplane photographs, defence schemes, Documents relating to the sector, Trench stores etc. will be taken over, and receipts obtained, and forwarded to Battn. H.Q. by 12 noon on the 16th inst.

f) On relief, the Coys will take over the same areas as last time. One officer per Coy and 1 N.C.O. per platoon will proceed in advance to take over, before 2 p.m. 15th inst.

g) CODEWORD for relief complete, to be sent to Bn H.Q. by WIRE and RUNNER — TUNE.
CODEWORD for Coys on reaching support line – HIST.

h) ACKNOWLEDGE.

Copies to:-
1. C.O.
2. Adjt
3.–6 Coys.
7. 2/7 R. War. R.
8.

(sd) W. R. T. WHATMORE,
Major,
Cmdg. 2/8 R. War. R.

SECRET.

Copy. No.

2/8TH BATTN. ROYAL WARWICKSHIRE REGIMENT

Battalion Order. No. 188.

Reference:- Map
FAMPOUX - GREENLAND HILL. (1/10000)

November. 20th 1917.

INFORMATION. 1. The Battalion will be relieved by the 2/7 WORCESTER RGT. in the GREENLAND HILL SECTOR on the afternoon of the 21 st. November.

INSTRUCTIONS. 2. (a) Table of relief.

2/8 R. WAR. R.	2/7 WORC. R.	present posn of 2/8 R. War. R. Coy H.Q
'A' Company	'A' Company	H. 11. b. 50. 60.
'C' "	'C' "	H. 11. b 20. 40.
'D' "	'D' "	H. 11. b. 44. 55.
'B' "	'B' "	H. 11. a. 90. 30.

(b) ROUTE AND TIME.

The incoming unit will enter via. CASTLE LANE - CABLE - NORTHUMBERLAND AV. Leading Coys will not pass TANK DUMP before 4 p.m.

(c) GUIDES.

One guide per platoon, 1 guide per Coy H.Q, and 1 guide for Battn. H.Q. They will report to 2/LT. DAVIS at TANK DUMP at 3.45 p.m. In addition 1 policeman will be on trench traffic duty at the junction of CASTLE LANE and CABLE to direct incoming companies.

(d) ADVANCE PARTY.

2/7 WORCESTERS will send in the undermentioned advance parties :-

(1) 1 Officer per Coy, and 1 N.C.O. per platoon.
(2) All Battalion and Company signallers.
(3) Battalion Observers.

(e) GUARDS.

2/7 WORCESTERS will relieve the following guards by 12 noon on the day of relief:-

(1) 2 L.G. teams in CAM VALLEY.
(2) 2 L.G. teams in CHALK RES.
(3) Water guard TANK DUMP (1 N.C.O. and 2 men)
(4) Ammunition guard at COOKHOUSE DUMP (1 NCO 2 men)

(f) All trench maps, aeroplane photographs, defence schemes, documents relating to the sector, trench stores, etc. will be taken over, and receipts ~~given~~ obtained and forwarded to Bn. H.Q. by 12 noon. on the 22 nd. inst.

(g) On relief, Companies will move independently to billets in ARRAS. Attention is directed to Traffic Control Orders.

(h). CODEWORD for Relief complete :- CHERRY BLOSSOM.

(i) ACKNOWLEDGE.

Copies to :-

1. C.O.
2. Adjt
3-6 Companies
7. 2/7 Worcesters
8. Q.M. & T.O.
9. R.S.M.
10. War Diary.
11. File.

(sd) W.E. PHILLIPS, Major,
Comdg. 2/8 R. War. R.

2/8th. Battn. Royal Warwickshire Regiment.

Supply Arrangements to accompany Battn. Order. No. 196.

November. 20. 1917.

Q.M. STORES. 1. The Transport and Q.M. stores will remain at ST. NICHOLAS, but the undermentioned will move to LEVIS BARRACKS on the afternoon of the 21st. inst.

(1) Tailors' shop.
(2) Bootmakers' shop.
(3) Field Kitchens
(4) Drums.

BILLETS. 2. Billets will be at LEVIS BARRACKS. Companies will occupy the same rooms as before.
Coy. clerks will report to LT. WOOLDRIDGE at Battn. H.Q. in the line at 8.30 a.m. on 21st. inst. LT. WOOLDRIDGE will report to the Adjutant for instructions
Q.M. will arrange with Transport Officer for conveyance of blankets etc. to LEVIS BARRACKS.

RATIONS. 3. Rations for consumption on the 21st. will be sent to the trenches complete. Men will have teas before leaving the line.
Q.M. will arrange for hot soup for Companies on reaching LEVIS BARRACKS.

TRANSPORT. 4. On 21st. inst., one limber per Company will be at TANK DUMP at 5.0 p.m. Mess Cart will be at CAM VALLEY at 11.30 a.m. and again at TANK DUMP at 5.0 p.m.

LEWIS GUNS etc. 5. Lewis Guns, ammunition, petrol tins etc. will be stacked into Coy. dumps near TANK DUMP, as Companies leave the trenches. This will be done under proper supervision by Companies, and a Guard will be placed by each Coy. on its own dump to await arrival of limbers.
Coys may make use of Mess Cart at 11.30 a.m. for sending out any Officers' mess properties they wish to. One servant per Coy. may accompany the mess-cart to ARRAS.

CANTEEN. 6 Canteen and recreation room will be as before.
C/C. Russell will arrange to have canteen open for men on their arrival in billets.

(Sd) W.P.T. WHATMORE,
Major,
2/8 R. War. R.

182/61 2044 21

Confidential

Vol 20

War Diary of:-

2/8th Battalion The Royal Warwickshire Regiment

Volume XX

Period:-

Dec: 1/17

to Dec: 31/17

Army Form C. 2118.

Instructions regarding War Diaries and Intelligence Summaries are contained in F. S. Regs., Part II. and the Staff Manual respectively. Title pages will be prepared in manuscript.

WAR DIARY
or
~~INTELLIGENCE SUMMARY.~~
(Erase heading not required.)

Place	Date	Hour	Summary of Events and Information	Remarks and references to Appendices
METZ-EN-COUTURE.	1st		Arrived by march from RUYAULCOURT 1-30 am. Conference at Bde Hdqrs. Battn	
			ordered to be in position in W14b in support of an attack by the Guards Division	
			in direction of VILLERS GUISLAN. Rested at HEUDICOURT – shelled – 1 Casualty.	W.R.O.D.
HEUDICOURT	2nd	8.30am	Left HEUDICOURT, marched VIA FINS + METZ to GOUZEAUCOURT WOOD. Transport	
			moved to ROYAULCOURT – Shelled in GOUZEAUCOURT WOOD – lost 1 Lewis Gun	App. 1.
			Conference in GOUZEAUCOURT WOOD – Orders received to take over front line	
			from mixed details of 20th Division under 7th KOYLI.	W.R.O.W.
FRONT LINE	3rd	2am	Relief complete. Line actually taken over ran from L.35 c 4.0 – R 5 a 0.3 –	
			R4 a 3.5 – R4 c 5.2 – R10 a 7.7 (Ref GONNILIEU 1/10000) with Battn HQ at R4 c 4.4	
			Dispositions "C" Left Front "A" Right Front "D" Left Centre "B" Right Centre.	
			2/7 R WARR on right + 1st KOSB 29th Div on left flank.	
			Enemy attacks continual throughout the day (see appendix attached.	
			2/Lt F J. STEPHENS wounded CAPT R.B GIBBINS. killed	W.R.O.W.
	4th		see appendix. 2nd Lt J.W. JESSOP wounded Lts. TOSLAND, WATSON + PHIPPS returned from leave	A.G. App. 2
	5th	5am	Battn Hdqrs moved to R3 b 7.2	W.R.O.W.
		10pm	The Battn was relieved by 10th Inniskillings who took over line intact.	W.R.W.
			Battn Moved Southwards and came under orders 2/6 WARWICKS and	

D. D. & L., London, E.C. (A7833) Wt. W509/M1672 350,000 1/17 Sch. 52a Forms/C2118/14

Army Form C. 2118.

Instructions regarding War Diaries and Intelligence Summaries are contained in F. S. Regs., Part II. and the Staff Manual respectively. Title pages will be prepared in manuscript.

WAR DIARY
or
~~INTELLIGENCE SUMMARY.~~
(Erase heading not required.)

Place	Date	Hour	Summary of Events and Information	Remarks and references to Appendices
LINE	5th		Battn HQ + remnants of 'A' Coy withdrew to RHONDDA TRENCH in R 7.d	
		5/6th	B. C. + D. Coys. were placed under orders of 4th BERKS then in front line.	WRW
RHONDDA TR.	6th		Enemy shelled RHONDDA + neighbourhood throughout the day.	
		8pm	Battn HQ + 'A' Coy moved to HAVRINCOURT WOOD.	WRW
HAVRINCOURT WOOD	7th		General cleaning up. 2nd Lt TYLER returned from course	WRW
"	8th	6am	'B' 'C' + 'D' Coys rejoined Battalion in HAVRINCOURT WOOD. 2ND LT. DAVIES TO 3rd Army [illegible]	WRW
"	9th	9am	The camp was heavily shelled, but the Batt suffered no casualties	
			Battn moved to Q 3 b (HAVRINCOURT WOOD). (See appendix) 2nd Lt. WAREHAM + SMITH to [illegible]	WRW
"	10th	10.30am	Battn was ~~inspected~~ addressed WRW by GOC Division.	
		4.30pm	The Battalion moved into Brigade Support with HdQrs in RHONDDA	APP 2A.
			TRENCH R y d. Night very quiet.	WRW
RHONDDA TRENCH	11th		Cleaning up + improving trenches. Heavy shelling by the enemy	
			throughout the day. Aircraft very active.	WRW
LINE.	12th		Battalion relieved 2/6 R.WARR in front line LA VACQUERIE - LEFT SUB-	App 3
			SECTOR. See appendix	
"	13th		Work on trenches. Cleaning up and improving	[illegible]

D. D. & L., London, E.C. (A7853) Wt. W593/M1672 350,000 4/17 Sch. 52a Forms/C/2118/14

Army Form C. 2118.

Instructions regarding War Diaries and Intelligence Summaries are contained in F. S. Regs., Part II. and the Staff Manual respectively. Title pages will be prepared in manuscript.

WAR DIARY
or
~~INTELLIGENCE SUMMARY.~~
(Erase heading not required.)

Place	Date	Hour	Summary of Events and Information	Remarks and references to Appendices
LINE	14th		Work on new trench (support) continued and completed. Wiring completed to same trench. Wounded prisoner belonging to 28th R.I.R. captured on left [illegible] coy. front. Died shortly after. No information or documents on body.	[illegible]
LINE to SUPPORT	15th		Battalion was relieved (night 15/16th) by 2/6th [illegible] R. Battalion proceeded to and occupied RHONDDA TRENCH in support.	APP. 4 [illegible]
HAVRINCOURT WOOD	16th		Battalion proceeded to HAVRINCOURT WOOD to bivouack camp (see appendix)	[illegible] APP. 5
	17th		Cleaning up	[illegible]
MANANCOURT	18th		Battalion marched to hut and tent encampment at MANANCOURT (see appendix) 2nd Lt. SCUTT to Div. Depot Batt.	[illegible] APP. 6
"	19th		Lt. Col. E.C. CADMAN DSO and CAPT. W.R.T. WHATMORE admitted to hospital Cleaning up and platoon training. CAPT. A.E. TONKS returned from course	[illegible]
"	20th		Platoon training & cleaning up	[illegible]
"	21st		Platoon & company training. LT. PHIPPS to M.G.C. 2nd Lt. TYLER proceeded on leave Capt. Dunlop R.A.M.C. to hospital	[illegible]
"	22nd		Platoon and company training. Inspection of Battalion by C.O. Area heavily bombed by hostile aircraft	[illegible]
"	23rd		Battalion moved by train & march route to CERISY (see appendix) LIEUT. E.K. WHITAKER MORC U.S. Army reported for regimental duty	[illegible] APP. 7

D. D. & L., London, E.C. (A7883) Wt. W803/M1672 350,000 4/17 Sch. 52a Forms/C/2118/14

Instructions regarding War Diaries and Intelligence Summaries are contained in F. S. Regs., Part II. and the Staff Manual respectively. Title pages will be prepared in manuscript.

WAR DIARY
or
~~INTELLIGENCE SUMMARY.~~
(Erase heading not required.)

Army Form C. 2118.

Place	1917 Date	Hour	Summary of Events and Information	Remarks and references to Appendices
	Dec.			
CERISY	24th		Resting, cleaning up and improving billets. Transport arrived.	[initials]
"	25th		Christmas day. Short parades and voluntary service in morning.	[initials]
"	26th		Platoon + Company training. Bombing ground prepared. L.G. classes continued	[initials]
"	27th		Platoon + Company Training. Musketry. Lewis gun + Bombing training	[initials]
"	28th		Training continued.	[initials]
"	29th		Training continued. 2nd LT. GILDERTHORP admitted to hospital.	[initials]
"	30th	8.30am	Battalion moved by march route to BEAUCOURT-EN-SANTERRE.	APP. 8.
BEAUCOURT		12.30pm	Billets good and clean. Move completed 12.30 pm. Transport arrived 1.30pm.	[initials]
BEAUCOURT	31st		Platoon and Company training continued. Specialist classes continued. Section commanders (R.G.) under Bombing Sgt Instructor. Other NCO's under Musketry Sgt Instructor.	[initials]

W. E. Phillips Major.
Commanding 1/8 Warwicks.

D. D. & L., London, E.C. (A7883) Wt. W8o3/M1672 350,000 4/17 Sch. 52a. Forms/C/2118/14

2/8 R. Warwick Regt.

Bn. Operation Order No 186 dated [illegible]

APP. I

Reference Sheet 57c (1/40,000)

INFORMATION. 1. (a) 182nd Inf. Bde. will relieve left sector (R.17 a.5.8 – R.5 c. [illegible]) of 20th Division on night of 3rd inst.

(b) 2/8 R. War. R. will move tomorrow morning to area between METZ + TRESCAULT.

INSTRUCTIONS. 2. (a) ORDER OF MARCH. H.Q. B, C, D, 'A' Coys. Transport.

(b) STARTING POINT. Cross roads [illegible] at W 14 c.8.4.

(c) TIME. 8.0 a.m.

(d) ROUTE. FINS – METZ.

(e) DRESS. Fighting Order.

(f) DISTANCE. A distance of 200x will be maintained between Coys. + equivalent bodies.

REPORTS. 3. Reports to head of Batt. Column.

(sd.) E. C. CADMAN Lt.-Col.
Cmdg. 2/8 Warwicks.

1/8 R. Warwicks Regt

Administrative Instructions to accompany B.O. 186

LEWIS GUNS. 1. Lewis Guns will be loaded by 7.0 am. LT. CHIDGEY will supervise.

MESS BASKETS. 2. Mess baskets & all surplus kit which will not be taken into the line, will be stacked by Coys. in R.S.M.s hut before 7.30 am. Transport Officer will afterwards make arrangements for their collection. O.C. D Coy will leave one unfit man behind as guard.

TRANSPORT. 3. Transport will move to RUYAULCOURT as ordered, but the following will accompany the Batt. on the march.

(a) Coy Cookers.

(b) Lewis Gun limbers, on which Coys. may put any stores they are taking up into the line.

(c) No 13 SAA. limber.

(d) Mess Cart

(e) 1 Water Cart.

(f) Maltese Cart.

(2)

RATIONS. 4. Rations for 2nd
Breakfast before leaving. Dinner on line of march. Arrangements for tea will be notified later, but tea, sugar & milk should be carried on cooker. Water bottles will be filled before leaving. Dixies will be carried on Coy. Cookers.

S.O.S. GRENADES. 5. Coys. will take into the line 2 boxes of S.O.S. Grenades. Ammunition above establishment will be returned to Batt. HQ.
2 days iron rations will still be carried.

STORES. 6. QM will take immediate steps to collect all men now at METZ & all stores, blankets etc. at METZ and BAPAUME, so that everything will be at a central QM Stores.

(sd.) E. C. CADMAN Lt Col.
Cdg. 1/8 Warwicks.

2nd 8th Battn the Royal Warwick Regt

APP. J

Summary from 30-11-17 to 12-12-17

Ref. MAPS GONNIZIEU 1/10000
GOUZEAUCOURT Ed 2c 1/20000

30-11-17 Entrained at BEAUMETZ-LES-LOGES at 3 pm
Detrained at BAPAUME at 7 pm
Embussed outside BAPAUME at 8 pm and
reached RUYAULCOURT about 11 pm debussed
& marched to METZ-EN-COUTURE

1-12-17 Conference at Brigade HQ – ordered to be in
position in W 14 b in support of an attack
by the Guards Division in the direction of
VILLERS GUISLAN Rested HEUDICOURT – shelled –
1 casualty.
1st line Transport parked at W 13 b.

2-12-17 Left HEUDICOURT at 8.30 am marched via FINS
METZ en route to HAVRINCOURT WOOD Battn was
diverted to GOUZEAUCOURT WOOD. Transport moved
to RUYAULCOURT – Shelled in GOUZEAUCOURT WOOD –
lost 1 Lewis Gun.
Conference in GOUZEAUCOURT WOOD – order received
to take over front line from mixed details of 20th
Division under 7th KOYLI

3-12-17 Relief complete at 2 am line actually taken
over ran from L 35 c 4 0 – R 5 a 0 3 R 4 a 3
R 4 c 5 2 – R 10 a 7 7 with Batt HQ at R 4 c 4
Dispositions "C" Coy – LEFT FRONT
"A" " – RIGHT FRONT
"D" " – LEFT CENTRE
"B" " – RIGHT CENTRE
Flanks RIGHT 2/7 R WAR R
LEFT 12 KOSB 29th DIV
The exact point of junction between ourselves
and 2/7 WAR was in doubt for a few hours
but by 4 am it was finally settled at R 10 a 1 6
Throughout the morning the enemy made
repeated bombing attempts to capture the
trench running from R 11 a 2 7 to R 10 b 3 7
During one of these attacks the OC 'A' Coy was
killed. Our counter attacks restored the
position and at 2 pm the line was intact,
although the enemy repeatedly tried to bomb
down the trench during the afternoon &
throughout the 4th

4.12.17. During the evening of the 4th the enemy fired several medium Minenwerfer. As this was the first indication of minenwerfers they were probably registering targets
At 3 pm the enemy put down a barrage of T.Ms and shells of all calibres in the area R 4 c This lasted until 5 pm when he again tried to capture the trench R 10 a 2 7 to R 10. b 3 7 He succeeded in reaching the W end of the trench but a hastily organised counter attack delivered by a mixed party of 2/7 2/5 + 2/8 WAR troops restored the position.
The position of 2/7 WAR on our right was now obscure and as the enemy still threatened to break through at junction of ourselves and 2/7 WAR the C.O. decided to form a defensive flank facing right and the following orders were accordingly issued.
(1) Section 2/5th + 1 Lewis Gun (Batt^n Reserve) moved to junction R 9 b. 8 7 with instructions to hold until arrival of 1 Coy 10th Inniskillings + to work E toward front line
(2) 20 men + 1 Lewis Gun moved to reinforce our right Coy
(3) O.C. A Coy to hold line from junction R 9 b 8 7 E to front line - R 10 a. 5. 8 His right posts must hold on or if impossible move back towards his Support Trench

5.12.17 At 5 am on 5th Batt^n HQ moved to R 3 b 7 2 from whence the CO was able to control the Support Coy of 2/5th RWR which had been attached the previous night.
At 10 pm on 5th we were relieved by the 10th Inniskillings who took over our line intact Batt^n HQ + remnants of A Coy withdrew to RHONDDA TRENCH in R 7 ? while B C + D Coys were placed under the orders of 4th BERKS, then in the front line.
At 8 pm Batt^n HQ + A Coy moved to HAVRINCOURT WOOD. B C + D Coys rejoined the Batt^n at 6 am 8-12-17

9-12-17 At 9 am the Camp was shelled but no casualties resulted. The Batt^n moved to Q.3. b where it remained until 11 30 pm 10-11-17 when it moved Brigade Support. Owing to casualties A + D Coys were amalgamated for the time + re-named X Coy

12/12/17

APP. 2A.

2

4. Boundaries

The Bgy will take over front [illegible] Bgy in BERKS [illegible] already in [illegible] [illegible] HQ in BEAUCAMP V LESBOEUFS [illegible] when the [illegible]

5. Time

Orders & warning should be issued as soon [illegible] taken.

6. Relief

[illegible] they have taken over their new areas.

(Sd) E C [illegible]
[illegible]
[illegible]

1/8th Warwicks Regt

Administrative Orders to accompany B.O. 189.

1. RATIONS.
Rations for consumption on the 11th & 12th will be carried on the man. For the 13th & subsequent days they will be dumped at R 8.c 6 4.

2. WATER.
Filled water bottles will be taken into the line. Water for 12th & subsequent days will be dumped as above.

3. S.A.A. etc.
Every man will carry (a) 170 rounds S.A.A.
(b) 2 bombs (No 5 or 23)
Rifle Grenadiers will carry 8 No 23s but will not carry the 50 extra rounds of S.A.A.
Coys will carry in at least 24 Very Lights & 1 box of S.O.S.

4. TRANSPORT
1 Limber for each of B & C Coys & 1 for A & D combined, will carry Lewis Guns etc. These limbers & the mess cart will report at 3 pm at [illegible] parade ground [illegible] to [illegible] camp.

5. BLANKETS
Blankets will be rolled & stacked at junction of rail road by 1.0 pm.
Officers' Mess Baskets etc will be stacked near Quarterly Room Tent by 4.0 pm.
Transport Officer will be responsible for their removal.

6. DRUMS.
10 drummers will report to Adjutant for fatigue at 11 am. tomorrow. Drums will be carried.

(sd) W R T WHETMORE
Capt & Adjt
1/8 Warwick

APP. 3

1/8th Royal Warwick Regt
O.O. No. 191. 12-12-17

Ref. [illegible] 1/20000

1. The Battn will relieve 2/6 [illegible] in the line tonight

2. Dispositions

LEFT FRONT	–	B Coy
RIGHT FRONT	–	C "
SUPPORT	–	X "

3. Guides
Guides for X & B Coys will be at Hdqrs of 2/6 R.War.R from 4 pm onwards. There will be no guides for C Coy

4. Tools
Each Coy will carry 30 Shovels & 5 Picks into the line

5. Ration Parties
[illegible] & water will be at RATION DUMP R.8.c.6.4 at 7 pm and Coys will send their own carrying parties to meet them at this time

6. Trench Stores
All Defence Schemes, Maps, Trench Stores &c will be taken over. A copy of the receipts being forwarded to Battn HQ

Army Form C. 2121
(in pads of 100).

"A" Form

MESSAGES AND SIGNALS.

No. of Message..................

Prefix..............Code..................m. Office of Origin and Service Instructions.	Words.	Charge.	This message is on a/c of: ....Service. .... (Signature of "Franking Officer.")	Recd. at............m. Date .... From .... By ....
	Sent At..................m. To .... By			

TO

Sender's Number. *	Day of Month.	In reply to Number.	AAA

From

Place

Time

The above may be forwarded as now corrected.

(Z)

Censor.

Signature of Addressor or person authorised to telegraph in his name.

*This line should be erased if not required.

(18965.) Wt. W12952/M1294. 187,500 Pads. 1/.7 M^cC. & Co., Ltd. (E. 818.)

7. [illegible]

[illegible] 136 [illegible]
[illegible] 135 [illegible]

8. Line Men

[illegible] will be reported by each unit [illegible]

9. Change of Front

Upon the relief is complete B Coy will exchange with C Coy to take over part of that Coy front so that length of each Coy front is in proportion to its strength.

10. Acknowledge

Sgd W E PHILLIPS Captn
for Lt Col Comdg 2/5 R Warw R

Army Form C. 2121
(in pads of 100).

"A" Form

MESSAGES AND SIGNALS.

No. of Message..................

Prefix..............Code..................m.	Words.	Charge.	*This message is on a/c of:*	Recd. at..............m.
Office of Origin and Service Instructions.	Sent		.................................*Service.*	Date ....
....	At....................m.			From ....
....	To		....	
....	By.......................		(Signature of "Franking Officer.")	By ....

TO

Sender's Number.	Day of Month.	In reply to Number.	AAA
*			

From			
Place			
Time			

The above may be forwarded as now corrected. (Z)

.... *Censor.*

.... Signature of Addressor or person authorised to telegraph in his name.

*This line should be erased if not required.

(18965.) Wt. W12952/M1294. 187,500 Pads. 1/.7 McC. & Co., Ltd. (E. 818.)

2nd 8th Battn The Royal Warwick Regt. APP. 4.

Order No 192. 15-12-17

1 The 2/6th R. WAR R will relieve 2/8 R. WAR R in the Left Sub-Sector on night 15/16th inst

2. DISPOSITIONS (a).

2/8	2/6	DISPOSITIONS
B	B & C	LEFT FRONT
C	D	RIGHT FRONT
X	A	SUPPORT

(b) "A" Coy of 2/6 R WAR R will take over WELSH TRENCH only, no relief will be provided for troops holding NEW trench who will be withdrawn when the relief of remainder of X Coy is complete

3. GUIDES Guides will be supplied by Battn Hdqrs. Relieving Coys may be expected from 5-15 pm onwards

4. TRENCH STORES All Defence Schemes, Maps, Air Photos, S.O.S Grenades &c will be handed over. A copy of Trench Stores to be handed over will be forwarded to Battn H.Q. before 1 p.m today.

5. CODE WORD Relief complete will be notified by code word "ZIG ZAG"

6. ON RELIEF On relief Batt will become Bde Support & Coys will withdraw to same Areas as occupied when previously in Bde Support. Coy Commanders will report to Support Battn Hdqrs when their Coys are all in.

7. RATIONS. Rations will be dumped at Ration Dump R.8.c.6.4 at 6 pm & a guard will be put on them by Battn H.Q. until Coys can send for them.

8 ACKNOWLEDGE.

SGD. W.E PHILLIPS.
MAJOR for Lt Col
COMM 2/8 R. WAR R.

2/8 Battn. The Royal Warwick Regt. APP. 5.
Order No. 193. 16th Dec. 1917.

REF: MAP. GOUZEAUCOURT 1/10000.

---

1. The Battn. will be relieved by 1. Platoon of 2/4. OXFORDS on night 16/17th Decr.

2. DISPOSITIONS
(a). The only Coy to be relieved will be "C" Coy who will report the arrival of relieving Platoon by codeword "BON", and relief complete by codeword "TOOT SWEET"
(b). 'X' & 'D' Coys will move off on receipt of orders from Battn. H.Q. The time will probably be about 7 p.m.

3. TRENCH STORES
All Maps, Defence Schemes, S.O.S Grenades will be taken out of the line and forwarded to Battn. H.Q. by 12 noon tomorrow 17th inst.

4. On relief Coys will move independently to. HAVRINCOURT WOOD.

2

5. TRANSPORT

One limber will be at the disposal of each Coy.

These limbers & Mess Cart will be on BEAUCHAMP – VILLERS PLOUICH ROAD where overland track commences, from 7-15 pm onwards.

6. ACKNOWLEDGE.

Sgd. W.E. PHILLIPS.
Major for Lieut Col
Comm. 2/8 R Warwk

APP 6.

2/8th Battn Royal Warwick Regt
Order No 194. 18 Decr 1917

REF:- MAP 57c.

INTENTION 1. The Battn will march to MANANCOURT today 18th inst.

INSTRUCTIONS. 2 (a) Order of March. H.Q. 'X' 'B' 'C' Coys.

(b) Starting Point Q.14.d. 2.5 (where Railway meets road)

(c). Time - 12-50 p.m.

(d) Distances. A distance of 200 yards will be maintained between Coys.

(e) Route. X roads Q20 c 7 7 - Fork Roads Q19 a 6.0. - X roads P35 central - EQUANCOURT - V.10.a 25.95. - V.9.b 50.55. - ETRICOURT.

(f) Dress:- Full Marching Order - Leather Jerkins will be carried in packs.

(g) Advance Parties. Billetting Parties &c are being provide by Brigade.

(h) Blankets &c. Blankets, Mess Baskets &c will be stacked as laid down in Standing Orders for the move.

REPORTS 3. Reports to head of column.

ACKNOWLEDGE.

Sgd. W.E. PHILLIPS. MAJOR
for Lt Col. Comm 2/8 R War R

SECRET.

App. 7.

2nd 8th Batt. The Royal Warwickshire Regt.
Battalion Order No by Major [illegible] Fuller [illegible] Comdg.
22nd Decr [illegible]

REF. Sheet 57c 1/40000. LENS & AMIENS 1/100000.

1. MOVE. The Batt. will move to CERISY tomorrow 23rd inst.

2. ENTRAINMENT. The Batt. less Transport will entrain at ETRICOURT at 12.30 pm. Detraining at CORBIE at about 3.30 pm.
Order of March: HQ & Drums A.B.C.D Coys.
[illegible] will be maintained [illegible]
Starting Point: MANANCOURT CHURCH V.3.c.7.8.
Time: Head of column to pass starting point at 11 am.
Dress: Full marching order. Steel helmets [illegible] packs. Jerkins will not be worn. Water bottles will be filled.

3. SHOVELS. 4 Shovels per Coy and HdQrs will be drawn from Batt. H.Q. at 9.30 am. These will be carried in Fighting Order.

4. OFFICERS KITS, BLANKETS &c. Officers' kits will be loaded on G.S. wagon at [illegible] HdQrs not later than 7 am.
All blankets will be dumped at Batt. H.Q. not later than 8 am.
Remaining stores as per Batt. Standing Orders for the move.

5. LORRIES. 3 Lorries will report at [illegible] MANANCOURT at 8 am tomorrow. QM will send guide to take them to QM Stores.
QM will send sufficient [illegible] the blankets. These lorries [illegible] after 8.30 am at [illegible]
[illegible] same.
Route for lorries [illegible]
[illegible] 23rd inst. [illegible]

6. PARADE STATE. Coys will report to Orderly Room not later than 8.30 am exact numbers of men proceeding by train.

7. MEALS. Breakfast [illegible]
Dinners [illegible] am
Unconsumed portion of days rations will be carried on the man.
Breakfast rations for 24th inst. will be carried on the lorries.

8. [illegible] PARADE [illegible] at [illegible]
[illegible] Post.

DETACHED PARTY — [illegible] Malpas [illegible] and [illegible] will [illegible] 6. [illegible] 9.30 am and will [illegible] STATION [illegible] at 0.15 am. [illegible] at 1.30 pm. [illegible] at CORK [illegible] [illegible]

[illegible]

[illegible]

[illegible]

[illegible]

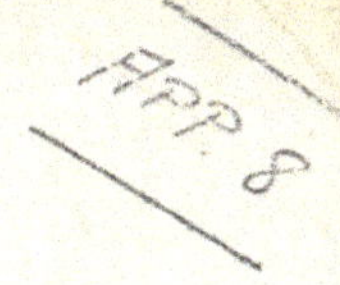

2nd 8th Battn The Royal Warwickshire Regt
Battalion Order 196. 29th Decr 1917.

REF:- AMIENS. 1/100000

1. The Battalion will move tomorrow by march route to BEAUCOURT-EN-SANTERRE.

2. ROUTE. MORCOURT - BAYONVILLERS - WIENCOURT - CAYEUX.

3. STARTING POINT Road junction W. of C in CHIPILY

4. TIME. Head of Column to pass starting point at 8-30 am

5. ORDER OF MARCH H.Q. Drums B.C.D. Coys. One Platoon of "A" Coy - first ten vehicles of Transport, second Platoon of "A" Coy - remainder of Transport
Interval of 25 yards will be maintained between Coys.
Dress:- Full Marching Order.

6. TRANSPORT (a). One Tool Limber will precede the Battn at a distance of 500 yards, carrying ten sandbags of cinders or earth. Regimental Police and Pioneers will march with limber and will spread cinders or earth over slippery portion of the roads. They will also clear a way through drifted snow where necessary.
(b). Remainder of Transport will march in rear of Battn in groups of ten vehicles with interval of 200 yards between groups.
Platoons of "A" Coy will be prepared to assist wagons up hills and over bad places, using drag ropes if necessary. Drag ropes will be provided on each vehicle.
(c). Cookers will march in rear of second group of Transport.

7. LORRIES. Two lorries will report at SAILLY LORETTE CHURCH at 8 am. and QM will detail a guide to report to 2/Lt GOUGH at rendezvous and conduct lorries to QM. Stores. These lorries will do one journey only to BEAUCOURT returning to lorry park as soon as work is completed. An additional lorry will be available at a later hour to take half load from 2/7 R. WAR R and half load from 2/8 R. WAR R

8 BLANKETS, OFFICERS' VALISES, MESS BASKETS &c. As per Battn Standing Orders for the move.

9. ROUTINE. REVEILLE 5-30 am
BREAKFASTS 6-30 am
SICK PARADE. 7-0 am

Haversack Rations will be carried.
Dinners on arrival.

10. Acknowledge.

Sgd. H.T. CHIDGEY. Lieut & Adjt
2/8 R. War

Sgd. W.E. PHILLIPS. MAJOR
COMM. 2/8. R War R.

21 H 17

Confidential.

Vol 21

War Diary of -

2/5th Battalion Royal Warwickshire Regt.

Volume XXI

Period.

Jan: 1/18 to
Jan: 31/18.

Instructions regarding War Diaries and Intelligence Summaries are contained in F. S. Regs., Part II. and the Staff Manual respectively. Title pages will be prepared in manuscript.

WAR DIARY or ~~INTELLIGENCE SUMMARY.~~

(Erase heading not required.)

Army Form C. 2118.

Place	Date	Hour	Summary of Events and Information	Remarks and references to Appendices
	1918			
BEAUCOURT EN SANTERRE	1st Jan.		Platoon and Company training. Musketry, range work for rifles and Lewis guns, specialist training continued. 2ND. LT. DAVIES returned from course	[initials]
"	2nd		Platoon, Company and Specialist training continued. 2nd. LT. PARROTT returned from XVIII Corps Rest Station, 2nd. LT. SCOTT returned from Divisional Depôt Battalion. Reinforcements, 2 O.R., reported	[initials]
"	3rd		Platoon and Company training continued. Field firing by Lewis guns. Specialist classes continued	[initials]
"	4th		Platoon and Company training. Draft of 43 O.R. arrived. 2nd Lt. C.H.B. KITCHIN returned from hospital. a/Capt. A.L. PROSSER returned from leave.	[initials]
"	5th		Platoon and Company training.	[initials]
"	6th		Baths at LE QUESNEL. Draft of 41 O.R. arrived. F.G.C.M. at MARCELCAVE for trial of 2nd. Lt. C. HARRIS.	[initials]
"	7th	8 am	Battalion moved by march route to RETHONVILLERS and MARCHE (See Appendix)	
RETHONVILLERS	"	4-30 pm	Move complete. CAPT. WHATMORE returned from hospital. 2nd. LT. TYLER returned from leave. Billets good – A Coy at MARCHE, remainder at RETHONVILLERS.	[initials]
"	11th		C.O. Adjutant and Coy. Commanders proceeded to reconnoitre line to be taken over at FAYET from 2nd. Batt. 74th Regt. French Army. Rejoined battalion at 11 pm	

T2134. Wt. W708–776. 500000. 4/15. Sir J. C. & S.

Army Form C. 2118.

Instructions regarding War Diaries and Intelligence Summaries are contained in F. S. Regs., Part II. and the Staff Manual respectively. Title pages will be prepared in manuscript.

WAR DIARY
or
~~INTELLIGENCE SUMMARY.~~

(Erase heading not required.)

Place	Date	Hour	Summary of Events and Information	Remarks and references to Appendices
RETHONVILLERS	8th		Resting and cleaning of equipment, Lewis guns etc. Short P.T. parade in afternoon. Capt. Ingle, Intelligence Officer and Transport Officer reconnoitred new line and approaches.	H.L.6
RETHONVILLERS	9th	9am	Battalion moved by march route to ETREILLERS. Capt. Slater & Lt. Whitaker to hospital.	
ETREILLERS		5.40pm	Move complete. Billets satisfactory. Capt. B.K. Parsons returned from hospital (see appendix)	H.L.6
"	10th	1pm	Advance party proceeded to line to commence taking over from French. Lt. Wooldridge in charge of party (see appendix). Capt. Bolster RAMC 1/3 W.M.F.A.M.C. reported for duty.	H.L.6
LINE	11th		Lieut. NORTH, MORC U.S. Army reported for duty replacing Capt. BOLSTER. Battalion relieved 3rd Batt. 76th French Regt. in the FAYET SUB-SECTOR of the line. Relief complete by 11-15 pm. (see appendix)	H.L.6 H.L.6
"	12th		Inter-company relief, front line being re-allotted to three coys. distributed in depth (see appendix) B Coy remaining in reserve	H.L.6
"	13th		[illegible] of wire started in front of WARWICK TR. [illegible] [illegible] post constructed at [illegible] [illegible] [illegible] 75.25. Considerable shelling of FAYET in afternoon and cemetery and neighbourhood of HOLNON.	
"	13th		Patrol from left coy reconnoitred enemy wire and found it strong and deep. [illegible] line of resistance - CAKAR TR. cleared for [illegible] [illegible] new posts constructed [illegible] in front of MORLAIX WORK strengthened and also in front of DUGUESCLIN WORK	H.L.6

T2134. Wt. W708—776. 500000. 4/15. Sir J. C. & S.

Army Form C. 2118.

Instructions regarding War Diaries and Intelligence Summaries are contained in F. S. Regs., Part II. and the Staff Manual respectively. Title pages will be prepared in manuscript.

WAR DIARY
or
INTELLIGENCE SUMMARY.
(Erase heading not required.)

Place	Date	Hour	Summary of Events and Information	Remarks and references to Appendices
LINE FAYET SECTOR	13th		MORLAIX WORK improved. Wire placed at M36 c 50.25 to fill up gap. 150x new C.T. constructed at S5 central. Aircraft of both sides active during daylight.	H.L.
"	14th		Day and night quiet. Local bomb stores completed at junctions of C.Ts with line of resistance. Centre coy's H.Q. removed to No. 7 post. Wiring in front of line of resistance on left coy. front continued 100x and strengthened and gap filled in. New C.T. from BREST TR. to No 8 POST constructed by W.P. from 7/5th R War R. All posts in line of resistance and WARWICK TR. improved and strengthened.	H.L.
"	15th		Slight hostile artillery activity in and around FAYET, during morning. Advance parties from 2/5th R. War. R. arrived during morning. 2nd. LT. PITT R. reported for duty.	H.L.
"	15/16th	4.25am	Battalion relieved by 2/5th R. War. R, proceeding after relief to support area about X 12 a. 9.2 (HOLNON WOOD) (See APPENDIX)	H.L.
HOLNON WOOD	16th		Resting and cleaning up. Inspections by platoon and coy commanders. Lt. Kitchen proceeded on leave. 2nd. LTS. MACMILLAN, BURGESS, SLICER, TOLSON, BATTYE, UNSWORTH, REECE, GROUTAGE & JONES reported for duty.	H.L.
"	17th		Improving and draining support area. Working party 150 OR. with 5 officers worked 4 hours (6.30 – 10.30pm) under Bde. Works Office clearing BRETON C.T.	H.L.
"	18th		Battalion relieved in support by 2/4th Gloucester Regt. Relief complete 6.45pm. Battalion proceeded to billets at VAUX. Billets satisfactory. All in 9-10 pm.	H.L.

T2134. Wt. W708—776. 500000. 4/15. Sir J. C. & S.

Instructions regarding War Diaries and Intelligence Summaries are contained in F. S. Regs., Part II. and the Staff Manual respectively. Title pages will be prepared in manuscript.

WAR DIARY

or

~~INTELLIGENCE SUMMARY.~~

(*Erase heading not required.*)

Army Form C. 2118.

Place	Date	Hour	Summary of Events and Information	Remarks and references to Appendices
VAUX	19th		Cleaning up and company inspections. Capt. TONKS proceeded on leave LIEUT. K.C.F. WATSON proceeded on Army Musketry Course	A.L.
"	20th		Baths for two companies. Platoon and company training (see Appendix)	A.L.
"	21st		Platoon and Company Training. Capt. Mingle proceeded on Sanitation Course at PERONNE	A.L.
"	22nd		Platoon and Company Training. Draft of 5 B1 men reported - sent to 2/2nd F.A.	A.L.
"	23rd		Digging trench for buried cable (whole battalion) for XVIIIth Corps Signals at ATTILLY. 2nd Lieut. R.O. LUNT and LT. W.R.T. WHATMORE proceeded on leave	A.L.
"	24th		Digging trenches on new INTERMEDIATE LINE astride SAVY - ATTILLY railway under R.E. (200th Field Coy.) supervision - whole battalion. Baths for remainder of battalion.	A.L.
"	25th		Work on INTERMEDIATE LINE continued - whole battalion. Capt. MINGLE returned from course. 2nd Lieut. C. HARRIS sentenced by F.G.C.M. to dismissal from H.M. services. Sentence promulgated.	A.L.
"	26th		Ex. Lieut HARRIS handed over to A.P.M. Battalion relieved 2/5th Gloucesters in right sub-sector of left brigade sector. (See Appendix) Relief complete 7.30 pm. Billets taken over by 2/5th Gloucesters. 2nd Lt. KIBBEY returned from hospital	A.L.

T2134. Wt. W708—776. 500000. 4/15. Sir J. C. & S.

Instructions regarding War Diaries and Intelligence Summaries are contained in F. S. Regs., Par. II. and the Staff Manual respectively. Title pages will be prepared in manuscript.

WAR DIARY

or

~~INTELLIGENCE SUMMARY.~~

(Erase heading not required.)

Army Form C. 2118.

Place	Date	Hour	Summary of Events and Information	Remarks and references to Appendices
Line. RIGHT SUBSECTOR. GRICOURT.	27.		Quiet day. Misty. Work done in improving posts, clearing trenches, constructing new latrines. Continuing wiring around CORNOUILLERS WOOD. Building new cook-house at Batt. HQ. Two patrols from left coy front (A Coy) one of which reconnoitred 3 SAVAGES. Two enemy seen who fled on approach of patrol. Second patrol proceeded to TOMAHAWK COPSE and located two enemy posts. Occupants ran back and M.G. fire was opened by them on patrol. Patrol also from right coy reconnoitred sunken road in M29d and M35b. No signs of enemy. Lt. Col. CADMAN DSO. returned from hospital. ~~Lt. AT KIBBEY~~	[illegible]
"	28		Slight shelling by 77s and 4.2s of FRESNOY cemetery and vicinity in morning. Considerable reciprocal aerial activity throughout day. Night spent in clearing and duckboarding posts in front line. Patrols reconnoitred S. end of TOMAHAWK COPSE and sunken road running E. from GRICOURT also 3 SAVAGES	[illegible]
"	29		Quiet day. Some aerial activity. Work by night, strengthening wire (front line) round CORN WOOD and in front of line of resistance (ARGONNE and AMBOISE TRENCHES) also MARRONNIERS WOOD.	[illegible]

A6945 Wt. W11422/M1160 350,000 12/16 D. D. & L. Forms/C./2118/14.

Instructions regarding War Diaries and Intelligence Summaries are contained in F. S. Regs., Part II, and the Staff Manual respectively. Title pages will be prepared in manuscript.

WAR DIARY
or
~~INTELLIGENCE SUMMARY.~~
(Erase heading not required.)

Army Form C. 2118.

Place	Date	Hour	Summary of Events and Information	Remarks and references to Appendices
LINE E	29th		Patrol reconnoitred TOMAHAWK COPSE throughout and penetrated to enemy front line, bringing back material. No enemy seen, but some MG fire. Other patrols reconnoitred sunken road E. of GRICOURT remaining out for 9 hrs. No sign of enemy patrols.	A.L.
"	30th		Quiet day, aerial activity only. Battalion relieved by 2/5th R.War.R (See Appendix) Relief complete 8.30 pm. Battalion withdrew to right support area on relief. Working party on PERONNE TR. area	A.L.
RT. SUPPORT QUARRY on FRESNOY RD and dug-outs by OTTER COPSE	31st		Misty day, very cold. Working parties on defences of FRESNOY wiring, – 300x wire put out, work on dug-outs in BADGER COPSE, also on PERONNE and AMBOISE TRENCHES.	A.L.

Ed. C. Cadman
Lt. Colonel
Commanding 2/8th R.War.R

A6945 Wt. W11422/M1160 350,000 12/16 D. D. & L. - Forms/C./2118/14.

2ND 8TH BATTALION THE ROYAL WARWICKSHIRE REGIMENT.

BATTALION ORDER No.198. 6th JANUARY 1918.

Ref. AMIENS. 1/100000.

1. The Battalion will move tomorrow the 7th inst. by march route to RETHONVILLERS and MARCHE.

2. ROUTE: BOUCHOIR - ROYE - CARREPUIS - RETHONVILLERS.

3. STARTING POINT: Road junction 550 yards South of A in CHAU.

4. TIME: Head of column to pass Starting Point at 8 a.m.

5. ORDER OF MARCH. H.Q. DRUMS. "D" "A" "B" "C" Coys.

6. DRESS; Full Marching Order, less packs. Jerkins will be rolled in packs. Water Bottles will be carried full. Mess Tins will be carried strapped to back of belt. Steel Helmets will be worn. Rifle Grenade Haversacks will be carried on the back by Rifle Grenadiers.

7. TRANSPORT. Transport will move in rear of the Battalion in groups of 6 vehicles. Interval of 25 yards will be maintained between groups. Cookers will move in third group of Transport. Transport will not be overloaded.

8. O.C. "C" Coy will detail 4 Sections of not less than 8 men each, to march 1 Section in rear of each group of 6 vehicles.

9. HALTS. In addition to the regular halts at 10 minutes to the clock hour, there will be a halt from 12-30 to 1-30 p.m. for dinners, and watering and feeding of horses. Water for horses will be carried in petrol tins.

10. PACKS. Packs (but no sandbags or other articles) will be carried on Q.S. wagons.
They will be brought to Q.M. Stores for loading at same time as blankets.

11. 2½ Motor Lorries will be available for carrying blankets etc.
Q.M. will send guides to be at LE QUESNEL CHURCH at 9 a.m. to conduct lorries to Q.M. Stores.

12. BLANKETS, OFFICERS' KITS ETC. As per Standing Orders for the move. Coys are reminded that blankets must be rolled, tightly and securely, in tens.

13. REVEILLE. 5-30 a.m.
BREAKFASTS. 6-30 a.m.
DINNERS. 12-30 p.m. en route.
SICK PARADE. on arrival.

14. ACKNOWLEDGE.

sgd. W.E.PHILLIPS. Major.
Commdg. 2/8th.R.WAR.R.

Copies. 1. C.O.
2/5. Coys.
6. Q.M.
7. T.O.
8. R.S.M.
9. Offrs.Mess.
10. File
11. War Diary.

2ND 8TH BATTALION THE ROYAL WARWICKSHIRE REGIMENT.

BATTALION ORDER 199.   8th JAN. 1918.

Ref. AMIENS – ST QUENTIN 1/100000.

---

1. The Battalion will move tomorrow the 9th inst. by march route to ETREILLERS.

2. <u>ROUTE.</u> NESLE – VOYENNES – MATIGNY – DOUILLY – GERMAINE.

3. <u>STARTING POINT.</u> Road junction 300 yards South of First E in RETHONVILLERS.

4. <u>TIME.</u> Head of column to pass Starting Point at 9 a.m.

5. <u>ORDER OF MARCH.</u> H.Q. DRUMS. "A" "B" "C" "D" Coys.

6. <u>DRESS.</u> Full Marching Order, less packs which will be carried on G.S. Wagons. Steel helmets will be worn. Ground sheets will be carried rolled on belts. Mess Tins will also be carried ~~on belt~~ on haversack. Water bottles will be filled. Jerkins will be rolled in Packs.

7. Transport will move in rear of the Battalion in groups of six vehicles, interval of 25 yards being maintained between groups. Transport will not be overloaded.

8. O.C. "D" Coy will detail 4 Sections of not less than 8 men each to march behind each group of vehicles.

9. <u>HALTS.</u> An additional halt from 1-30 to 2-30 p.m. will be made for dinners and watering and feeding of horses. Water for horses will be carried in petrol tins.

10. <u>BLANKETS.</u> OFFICERS' KITS &C as per Battalion Standing Orders for the move.
Packs will be loaded at Q.M. Stores at same time as Blankets.

11. REVEILLE. 6 a.m.
BREAKFAST. 7 A.M.
DINNERS on route. 1-30 p.m.
SICK PARADE on arrival.

12. ACKNOWLEDGE.

sgd. W.E. PHILLIPS. Major.
Comndg. 2/8th. R.WAR.R.

Copies.
1. C.O.
2/5. Coys
6. H.Q. Mess.
7. R.S.M.
8. T.O.
9. Q.M.
10. File
11. War Diary.

2/8th Bn. Royal Warwickshire Regt.

Battalion Order. No. 201.

by Major. W.E. PHILLIPS, Comdg.

10 : 1 : 1918.

1. The following will proceed to FAYET sector [illegible] as an advance party, today.

"A" Coy.	1 Off.	2 N.C.O.'s.
"B" & "C" Coys	1 "	4 "
"D" Coy	1 "	3 "

Not more than 2 runners per Coy.

2 Battalion runners.

LT. WOOLDRIDGE who will be in charge of the party.

2. The above party will report to LT. WOOLDRIDGE on road outside Q.M. Stores at 1 p.m., ready to move.

3. Dress : Fighting order with great-coats in packs. Jerkins will be worn.

4. Rations, up to and including those for 12th inst., will be carried.

5. Advance party will obtain as much information as possible from the French, and arrange details as to guides for their respective Coys from Bde. H.Q. forward on the night of relief 11/12th inst.

Copies to :-

1-4. Coys.
5. C.O.
6. Adjt
7. LT. WOOLDRIDGE.
8. File
9. War Diary.

H.T. Chidgey
Lieut & Adjt
2/8 R. War. R.

SECRET.

Copy No.

2/8th Bn. Royal Warwickshire Regiment.

Battalion Order. No. 202. dated 10-1-1918.

Reference
map sheet 62 B. S.W. } 1:20,000
62 c. S.E }

1. The Battalion will relieve the 2nd. Battalion 7th Regt. [illegible] French Division in the FAYET SECTOR on the night of the 11/12th. January 1918.

2. RELIEF TABLE.

RELIEF	RELIEVING
"D" Company.	Compagnie de GAUCHE (LEFT)
"A" "	" " DROITE (RIGHT)
"B" "	" " SOUTIEN (support)
"C" "	

Note:- The whole of "B" Company will be accommodated in the [illegible] of SOUTIEN.
One platoon of "C" Coy. will take over dug-outs in sunken road in M.35.c. Two sections will take over the sections of the compagnie de SOUTIEN in the TR. DES EPARGES in M.3.c. The remaining two sections will be accommodated in FAYET. "C" Coy's [illegible] will be at M.35.c.

3. Companies will move off by platoons in the following order :- "D" Coy. "A" Coy. "C" Coy. "B" Coy. H.Q. Intervals of 50 yds to be maintained between platoons and 200 yds between Companies.
The leading platoon of "D" Coy. will pass road junction at R. 3[illegible] at 4-30 p.m.
Route – ETREILLERS – SAVY – [illegible] road.

4. GUIDES. Guides will be met at road junction S.7.d.4.4., one per platoon and one for Battn. H.Q.

5. DRESS. Fighting Order, with greatcoats in packs. Surplus kit and [illegible] to be disposed of in accordance with supply arrangements, [illegible] jerkins will be worn.

6. Lewis Gun limbers (one per Coy) will move in front of leading platoon of each Company. Twelve drums per gun will be taken into the line by the teams. Additional drums, to bring total to 20 per gun, will be brought up by [illegible] on the night of 11/12th. and dumped at Battalion H.Q. whence Coys will draw as early as possible.
Coys must make arrangements for the rapid unloading of limbers. [illegible] will be loaded before 3.30 p.m. under supervision of L.G. sergeant.

7. Bombs. Each [illegible] section will carry [illegible] No. 23's per man, [illegible] per man.

8. Relief complete to be reported by [illegible] to Battn. H.Q.

9. Movement by daylight in places under enemy observation is absolutely forbidden. Ration and water carrying must be arranged accordingly.

10. Telephone communications in daylight are absolutely forbidden [illegible] must be sent by runner.

11. Companies will not leave any personnel out of the line, other than C.Q.M.S., Coy. Storeman, and one cook, without reference to Battn. H.Q.

12. ACKNOWLEDGE.

Issued at [illegible] p.m. 10-1-1918.

Copies to :-

1. C.O.
2-5. Coys.
6. Second in command.
7. Transport Officer
8. Q.M.
9. Intelligence Officer
10. A.S.M.
[illegible]

(Sd) W.R. PHILLIPS,
Major
Comdg. 2/8 R. Warw. R.

[illegible] Bn. Royal Warwickshire Regiment.

Administrative Orders (to accompany B.O. No 202.)

1. Q.M. STORES. Q.M. Stores and Transport will remain at ETREILLERS.

2. RATIONS. Rations for consumption on the 12th will be carried on the man.
Rations for consumption on 13th and subsequent days for 'A', 'C' and 'D' Coys will be brought on limbers to Battn. H.Q. at S.5. a.8.7., whence they will be carried to Coy. H.Q. by Coy ration parties.
Rations for 'B' Coy will be brought to road junction at S.4.c.0.4.
Rations will arrive at Battn. H.Q. at about 6 p.m.

3. WATER. There is a supply of water at Battn. H.Q. Coys will take into the line 6 empty petrol tins for water carrying. These may be drawn from Q.M. Stores.

4. COOKING. Cookhouses are available for each Coy. These will not be used in daylight, unless adequate arrangements can be made to prevent smoke being seen by enemy.
Dixies may be taken into the line. One cook per coy will be left out of the line. These cooks will report to the Q.M. on departure of their coys.
Sgt. master cook will go into the line, and live at Bn H.Q.

5. TRANSPORT. 1 limber per coy and one for H.Q. details will report to each coy H.Q. at 2.45 p.m. for carrying Lewis Guns, ammunition, gum boots etc.
1 limber will report to Battn H.Q. at 4.0 p.m. for Bn. H.Q. and M.O.'s properties.
The four Company limbers will accompany infantry as far as road junc at S.5.a.1.6. The two H.Q. limbers will proceed as far as Battn H.Q.
Transport Officer will arrange for limbers to carry up 8 drums per gun to Battn H.Q. on night of 11/12th.

6. BOMBS. Each man of the Rifle Grenade sections will carry five No. 23 Grenades and blank cartridges. Remainder of mobile No. 23 Grenades will be distributed equally between 'A', 'C' and 'D' Coys.

[P.T.O.

7. GUM BOOTS. Gum Boots will be taken on Lewis Gun limbers. They may be drawn from Q.M. Stores after 12 noon tomorrow.
Receipts will be given to Q.M. for gum boots. Any loss will be made good by the men concerned.

8. SURPLUS KITS. Surplus kits will be packed in sandbags, and clearly marked with Regtl number, name and Company of each man.

9. BLANKETS etc. Blankets, Officers' kits, men's surplus kits, mess baskets etc. will be left at Coy. H.Q. before going into the line.
Transport Officer will arrange for collection and Q.M. for storage of these.

10. DUMPS. The Battalion dump will be at Battn H.Q. Steps must be taken to form Coy dumps as early as possible; and Battn. dump may be drawn on for this purpose.

10:11:1918.

(sd) W.R.T. WHATMORE, Major,
2/8 R. War. R.

SECRET.

2/8th Battn. Royal Warwickshire Regiment.

Battalion Order no. 202/1. d/ 12.1.1918.

Ref. map, no HWB/3/:8.

1. The following inter-coy relief will take place tonight:-

1. 'C' company will take over the centre sector of the Battalion front.

Boundaries. Northern.— From junction BOYAU-BRETON and sunken road M.35c — BOYAU BRETON to M.35.d.2.0. — road running to M.36.c.4.3. inclusive — DUGUESCLIN WORK inclusive to intersection with front line at M.36.c.75.40

Southern — a line through S.5.a.8.5 to dug-out no. 37 in BREST TR. continued to front line at S.6.b.2.7. Dug-out inclusive to 'C' Coy.

2. Relief Table, as below, details to be arranged between Coy. Cmdrs concerned.

Relief	Relieving
† 1 platoon 'C' coy in M.35c	1 pl 'D' Coy in DUGUESCLIN work.
1 section 'C' coy in M.35.c.	1 section 'A' Coy in Dug-out no. 37.
3 sections of 'C' coy in EPARGES TR. move to main line of resistance in S.5.b. *	
1 section of 'A' coy from BREST TR. moves to TR. des EPARGES.	

† replaces 1 pl. 'D' Coy in M.35.c.

* NOTE. From platoon of 'C' coy in main line of resistance in S.5.b., local supports must be found & accommodated in rear.

3. Relief to be commenced immediately after dusk. Disposition map to reach Battn H.Q. by 6 p.m. Details of work in hand must be taken over.

4. Relief complete to be notified to Battn. H.Q. by runner.

5. ACKNOWLEDGE.

Issued at 1.30 p.m.

(sd) W.E. PHILLIPS, Major,
2/8 R. Warwick. Regt.

Copy to.

1. C.O.
2.-4. 'C', 'D' & 'A' Coys
5. War Diary
6. File
7. 'B' Coy (for information).

SECRET. Copy. No

2/8th Battn. Royal Warwickshire Regiment.

Battalion Order. No. 203.
Dated 14-1-1918.

1. The Battalion will be relieved in the FAYET sub-sector on the night of 15/16th January 1918 by 2/5 R.WAR.R., in accordance with the following relief table.

RELIEF	RELIEVING
'A' Coy. 2/5th	'A' Coy. 2/8th (2 platoons)
'B' " 2/5th	'B' " "
'C' " 2/5th	'C' " "
'D' " 2/5th	'D' " (2 platoons).

2. The following personnel of 2/5th R.WAR.R. will report on the morning of 15th inst.

   1 Officer + 1 N.C.O. per Coy.
   1 N.C.O. to take over from R.S.M.
   2 Battalion signallers.
   1 " observer.
   Battn. police to take over traffic control.

3. Guides, one per platoon and one for Battn. H.Q. will report to Lt. WOOLDRIDGE at 3 p.m., each guide to have written instructions provided by O's C. Coys concerned.
   Incoming units will be met at X roads, S.2.c.8.9, near Bde. H.Q. from 4.30 p.m. onwards.

4. All Trench Stores, including trench documents, maps, [illegible] tins, food containers, S.A.A., grenades, Very lights, rockets and Defence Schemes will be handed over to relieving unit and receipts obtained.
   The fullest information concerning the sector will be handed over to incoming Coys.
   Note:- The bombs that were carried in the men with the line will be handed over in dumps. Rifle Bombers will take out with them the same number of rifle grenades as they carried in.
   All L.G. Drums MUST be brought out.

5. Gum Boots will be brought out and dumped at Coy. H.Q., and handed over, receipts being obtained.

6. One officer per Coy, one N.C.O. per platoon and two Battn. signallers will report at 10.0 a.m. to CAPT. MUNGLE at Bn. H.Q., and proceed to take over area at present occupied by 2/5 R.WAR.R. These men will act as guides for their respective Companies, and will meet them at the QUARRY, S.4.c.8.8 from 5.30 p.m. onwards.
   Coys will take over from 2/5th as follows:-
   'A', 'C' and part of 'D' Coy. dugouts near X.12.a.9.2.
   'B' Coy. dugouts in M.31.d.
   'D' " (2 off. + 30 O.R). dugouts at S.9.a.4.9

7. Relief complete to be reported by runner to Battn. H.Q.

8. ACKNOWLEDGE.

P.T.O

Issued to:-
1. C.O. 9. R.S.M.
2-5. Coys. 10. T.O.
6. 2/5 R.War.R. 11. Q.M.
7. Capt. MUNGLE. 12. War Diary
8. " WOOLDRIDGE 13. File.

(sd) W.E. PHILLIPS,
Major,
Comdg. 2/8 R.War.R.

Supply Arrangements to accompany B.O. 203.

14.1.18.

1. RATIONS. Rations will be brought up for all Coys to their new areas. C/Q.M.S.'s will stay with their rations until Coys are able to send for them.
Coy. advance Officer will find out from Coy of 2/5th where rations are brought up to.

2. TRANSPORT. Limbers will report as under:-

COY.	No. of limbers	PLACE	TIME
'A' & 'C'	ONE	S.4. b. 9.6.	6.15 p.m.
'D'	HALF	S.4. b. 9.6.	6.15 p.m.
Bn. H.Q.	TWO	present Bn Hq.	6.15 p.m

3. WATER CARTS. Water carts will be used if necessary.
Transport Officer will enquire from 2/5th what are the water arrangements.

4. FOOD CONTRS. Food Containers will be handed over on relief.

5. COOKS. Coy. Commanders will make arrangements, if possible to have something hot for the men on their arrival at their new areas. To do this, one cook per Coy may be sent out with advance party.

(sd) W.R.S. WHATMORE
Major,
7th R. War. R.

2CR

Copy No.

2/8th Bn. Royal Warwickshire Regiment.

Battalion Order No. 204

Ref. map sheet 62 C. S.E. January. 17th 1918.

1. The Battalion will be relieved in the support area tomorrow, 18th January 1918 by 2/4 GLOSTERS, proceeding after relief to billets in VAUX.

Relief	Relieving
"A" Coy 2/4 Glosters.	"A" Coy. 2/8 Warwicks
"B" "	"B" "
"C" "	"C" "
"D" "	"D" "

2. Guides as follows will meet incoming Coys of 2/4 GLOSTERS at Railway Crossing X. 10. b. 1. 1. from 5 p.m. onwards.

   1 guide per platoon (2 platoons per Coy.)
   1 " " Coy H.Q.
   1 " " Battn. H.Q.

   Guides as detailed will report to 2/LT. DAVIES at Bn. H.Q. at 4 p.m.

3. Advance parties from 2/4 GLOSTERS will report tomorrow morning.

   1 Officer per Company & 1. N.C.O. per platoon.
   1 Officer & 1 N.C.O. per Battn H.Q.

   Two Battalion runners will be detailed to meet this party at railway crossing at X. 10. b. 1. 1., and guide them to Coys.

4. All trench stores, including stoves, braziers, beds, S.A.A. etc. will be handed over, and receipts obtained.

5. Relief complete will be reported by runner to Bn H.Q. (B Coy by telephone)

6. After relief, Companies will proceed independently, via ETREILLERS, to VAUX. Intervals of 50x between platoons, and a minimum of 200x between Coys. on the march. Limbers have been detailed in administrative orders herewith.

7. Billeting party of two O.R.'s per Coy. and two signallers for Battn. H.Q. will report to LT. WOOLDRIDGE at H.Q. at 9-30 A.M., and proceed to VAUX.

8. ACKNOWLEDGE.

Issued at 6.15 p.m.

Copies to:-

1. C.O.
2-5. Coys
6. 2/4 GLOSTERS.
7. T.O.
8. Q.M.
9. H.Q. Mess.
10. Lt. Wooldridge
11. 2/Lt. Davies
12. R.S.M.
13. War Diary
14. File.

(sd.) W. E. PHILLIPS, Major,
Cmdg. 2/8 R. Warwick. Rgt.

[illegible]

Administrative Orders to accompany Bn. Order. 204

17-1-1918.

1. TRANSPORT & Q.M. STORES. Transport & Q.M. Stores will remain at VILLEVEQUE. The tailor's shop, bootmaker's shop, and Barber will move to VAUX, and will be ready to start work on morning of 19th inst.

2. BLANKETS, etc. Blankets, surplus kits, officers' kits, Mess Baskets etc will be delivered to Coy. headquarters before arrival of Companies.

3. RATIONS. Rations for consumption on 19th will be delivered to companies at VAUX.

4. WATER. Water carts will be taken from present area after 2.0 p.m. and will be at VAUX filled in sufficient time to allow cooks to prepare hot food for incoming companies.

5. COOKING. Field Kitchens will be sent to new area. Sgt. FINNEMORE will proceed in advance of Batn. to new area, and will make all necessary arrangements in consultation with Q.M.

6. TRANSPORT. Transport will report as under for carrying Company stores from the line to new area.

Coy.	Nature of vehicle.	Place	Time
A.	1 limber	Present Bn. H.Q.	5.0 p.m.
B	1 limber	S.2.C.7.9.	5.30 p.m.
C	1 limber	Present Bn. H.Q.	5.0 p.m.
D	2 half limbers	Present Bn H.Q.	5.0 p.m.
H.Q.	{ 1 limber { Mess cart	Present Bn H.Q.	5.0 p.m

O.C. 'D' Company will provide guide for half limber for his detached platoon. Medical equipment will be carried on Mess cart.

(sd). W.R.T. WHATMORE, Major
2/8 R. War. R.

[P.T.O.

1/8 R. Warwicks Regt.

[illegible] Order No. 205 by Major W.E. PHILLIPS, M.C. Commanding. Jan: 24/18.

Reference: [illegible] 62B S.W. 1/20,000.

1. The [illegible] will [illegible] the line on the night Jan. 26/27th.
2. The following will proceed to the right sub-sector of the left Brigade front tomorrow:

   Coy. Commanders.
   1 N.C.O. per Coy.
   1 runner or signaller per Coy.
   2 signallers of Batt: Headquarters.
   1 runner " "

3. Coy. Commanders will rejoin Batt: after reconnaissance. The N.C.O's etc. will remain in the line, & be prepared to assist in guiding the Coys. on night of 26/27th. They will take in rations for remainder of 25th, & for the whole of 26th & 27th.
4. A 'bus will convey N.C.O's & men (not more than the above numbers) as far as GARDE MAISON, whence they will proceed on foot to FRESNOY (Batt. HQ). 'Bus leaves VAUX Cross Roads shortly after 9am. NCOs & men proceeding to the line will parade at HQ at 9am.

   Officers will ride (either horse or bicycle), & will pick up remainder of party at GARDE MAISON.

   Guides will be obtained at Batt. HQ P.C. SAMSON M.21.C.9.0.
5. Dispositions will be as under:

	1/8th R. War. R.		1/5th Glosters
	'A' Coy.	Left front.	'B' Coy.
Trimble → to stay with Coy. HQ.	'B' "	Right "	'C' "
'C' Coy	No. 9 platoon		No. 1 platoon
	" 10 "		" 2 "
	" 11 "		" 14 "
	" 12 "		" 16 "
'D' Coy.	" 13 "		" 3 "
	" 14 "		" 4 "
	" 15 "		" 13 "
	" 16 "		" 15 "

'C' Coy. = Counter-attack Coy.
'D' " = Passive Defence

6. Dress for N.C.O's & men:- Fighting Order. Greatcoats will not be taken into the line. Water bottles will be carried filled.
7. Acknowledge.

(sd.) W. E. PHILLIPS,
Major
Cdg. 1/8 Warwicks.

To report to T. M. S. to-day
29643 Pte H. Harrison

[illegible] Battn. Royal Warwickshire Regiment.

Battalion Order. No 206.
dated 25-1-1918.

Reference.
Maps 62 B. S.W. } 1/20,000.
62 C. S.E. }

1. The Battalion will relieve the 2/5th GLOSTERS in the right sub-sector, left Brigade sector on the night of 26/27th January 1918.

2. Relief Table.

Relief	Relieving	Relief	Relieving
'A' Coy + 1 L.G. sec. of 'D' Coy.	'B' Coy (left front Coy)	'B' Coy.	'C' Coy (right front Coy.)
'D' Coy: No. 9 platoon, 10 ", 11 ", 12 "	No. 1 platoon, " 2 ", " 14 ", " 16 " ([illegible] attack Coy)	'D': No. 13 plat., " 14 ", " 15 ", " 16 "	No. 3 plat., " 4 ", " 13 ", " 15 " } passive defence Coy.

Note:- 'D' Coy. will provide one Lewis Gun section to be attached to 'A' Coy. for the tour. This section will move off with 'A' Coy. Rations to be sent up with those for 'A' Coy.

3. Guides will be at X roads, near S.2. central from 5 p.m. onwards as follows:
1 guide per platoon.
1 " " Coy. H.Q.
1 " " Battn. H.Q.

4. Coys will move off from VAUX at 15 minute intervals in the following order, 'A', 'B', 'C', 'D', H.Q., leading Coy. starting at 3.45 p.m. Platoons will march at head of Coys. 50 yds will be maintained between Coys on the march. Route:- ETREILLERS – SAVY – SAVY WOOD [illegible] – X roads near S.2. central.

5. Dress – Fighting Order [illegible] to be worn, water bottles filled. Greatcoats will not be carried.
Meals:- Tea before starting.

6. Lewis Guns. 20 drums per gun will be carried into the line. Limbers must be unloaded as rapidly as possible.

7. Gumboots will be issued to front line Coys tomorrow afternoon.

8. Battn. Intelligence Officer and three observers will proceed to the line before noon to take over O.P.s.
1 officer per Company and L.G. section commanders of front line Coys (including one section from D Coy) and three Battn. signallers, will also proceed in advance.

9. A lorry leaves VAUX at 9 a.m. and will carry this party to [illegible] MAISON. Lieut. HOLDRIDGE who is in charge of the party which will rendezvous at X roads VAUX at 8.30 a.m.

9. S.A.A., Bombs, S.O.S. [illegible], Food containers, petrol tins, trench maps and all information will be taken over, and receipts for trench stores obtained and sent in early to Batt. H.Q.

10. Relief complete by code word 'CASCARA' to be telephoned.

11. Movement in daylight is to be restricted to the minimum limits in this sector.

12. Acknowledge.

Issued at 7 p.m.

Copies to:-

1. C.O.
2-5. Coys.
6. 2/5 Glosters.
7. T.O.
8. Q.M.
9. Intelligence Off.
10. R.S.M.
11. H.Q. Trans.
12. War Diary
13. File.

for H.E. PHILLIPS,
Major,
2/8 R. War. R.

2ND/8TH BATTALION THE ROYAL WARWICKSHIRE REGIMENT.

BATTALION ORDER NO.207. 29th JANUARY 1918.

Ref. Map 62B.S.W. 1/20000.

1. The Battalion will be relieved in the Right Sub-Sector by the 2/5.R.WAR.R on the night of 30/31st January 1918 in accordance with the following relief table.

RELIEF.	RELIEVING.
"A" Coy. 2/5.R.WAR.R.	"A" Coy 2/8. R.WAR.R.
"C" " do	"B" " do
"B" " do	"C" " do
"D" " do	"D" " do

2. GUIDES. As arranged between Coy Commanders concerned.
NOTE. No movement in connection with relief before 5-30 p,m.

3. Advance parties of 2/5 R.WAR.R., 1 Officer and 2 o.r. per Coy will report to "A" "B" and "C" Coys tonight and to "D" Coy on the morning of 30th inst.

4. All Trench Stores including French documents and maps, S.A.A., Grenades, S.O.S. Grenades, Very Lights, Trench Maps, Food Containers &c will be handed over and receipts obtained.
Coys will take out of the line the five petrol tins brought in and will hand over to 2/5 R.WAR.R. the exact number taken over from 2/5 Glosters, obtaining receipts for same.
Complete lists of stores to be handed over will be sent in to Batt H.Q. by 10 a.m. tomorrow.

5. All Gum Boots will be handed over at Batt H.Q..

6. On relief the Battalion will withdraw to Right Support Battalion Area. 1 Officer per Coy and 1 o.r. per Platoon will report to H.Q. 2/5.R.WAR at 10 a.m. tomorrow and take over area at present occupied by 2/5.R.WAR.R.
The 4 o.r. will act as guides to their respective platoons and will meet them at northern extremity of FRESNOY village at M.27.a.8.2. from 6 p.m. onwards.
Coys will take over as under:-

"A" Coy 2/8.R.WAR.R.	area occupied by	"A" Coy	2/5.R.WAR.R.
"B" " "	" "	"C" "	"
"C" " "	" "	"B" "	"
"D" " "	" "	"D" "	"

7. Relief complete by code word "CASCARA" to Battalion H.Q.

8. RATIONS. Coys will send guides to meet ration limbers at 8 p.m. at M.26.d.9.0. (near KIRCHNER COPSE). These guides will accompany advance party detailed above.

9. ACKNOWLEDGE.

sgd, R.C.CADMAN. Lieut.Col.
Commdg. 2/8.WARWICKS.

Issued at 9 p.m.

Copies. 1. C.O. 2. 2nd in Command.
3/6 Coys. 7. Intell.Off.
8. R.S.M. 9. Quartermaster.
10. Transport.O. 11. O.C.2/5.R.WAR.R.
12. War Diary 13.

Instructions regarding War Diaries and Intelligence Summaries are contained in F. S. Regs., Part II. and the Staff Manual respectively. Title pages will be prepared in manuscript.

INFANTRY RECORD OFFICE No. 7 DISTRICT 1 MAR 1918 13829 WARWICK

WAR DIARY
or
~~INTELLIGENCE SUMMARY.~~
(Erase heading not required.)

2/8 R Warwicks

Army Form C. 2118.

182 / 61

Place	Date	Hour	Summary of Events and Information	Remarks and references to Appendices
	Feb.		Ref. Sheet 62 B S.W. 1/20000	
SUPPORT AREA	1st		One coy (A) working on defences of FRESNOY, northern end – wiring and filling-in	
BADGER COPSE			disused trenches. One coy (D) wiring S-E end of FRESNOY defences and draining	
nr FRESNOY-LE-PETIT			and improving CHAMPAGNE and AMBOISES trenches. One coy (C) making dug-outs	
			in M26c. Remaining coy (B) clearing up QUARRY (Batt. H.Q. M26.d.9.7), filling	A.L.
			up shell-holes in and repairing FRESNOY – HOLNON road. LT. WHITELEY to England (Courses)	
"	2nd		A, C + D Coys. as above. B Coy. thickening and strengthening wire to	
			CHAMPAGNE TRENCH. 2nd Lts. GUNTER and SCOTT proceeded on leave.	
			2nd Lieut. GILDERTHORP returned from hospital. Lt. Kitchin returned from leave	A.L.
"	3rd		A, B and C Coys. as above. Battalion relieved 2/5th R. War. R	(See Appendix)
GRICOURT			in the line. Relief complete 8.10 pm. Quiet night. Four patrols out –	
SECTOR			two to 3 SAVAGES at different times during night, one to TOMAHAWK COPSE	
			one to sap in M36a. Small hostile patrol scattered by a bomb.	
			No other trace of enemy.	A.L.
"	4th		Quiet day. Corps Commander (SIR IVOR MAXSE LT. GEN.) visited line. B Coy.	
			working on FRESNOY DEFENCES, wiring. Patrols reconnoitred 3 SAVAGES and C.T. east	
			of same, also TOMAHAWK area. 2nd Lt. Bevan [illegible] from [illegible] returned from leave.	A.L.

A6945 Wt. W11422/M1160 350,000 12/16 D. D. & L. Forms/C./2118/14.

Instructions regarding War Diaries and Intelligence Summaries are contained in F. S. Regs., Part II. and the Staff Manual respectively. Title pages will be prepared in manuscript.

WAR DIARY
or
INTELLIGENCE SUMMARY.
(*Erase heading not required.*)

Army Form C. 2118.

Place	Date	Hour	Summary of Events and Information	Remarks and references to Appendices
			Ref. Sheet 62B S.W. 1/20000	
LINE	5th Feb.		Quiet day. B Coy. + H.Q. details wiring W. side of FRESNOY defences. Silent raid	
GRICOURT			on 3 SAVAGES carried out by D Coy. No enemy. Fighting patrols of A + C Coys reconnoitred	
			TOMAHAWK COPSE and line to north of same. Machine-gun opposition. Our patrols	
			located enemy posts and fired LGs and salvoes of rifle grenades.	[illegible]
do	6th		Quiet day. B Coy. + H.Q. details again wiring FRESNOY defences. B Coy clearing	
			timber from cemetery, FRESNOY. Night D Coy reconnoitred sunken road	
			M23a 2.0 to M18.c.7.8. Road well-wired, no enemy. A Coy. + C Coy.	
			each fighting patrols with LG approached enemy lines opposite our right and	
			awaited enemy patrols. None appeared. Salvoes of rifle grenades dropped on	[illegible]
			TOMAHAWK COPSE and sap in M36a 2.8	
do	7th		Quiet day. B Coy. and ~~the~~ H.Q. details on FRESNOY wiring and clearing	
			cemetery as on 6th. Battalion relieved by 2/5th R.War.R. (See Appendix)	
			Lt. Wooldridge proceeded to England for 6 months' rest. After relief (Relief complete 8 pm) battalion	
			took over OTTER COPSE area and remained in support. D Coy on	
			FRESNOY defences and AMBOISE TRENCH wiring by night.	[illegible]
OTTER COPSE in support	8th		One coy. on new dug-outs near Batt. H.Q. continuously; one coy wiring FRESNOY	

A6945 Wt. W11422/M1160 35,000 12/16 D. D. & L. Forms/C./2118/14.

Instructions regarding War Diaries and Intelligence Summaries are contained in F. S. Regs., Part II, and the Staff Manual respectively. Title pages will be prepared in manuscript.

WAR DIARY
or
~~INTELLIGENCE SUMMARY.~~
(Erase heading not required.)

Army Form C. 2118.

Place	Date 1918	Hour	Summary of Events and Information	Remarks and references to Appendices
	Feb			
OTTER COPSE	8th		defences, one coy digging and wiring AMBOISE and FRESNOY.	
in support			Lt. W.R.T. WHATMIRE, 2nd Lt. R.O. LUNT returned from leave	F.L.
Do.	9th		Coys working as on 8th CAPT. MUNGLE, 2nd. LT. BEVAN proceeded on leave	
			LT. S. WALKER, 2nd. LTS GROUTAGE and MACMILLAN proceeded to courses	F.L.
Do.	10th		~~Coy~~ working as on 8th + 9th. Quiet day	F.L.
Do.	11th		Work as above. Area about Batt. H.Q. shelled for 2½ hrs intermittently with 77mm and 4.2s. Batt. relieved (3 coys) by 9th Royal Scots and (1 coy + H.Q.) by 5th Gordons. Relief complete 8-5 pm. (See appendix) After relief battalion marched to huts at UGNY L'EQUIPEE. Billets poor.	F.L.
UGNY	12th		Rest and cleaning-up. Preparation for disbandment	F.L.
do	13th		Battalion parade in morning. Addresses given by B.G.C. and Commanding Officer. Preparations for disbandment	F.L.
"	14th		17 officers 350 o.R. transferred to 2/7th R.War.R. Handing-in of regimental stores. Surplus remaining at UGNY	F.L.
"	15th		Q.M. Stores and Transport rejoined battalion from VILLEVEQUE	F.L.

A6945 Wt. W11422/M1160 350,000 12/16 D. D. & L. Forms/C./2118/14.

Instructions regarding War Diaries and Intelligence Summaries are contained in F. S. Regs., Part II. and the Staff Manual respectively. Title pages will be prepared in manuscript.

WAR DIARY
or
~~INTELLIGENCE SUMMARY.~~
(Erase heading not required.)

Army Form C. 2118.

Place	1918 Date	Hour	Summary of Events and Information	Remarks and references to Appendices
UGNY	Feb. 16th		Working parties 7 off 150 O.R. for Corps H.A. constructing new gun-pits near BEAUVOIS–VAUX road and at MARTEVILLE. 2nd Lts PARROTT + DAVIES proceeded on leave	A.L.
"	17th		Work continued as above parties remaining billeted at VAUX and VILLEVÊQUE (16th–18th) Headquarters remained at UGNY	A.L.
"	18th		Work on gun-pits &c. continued as above. Parties returned to billets at UGNY	A.L.
"	19th		Work on gun-pits etc. continued	A.L.
"	20th		Work continued as above	A.L.
"	21st		Preparations for final disbandment	A.L.
"	22nd		Battalion finally disbanded. Remainder formed, together with 2/1st Bucks Batt. into No. 25 Entrenching Battalion	A.L.

Ed. C. Cadman Lt Col
Comm 2/8 R War R

A6945 Wt. W11422/M1160 35,000 12/16 D. D. & L. Forms/C./2118/14.

2ND 8TH BATTALION THE ROYAL WARWICKSHIRE REGIMENT.

BATTALION ORDER 208. 2nd FEBY 1918. SECRET

Ref. Sheet 62B.S.W. 1/20000.

1. The Battalion will relieve 2/5.WARWICKS in the RIGHT SUB-SECTOR on night of 3/4th FEBY. 1918, in accordance with following relief table:-

RELIEF.	RELIEVING.	
"D" Coy. 2/8.WAR.	"A" COY. 2/5.WAR.	LEFT FRONT.
"C" do	"C" do	RIGHT FRONT.
"A" do	"B" do	COUNTER ATTACK.
"B" do	"D" do	PASSIVE DEFENCE.

NOTE. "A" Coy will detail 1 complete Lewis Gun Section to be attached to "D" Coy for this tour. This Section will report to O.C."D" Coy before 6 p.m. tomorrow 3rd inst. and will move off with "D" Coy.

2. Guides as arranged today between O.C.Coys concerned.

3. Coys will move off at 15 minute intervals in the following order, 50 yards being maintained between Platoons.
"D" "C" "B" "A", H.Q.
"D" Coy will move off at 5-30 p.m.

4. DRESS. Fighting Order, Jerkins worn, water bottles filled.
TEAS before starting.

5. Lewis Guns will be overhauled and inspected together with Drums and ammunition (20 Drums per gun) during the day.

6. Advance Parties of 1 Officer per Coy and 1 N.C.O. per Platoon will be detailed and proceed to the line before noon.
R.S.M., 3 Observers and Batt Signallers will take over during afternoon.
No other movement in connection with relief will take place before 5-30 p.m.

7. Officers proceeding in advance will take over and carefully check all Trench Stores including Coy Defence Schemes, Trench Maps, Aeroplane Photos, Gas Rattles, Petrol Tins, S.A.A., Bombs, Rifle Grenades, S.O.S. Grenades, Food Containers etc.
Signed receipts will be sent in to Batt.H.Q. as early as possible.

8. Relief complete will be notified by Fullerphone, Codeword "JOCK".

9. Blankets of "A" "B" "C" Coys will be rolled and stacked outside "B" Coy H.Q. O.C."B" Coy will detail a Guard of 1 N.C.O. and 2 men to remain until blankets are collected.
Blankets of "D" Coy and Hdqrs will be rolled and stacked at Batt.H.Q.
Two Batt.Police will remain as Guard.
Returning Ration Limbers will collect all blankets after which Guards will rejoin their Units.

10. Rations will be delivered at 8 p.m. at dumps as in last tour:-

LEFT FRONT COY.	GRICOURT.
RIGHT FRONT COY.	MONT NEEDLE.
COUNTER ATTACK. }	{ MONT NEEDLE.
PASSIVE DEFENCE. }	{ CRATER, FRESNOY.
HEADQUARTERS.	Batt.H.Q.

ACKNOWLEDGE.

sgd E.C.CADMAN. Lieut.Col.

Comdg. 2/8.WARWICKS.

2ND 8TH BATTALION THE ROYAL WARWICKSHIRE REGIMENT. SECRET

BATTALION ORDER 200. 2nd FEBRY 1918.

Ref. Sheet 62B.S.W. 1/20000.

1. The Battalion will relieve 2/5.WARWICKS in the RIGHT SUB-SECTOR on night of 3/4th Febry 1918, in accordance with following relief table:-

RELIEF.	RELIEVING.	
"D" Coy. 2/8.WAR.	"A" Coy. 2/5.WAR.	LEFT FRONT.
"C" " "	"C" " "	RIGHT FRONT.
"A" " "	"B" " "	COUNTER ATTACK.
"B" " "	"D" " "	PASSIVE DEFENCE.

NOTE. "A" Coy will detail 1 complete Lewis Gun Section to be attached to "D" Coy for the tour. This Section will report to O.C. "D" Coy before 5 p.m. tomorrow 3rd inst and will move off with "D" Coy.

2. Guides as arranged to day between O.C.Coys concerned.

3. Coys will move off at 15 minute intervals in the following order, 50 yards being maintained between Platoons.
"D" "C" "B" "A" H.Q.
"D" Coy will move off at 5-30 p.m.

4. DRESS. Fighting Order, Jerkins worn, water bottles filled.
TEAS before starting.

5. Lewis Guns will be overhauled and inspected together with Drums and ammunition (20 Drums per gun) during the day.

6. Advance Parties of 1 Officer per Coy and 1 N.C.O. per Platoon will be detailed and proceed to the line before noon.
R.S.M., 3 Observers and 3 Batt Signallers will take over during afternoon.
No other movement in connection with relief will take place before 5-30 p

7. Officers proceeding in advance will take over and carefully check all Trench Stores including Coy Defence Schemes, Trench Maps, Aeroplane Photos, Gas Rattles, Petrol Tins, S.A.A., Bombs, Rifle Grenades, S.O.S. Grenades, Food Containers etc.
Signed receipts will be sent in to Batt H.Q. as early as possible.

8. Relief complete will be notified by Fullerphone, Codeword. "JOCK".

9. Blankets of "A" "B" "C" Coys will be rolled and stacked outside "B" Coy H.Q. O.C."B" Coy will detail a Guard of 1 N.C.O. and 2 men to remain until blankets are collected.
Blankets of "D" Coy and Hdqrs will be rolled and stacked at Batt.H.Q.
Two Batt.Police will remain as a Guard.
Returning Ration Limbers will collect all blankets after which Guards will rejoin their Units.

10. Rations will be delivered at 6 p.m. at dumps as in last tour:-

LEFT FRONT COY.	GRICOURT.
RIGHT FRONT COY.	MONT NEEDLE.
COUNTER ATTACK.	MONT NEEDLE.
PASSIVE DEFENCE.	CRATER, FRESNOY.
HEADQUARTERS.	Batt.H.Q.

11. ACKNOWLEDGE.

sgd, E.C.CARMAN. Lieut.Col.

Commdg. 2/8.R.WAR.R.

2ND 8TH BATTALION THE ROYAL WARWICKSHIRE REGIMENT.

BATTALION ORDER No.211. 10th FEBRUARY 1918.

Ref.Maps. 62B.S.W. 1/20000
62C.S.E. 1/20000, and ST.QUENTIN. 1/100000.

1. The Battalion will move on night 11/12th inst. to billets at UGNY.

2. A.B.C.Coys will be relieved by two Coys of 9th R.SCOTS. Batt.H.Q. and area occupied by "D" Coy will be taken over by 5th GORDONS.

3. Coys will move independently as relieved to UGNY, at intervals of not less than 15 minutes. 50 yards will be maintained between Platoons. "D" Coy and Headquarters will not move before 7 p.m.
ROUTE TO UGNY:- OTTER COPSE - KEEPERS HOUSE - MARTEVILLE - VILLEVEQUE - BEAUVOIS - LANCHY - UGNY.

4. Half an hour's halt will be made at Q.M.Stores VILLEVEQUE for hot soup etc.

5. Billets and area stores will be taken over at UGNY before 12 noon tomorrow. 2/LT.DEVERELL will proceed in advance to take over.

6. Transport is allotted as follows for the move: Each Coy 1 limber.
Headquarters. Mess Cart and 1 limber.
These will report as soon after 5-45 p.m. as possible.
Blankets will b e rolled in bundles of ten and loaded in front halves of limbers. Rear halves of limbers will contain Lewis Guns, drums, and S.P.Bags only. Rear halves will be detached at VILLEVEQUE and Lewis Guns etc handed over to Q.M. Water Carts will proceed to UGNY.

7. One blanket per man additional, and rations for 12th inst will be conveyed to UGNY during daylight and dumped at Coy billets in charge of Q.M.S's.

Permanent R.E.party will join Battalion at UGNY proceeding in advance tomorrow 11th inst.

9. All Trench Stores including S.A.A., Grenades, S.O.S.Grenades, Gas Rattles Tools etc. will be handed over to incoming Units and receipts obtained. All Defence Schemes will be returned to Battalion Headquarters by 4 p.m. tomorrow 11th inst.

10. Relief complete will be reported by A.B.C.Coys by codeword "ROCK" by wire to Batt.Headquarters.

11. ACKNOWLEDGE.

Issued at 8 p.m.

sgd. E.C.CADMAN. Lieut.Col.

Commdg. 2/8.R.WARWICK.REGT.

Copies. 1. C.O. ✓ 2. 2nd in Command. ✓
3/6. Coys. ✓ 7. 9th.R.SCOTS. ✓
8. 5th GORDONS. ✓ 9. 2/LT.DEVERELL. ✓
10. Quartermaster. ✓ 11. Transport Officer. ✓
12. R.S.M. ✓ 13. War Diary. ✓
14. File. ✓

War Diary

2ND 8TH BATTALION THE ROYAL WARWICKSHIRE REGIMENT.

BATTALION ORDER 212. 13th FEBRUARY 1918.

Ref. Map. ST.QUENTIN. 1/100000.

1. A proportion of Officers, N.C.Os and men already detailed will be transferred to 2/7.R.WAR.R. tomorrow 14th inst, proceeding to MDE. HOLNON WOOD.

2. Parties detailed will parade in line facing North on LANCHY ROAD opposite Batt.H.Q. ready to move at 1-30 p.m. CAPT.A.E.TONKS will command the whole.
ROUTE. LANCHY - BEAUVOIS - VILLEVEQUE - ATTILY - MDE DUGOUTS.
ORDER OF MARCH: DRUMS & DETAILS. "A" "B" "C" "D" ~~Coys~~. Platoons
DRESS: Full Marching Order. Steel Helmets to be worn.

3. Drums will be detached at VILLEVEQUE and report to Q.M. 2/7.R.WAR.R.

4. Transport Officer will detail transport to carry Blankets and Officers valises. Blankets will be rolled in tens and labelled ready for loading at 12 noon. An additional limber will be detailed to convey necessaries to MDE, HOLNON WOOD.
Blankets and Officers valises will be handed in to Q.M.Stores, 2/7th R.WAR.R. at VILLEVEQUE.

5. CAPT.A.E.TONKS will take nominal rolls and A.F.B.122 for whole of dra[ft] including those proceeding to 2/7.R.WAR.R. at a later date.

6. Marching Out State to be rendered and numbers carefully checked.

7. Nominal Rolls will be handed in to Orderly Room not later than 10 a.m. tomorrow showing N.C.Os and men forming part of the draft but not actually marching out tomorrow. These rolls will be compiled from the proforma lists A.B.C.D.

sgd. E.C.CADMAN. Lieut.Col.

Commdg. 2/8.R.WARWICK.REGT.

Copies to. 1. C.O. 2. MAJOR.PHILLIPS.
3/6. Coys. 7. O.C. 2/7.R.WAR.R.
8. Q.M. 9. T.O.
10. CAPT.TONKS. 11. R.S.M.
12. War Diary. 13. File.

Major [illegible] M.C.

War Diary

2/6th BATTALION THE ROYAL WARWICKSHIRE REGIMENT.

BATTALION ORDER No. [illegible] 16-[illegible]

1. 1 Officer and 50 men of A Coy will proceed to billets at VILLEVEQUE and 2 Officers and remainder of A Coy and the whole of C Coy will move to billets at VAUX.

2. One Officer of A Coy will report to Town Major of VILLEVEQUE at 6-30 a.m. tomorrow morning 17th inst to obtain information for billeting.
An Officer from C Coy will report to Area Commandant, VAUX at 6 a.m. tomorrow for same purpose.

3. Parties as detailed above will march off from UGNY in order A - C Coys to new area at 7-45 a.m.
DRESS. Full Marching Order less packs, Steel Helmets will be worn.

4. 2 G.S. wagons will be at UGNY at 7-30 a.m. to carry valises and the blankets per men. One wagon proceeding to VAUX and one to VILLEVEQUE. Blankets will be rolled in bundles of ten and loaded immediately on arrival of G.S. wagons. Officers valises will be loaded and ready at same time.

5. Both parties will carry unconsumed portions of the day's rations. Rations for 18th will be sent on during the morning and one Field Kitchen will move to VAUX.
VILLEVEQUE party will take three Camp Kettles on G.S. wagons.

6. From and including the 18th inst. parties will be attached for rations as under:-

VAUX PARTY.	[illegible] Brigade A.F.A.
VILLEVEQUE PARTY.	[illegible] Bde. A.F.A.
	[illegible]

7. Transport Officer will detail two limbers to carry rations daily from 18th inst. inclusive from Refilling Point for party at VAUX.

8. Officers from [illegible] Bde. A.F.A. will meet parties on arrival at VAUX and VILLEVEQUE.

9. C.Q.M.Ss A and C Coys will remain at UGNY. All other N.C.Os and men will proceed with their respective Coys to new areas. CPL. FISHER will remain at UGNY.

10. Marching Out States will be rendered.

11 ACKNOWLEDGE.

sgd. [illegible] Lieut.Col.

Comdg. 2/6 R.WAR.R.

Copies. 1. C.O.
2/3 Coys.
4. Adjutant.
5 T.O.
6 Q.M.
7 R.S.M.
8 File.

2ND 8TH BATTALION THE ROYAL WARWICKSHIRE REGIMENT.

ORDER No.214. 21st.FEBRY.1918.

Ref.Sheets. ST.QUENTIN & AMIENS 1/100000.

1. Companies, as re-organised today, will move by march route to the CURCHY -ETALON area tomorrow 22nd inst. where they will join 2/1st BUCKS BATTN.

ROUTE. UGNY - MATIGNY - VOYENNES - NESLE - CURCHY - ETALON.

2. Coys will parade in close columns facing Battalion Headquarters at 8-45 a.m.
DRESS: Full Marching Order, Steel Helmets on pack.

3. Cooker will move in rear of column.
A Halt will be made from 12-30 to 1-15 p.m. for dinners.

4. Blankets, Officers Kits and Mess Baskets will be dumped at Headquarters by 8 a.m.

5. 2/LT.J.G.REECE and CQMS.E.A.CLIVE will proceed in advance by bicycle to Town Major's Office, ETALON for billeting. They will meet there an Officer of 2/1st BUCKS at 11 a.m. who will give further instructions.

6. ACKNOWLEDGE.

sgd. E.C.CADMAN. Lieut.Col.

Comdg. 2/8.R.WARWICK.REGT.

www.ingramcontent.com/pod-product-compliance
Lightning Source LLC
Chambersburg PA
CBHW080803010526
44113CB00013B/2317

* 9 7 8 1 4 7 4 5 3 3 1 3 3 *